Saint Raphael Kalinowski

Apprenticed to Sainthood in Siberia

Timothy Tierney

BALBOA.
PRESS
A DIVISION OF HAY HOUSE

Balboa Press books may be ordered through booksellers or by contacting:

Balboa Press
A Division of Hay House
1663 Liberty Drive
Bloomington, IN 47403
www.balboapress.com.au
1 (877) 407-4847

Print information available on the last page.

ISBN: 978-1-5043-0434-4 (sc)
ISBN: 978-1-5043-0435-1 (e)

Balboa Press rev. date: 10/12/2016

Contents

Part 2 Religious Life of Raphael Kalinowski

Acknowledgements

First of all I would like to thank profoundly Fr. Saverio Cannistrà OCD, Superior General of the Discalced Carmelites, for taking time off from his busy schedule to provide me with a Preface for this book. In those circumstances his kindness is all the more appreciated.

I have also been helped by the kindness of Fr. Albert S. Wach OCD and Fr. Rafal Wikowski OCD, a member of Fr. General's staff.

I would like also to express my indebtedness to Fr. Szcepan T. Praskiewicz for his invaluable help, support and encouragement to me in writing this biography. He has allowed me to draw freely on his own considerable writings on St. Raphael Kalinowski.

My thanks also go to Adrian Doesburg who edited the whole text and offered many helpful suggestions and corrections which I have incorporated in the finished product.

Thanks also to Bernadette Micallef OCDS who helped on part of the text.

I would also like to thank our office staff, friends and parishioners whose generosity made possible this publication.

Finally grateful thanks to my colleague Fr. Sunny P Abraham OCD who has checked the text thoroughly and made many useful suggestions which I have adopted.

Note. I have used American spelling in this book, eg., `favor` rather than `favour`.

Preface

$\mathcal{S}$t. Raphael (Joseph, in secular life) Kalinowski during his earthly life, and especially before joining the Order of Discalced Carmelites at the age of 42, travelled widely, covering great geographical distances both in Europe and in Asia. Suffice it to simply name the countries of his long itinerary: Lithuania, Russia (as far as distant Siberia), Poland, France, Austria, Italy, Switzerland, Hungary and again Poland. For the most part he went on foot, as well as by carriage or by train – this latter was then becoming the most modern means of travel. From the time of his conversion at the age of 28, he never undertook a journey of his own will, but always because of the circumstances of his life – adverse historical events, or on the orders of his religious superiors who sent him to different places to accomplish some mission or other. Throughout all his travels, however, he always had a sense of the guiding hand of Providence and that he was fulfilling God's will in his life. Wherever he stayed – as observed by the Polish Provincials in their joint letter on the occasion of the first Centenary of his death (1907-2007) – "he took up office without ceremony, offering – in so far as he was able – different services to the people about him. Complete openness and kindness marked him out. This was how he dialogued with his contemporary. He made no distinction between people because of their religion, language, tradition, social status or education."

However, Raphael Kalinowski was never in Britain, Australia, America, Africa or in other countries where English is spoken, even though he liked the language a lot and knew it well. Besides, when he was young he was curious about English literature and culture in general. He missed no opportunity to come to know it better and to share it with others. We cannot rule out that as a good mathematician and analyst, with a bent towards the concrete and empirical, that he would have found a certain liking for the Anglo-Saxon world, for its rich scientific tradition; temperamentally, however, he was much closer to the Latin world with which he was more strongly linked historically in an almost continuous and direct way.

Having been already introduced to the public as a canonized saint, the time has now come for diffusing a wider and deeper knowledge of Raphael Kalinowski in the Anglo-Saxon world. All thanks to this fine book by Fr. Timothy Tierney, an Irish Discalced Carmelite, currently resident in Australia, which I have the joy of introducing and recommending to readers. Fr. Timothy knows how to combine in his work a rich, detailed and interesting collection of biographical material, probably unknown to many, with a penetrating analysis of the spiritual life of Fr. Raphael Kalinowski. The history and culture of Central and Eastern Europe, marked by so much suffering and contradiction, emerge simultaneously with the attempt to decipher the enigma of the personality of his (and now our) Hero and Protagonist. The story of everyday life, grey and seemingly meaningless, is related to descriptions of dramatic and moving adventures, where human weakness is certainly not lacking; but without doubt these anecdotes are full of great passion and aspiration, which alas, a cynical age seems to want us to prohibit in our day.

In short, we have before us a biography that shows us a living Saint, inserted into the history of different peoples, close to those who are seeking for meaning in life. A Saint who knows no distance between God and people, or at least does not measure it in kilometres and years. A Saint who after the agonizing events of his own life has finally found, like Saint Teresa of Avila, St. John of the Cross, St. Thérèse of Lisieux, Saint Faustina Kowalska, his rest in the divine mercy.

Fr Saverio Cannistrà OCD Superior General, November 19, 2015, Feast of St. Raphael Kalinowski

Introduction

*P*oland and Polish names made a debut, if not a comeback, in the universal church with the election of Karol Wojtyla as Pope in 1978. St. Raphael Kalinowski, is a distinguished Discalced Carmelite priest of Polish descent, only the second male member of the Teresian Reform to be so honored, since John of the Cross was canonized by Pope Benedict XIII in 1726. He was named a Doctor of the Church by Pope Pius XI in 1926.

A canonized saint belongs to the universal Church and offers a model of holiness to all its members. By the same token that gives Raphael Kalinowski a pronounced importance for Carmelite friars worldwide as well as for the whole Carmelite Family.[1] His spiritual links with the late Pope John Paul II (only recently canonized), and the Pope who both beatified and canonized him, make him a topical figure for the present day. Saint Pope John Paul II freely acknowledged that Raphael Kalinowski was for him a boyhood hero. Karol Wojtyla was born in Wadowice, the town where Kalinowski founded a Carmelite Church, a priory and school and the place where he died. The young Wojtyla had a passion for acting and

---

[1] Spaniard Henry de Ossa Y Cervello, figures in the Carmelite calendar but only because he founded a congregations of Carmelite Missionaries. Five years younger than Kalinowski, he was born in Catalonia on 16th October, 1840. He died on January 27, 1896 and was canonized by Pope John Paul II on July 16, 1993.

drama and indulged in writing plays and poetry. As a young man during World War II, together with some friends, he formed the Rhapsodic Theatre in Kraków. They wrote and performed their plays underground as a protest against Nazi destruction of Polish culture. One of his plays, known as 'Our God's Brother' was written in 1944. It tells the story of Adam Chimielowski, the nineteenth century Polish artist who like Kalinowski had been a freedom fighter caught up in the failed insurrection of 1863. Later on Chimielowski was inspired by Kalinowski's example to dedicate his life to God, and founded two Congregations of religious, male and female, to serve Christ in the poor and homeless.[2] As Pope John Paul II in 1983, Wojtyla would beatify Chimielowski, Kalinowski and a third Polish candidate, Ursula Ledochowska, before a gathering of two million people in the Bronia Meadow, Kraków on June 22, 1983.[3]

Kalinowski has Lithuanian-Polish origins but his appeal goes far beyond his background. His story certainly has dramatic overtones,

---

[2]   See Michael Walsh, *John Paul II* (London: HarperCollins, 1994). Chimielowski adopted the religious name Albert, which may have been in deference to Kalinowski who had joined the Carmelites ten years earlier. St Albert of Jerusalem was the author of the Carmelite Rule. The members of Chimielowski's Congregation were known as Albertines.

[3]   Pope John Paul II also beatified a follower of Raphael Kalinowski, namely Joseph Mazurek. He was born in 1891 at Baranowka, near Lubartow, Poland. He entered the Discalced Carmelites in 1908, the year after Kalinowski's death, taking the religious name Alphonsus Mary. He was ordained a priest and appointed a professor and worked in the education of youth. Afterwards he served in his Order as prior and bursar. In 1944, after having been arrested by the Nazis who had invaded Poland in 1939, causing the outbreak of World War I, he was murdered by them on August 28, at Nawojowa Gora, near Krzeszowice. He was beatified by Pope John Paul II on June 13, 1999, together with many other Polish martyrs. One of those was an O. Carm friar, Hilary Januszewski who died in Dachau. Alphonsus' memory is observed on June 12. Relics of St. Alphonsus, together with those of two other Carmelite saints, were placed in the newly consecrated altar of the Oratory in the new priory at Varroville, Sydney, Australia.

of which one-time rebel and political prisoner is only one aspect. His brief involvement in the insurrection of 1863, as we shall see, led to further drama, joining the throng of exiles for an extended stay in Siberia.

Kalinowski was an extremely cultured man, fluent in several languages, including English. In fact he read Shakespeare avidly and quotes a poet like the romantic Lord Byron and novelist Sir Walter Scott. He occasionally includes English phrases in his letters, including allusions to Shakespeare.

Poland too had strong and close ties with France stretching back many centuries. Much of Kalinowski's spiritual reading would derive from French sources and French authors, and consequently a French devotional tone can be readily detected in his spirituality. This was reinforced by over two years based in Paris as tutor to Prince Auguste Czartoryski, and a period of travel accompanying his protégé throughout much of France and surrounding countries. Many Irish people can empathize with Poland and Polish people as well, having also struggled to preserve their culture and identity for centuries against superior odds.

Kalinowski was deeply influenced by Hermann Cohen, the Jewish convert and Carmelite founder. In many ways Kalinowski would have seen his own life as following the same trajectory as Cohen's – neglect of religious duties in early life, followed later by a thorough-going conversion to Christ. This eventually led to a rebuilding of the Carmelite Order by Kalinowski, not only spiritually but also physically, through establishing new Carmelite houses in Poland, and through his work for the Carmelite nuns and Carmelite Secular Order both in Poland and further afield.

There is a scarcity of material in English on this great male Carmelite figure from the nineteenth century. In writing this account, I am indebted to a biography of the saint written by a French-born contemporary of his, Père Jean-Baptiste Bouchaud OCD, who had been his colleague in Czerna and Wadowice.[4] Part One of this book is based on Père Jean-Baptiste Bouchaud's book: *Joseph Kalinowski* (Liège: Arts et Métier, 1923). However, his biography is incomplete in the sense that it deals mainly with Kalinowski's life up to the time he joined the Carmelite Order. Bouchaud intended it as Volume 1 though he does not call it such. He does have a section on 'The Religious Life' of the saint, but this consists of less than 100 pages as compared with 450 in the earlier part of the book.

Bouchaud did write a second volume in French on Kalinowski's life as a Carmelite; the original is now lost but was translated into Polish early on and has now been published by the Carmelites in Kraków: *Miłość za Miłość* (Love for Love).[5] Part Two of my account is based on the above. I am also fortunate in having to hand an English version of Kalinowski's *Wspomnienie* or Memoirs. These were translated for the first time into English from a reliable Italian version some years ago by Sr. Miriam Quinn OCD, Founder of the Carmel of Maria Regina, Eugene, Oregon, USA. The Italian text was edited and introduced by Szczepan T. Praskiewicz OCD.[6]

I have drawn copiously on the work of Père Jean-Baptiste Bouchaud in this biography, so I need to say something about him here. Born on October 11, 1851 in La Haie-Fouassière in Brittany, France, Bouchaud graduated with a teaching degree from the Institute of St. Joseph in the nearby town of Ancenis. He served as a volunteer in the Franco-Prussian War (1870-1871). In the autumn of 1872 he entered the Carmelite novitiate in the province of Aquitaine at Le Broussey, near Bordeaux, where Hermann Cohen had also been a novice. On October 15, 1873 Bouchaud made first vows,

---

[4]   P. Jean-Baptiste Bouchaud, *Joseph Kalinowski* (Liège: Arts et Métier, 1923).

[5]   P. Jean-Baptiste Bouchaud, *Miłość za Miłość* (Kraków: Wydawnictwo Karmelitow Bosych, 2006).

[6]   I am indebted to Sandra Malkovsky for sending me the file of Kalinowski's *Memoirs* in English.

then went to the priory in Agen, where he studied philosophy and theology. He was ordained a priest on June 10, 1877.

In the fall of 1913, Bouchaud and Bartholmew Diaz de Cerio received a request from Fr. Gregory Joseph, the French Provincial, to leave Poland and return to France. At this time Religious Orders in France again experienced a period of severe persecution. In 1901, following a law requiring the registration of all religious Orders, numerous monasteries were closed, and religious personnel emigrated to other countries, including neighboring Belgium and across to Britain. On November 15 the two friars passed through Vienna and Luxembourg and reached the Carmelite Priory at Marche-en-Famenne in Belgium, where there was a small French novitiate and student house. Only in 1920 were they able to return to France and lived in the novitiate house in Avon, near Paris. Here Bouchaud died on January 6, 1932.

Bouchaud maintained close contacts with Polish Carmelites after leaving Poland. On November 28, 1913, he wrote from Belgium to the Carmelites in Kraków: "Always, always and forever I will remember with love our most dear Polish Carmelites." A few months later he wrote to Kalinowski's friend Benedict Dybowski: "I lived for 33 years in Poland, which I loved, my second home where I left more than half my heart."[7]

Undoubtedly Bouchaud's most important writing was his biography of Raphael Kalinowski. He began to gather material for this immediately after Kalinowski's death. At his request, Kalinowski wrote down memoirs of his early life in Lithuania and exile in Siberia, his life as a Carmelite, his penitents, the priests, sisters and lay people he knew, especially colleagues from Siberia. Family background was supplemented by the saint's brother Fr. Jerzy Kalinowski, who invited some relatives to share their own memories. In addition Jerzy helped in making contacts with Siberian exiles. Jerzy was also the source of information about his brother's life in the

---

[7]   P. Jean-Baptiste Bouchaud, Miłość za Miłość, p. 10.

Hôtel Lambert in Paris, and the Carmelite foundations in Poznan[8] and Ulica Łobzówska in Kraków. Finally Jerzy provided information on the reform of the priory in Czerna. Bouchaud explicitly states that without Jerzy's help writing his book would be impossible. Bouchaud made a collection of Kalinowski's vast correspondence though not complete. Many letters, especially to religious order personnel concerned confidential matters, and some letters to his family in turn were very personal, so recipients either destroyed them or just made partial copies. Nevertheless, this collection, supplemented later by the vice-postulator of his Cause was impressive: nearly 1750 letters and postcards for a period of over 50 years. (1856-1907) Furthermore Bouchaud had access to Kalinowski's other writings and texts for conferences and so on.

Bouchaud's biography of Kalinowski became part of the history of the Order in Poland, and even – somewhat artificially – was incorporated into the history of the entire Order.

The manuscript of the first part of the biography of Kalinowski was not preserved. In 1947 Anselm Gądek recalled: "When in 1932 [1930!] I visited him in Avon in France, he not only claimed that Raphael is a great saint, but he earnestly insisted on the fact, and asked that the beatification process should start as soon as possible. This would bring to completion what he himself had not been able to do – treat of the inner religious life of Father Raphael. For this purpose, in addition to the biography which he wrote in French, he passed on all his records and documents to the Polish Province.

The second volume on Kalinowski's religious life, *Miłość za Miłość*, was completed in 1919 at the priory in Marche-en-Famenne. Bouchaud's work became for many years practically the only source of knowledge about Kalinowski. He hoped that both would eventually be published in Polish translation.

---

8   Hermann Cohen preached here on occasion. It was then known as Posen and under German control.

As Bouchaud spent many years in the company of his hero, his personal opinions are also of value as a source text. The second volume of Bouchaud's was entitled as we saw, 'Love for Love.' The Mercy Sisters first heard this phrase from Kalinowski when they asked him for some 'words of wisdom.' Another Mercy sister stated that Kalinowski used the motto 'Life for Life, Heart for Heart, Love for Love,' in a letter to his brother Gabriel's wife Helena, who had accused him of exaggerating the value of religious life. As Kalinowski explained it through one of his letters to her: "God gave all up for us, how can we not give all to God?"

Reading Bouchaud's work it should be remembered that the author wrote from the heart. This has its drawbacks, but also gives his complete work an authentic feeling, especially with regard to the person of Kalinowski. Bouchaud was fascinated by him, and was charmed by Polish culture, and convinced of the unique mission of the Poles vis-à-vis other nations, especially towards the Russians and the Russian Orthodox Church. In his view: "Carmel and Poland had one and the same mission. What Teresa of Avila did in Spain in the sixteenth century, Carmel did in Poland in the twentieth century through suffering and prayer. It would besiege heaven and implore mercy for the peoples of the East and the triumph of the holy Church."

Bouchaud was as much interested as Kalinowski in the restoration of Christian unity. In their opinion the only way to unity – in accordance with the concepts of the time, generally accepted in the Roman Catholic Church – was the return of the Orthodox (and Protestants), to the Catholic Church. Their opinions on this subject should be taken in their historical context. It should however be noted that Kalinowski had lifelong close friends among Christians whether Protestants or Orthodox, and also among Jews.

In Bouchaud's work we meet a priest who wished to imitate Christ the priest perfectly, not only while celebrating the Eucharist, but also by the gift of sacrifice through spiritual and physical suffering; in addition there was Kalinowski's contribution by exhausting work in the confessional, and in producing spiritual books.

We should appreciate Bouchaud's efforts to gather sources for the public on the life of Raphael Kalinowski. They come primarily from those who did not live to see the opening of the beatification process, for example his brother Jerzy, Sr. Mary Xavier Czartoryska, Benedict Dybowski and many others.

And one final remark: the Polish Carmel and the wider Carmelite Family owe a debt of gratitude to Père Jean-Baptiste Bouchaud for giving us such a full account of St. Raphael Kalinowski.

Timothy Tierney OCD.

Part One

Kalinowski Family Tree

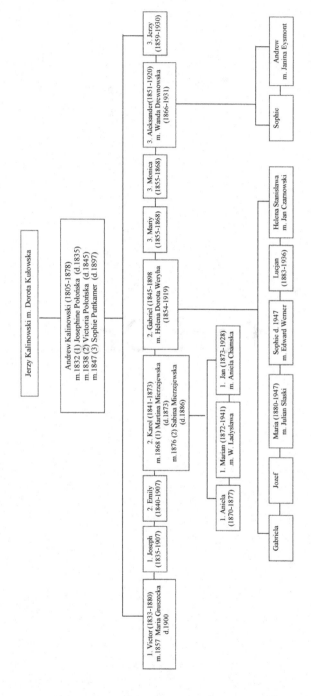

Jerzy Kalinowski m. Dorota Kułowska

Andrew Kalinowski (1805-1878)
m.1832 (1) Josephine Połońska (d.1835)
m.1838 (2) Victoria Połońska (d.1845)
m.1847 (3) Sophie Purtkamer (d.1897)

1. Victor (1833-1880)
m.1857 Maria Gruszccka
d.1900

1. Joseph
(1835-1907)

2. Emily
(1840-1907)

2. Karol (1841-1873)
m.1868 (1) Martina Mierzejewska
(d.1873)
m.1876 (2) Sabina Mierzejewska
(d.1886)

2. Gabriel (1845-1898)
m. Helena Dorota Weryha
(1854-1919)

3. Marry
(1855-1868)

3. Monica
(1855-1868)

3. Aleksander(1851-1920)
m. Wanda Drewnowska
(1866-1931)

3. Jerzy
(1859-1930)

1. Aniela
(1870-1877)

1. Marjan (1872-1941)
m. W. Ladysława

1. Jan (1873-1928)
m. Aniela Chamska

Gabriela

Jozef

Maria (1880-1947)
m. Julian Slaski

Sophie d. 1947
m. Edward Werner

Lucjan
(1883-1936)

Helena Stanisława
m. Jan Czarnowski

Sophie

Andrew
m. Janina Eysmont

* See Footnote 7, Chapter 4 (Part 1)

xxii

Chapter One

Setting the Scene

$\mathscr{D}$igging round the family tree, we find the surname Kalinowski occurring frequently in the annals of Poland, Lithuania and Ukraine. Since the 17th century various highly placed members of the family have struggled bravely against external enemies.

In the 18th century the Kalinowskis distinguished themselves by their charity and generosity. Jan Kalinowski created a foundation for Jesuit missionaries in Eastern Galicia,[9] known at the time as Red Ruthenia and now part of Ukraine. Another Kalinowski, Joseph, after whom our saint would be named, equipped a regiment of soldiers at his own expense and offered his services to Napoleon I. The regiment served in the army of Napoleon's brother Jerome. Joseph's immediate ancestors hailed from the city of Grodno[10] in Belarus, close to the Polish and Lithuanian borders.[11] Kalinowski

---

[9]   The area was given this name by Austrian overlords.

[10]   Belarus was also known as White Russia or Bylorussia. Grodno or Hrodno was formerly in the Polish –Lithuanian Commonwealth but is now in Belarus. There was an ancient Carmelite house there from 1668 – 1845. Grodno was the birthplace of Olga Korbut, whose gymnastic feats at the 1972 and 1976 Olympics took the world by storm.

[11]   They were known as *Szlachta* or members of the gentry. However, the *Szlachta* were nearer to the Samurai tradition of fighters than to nobility.

possessed several properties but these, like so many others that belonged to Polish families, would be confiscated by the authorities in successive acts of oppression and spoliation.

Joseph Kalinowski's grandfather Jerzy sent his son Andrew to the University of Vilnius[12] founded by Prince Adam Czartoryski. After graduation Andrew was appointed Professor of Mathematics at the College of Vilnius. Charitable and generous, he often gave additional instruction to needy pupils at his own home without remuneration.

Around 1832, Andrew met and married Josephine Polonska, eldest daughter of Joseph Polonski, who had several properties in the Sluck district near Minsk.[13] She had a sister Victoria and two brothers, Karol and Ladislaus.

Joseph Kalinowski was born on September 1, 1835 in Vilnius, capital of Lithuania. Andrew and Josephine Kalinowski already had a son named Victor and the second boy to come along was christened Joseph. As was customary among Carmelites and other Orders in the pre-Vatican II era, he was given the name Raphael in religious life, the name by which he is now known. Sadly, Josephine died only two months after Joseph's birth. After Josephine's death, Andrew married Victoria Polanska. She also died, when Joseph was about nine years old. She had already imparted to him her own strong faith and devotion.

Joseph, in his *Memoirs*, tells us that he was born in a house that had belonged to the Dominican Fathers, situated beside the Dominican residence and adjacent to the Church of the Holy Spirit on *Ulica Swietego Ducha* [Holy Spirit Street]. After the expulsion of religious personnel, the residence had been turned into a jail for political prisoners. The Kalinowski home was located not far from a former Carmelite Church dedicated to St. Teresa of Avila that had been founded by the Carmelites in 1633. This church was associated

---

[12]   Also known as Vilna or Wilno in Poland.
[13]   He was the administrator of Prince Leon Wittgenstein's estate at Musizce.

with the nearby Chapel of Our Lady of the Gate of Dawn, also known as Our Lady of Mercy or *Ostra Brama*; this shrine displayed Lithuania's most renowned icon of that name. The chapel was built into the last of nine defensive gates left standing in the city, called the *Spiked Gate*. It enjoys the same esteem in Lithuania as that of Our Lady of Częstochowa in Poland, or looking further afield, is venerated on a par with Lourdes in France or Guadalupe in Mexico.

It doesn't appear that the Carmelites as such created a great impression on the young Kalinowski, as there were numerous other competing churches and religious Orders in Vilnius. The city itself developed on the banks of the Wilia, where it joins another river, the Wileika; the two rivers combine to flow into the Niemen at Kaunas, Lithuania's second city. Vilnius lay along a route that would soon become the railway line between Warsaw, capital of Poland, and St. Petersburg in Russia. As an engineer in later life, Joseph would work on the expansion of the railway system on this line and in other regions. The city of Vilnius was surrounded by picturesque hills overlooking the two rivers.

Lithuania, of course, was neighbor to Poland and had political associations with Poland for centuries, especially for a period of over two centuries since the Polish-Lithuanian Commonwealth was established in 1569. This arrangement came to a definitive end in 1794-1795 with the defeat of an insurrection against powerful enemies by whom they were surrounded – Russia, Prussia and Austria. One of the leaders in this rebellion was Tadeusz (*or Thaddeus*) Kosiuzko, who, like Irishman Thomas Francis Meagher, was a veteran of the American War of Independence; both fought alongside George Washington.[14] In what is referred to as the *third partition*, Poland was effectively wiped off the map by the three above-named great powers.[15] As a result of their handiwork, from

---

[14]   Kosciusko County in Indiana is named after him as is a small town in Texas. The highest mountain in Australia is called Mt. Kosciusko.

[15]   So as to ensure complete annihilation of Poland, the big three drew up a secret plan two years later to do whatever was necessary to extirpate every

that time, until 1918, there was no independent Polish state. The Poles had, like the Irish, engaged over the years in various ill-fated rebellions against an oppressor.[16] The final revolt took place in 1863. But after the failure of the January uprising of that year, the nation came under Russian control. The opportunity for freedom appeared only briefly again after World War I, when the imperial powers were defeated. Then it was back again under subjection to the Russians, the colors of the tyrant having changed to red. Modern Poland begins in 1989.

We shall see Joseph Kalinowski, future Carmelite saint, was caught up in the final rebellion, which erupted on January 22, 1863.

The close bonds between Poland and Lithuania explain why you find staunchly patriotic Polish people like the Kalinowskis born in Vilnius, the capital: it had an overwhelmingly Polish population. Polish families were also found in Ukraine, including members of the Kalinowski family. A certain Valentin Kalinowski, *staroste* or prefect of Braclaw and Winnica was the hero of bitter battles at the beginning of the 17th century. He was rewarded with immense estates in Ukraine.

Foremost among the Lithuanian Poles was Adam Mickiewicz (1798-1855), the great, if not the greatest Lithuanian-Polish poet, also born in Vilnius. He was the star-crossed lover of Marie Wereszczak, mother of Sophie Puttkamer, Joseph's stepmother.[17] Sophie was

---

vestige of nationhood from the former Poland.

[16] In his classic two-volume work on *Poland, God's Playground*, Norman Davies writes: "In the British Isles, the only comparable experience was that suffered by the Irish, whose own loss of statehood lasted from 1800 – 1921 and who strove to preserve their own sense of identity from within another rich, confident, and expansive empire. But if the Irish were faced with one imperial enemy, the Poles were faced with three." Clarendon Press, Oxford, UK, Vol. 11, 1981. Davies goes on to quote a contemporary Polish writer who said he would gladly have exchanged places with the Irish any time.

[17] Mickiewicz would immortalize Marie in his works under the name *Maryla*, also the name of the poem.

Kalinowski senior's third wife. She was a deeply religious woman and became a second mother to her stepchildren. Indeed, from his letters we can see how Joseph treated her like his real mother, though in fact she was only seven years older than he. Through Sophie, Joseph would come under the influence of the poet Mickiewicz's intense Polish patriotism. Saint Pope John Paul II would also be greatly influenced by this poet patriot and refer to him in his inaugural speech as Pope in 1978.[18]

In 1844 at the age of 9, Joseph was enrolled by his father in the Institute of Nobles. The school was established by the Russian government in a former house of the Piarist Fathers. As the name suggests, it was meant to cater for the sons of Lithuanian nobility. It was situated near the former Dominican Priory of the Holy Spirit. Andrew eventually became headmaster of the school. During his tenure between the years 1847-1857, the Institute was highly successful. It was a boarding school and the boys were only allowed home on Sundays and Feast days. In his *Memoirs*, Kalinowski observes: "Within the college severe discipline was enforced. With the exception of the director – a certain Haller, probably of German descent, it was Russianized in everything else…"[19] Kalinowski tells us that some teachers were French and had been officers of Napoleon I in 1812. Three of the teachers were Russian, the rest Polish. However, he was under his father's direction for five years

---

[18] So let us leave aside words. Let there remain just great silence before God, the silence that becomes prayer. I ask you: be with me! At Jasna Gora and everywhere. Do not cease to be with the Pope who today prays with the words of the poet: "Mother of God, you who defend Bright Czestochowa and shine at Ostra Brama. And these same words I address to you at this particular moment." Karol Wojtyła grew up in the shadow of the Carmelite School and Church founded by Raphael Kalinowski and here he would often come to pray.

[19] *St. Raphael Kalinowski, Memoirs* (Unpublished translation by Sr. Miriam Quinn OCD from an Italian version with Introduction by Szczepan T. Praskiewicz, OCD). [Hereafter the references to *Memoirs* of Kalinowski will be referred to in the text with its chapter number inside brackets].

of his time there. A white habited Dominican, Fr. Mokrzewski, chaplain at the school, who greatly impressed the young student, was later, like so many others found guilty of "patriotism." He was deported to Siberia where Kalinowski would briefly meet up with him in Irkutsk.

In his *Memoirs* Kalinowski also relates that during the reign of Czar Nicholas there had been many anti-government conspiracies; he remembered how, as a boy, he had witnessed condemned rebels being led along the nearby street to execution by Russian soldiers. Kalinowski also states that not only were the Poles persecuted but also the Jewish population [*Memoirs*, ch.1].[20]

He notes that many of the inhabitants including the metropolitan archbishop, a man he refers to as the apostate Joseph Siemaszko, together with other bishops and several members of the clergy, had been enticed into the Russian Orthodox Church from the *Uniate* Church.[21] And he adds that the Church of the Holy Trinity became an Orthodox one as well as the Basilian Church and monastery. The latter now housed Russian monks, especially sad for him because it had been hallowed by the presence of the first three martyrs of Vilnius. The Dominican house and that of the Jesuits had been converted into a prison and an army barracks respectively. The University of Vilnius itself had been downgraded to college status.

In the College of Nobles, the boys on the whole were well-behaved, but Kalinowski notes a lapse on one occasion when the professor of French was pelted with pillows! The boys suspected him

---

[20] As is the case with Australia's *stolen generation* of Aborigines, at one point Jewish children were stolen from their homes and from the arms of their weeping mothers, and taken to Russian military schools where they were forced to become Orthodox Christians. Kalinowski himself witnessed one such scene.

[21] Siemaszko resembles somewhat the case of Hyacinthe Loyson, a former Carmelite, who figures in the life of St. Thérèse and that of Hermann Cohen.

of being a Russian spy and it was their way of expressing patriotic feelings.

Kalinowski described the usual religious exercises, which took place such as retreats at Christmas and Easter. They were also given spiritual direction by Constance Eymont, a devout Vincentian or Lazarist priest, as they were known. In his *Memoirs* Kalinowski recalls:

> There was a conference of St. Vincent de Paul in Vilna and the women were allowed to visit the Institute and give us our *obole*.[22] We also celebrated Eucharistic processions with great solemnity throughout the city, while Russian military maintained order. I often observed Bibikow, the governor of Vilna, watch the Blessed Sacrament respectfully from the balcony of his palace, formerly that of the bishop. It was a joy to behold, but also somewhat hard: when we walked along the streets of the city, we saw Russian soldiers on guard at the doors of ancient religious houses: when we reached the rural areas, on the hill of the Three Crosses,[23] raised in honor of the three martyrs murdered by pagans, we saw cannons at the top with their barrels trained on the city; this filled our hearts with sadness and dread.[24]

Kalinowski tells us that in his seventh and final year there were eighteen students. At the end of the year they had to undergo

---

[22] The *obole* was a small coin.

[23] Situated in area known as Siauliai, Pope John Paul II prayed here during his visit to Poland on September 7, 1993. There are now 100,000 crosses on the hill as Lithuanians replaced and enlarged the number of those destroyed by the Soviets.

[24] P. Jean-Baptiste Bouchaud, *Joseph Kalinowski* (Liège: Arts et Métier, 1923) p. 23. [In the first part of this book I refer mostly to the above mentioned work of Bouchaud and references to this book will be cited in the text with its page number/s].

an examination for their graduation diploma. Emperor Nicholas I 'graced' them with his presence. The meeting took place on the first floor of what had formerly been a Piarist church. He tells us the entry of the emperor filled them with dread, as he appeared as a tyrant in their eyes. He told them they had acquired sufficient knowledge and they ought to now take up a military career. Some joined the army, others took a different course.

Joseph was an outstanding student and one of his colleagues at the school testifies that he received an award each year and at the end of his final year was given a gold medal and had his name inscribed on a marble plaque at the Institute. This colleague, Stanislaus Slawinski, further testifies that Joseph "was distinguished by his affability, his application to work, his sensitivity and the goodness of his character. He was esteemed by all his comrades." [p. 24].

When Joseph completed his studies at the Institute of Nobles, he decided to continue studies at the Agronomical School at Hori-Horki near Orsza. The reason for this was that the Russians did not allow students to attend colleges in the Kingdom of Poland – it was either Russia or elsewhere in exile. So Joseph and his elder brother Victor made their way to Horki. He tells us that they stayed over at Minsk for some time where he met his former professor of Russian at the local school, and although they had been treated coldly there, he was sorry to leave because of his filial attachment to this particular man.

Again in his *Memoirs*, Kalinowski tells us that at Horki they lived some distance from the church which made it difficult to attend to religious duties; this, he felt, was unfortunate. He tells us that they attended some "worldly entertainments" without specifying what these were. He insists however, that they were merely spectators and took no active part in these goings-on. "At the school," he writes, "we studied agronomy, zoology, chemistry, apiculture and horticulture. After the second course, we were invited to make excursions to country areas to make practical application of different systems of agriculture. Such work was beyond my energies and tired me; I had a greater aptitude for abstract sciences." [p. 26].

After this period, Joseph transferred to St. Petersburg, at that time capital of Russia, and tried to enroll in the School of Roads and Bridges, but there was no place available. Instead, he entered the School of Military Engineering. Kalinowski continues his story:

> Everything in this school was explained with due care, and Dominic Stankiewicz, a Dominican father from St. Catherine's priory came to teach catechism from time to time. As well as three Polish people, I had many friends there to whom I became very attached. One day one of them contracted cholera; during the course of his illness we stayed close to him and his death caused us much sorrow. At the final examination our Dominican father put a question to me in the presence of the Orthodox officers, which embarrassed me. He asked me if it were possible to be saved outside the Catholic Church. I didn't know how to reply.[25] After this examination I was admitted with the three Poles to the school of engineering. Here again the chaplain was a Dominican who ministered at the church in Prospekt-Newski. This school was situated in the ancient palace of the Grand Duke Michael, brother of Czar Nicholas. The palace was the residence of the emperors in the 13 century and it was here that the Emperor Paul I was assassinated. It was an immense building surrounded by a large and deep trench, and an interior court with tortuous corridors and limitless stairs. Before being admitted we were asked, as in the manner of making religious profession, whether we intended to persevere. Here and now, we were told, you can withdraw, but once admitted you will not be allowed to.

---

25   This priest was not popular with the church authorities, being considered somewhat liberal in his approach to mixed marriages.

> Everything repelled me, everything annoyed me, but what could I do? I gave a response in the affirmative, but with much reluctance, like a man who is condemned to servitude. [*Memoirs*, ch. 1].

There was a harsh discipline in this school and moreover the higher classes were allowed to dominate those below them and treat them in a savage way. However, Kalinowski himself soon passed into the higher class. There were a lot of students from Lithuania, Ruthenia and Poland. They also got on well with the German and Russian students and during the summer went camping under vast tents in Tsarkie-Siolo. [*The palace of the Czars was located here*].

Kalinowski relates that Czar Aleksander II, who succeeded Nicholas, visited them one day and reviewed the students. [*Memoirs*, ch. 1].[26] "When he saw me looking puny and pale he asked me what was wrong? Sir, I replied, I have a toothache. He then spoke a few words to the officer who accompanied him and continued the review. Before leaving he told us that he was satisfied with us." [pp. 27-28].

Kalinowski goes on to tell us that he was once guilty of a breach of discipline by wearing gloves. The director of the school placed him under three days arrest and made him do guard duty during recreation. He was gratified by the support of his comrades who came to visit him and sprinkled eau de cologne in his dank cell. They laughingly saluted him on guard duty outside the recreation hall, but he took it in good part.

He continues in his *Memoirs*: "Our professor of religion was again a Dominican father from the church of Prospekt-Newski where we went to attend Mass. From the point of view of religion

---

[26] Aleksander Romanov survived several assassination attempts before a successful final attempt on March 13, 1881. Kalinowski informs us: "The figure of Aleksander II was very different to that of Nicholas I. Of handsome features, a little affected in gestures, he presented a self-possessed and attractive image.

we were given plenty of freedom. I read *Genie du Christianisme* [The Genius of Christianity] by Chateaubriand and other similar books." [*Memoirs*, ch. 1].

At this time Kalinowski mentions an incident that points to his courage and integrity. The French professor Monsieur Bougeaud gave one of the students a bad report, which he had indeed merited. The students were furious, however, and threw it away. M. Bougeaud questioned them individually but no one owned up. When it came to Kalinowski's turn he stood up and admitted the truth. Needless to say he became the butt of many reproaches. "That was the only courageous act of my life," [p. 28] Kalinowski modestly comments.

Kalinowski goes on to relate how the students were introduced to manual work and a school was established for this purpose. There were workshops for carpentry, wood turning, locksmiths, etc. On the day of the solemn opening the director wished to test the aptitudes of the students with practical experience. As a first-rate student, Joseph was given a small hatchet for squaring beams. He accidentally wounded his leg with the hatchet, which of course caused alarm and he was rushed to hospital and treated by the imperial doctors. He tells us: "I was out of bounds for some months and as it included the feast of Easter, it was the saddest time of my life." [p. 29].

When he finished his studies at the engineering academy he graduated as a lieutenant with distinction. His director then decided to keep him on at the school teaching mathematics. He began on June 1, 1857 at the age of 22. He tells us in his *Memoirs* that he had no great enthusiasm for this task. He liked to indulge in reading instead. "My pleasure," he goes on, "was in reading. I read many books, many edifying, and others which were forbidden by the government." In fact, his preferences were for books in English, such as works of Shakespeare, Byron, Walter Scott and others.

Kalinowski liked to attend ballet and theatrical performances. We don't have a great deal of information, however, about his youthful relationships. Ceslaus Gil tells us he met his first girlfriend in 1854, but nothing is known of her or her successor. Gil writes:

"Later, he became interested in Celina Gruszewska. They knew each other since childhood and had vacations together at the home of his grandmother Caroline Polonska. Celina's mother would not give her permission to marry Joseph because he lacked the means to support a future family. Joseph accepted that decision quite readily. In a letter to family friend Louise Młocka he said, "My heart has now cooled down and I have little regret." He further remarked that he was happy to hear Celina had found a suitable partner and had married.[27]

Gil comments further: "His opinion of marriage became very pessimistic as he observed the life of married persons around him. 'Everything is ideal in dreams because what can be more sweet than the union of two people in a completely mutual attraction. In reality, however, all the poetry of married life disappears before the prose of reality.'"

Some years prior to this, the young Kalinowski grew careless.[28] Later in his *Memoirs* he recalled: "I abandoned religious practices, but from time to time a craving for these things awakened in my soul. But I was not faithful to that interior voice." [*Memoirs*, ch. 2]. Like many enquiring students he underwent some soul-searching and eventually came to the conclusion that only faith can form a stable basis for one's life.

Kalinowski availed himself of the presence and performances of an English Shakespearean actor to deepen his appreciation of the bard. This was the time when he went through an Anglophile period and became infatuated with a girl called Margaret, an English actress. He makes a short but tantalizing comment on that early dalliance, which also went nowhere – he allowed himself to be smitten by an English Rose, but it seems to have been an unrequited love. Writing to his brother in December 1858, when he was 23 years

[27] Gil Czeslaus OCD, *Father Raphael Kalinowski* (Translated by Sr. Czeslava of Divine Mercy OCD. Carmelites, Kraków, 1979).
[28] Praskiewicz, Szczepan T. OCD, *Saint Raphael Kalinowski* (ICS Publications, Washington D.C., 1998).

of age, he had this to say: "An English arrow has dealt me a slight wound. I adore Margaret, but have no hope of being loved in return. I search for soul and I only find something of a material kind."[29] Kalinowski seems then to have thought seriously of marriage at this time, but hesitated at the idea of commitment. A year earlier he had written to his brother Victor:

> At Petersburg people only talk of outlaws, assassinations and daylight robbery. Corrupted by life in the capital, I have become completely sceptical about the marriage state, which has for me little charm. I know that I will not find peace and that I will always be lacking something. My imagination is so vivid that it makes me sway from side to side. I am inclined towards worldly diversion, but I do not find the peace that I seek and there is always something lacking. My extremely vivid imagination tosses me to and fro. On the other hand, I suppress the impulses that would prompt me to study. The only plus I experience is when I can enjoy peaceful sleep after being distracted and fatigued. I confess that I have never come across anyone as volatile as myself in my attitudes. I sway carelessly from one extreme to the other. But it's a good thing that I recognize this defect in myself and quickly return to my normal state. I'm surprised at my moderation. I have so much temptation to cope with at every turn that I don't know where to look for an escape. [p. 30].

Then he tells us he engaged in some serious reading: "Evenings in St. Petersburg, *(Pope and Papability)*, by Joseph de Maistre gave me plenty to think about, as did the *Confessions* of St. Augustine." [p. 31]. He attended Lenten conferences preached in French by a

---

[29]   An unidentified English actress. He would have encountered her at the English Theatre in St. Petersburg.

Dominican priest, Dominic Souaillard.[30] It will be obvious that Kalinowski was gifted at languages as he seemed equally at home reading French and English in addition to his native languages Lithuanian and Polish. French, of course, was a second language for the educated classes at that time. But, he tells us: "the good effects of the lectures didn't endure. I neglected religious practices. These lectures awoke in me a taste for piety, but I didn't always obey the voice of my conscience. One day I passed by the *(Dominican)* church of St. Stanislaus. The thought struck me to enter the church. I knelt down before the confessional, unfortunately it was empty and there wasn't a person in the church. I burst into tears and a feeling of sadness and tedium enveloped me..."[31] Again referring to reading the Dominican's lectures, he continues:

> But in spite of that I didn't find the impetus I needed and my life continued in hesitant vein. I daresay I would have been on more of an even keel in my homeland, when I reflect on what a sad situation had unfortunately overtaken so many of my comrades, people who were more devoted, more capable and more virtuous than I; this made me conclude that we were like young plants uprooted from our native place and planted in a strange soil, where eventually we wilted completely. We were indeed like plants suffocated in this strange land, where certainly if we did take root we bore fruit for aliens and not for our own country. And I say nothing of the hardships of souls, or the neglected goal of our lives, which should be a progress towards eternal life. If we were sons of Holy Church, where were the signs of our sonship? [p. 31].

---

[30] Souillard also known as Soyard.

[31] Surprisingly he deferred trying again at a suitable time, and it was not until much later when he returned to his family in Vilnius, where he made his peace with God by means of the sacrament of penance.

Kalinowski had now become an army engineer and he served briefly building fortifications at the island of Kronstadt, near St. Petersburg, during the Crimean War; he had to withdraw from there through illness, and returned on leave to stay with his family. Apparently the intense summer heat had caused him to take ill. Kalinowski goes on to comment that the first years of Czar Aleksander II were a time of reprieve all round and there was a perception that the Catholic Church might enjoy a period of freedom. He continues:

> At this time P. Souaillard gave Lenten conferences every Wednesday in St. Petersburg. The surroundings of the church were full of coaches from the imperial court. It was at the Catholic Church that people came in search of light. The Orthodox tried to set up a rival effort but nobody listened to them. They were annoyed and after Lent lodged complaints telling P. Souaillard not to return to Russia. I will repeat again a passage from the conferences on the works of charity in the heart of the Church where one sacrifices one's very person and not just one's resources as the Protestants do. [p. 32].

This remark seems to prompt Kalinowski to observe about those who attended the lectures:

> Among these, distinguished for exceptional recollection and her spirit of devotion, was Catherine Narischkin, a convert from the Russian Orthodox Church inspired by the example of Sister Natalie. Just the sight of her raised the soul to God: her features gave evidence of interior silence and peace of heart, nobility joined with simplicity. She looked like an angel. The figure of Catherine had elements in common

15

with the sister that Augusta Craven described for us in the Life of Sister Natalie Narischin." [*Memoirs*, ch. 2].[32]

At this time Kalinowski made the acquaintance of the Russian aristocratic Imeretynski family whom he met through General Zurov, a relative of theirs. The two young princes in the family, Aleksander and Dimytri, were students in the Page Corps in St. Petersburg. Kalinowski was asked by the boys' professor to stand in for him during holidays. The grandfather of the princes was an ex-Adjutant-General of the Emperor and liked to play chess with Kalinowski. Amusingly, Kalinowski tells us that he made overtures to this man to convert him to Roman Catholicism, but admitted that the General was more likely to have been successful the other way round.

Kalinowski was particularly impressed by Aleksander, who he saw was *richly endowed*, and tried to instil in him upright principles, warning him also to avoid bad companions. Aleksander grew up to attain the highest positions in the Russian Army. Ironically, he was involved in the suppression of the 1863 Polish uprising in which Kalinowski took part. However, Aleksander was a moderate; he lifted some restrictive laws such as a prohibition on using the Polish language. He allowed the Poles to erect a monument to the great poet Adam Mickiewicz and as a result of these moderate policies was eventually removed from office. Perhaps we have Kalinowski to thank that this man would prove favorable to Polish aspirations in later life. [p. 33].

---

[32] Kalinowski tells us that Natalie was Superior of the Sisters of Charity in Paris and because of her contacts with the Russian court she arranged for Souaillard to deliver these lectures in St. Petersburg. I will provide an account of Natalie Narischin in a later chapter. She was a friend of Hermann Cohen, whom she greatly admired. Kalinowski produced an edition of Craven's *Life of Natalie* in Polish in Kraków in 1903.

Around this time he met Balthasar Kalinowski,[33] and though not directly related to him, he proved to be a good friend and very helpful to Kalinowski when he returned from exile. At this time there were a number of possibilities opening up for the young engineer. There was mention of him being sent to plan the railway line to Pskov on the link from St. Petersburg to Vilnius and on to Warsaw. There was even a possibility of him being sent as an ambassador to Beijing. But both of these fell through possibly because Kalinowski fell ill. A heavy winter fog blanketed St. Petersburg and this was reflected in his own life. Uncharacteristically he gives us a litany of maladies afflicting him: headache, toothache, eye problems, irregular heartbeat and painful spleen, all of which were plunging him into a fit of depression. The high mortality rate in the area induced a feeling of foreboding and he contemplated the possibility of death, adding: "If only death would deliver me from this fog in Petersburg." To cap it all he grumbles: "The English theatre has burned down, our Polish journal has been suppressed, only sad news from Vilnius, is it really life when one is separated from all one loves?" [p. 34].

Kalinowski continues his story in Chapter Two of his *Memoirs*, telling us that after spending a year and a half teaching mathematics at the Academy in St. Petersburg, he was given an engineering post there. At that time the construction of a railway line from Kursk to Odessa was undertaken.[34] Due to the good graces of his old teacher of mathematics, he was given the job of planning the direction the new railway line had to take, and for this purpose he was sent to Kursk. It's worth noting Kalinowski's spiritual development at this time:

---

[33] Kalinowski tells us they discussed the writings of Aleksander Herzen, an exiled Russian who lived for a time in London.
[34] The city of Kursk is about half way between Moscow and Odessa, the Ukrainian port on the Black Sea.

My job at Kursk was to draw up the necessary plans for carrying out the work. It was necessary for me to make many journeys to Putywl and other places to pick up statistical and geographical ideas of which I was in need. Nowhere did I find a Catholic church... At Kursk I lived near the Orthodox Church. I only set foot in there once, invited to a wedding by a family who were known to me. Perhaps here I could do some praying. That evening, the thought of the cemetery which was close to my room, and the cry of the owls that inhabited the neighbourhood, exercised a salutary impression on my mind. The old sacristan who was a very honest man became a friend. When I returned after a long absence and asked him how he was, he would reply, 'I am very well, thanks be to God and to your prayers.' In all this expedition I can report only one benefit, not from my work, but from a little religious book, an anthology of prayers to the Blessed Virgin. It had been given to me by a young Polish man who helped me draw up the plans and had been a keepsake of his mother. The reading of this little book had a great influence on me. It instilled in me particularly a lively trust in the intercession of the Holy Virgin. One remark on the efficacy of the Hail Mary remained deeply engraved on my memory, and on one occasion when I found myself exposed to imminent danger, I recited the Ave and I emerged safe and sound. What a powerful weapon prayer is! How easy it is to obtain everything through the intercession of Mary! What efficacious means of salvation Holy Church places in our hands through these religious books, which open the eyes of our souls to the splendor of divine truth! [*Memoirs*, ch. 2].

In a letter to his brother Victor dated September 25, 1859, Kalinowski demonstrates how grace was beginning to take hold in his life. Having referred to himself as living a bohemian life or worse at this time, he goes on to mention a feeling of homesickness when he reflected on the happy families whom he encountered. Being on the move, he was soon separated from new friends, but now something else was happening. "Being deprived of their company nevertheless did not cause me to lose my good humor." Then he continues:

> In my solitude, I have always been able to turn inwards on my interior life, and I can openly say that this constant work with myself and on myself, far from the world, has produced in me a great change for the better... I have recognized the great need for solid religious convictions and I have finally formed them on myself. I am indebted to one book in particular of inestimable value, the *Confessions of St. Augustine*; from this I have richly drawn new life for myself. I look upon life more calmly now and its allurements have lost much of their charm for me. There remains much for me to do, however, and I tremble when I think of the whirlwind life of the capital, which I am obliged to visit often; I know only too well its strong attractions. [p. 37].

Kalinowski was allowed a holiday in early August and went to visit his father who was staying at his brother Victor's home known at 'Studzionki.' From there he went home to Vilnius and then on to Kaunas. An interesting development at this time which shows Kalinowski's growing charity is the following anecdote. Writing to his brother Victor on August 10 he adds this postscript:

> P.S. I re-open my envelope and do you know the reason? I do this in order to greet you concerning a nephew and for myself about a son, whom God willed to send me today. I went on a walk today to Rosa. Passing near a garden, I heard a little infant wailing: I approached and found a little creature near the path. Thankfully it was not far from

the Foundlings Home. I found a baptismal certificate and some nappies beside him. I saw the hand of providence in this event and I adopted my little Jean and my life from now has one aim – I work for him. However, I am a little embarrassed now not knowing what to do with him. It would be lovely if you could take him into your home! Write to me on this subject to Vilna, to father's address, but frankly and openly. If you agree I will arrange to transfer him to Glaskowszczyzna. He is a little infant with blue eyes, shining and bright. The tiny mite was frozen because the rain had soaked him and the morning was cold. In my present circumstances of being unmarried, I am happy at the way Providence has dealt with me. I am a child without a spouse, a rose without a thorn. I am curious to know what Mary (*Victor's wife, they had no children*) will say on the matter. I kiss your hand and ask for shelter for my little child. Father is not at Vilna and knows nothing about this: when he returns I will congratulate him about his little son. As for you, I must be perplexing you. Keep well and reply to me without delay. [p. 37].

Back in St. Petersburg he writes to Victor again on September 17. He must have had a favorable response: "Many thanks for your good will, and for the compassionate welcome your noble heart has held out for my little child. In a few weeks I will leave for the fortress of Brest-Litewski. I will then be nearer to you and I will try to obtain some week of leave to see you." [p. 37]. It seems that he had been quite ill and was awaiting an operation. He writes: "I will not let myself be photographed at this time because my face is swollen and deformed for an uncertain period and I wouldn't like to appear in this state in your halls."[35] Twelve days later he wrote:

---

[35] In later life as a Carmelite Kalinowski would be averse to being photographed and would turn his head away from the camera. He was also known to avoid the use of mirrors and even to shave without one!

I am still in my prison in Petersburg, and I have no idea when I can leave for Brest. Pity me: I'm sitting in my room all day, my head shrouded in bandages, I wait for the end of my treatment with a patience and resignation that is not at all like me. The doctors in St. Petersburg, like those in Vilna, contradict each another and seem to have no idea about my illness. My diversion consists in reading and meditation; I have plenty of books and I am now making provision for the scarcity of books that will await me in Brest. I'm hoping that down there I will be able to engage in writing; hence, I'm buying paper and pens. Joking apart, when I consider the piles of books I have read and the knowledge I have gained, I feel like a crook who steals from others and I don't give anything to anybody. That uselessness of my life is often a cause of remorse for me: what consoles me is my tranquillity, that I have good will. [p. 39].

Chapter Two

Reluctant Rebel

*W*e now follow Joseph Kalinowski in a new chapter of his life. The story unfolds in his *Memoirs:* "On September 1, 1860 I was transferred as Commandant of Engineering to Brest. All the officers were German and I had a good rapport with them, though I rarely took part in their recreational activities. I also had more frequent and closer relationships with some Polish families, who lived in the area." [*Memoirs*, ch. 2. This was his 25th birthday]. Kalinowski gives us a snapshot of the area in his *Memoirs*:

> The population at Brest is mainly Jewish; the country folk, at one time Uniate, were forcibly made to join the Sect after the apostasy of the metropolitan Siemaszko. The people are peaceful but the police stir up trouble against Catholics and they become discontented. The suppression of the Uniate Church has been a terrible calamity for the country from a religious and social point of view: discord and hatred is rife among the different classes of society. In the rural areas morals are corrupted because the people, deprived of the help that the Catholic religion provides, no longer have the moral fiber to withstand the daily challenges of life. The

Brest Fortress was built on the ruins of the ancient town where the Union of Brest was ratified. All that reflected our national and religious past was destroyed. The monastery of the Basilians was turned into a prison for delinquents who were forced to work in the fortress; the Jesuit College became a military hospital. The Ruthenian Catholic Church was changed to the breakaway one. In the part of the fort that I was engaged to survey, a storeroom for gunpowder had to be constructed. I was given a group of prisoners to help in strengthening the foundations. In seeing the wretched state of their souls *(for the government did not care about them)*, one's heart was moved to compassion. The thought struck me that these unfortunates were less culpable before God than us, because we do not profit from the help we receive for our own spiritual good and that of our neighbor. [*Memoirs*, ch. 2].

Here we see Kalinowski's heart expanding and responding to the spiritual need he noticed around him. He wrote: "Involvement in service meant nothing for me but trouble. But the friendship of a few people and some intimate exchanges with them was my only joy. That is the feeling that provides a goal in life for us, which builds up society and fully animates me. I like to think that this love of neighbor which enlivens us is like a bond that reconnects us to life." [p. 44].

An example of this love in action was when he adopted another youth called Louis and took the boy's education in hand. He wrote to his friend Louise Młocka[36] in February 1862: "Louis' education is going well. Little by little he is mastering the elements of primary education and he is a great help to me in our little school." [p. 42].

---

[36] Around this time (1861) Kalinowski made the acquaintance of Louise Młocka, a relative of his sister-in-law Marie, and she would exert a good influence on him from now on. She would later send him a beautifully bound copy of the New Testament.

Another example of his selfless nature was that when the opportunity arose for 'taking the waters,'[37] of which indeed he had great need, he sent Louis instead who he felt needed them more. Later on when leaving Brest, he entrusted Louis to the care of a good family.

On April 7, 1862 Kalinowski was appointed Captain of General Staff. However, life was very frustrating for him in Brest. He ought to have been given a post in the Higher Institute of Engineering in Warsaw, but his requests fell on deaf ears. He expressed his frustration in these words: "I am like a fish banging his head on the glass. I find myself very isolated! Incessant work, feeble health, nothing but sadness within and without. There is nothing on which I can fix my thoughts with satisfaction." Yet he could also say: "Let us allow God to direct our barque." And again: "It is only in prayer – if indeed one still knows how to pray – that one is able to find peace, if only for a few moments. God gives courage and perseverance to the unhappy and the suffering. I'm sadder at the lot of the blind who reject suffering and seek comfort in diversions, which they ought to avoid." Another remark shows Kalinowski's innate sensitivity: "When digging out the soil we unearthed many bones and I asked the pastor to take them to the cemetery, which was done. While the work was going on one of the men gave this sad pile of bones a kick saying 'away with you noble bones.' This vulgarity caused me great sorrow and I commanded him to show respect at least in death." [*Memoirs*, ch. 2]. Kalinowski now gives hints of immense trouble to come:

> During my time at Brest-Litewski trouble began in Warsaw. A hidden and invisible hand stirred up the spirit of insurrection in the Kingdom of Poland, and among the students in the universities of Moscow, Kiev and as far as St. Petersburg. It happened also in Brest and its surroundings.

---

[37] This entails the popular practice of visiting spas in various places and bathing in sulphurous springs.

At the beginning people talked only of the public good, of beneficial works, but that was only among us engineering officers. No one knew who among the young people were indulging in activist propaganda. Proclamations which stirred up insurrection were secretly printed. Meetings were held here and there for the same purpose. One day I myself was invited along and I joined in with them. One young speaker addressed us, 'don't worry, Napoleon III and Turkey are with us.' I stood up in my turn, and after pointing out the tragic and dire consequences of such empty-headed stuff, I left the hall, my heart full of sadness and bitterness, at seeing the abyss into which people were blindly throwing themselves. What could Poland do without arms, against a power as strong as Russia? I again asked for a transfer from military engineering back to the railway section, but my request was not granted. [*Memoirs*, ch. 3].

Prince Adam Czartoryski is undoubtedly one of Poland's great heroes. He took part in the famed – but failed – insurrection of 1794, led by Tadeuz Kosciusko. He was then sent to St. Petersburg as a kind of hostage, where he became a friend of the Grand Duke Aleksander. When Aleksander became Czar in 1801, he appointed Czartoryski Minister for Foreign Affairs in addition to giving him an education portfolio in the former Polish territories. After Napoleon's defeat, Aleksander brought Czartoryski along with him as a negotiator to the Congress of Vienna. Later Czartoryski drew up a constitution for the new Kingdom of Poland, or the Congress Kingdom as it was called. Moreover, he was Curator of the University of Vilnius, which had an excellent reputation. Meanwhile Aleksander died and the new Czar Nicholas adopted a tough line against the Poles.

In November 1830, an assassination attempt was made on the Grand Duke Constantine. The Polish authorities tried to contain the situation and Czartoryski joined a National Council, but Aleksander refused to be placated. As the situation deteriorated a new government was formed and led by Czartoryski and Michal Radziwill, who was appointed commander-in-chief. There were opportunities for the Poles to gain the upper hand on Russia at this time, but strategic mistakes were made by the Polish forces and the opportunity passed them by.

Their military cause was not helped by the fact Czartoryski was leaning towards a diplomatic solution, which didn't endear him to the hotheads. This indecision and hesitation at the top bought time for Russia and they used it to achieve a military solution themselves. Many of the leaders including Czartoryski were captured and condemned to death. Tens of thousands ended up in Siberia. Czartoryski's sentence was commuted to exile and he made good his escape to Paris. These events signaled the end of what was called the *First Insurrection* against the Russians. Czartoryski set up a government in exile in the Hôtel Lambert in Paris and published a paper for Polish exiles called *Wiadomosci Polskie* or *Polish News.* He was the leader of what was known as the aristocratic or White Party, while there were numerous adherents of a radical or Red Party among the Polish émigrés.

Events of course kept moving forward at a fast pace and Europe was again in turmoil with the emergence of European-wide revolution during the upheavals of 1848, The 'Springtime of Nations.'[38] Poland again had the opportunity to make a play for freedom. Even the diplomatic-minded Czartoryski made his way from Paris to Poznan, a revolutionary center with forces commanded by General Ludwik Mieroslawski. But as so often in the past and as happens in the present, the tide was turning under the pressure of politics. Both Napoleon III of France and Lord Palmerston of Britain now pulled back so as not to alienate the Prussians and Austrians, as they both faced a common foe in Russia in the run up to the Crimean War.

---

[38] This phrase has gained currency again with what has been called *The Arab Spring* in 2011, referring to insurrection in Tunisia, Libya, Syria and other places.

Meanwhile, Aleksander Wielopolski, a capable, intelligent and prudent Pole trusted by the Russians, had initiated reforms from St. Petersburg. Though he had taken part in the 1830 uprising, he had come to see the futility of this approach. In 1862 he was appointed head of the civil government in the Kingdom of Poland. He obtained the agreement of the Czar for the appointment of Bishop Felinski as Archbishop of Warsaw and the Czar's brother Constantine as viceroy in Poland. Wielopolski was not universally popular because of real or apparent arrogance. Kalinowski himself took a more charitable view of him: "He is a reasonable man who has the interests of his country at heart, and tried to obtain from Russia whatever was possible for the country. Unfortunately, he was too attached to his personal opinions." [p. 49].

Before he died, Prince Adam Czartoryski advised his son Ladislaus to follow the policies of Wielopolski. Though Czartoryski didn't condemn the patriotic demonstrations, he nevertheless advised against armed insurrection. But Wielopolski had rivals in the reform movement such as Andrew Zamoyski, less capable but more popular than he. On February 25, 1861 a meeting commemorating the uprising of 1830 was broken up by the police. Two days later they opened fire on a religious procession, leaving five dead. This approach, highhanded to say the least, led to additional demonstrations throughout the Kingdom of Poland as well as Moscow, Kiev and even St. Petersburg. Thousands of people were picked up by the police and imprisoned.

Agitation was under way and in 1859 and 1860 groups of students as well as women's groups initiated political and religious demonstrations in the streets of Warsaw. Mieroslawski set up an Italian-style secret society called a *chapter,* in Warsaw. He was in touch with international radicals and was a friend of Garibaldi who was working for the reunification of Italy. Garibaldi's successes were a source of encouragement for rebellious-minded Poles. Adam Zamoyski writes: "While liberals saw a Polish Cavour in Czartoryski, radicals saw a Polish Garabaldi in Mieroslawski, who was a friend of Prince Napoleon, nephew of the Emperor of the French."[39]

Russia had been weakened by defeat in the Crimean War and this was an additional source of hope for Poles. Mieroslawski set up a provisional government in Warsaw with the aim of coordinating an insurrection in 1862. Kalinowski fills us in on his part in the lead-up to insurrection, so providing us with a slice of Polish history. He writes:

> Taking the waters at Ciechocineck, I saw Russian soldiers on Sundays and Feast days singing insulting anti-Polish songs. A young artist came to see me one day and talked to me about insurrection. He advised me to visit Warsaw and meet the leaders of the revolutionary movement. I took his advice, but the man I spoke to was such a demagogue that I got up and left. I had never come across anyone with such theories. Events followed one another quite rapidly. At the beginning of the year 1863, a National Government was set up in Warsaw and a state of insurrection was proclaimed. I was assured by Awejde that this measure was taken on the authority and at the threats of the conspirators themselves, when Wielopolski ordered the young people of Warsaw to join the military. [p. 50].[40]

Exacerbating the situation was the fact that Wielopolski had ordered the execution of the young men who had made an assassination attempt on the Grand Duke Constantine and on himself. This backfired on him and he was accused of not treating the conspirators as harshly as the would-be assassins. Then on January 22, 1863, Mieroslawski and the National Council declared

---

[39]   Adam Zamoyski, *Poland, A History* (London: Harper Press, 2009).

[40]   Oskar Awejde took part in the revolution of 1963 and was a leader of the National Government.

an insurrection, calling to arms "all the youth of Poland, Lithuania and Ruthenia."

Kalinowski consistently disapproved of armed insurrection and had what amounted to a premonition of the doom hanging over the whole enterprise. At the beginning of January he had in fact written to his friend Louise Młocka: "I have been so unhappy with the year that's just passed that I don't greet you on the one to come. I just send good wishes for your happiness. I cannot wait to leave military service and return to my loved ones … Groups of insurgents have formed in the Kingdom of Poland and blood is beginning to pour. I refrain from passing judgment on these happenings, and today I view things from a wider perspective. If I could have foreseen what I know today, I strongly doubt if the proclamation of the National Government would have produced the results that it has produced." [p. 52]. After relating some details of the turmoil that was now in full swing, Kalinowski tells us about the activity of one of the insurgent leaders and the effect it was having on himself:

> A party of insurgents, under their leader Roginski crossed the border to find refuge in Lithuania in the canton of Pinsk. It would be difficult to describe what was going on in my mind. It was a terrible struggle. My heart was profoundly moved when I considered that the blood of my brothers was being shed, and it was impossible for me to be at ease in a military uniform. The next development was enough to tip the scales. The Czar appointed Baron Nostitz to repress the rebellion and he delivered a hate-filled speech to the military (of which Kalinowski was one), insisting that no quarter be given, except to old people and women, as if the whole population were insurgents. [p. 53].

The upshot was that Kalinowski immediately demanded his commission to be withdrawn. He had been deeply moved by a patriotic demonstration on the occasion of the funeral of Prince Adam Czartoryski, who died in exile in France in 1861.

Then he reports on an atrocity: "But altogether different was the effect produced on the Russian soldiers by it (*the speech*). One day coming across a farm wagon loaded with grain, together with some barrels of brandy, they assumed it was destined for the insurgents. They raided the brandy and then in a drunken state murdered the proprietor of the farm. They would also have demolished his house had not a Russian officer diverted the cannon pointing at it." [p. 54].

He then tells us that after the dispersion of the insurgents, Nostitz returned to Brest with 100 prisoners, including their leader Roginski. Kalinowski mentions that he would meet Roginski again in Siberia. That was the end of insurgent action in the Brest area. It was rumored that the insurrection was over in the Kingdom of Poland and in Lithuania, but often pockets of rebels held on as long as possible, hoping for outside intervention in favor of Poland. But resistance was futile and the country was exhausted.

Napoleon III was not in favor of insurrection early on but changed his mind. The word from Czartorysk in the Hôtel Lambert in Paris suggested that they should be grateful for the autonomy Russia had accorded, and "that the insurrection was an unreasonable and deplorable enterprise, which could not count on French support." [pp. 54-55]. Soon, however, that advice changed. Bismarck, the Iron Chancellor, resented the friendship between Napoleon III and the Czar Aleksander II. He hoped to reverse the defeat at Jena and reclaim Poland as far as the Vistula River. He made overtures to the Poles to this effect but was indignantly rebuffed. Then he turned his attention to the German provinces, but to achieve this he needed the help of Russia. He craftily promised support to Russia in any Polish rebellion, which he suggested would be a signal for revolution in Russia and throughout Europe. So on February 8, 1863 he made a military pact with the Czar to suppress the revolution. Many young

Polish officers who had done their military training in France were arrested in Prussia and handed over to Russia.

This move, of course, prompted Napoleon III to change tactics and in concert with Britain and Austria signaled support for Poland. But he wanted it publicized as an anti-Russian move, upholding Polish nationhood and not as a revolutionary one. This had the effect of stirring up the nobility, quite inactive up to this point, to join the uprising. Soon the strongman Mieroslawski was replaced by Marian Langiewicz and when he was toppled also, the National Government looked to Ladislaus Czartoryski, Adam's son, and soon money was pouring into Poland. Kalinowski comments: "In Lithuania no attention was paid to social position, personal fortune or family bonds; everything was sacrificed for a cause considered to be truly national. In this situation I couldn't remain inactive. I consulted influential people on this but received an evasive answer because the insurrection had no chance of success. At Vilna the National Government section was replaced constantly because the police had caught the members in a net thrown widely across the country." [p. 56]. Kalinowski describes how things were developing:

> Groups of insurgents, decimated and few in number, darted here and there holding the Russian troops in check, until the endeavor was completely suppressed. After the defeat of the commandant Sigismond Sieralowski at Birze in Samogitia, the forces of the priest Mackiewicz and of de Dluski, held on for some time but they were not able to last long. In certain communities who had organized an insurrection, whole villages were burnt and the people deported to Siberia and were forbidden to return. The student revolt at the Agronomy Institute in Horki also ended in disaster. All the details were not immediately evident to me but the general situation was quite clear. You had to give yourself and sacrifice yourself without hope of success but only

from a sense of duty. Others were sacrificing themselves, could I be allowed to remain indifferent? There was much sentimentality in this, of course, but I knew I would have to take a definite decision. In May I received my de-mobbing and I left for Warsaw with the idea of returning to Vilna, where my father and the rest of the family lived. I didn't say goodbye to my friends in Brest, especially the Wiesniowski family. [p. 57].[41]

When Kalinowski arrived in Warsaw, he met two of his old friends in the street. One of them belonged to the Ministry of War in the National Revolutionary Government. Kalinowski remembers that one of these enlisted him to follow his example; this friend was serving under Wielopolski. The other friend he mentioned suddenly disappeared. The government member told Kalinowski about the first organizers of insurrection and it was not very positive. Two or three of them had been his colleagues in a school and they didn't enjoy a very good reputation. When the insurrection broke out, they promptly took flight across the frontier. But Kalinowski notes: "I closed my eyes to the faults of those who had ignited the rebellion and thought only of those who had become involved and gave their lives for it." [p. 58].

Kalinowski tells us that an officer in the Ministry of War, into which he was being co-opted, tried to get him to agree to pass sentences of death on anyone who proved to be a traitor. He refused. He continued to have qualms about becoming involved and needed to consult a confessor before making a final decision.

Kalinowski arrived back in Vilnius in May 1863. He had an additional reason for coming to the aid of his comrades in Vilnius, which he found to be, in his own words, "a gigantic prison." [p. 60]. It was a good preparation for what would come later in Siberia. It was

---

41 Kalinowski was godfather to Wiesniowski's child and had asked his friend Louise Młocka to send him a little gold cross or a medal of Our Lady of Czestochowa to give to the child.

also a foretaste of what would happen in the future in Nazi Germany and its occupied countries, or in Stalinist Russia, not to mention other totalitarian regimes. The Czar had installed the notorious Mikhail Muravyov in Vilnius to suppress the insurrection. He was good at this. Muravyov goes down in history with Judge Jefferies in England or Judkin Fitzgerald in Ireland as *The Hanging Judge*, or *The Hangman*, a sobriquet he would probably not have chosen for himself.

When Kalinowski reached Vilnius, Muravyov had only just begun his bloody business. He had absolute power and he used it indiscriminately. One of his first acts was to hang four priests "as a salutary example." [p. 61]. One of his aims was to extirpate the Roman or Uniate Church at all costs and compel people to join the Orthodox Church. He sent Krasinski, Bishop of Vilnius into exile, in accordance with his view that the Catholic Church was the greatest enemy of Russia in Lithuania. He also wished to hang the Catholic nobility of Lithuania, whom he perceived as preventing the peasants from joining the Orthodox Church. He also bribed the peasants to turn in anyone under the faintest suspicion of being an insurgent. The bribe was carefully scaled depending on the importance of the person delivered up. Entire villages and country houses suspected of being involved in insurrection were burned and destroyed. Those who were not killed were sent into exile under the lash. He was reputed to have personally hanged 128 people in less than two years. He had ordered more than 10,000 people into exile.

Kalinowski's three brothers, Karol, Victor and Gabriel had also become involved in the insurrection. The fourth, Aleksander, was attending the University of Moscow and left with the intention of taking part also. Karol suddenly left the University of Kiev, before his exams, with the same purpose. We know from a letter Kalinowski wrote to Victor that he, like many other thinking Poles at the time, was not in favor of young people from the colleges jumping headlong into the fray. Referring to the above-mentioned young man Roginski, he commented: "It is not blood that Poland needed – too much of that had already been shed, but sweat. But alas, youth do not wish to understand." [p. 59]. Muravyov's tyranny was such that Czar Aleksander recalled him and, in fact, the Russian people themselves were outraged at his conduct. This was the Tiger of Vilnius whom Kalinowski would face on his return home.

Chapter Three

Abortive Rebellion

A bout the forthcoming rebellion, Kalinowski writes:

> I had little confidence in the members of the National
> Government in Warsaw. Having made the acquaintance
> of Laurent, its commissary in Vilnius, I was confirmed
> in my fears. It's true I often wavered in my opinion, but
> my overall impression held good. One thing put my mind
> at ease and that was the integrity of the members of the
> National Government in Vilnius, who to tell the truth, were
> people called on to heal the wounds of the public and bring
> help to individuals. [*Memoirs*, ch. 2].

Kalinowski was also confirmed in this opinion by the arrival
of an official from Warsaw who did not go down well with the
Lithuanian group, and so the man quickly returned by the same route
as he came. He was replaced by Oskar Awejde, a young socialist who
had been finishing his studies in St. Petersburg. He tried to evade
the police by cutting his hair and assuming a false name. However,
it didn't work and Awejde was arrested. He remained silent for a time
but eventually gave the police the information they were looking for.

By the time Kalinowski returned to Vilnius, the National Government had given way to the followers of the revolutionary Mieroslawski. This led, of course, to complete confusion and lack of direction. They didn't last long and were replaced by a more moderate faction. In 1862 a committee had been formed in Lithuania to struggle for national and religious freedom. It recommended a prudent approach and warned that if the insurrection was started prematurely and without sufficient preparation, it would withdraw from the movement. However, as soon as blood began to flow in the Kingdom of Poland, the provinces of Lithuania couldn't remain indifferent. A call went out and the peasants rose, armed only with pikes and hatchets. Groups were successively organized under the direction of such leaders as Clet Korewa, Louis Narbut, Sigismond Sierakowski, Anthony Mackiewiez, Boleslaus Dluski, Romuald Traugutt and others. From February to May this group harried the Russian troops with some notable successes, but eventually were outnumbered. Many scattered and some fled to the Kingdom of Poland. Others, including a priest named Mackiewiez, continued the struggle until the spring of 1864. They were directed by Kalinowski who had been co-opted to head a Ministry of War. Korewa was arrested and shot at Kaunas in March 1863. Sierakowski was wounded at the battle of Birze and captured by the Russians, and in June he was hanged in Vilnius. Kalinowski witnessed the execution; apparently on this occasion he fell on his knees and consecrated his life to the service of God. Narbut died on the field of battle on May 13, saying he was happy to die for the fatherland. So one by one the leaders were picked up and executed. The priest Mackiewiez was hanged in Kaunas on December 28, 1863, together with many others. Early in June Muravyov's police arrested several members of the national government, including Aleksander Osierko, who was sentenced to death.

It was said an appeal for mercy was made to Muravyov who responded: "No mercy for Osierko." [p. 66]. However, for some reason, he relented and the sentence was commuted to exile in

Siberia. The rebel government in Vilnius regrouped and now included Joseph Kalinowski, still heading the Ministry of War, Constantine Kalinowski,[42] Jan Giejsztor, Felix Zienkowicz and a person named Weryho.[43] They met clandestinely by night in the Protestant cemetery. In the circumstances Kalinowski was confined to be providing help and support to the combatants. He was in constant danger. On one occasion he sought out a wounded insurgent in a safe house. He carried his identity papers with him including his recommendation from the Czar, the so-called *Ukase*.[44] Kalinowski managed to pass the first scrutiny but soon after he was stopped by the military again in Vilnius railway station. Though he also waved his commendation from the Czar to this official, it didn't work this time and he was further delayed. Eventually, however, he was allowed to pass. The next checkpoint was manned by municipal officials who appeared to Kalinowski to be less than enthusiastic about their role. He greeted them politely and they let him pass. A little later he arrived at a house where he was to pick up some information. This turned out to be the home of a family who belonged to the Starowiercy sect. The man of the house spoke to him in Russian. He was a good worker and his house, though modest, was well-kept. He possessed a carriage with good horses and he very generously lent them to Kalinowski to return to Vilnius during the night. Naturally his family who had no idea what he was up to were quite apprehensive. "This," Kalinowski concludes "is enough to give an idea of the dangers to which each one is exposed." [p. 68]. Kalinowski continues to record developments in his *Memoirs*:

> Also in Lithuania there was an insurrection committee, in addition to the National Government. Its president was M… an ex-Lieutenant of Roads and Bridges. I had nothing to do

---

[42]   He was not related to Joseph.

[43]   It is likely that this man was a relative of Helena Weryha who later married Gabriel Kalinowski.

[44]   Name for Czarist Decrees.

with him and he acted independently of me… I emphasize the fact that Lithuania did not voluntarily take part in the insurrection movement of 1863. But when it was resolved to initiate (rebellion), that part of the nation belonging to the Kingdom of Poland, which had been inactive until now, mounted a zealous campaign in Lithuania. I speak about the great landowning class. Muravyov determined to annihilate them and focused all his efforts to this end. In order to know whom to strike at, he required all the nobility to sign an address to the emperor in which they clearly expressed submission and fidelity. To facilitate this move he appointed as president of the nobility a person from Vilna named Domeyko who was loyal to the government. Soon after this, a certain individual came to his home asking to speak with him. As they began to talk he suddenly stabbed him with a dagger and fled.[45] He was found after two weeks of searching and hanged. He had already been interrogated by the commission of enquiry in Warsaw and revealed the names of those involved. The President M…fled and took refuge in London. From that time the municipal organization which he had directed ceased to exist. Attacks of this kind were unknown in Lithuania and we were widely reproached. One day I was given a letter from Piotrowski which stated simply, '*you will hang soon.'* I heartily wish that such crimes didn't happen! While I was still at Brest our people hanged a schismatic priest, and in revenge Muravyov hanged two priests in Vilna. [*Memoirs*, ch. 2].

In his *Memoirs* Kalinowski continues to describe events in the lead-up to his own arrest. He had nothing but admiration for the young people who stood up against tyranny, those who "with heroic

---

45   In the event Domeyko only sustained a wound in the attack from which he recovered.

forgetfulness of themselves, preferred to die rather than sin against their brothers." He offers examples. One day the authorities searched the room of a young man called Zdanowicz, the son of a university professor and nephew of a future bishop of Vilnius. He had just finished his degree and was known as a person of outstanding qualities and character. Some compromising letters were found in his room, which led to his arrest. Before the commission of enquiry the judges were moved by the plight of such a boy and tried hard to get his parents to force him to give the names of his accomplices. This he refused to do. Kalinowski tells us "he persevered courageously and died as a true martyr." He gives a second example – that of Titus Dalewski who remained silent before the judges and suffered the same fate. Kalinowski leaves us in no doubt as to where his sympathies lay: "If there are martyrs among us, these two assuredly were such and we can think of them as our intercessors before God." [p. 70]. Kalinowski relates other happenings connected with the insurrection such as an accident in which three young people were killed while printing rebel material, and another incident when a young man who hadn't taken sufficient precautions with damp gunpowder was also killed. These were everyday occurrences and Kalinowski knew nothing about them until the news leaked out. But he could not help but admire the heroism of these young men who didn't hesitate to sacrifice their lives for what they believed. Indeed, he continued to feel frustrated at his impotence to remedy the situation.

By this time the members of the National Government had dispersed. Kalinowski gives us an amusing anecdote concerning his height-challenged friend Felix Zienkowicz, the secretary of the National Government, who had been underestimated by the authorities. When he was hauled before a commission, the president scoffed: "What's the point of bringing this little man here?!" An assistant who had a great respect for the threat posed by Zienkowicz, replied, "Just wait and see what eyes this little man has!" Joseph and Felix would meet up again in exile, in Siberia.[46]

Kalinowski takes up his pen again: "At the beginning of August 1863, an inhabitant of Samogitia, Jan Giejsztor,[47] was taken in by the police and condemned to exile in Siberia and he was awaiting the signal from the police to leave his prison." [*Memoirs*, ch. 3].

A good friend of his, Kalinowski wished to give Jan a keepsake and asked his family to obtain a cross replenished with relics. We know that for a long time Kalinowski's family, especially his young sister Mary, had pressed him to go to confession. He had promised to do so but nothing happened. Now their opportunity came again and they agreed to his request provided he goes to confession. To this Kalinowski agreed. He arranged a meeting with Giejsztor, handed over the cross and took his farewell. Then on the Feast of the Assumption 1863, he received the sacrament of reconciliation in the church of the Vincentians. His comment on his confession:

> What God was pleased to do in my soul when I was at the feet of my confessor, the revered Monsieur Eymont,[48] the last Vincentian in Lithuania, only he knows what I experienced. I was under the spiritual direction of M. Felicien Antoniewicz, professor in the major seminary. Weekly confession and frequent communion refreshed my soul and I maintained my peace. The Church of the

---

[46] Zienkowicz had gone to England to organize a shipment of arms for the rebels at the start of the Insurrection. He engaged a steamship named the *Ward-Jackson* for this purpose and sailed with her. However, they were attacked by a frigate as they neared Poland and they took refuge in the port of Malmö in Sweden. The *Ward-Jackson* was built in Dumbarton in Scotland for Ward-Jackson and Watson, of West Hartlepool in North East England. The ship went missing in 1874.

[47] Back home after his exile, he would die on exactly the same day and date as Kalinowski.

[48] Constant Eymont was the priest who taught him at the Institute of Nobles.

Benedictines of St. Elizabeth was my favorite one and it was close to our house. I loved to attend morning Mass there every day. I also went sometimes to the chapel in the old house of the Friars of St. John of God, now long since changed into an alien one. [*Memoirs*, ch. 3].

He comments further here on the devotion of the local people who frequented the churches in the morning and participated in Holy Communion. Generally there was a strong spirit of piety there and especially during Carnival time people attended spiritual exercises and instructions from morning to night.

Kalinowski attributed his conversion to his sister Mary and to his stepmother. Writing from Siberia to Mary on November 11, 1868 he had remarked: "It is now four years since I left you and you were a child,[49] today I can see from your letter that you are a serious and experienced girl. Tears come to my eyes when I recall the last moments of my stay in Vilnius, the walks and excursion I made with you, our recreations at home and the little discussions which added new charm to our friendship itself. All this will not return here below, but the memories sweeten the bitterness of exile." [p. 72]. Writing from Perm in 1873 he said, "You yourself dear Mary and Mama have obtained my conversion." The same comment had already been made from Sieniawa in 1870: "It was to you, my angel, that I owe my return to God and Holy Church." [p. 73].

In September 1863, he wrote to his friend Louise Młocka: "Consider myself, at least for some time as definitively settled in Vilnius. One change has overtaken me. After 10 years of apostasy, I have returned to the bosom of the Church. I have confessed and now I am going well. I greet you Madam, because I consider this a very important event in my spiritual life. I want to make you part of all that has transpired."[50]

---

49 She was 15 years of age.
50 Czeslaus Gil OCD: *Father Raphael Kalinowski* (Kraków: Carmelite Fathers, 1979).

When we look at things objectively, however, we can easily see how Kalinowski had prepared the way for his 'conversion.' He had undergone a conversion of heart all along. He read spiritual books, attended the conferences of St. Vincent de Paul, made an abortive attempt at going to confession, and practiced unselfish charity towards orphans. But Kalinowski's definitive conversion grew out of a wish to give a religious relic to a friend.

At this point we need to backtrack a little in the context of the Polish Insurrection of 1863 in which Kalinowski found himself embroiled. One traditional vexed question revolved around the possibility of lifting the peasantry from their centuries-old state of serfdom. As in other parts of Europe, peasants had lived relatively peacefully in the Polish Commonwealth under a benign patriarchal system. However, in more recent times, things had deteriorated and the peasants felt oppressed. Resentment against the nobility and the clergy gathered momentum as happened in France before the Revolution. In fact, many young Poles had been educated in post-Revolution France and returned home imbued with ideas of liberty, equality and fraternity.

Moreover, the surrounding great powers, Austria, Russia and Prussia, saw that they would have to negate the influence of the nobility and the clergy, if they were to carry out their plans for a takeover of the Polish Commonwealth. Ironically, though diametrically opposed to one another, both the young revolutionaries and the foreign invaders had the same twofold aim: destroy the influence of the nobility and the church. To this end they both promised the peasants they would give them land and privileges. This explains the Massacre of members of the nobility in Galicia in 1846 and the persecution of the landowners by Muravyov in 1863.

Many of the noble families read the situation clearly and tried to avert disaster. Such were Prince Czartoryski, Count Fredro, Wasilewski; later on these were joined by Count Andrew Zamoyski, Aleksander Wielopolski in Poland and Count Lawrence

Puttkamer,[51] Appolinaris Hofmeister and others in Lithuania. These landowners set about abolishing serfdom on their estates by handing over the land to the peasants. In return they would receive a modest contribution from the peasants. Moreover, they undertook to set up agricultural schools to train the peasants in the administration of the land. Certainly Kalinowski inherited these ideas of reform, which his stepmother had learned from her father who came to be known as the 'Champion of the Peasants.' Sophie herself taught the peasants the elements of Christian doctrine. On December 26 1873 Sophie wrote to her stepson Kalinowski: "Yesterday I spent the morning reading to and praying with my domestics. It was a pleasure to see how attentive they were when I explained the mystery of our Savior's birth, and nothing was better calculated to soften the harshness of their work and poverty than that first appearance of Jesus and a reflection on his poverty." [p. 76].

While her mother was thus occupied, her young daughter Mary was busy in the kitchen preparing dinner, which would be shared in common. A spiritual benefit seemed to have resulted on that particular Christmas Day as Sophie goes on to mention that the son of the estate manager who was on the point of death was cured after a promise had been made to Our Lady of Ostra Brama, Lithuania's national patron.

On the political front, as we saw earlier, Napoleon III, initially hesitant about intervention in Poland, now changed tactics. He advised the Poles to continue the struggle at all costs and overturn the government of Constantine the viceroy and Wielopolski the civil director of government. So to advance this cause, the members of the Council of State and the members of Departmental and Municipal Councils tendered their resignation.

In April 1863, the Czar offered the Poles a general amnesty together with new freedoms, on condition that they laid down their arms, but this was to no avail. The insurgents had, of course, been

---

[51]   Father of Kalinowski's stepmother Sophie Puttkamer.

hoping for European intervention. In June, France, Britain and Austria made representations to the Czar in St. Petersburg, but his minister Gorczakow, strongly supported by his friend Bismarck, fobbed them off. In his book on Poland, Adam Zamoyski describes the course of events:

> Wielopolski still hoped to avoid insurrection. He brought forward the annual selective conscription into the Russian Army and excluded landowners and settled peasants from the lists. By concentrating the draft of more than 30,000 on the educated young and the cities, he calculated the majority of the conspirators would be caught in the net, while those who purposely avoided it would reveal their identity. In the event the majority slipped away from home as the draft drew near. On January 22, 1863 the National Committee proclaimed the insurrection, and that night small units attacked Russian garrisons around the country.[52]

At this turn of events, Wielopolski who could see the way things were going, resigned from the government and retired to Dresden, where he died 13 years later. In August 1863, Czar Aleksander II began the suppression of Warsaw. The Czar's brother Vice-Roy Constantine who disagreed with this development, also resigned and retired to Crimea on September 8. He was succeeded by General Berg who proceeded to give effect to the Czar's orders for suppression, putting them into effect in Warsaw; it was the same policy that the tyrant Muravyov had imposed on Vilnius.

The Polish cause drew sympathy from around Europe and many young people descended on Poland from Russia, Ireland, England, France, Germany and especially Italy. In fact, the biggest contingent came from Russia. The government of the insurrection was vigorously pursued and the members withdrew, leaving the door

---

[52] Adam Zamoyski, *Poland, A History* (London: Harper Press, 2009). See Ch. 15, Insurgency.

open for revolutionary extremists led by Ignatius Chmielenski 'the little Polish Mazzini.' Two days later an assassination attempt was made on the life of the Vice-Roy, as we mentioned earlier, and this only attracted further repression and discredited Poland in the eyes of Europe.

Soon these extremists also withdrew and on October 10, 1863 a moderate by the name of Romuald Traugutt assumed control.[53] Though only 34 years old, he had been Adjutant of Major Staff at the siege of Sebastopol. He was married to a grand-niece of Tadeuz Kosciusko. Traugutt was a fervent Catholic, much given to personal prayer and believed that national well-being depended on the people's adherence to their faith. He went to Paris to consult Ladislaus Czartoryski and Jerome Bonaparte. On his return to Warsaw, confident of French assistance, he set himself up as a dictator. He ruled with a firm, if not an iron hand. He began to organize an army along strict disciplinary lines, wanting a Polish soldier to be a 'soldier of Christ.' However, political events went badly for Poland. Seeing that Russia was supported by Prussia, Austria abandoned the Polish cause and Britain quickly followed suit. Napoleon alone remained. He called for a congress to address the Polish question as well as others, but this was not taken up. At this the insurgents turned to the revolutionaries of Italy and Hungary. Garibaldi began an assault on Austria, but was arrested by Bismarck. Bismarck promised support to Austria on condition that it placed Galicia under a state of siege, which was done on February 20, 1864. So the insurrection fell through. The Poles were encouraged by Napoleon and Czartoryski not to lose hope. But it was indeed a hopeless struggle. Kalinowski himself sums up the situation in regard to his unrelated namesake:

> The final act in this sad drama, before my own arrest, was that the Russians arrested Constantine Kalinowski, whom they had been tracking for a long time. The insurrectionary

---

[53] The Cause for his sainthood has been introduced.

forces were completely spent, and the national government had given him unlimited powers, because he alone was engaged in continual and unremitting activity. He was persevering, tireless, showed initiative and skill. He took no account of the fact of the absolute impotence to which we were reduced, and was faithful to hold firm and know that nothing had changed in the organization of the insurrectionary movement. Traugutt hid behind various pseudonyms, and used various passports and identity papers. Though based in Vilnius, he still moved around to plenty of other localities. For many months his photograph was displayed at the corner of the streets, but I don't remember what reward Muravyov had offered for his capture. Though I sometimes couldn't share the extreme principles this tireless worker espoused, still I admired his courage, his heroism, and his ingenuity in the midst of the constant risks to which he was exposed. The work consisted for the most part of making use of a small number of people at the coal-face. I asked Constantine to moderate his zeal, foreseeing the trouble that all the preceding events led to, which had such dire consequences and lost so much, but he paid no heed. [*Memoirs*, ch. 3].

Kalinowski goes on to relate the events leading up to Constantine's arrest and death. He sent a young university student to the province of Mohilev, providing him with the necessary papers. The young man failed to conceal the papers and he was arrested. Soon after, Constantine was also arrested, together with the family with whom he had been staying – father, mother, sons, two daughters and many other people. Shortly afterwards Constantine was condemned to death. The convoy to the place of execution passed the home of Joseph Kalinowski. As it passed he knelt down with his friends and recited the litanies of the Blessed Virgin and other prayers commending the condemned to the Lord. His was the last execution in Vilnius. At this point Kalinowski was the only remaining member of the insurrectionary government in Vilnius still at large. He was pressurized to continue the struggle, but he sent an account of the state of things to Warsaw. Kalinowski's conscience would not allow him to continue. Soon afterwards Traugutt sent out a decree announcing the end of the insurrection.

On Sunday April 10, Traugutt's secretary Marian Dubiecki was arrested and on April 11 Traugutt himself. He wrote a heartfelt letter to his wife later in June, expressing his profound faith. On August 4 a Capuchin friar heard his last confession. A scaffold was erected at the foot of the citadel in Warsaw guarded by a detachment of Russian soldiers. An immense crowd of spectators gathered round. Then a convoy of prisoners drew up consisting of five carriages, as four others were marked down for execution with Traugutt. The sentence of death was read out and the five were hanged together on the same scaffold. Traugutt's confessor wrote that "his death was that of a Christian hero and of a true saint." [p. 85]. That was the end of the Polish Insurrection of Warsaw in 1863.

The consequences for Poland and Lithuania were tragic. The nobility were decimated. In Lithuania alone, 800 properties were confiscated and their owners either hanged or exiled. The Church came under intense persecution; all the bishops of Poland, Lithuania and Ruthenia (Ukraine) were expelled, with the exception of two! Numerous obstacles were put in the way of the recruitment and formation of clergy. The Ruthenian-Catholic Church was definitively suppressed; members of religious Orders were expelled. Poles were excluded from employment and especially from the schools, as part of the Russification programs, which were aimed at brain-washing the youth. The tyrant Muravyov could not have been happier with the overall result.

Chapter Four

Imprisonment and Exile

*A*s we saw earlier, Kalinowski, though initially against such a course of action as rebellion because he realized its futility against superior odds, nevertheless was prevailed upon by the rebels to head a Ministry of War. He consented on condition that he would never be required to pass sentence of death on any prisoner. Kalinowski later reflected on the turn of events:

> I don't know what attracted the attention of the government to me, and nothing can be sure, so I have to resort to conjecture. An employee of Muravyov came looking for me one day. As I was not in the house he left an order for me to report to the police when I returned. I did report and I don't know what would have happened if no one I knew had been found there. I was given a favorable report and sent away politely. [p.87].[54] Soon afterwards I was told that there was a Jewish man waiting for me on the stairs and that he had something important to tell me. In fact he was a tall spy, with a half-Jewish, half military look. He told me that he had important documents for a certain Joseph Kalinowski.

---

[54] The implication seems to be that he knew someone at the police station.

I managed to get rid of him by saying that without doubt they were for someone else and not for me. I overlooked this incident and enjoyed peace for a while, but deep down I suspected that prison awaited me. Some artillery officers whom I had known previously came to visit me one day and brought some documents from the staff major, which they were not permitted to communicate with anyone. As they pretended to forget they left them in my room, I asked them to take them back with them. On the night of March 12 or 13 according to the old style calendar,[55] at midnight I was woken suddenly: "is Joseph Kalinowski, a former captain of engineering here?" I was asked in a loud voice, "this is the police chief." He asked me to open my desk, then he grabbed some papers that fell into his hands; this job didn't seem to please him much and after this exercise he said to me somewhat apologetically, 'Pardon me, I have been ordered to arrest you.' I gave in without objection. [p. 87].

Kalinowski's charitable nature is also revealed in his account. His first concern on being arrested was the welfare of a child called Francis, the son of Count Moriconi whom he was temporarily taking care of in the family home, as in the case of the child Paul he had cared for previously. The child slept through the procedure and didn't waken when Kalinowski gave him a kiss on the forehead. Kalinowski also asked permission to say goodbye to the rest of his family. Permission was willingly granted after which he left his home, never to see it again. [*Memoirs*, ch. 3].[56]

As we shall see also, Kalinowski's spiritual growth would deepen enormously during his years of exile and imprisonment.

---

55   In fact it was 25/26 March.
56   Czeslaus Gil suggests he was betrayed by Witold Parafionowicz, a collaborator of Constantine Kalinowski, whom he also betrayed. He was exiled to Tomsk where he joined the Russian Church and was employed by the government.

His devotional life would center on the Eucharist and dedication to Mary the mother of Jesus, so natural for a Pole.

First of all he was taken to the Dominican house, by now transformed into a prison. This was a religious house commandeered by the authorities but the attached church still functioned, so he could hear Mass being said from his open window. From here there was no escape, however,. He was locked in a religious cell which was well heated and lit by a lamp suspended from the wall. He was not allowed out by night or day for two weeks, but was given sufficient food. Kalinowski began to regulate his life according to a strict regime of prayer and meditation. He could also hear Mass being said in another nearby church. During the day he began to study Latin from his missal. He tried to avoid taking a siesta after lunch and instead recited the Litany of the Blessed Virgin. Afterwards he would engage in physical exercise in order to keep fit. Later a friendly officer brought him some spiritual books such as the work of St. Alphonsus de Ligouri on the 'Passion and Death of Jesus.' The book also contained pious exercises composed by King Stanilaus Leszczynski.[57] The book was called, *The crown of the passion of our Lord Jesus Christ.* On the first page there was a crown of thorns with an image of Our Lady of Częstochowa. The following pages of the book also contained pious dedications.

One of his concerns was that his parents, who had taken no part in the insurrection, would be incriminated because of him. When a few weeks had passed in this way, Kalinowski was roused at a late hour and taken by armed soldiers to a place of interrogation. He recited the *Sub tuum praesidium* (Under your protection) on the way and admitted he was very frightened. He remembered one of his interrogators was a General Szelgunow. They told him to sit down and asked if he knew a certain Milewicz. This he denied.

---

[57] Leszczynski's daughter Marie married King Louis XV and their daughter Princess Louise became a Carmelite nun at the convent of St. Denis with the name Teresa of St. Augustine.

They told him they knew everything and he would be better off to make a confession. He didn't suspect they were lying. He gave them no information, however, and was returned to his cell. Although Kalinowski was brought before the judges, Russia had nothing to fear from this man who had voluntarily laid down his arms. His enemies, however, were determined to root out any Polish sympathizers in Lithuania and destroy the Catholic religion. In fact Kalinowski, very nobly indeed, was ready to accept blame for whatever they wished to accuse him of, rather than incriminate others, especially his family. He was transferred to another cell and even though it was more spacious, he missed being able to follow the Mass from there.

After some intervention by influential friends, the death penalty was commuted to ten years hard or forced labor in the salt works of Siberia. Kalinowski was transferred to another prison where he did have access to Mass and sacraments. In comparison to Kalinowski's reprieve we reflect that in the fallout from the uprising about 130 rebels had been executed by hanging and 12,000 more were sentenced to transportation, and their property confiscated.

The time for departure duly arrived. He took with him into exile a copy of the *New Testament* together with the book of Job and the Psalms, the *Imitation of Christ* and his crucifix. Having in mind the biblical command ('pack your bag for exile' – Jer 46:19), Kalinowski relates:

> On June 29, 1864, the long terrible march began. On the very feast of the solemnity of the Holy Apostles Peter and Paul, near midday, the long file that we made up snaked its way through the streets of Vilnius toward the train station. An enormous crowd lined the streets and Cossacks on horseback prevented anyone from coming close to us; many people were watching from their windows. It looked like a funeral cortège. But from the beginning of the insurrection how many such convoys had preceded us! Among us were people of every age and every condition ... We took our

places in the train cars, where they piled one person on top of another. ... When the train departed, people moving along the heights that dominated the railway threw flowers on it as they do on graves of the dead at cemeteries.[58]

The journey to their destination, which was the salt works of Usolye near Lake Baikal lasted almost ten months; they arrived there on April 15, 1865. Some of the prisoners died along the way. The trip itself was quite varied. First St. Petersburg and then on to Moscow, the capital of the Czars with its shades of Peter the Great. They were housed and guarded in a vast shed, which inspired some fear that they might be detained in such a place. People, however, were good to them along the way and they found that many sympathized with their plight. Near Moscow Kalinowski again refers to the religious sect known as the *Starowiercy,* founded by a rich person with the aim of helping what they called the 'unfortunates' deported to Siberia.

From there they proceeded to Nizhny-Novgorod. An example of Kalinowski's growing heroism can be gleaned from a couple of anecdotes from this part of the march to exile. The bedraggled and starving crowd hobbled into the town on a Friday in July. Some meat was provided with the meagre meal and though in the circumstances, Friday abstinence could of course be disregarded, Kalinowski took his meat dish to a neighbor. Later that evening he had the opportunity of writing home. In a humorous aside at the end of his letter he remarked: "Immediately I was rewarded because it was possible for me to take my meat dish to a person who did not

[58] Praskiewicz Szczepan, T. OCD, *St. Raphael Kalinowski* (Washington DC:, ICS Publications, 1998). In this passage we have intimations of even worse violations of human rights in the following century under the Stalinist and Nazi regimes. A certain degree of humanity prevailed in the Czarist regime but none in the latter two.

have any meal at all, so this demonstrates that scruples can be very valuable."[59]

Here they embarked on a steamer, in reality a prison ship, which sailed down the Volga and the Kama rivers on the way to Perm which they reached at the end of July. The magnificent views on the river went some way to distract them from their predicament. At night a tremendous thunderstorm struck and the steamer had to moor by the shore. For Kalinowski it was a manifestation of the awe and beauty of nature. Though it became extremely dark the lightning played on the houses and cottages perched on a hill surmounted by a Greek church. In his *Memoirs* Kalinowski continues the story of their arduous journey:

> By the end of July we had reached the town of Perm and there I fell into the arms of my young brother Gabriel[60] also condemned to deportation to Siberia, from his agricultural college residence in Horki, on suspicion of having been part of the insurrection. The town of Perm was a distribution center for prisoners to other parts of Russia. Convoys of deportees headed from here to the East itself and beyond the Ural mountains. [*Memoirs*, ch. 4].

---

[59] Monk Matthew ODC. Tert. *Saint from the Salt Mines*, Ch11. 1986. The same writer relates a touching example of Kalinowski's charity. In Nizhny-Novgorod he also encountered a woman from Vilnius whose exile appeared to have been occasioned by her way of life back home! Kalinowski gave her some money and again when writing home asked his parents to "include at least one rouble for that poor girl," whenever they sent money to his brother-in-law (who was deported here.)

[60] He was known in the family as Bunio. Gabriel Kalinowski's daughter Sophia would later marry Edward Werner who became a Polish Vice-Finance minister. A great niece of Raphael Kalinowski, Marie Gabriela Werner was an Auschwitz survivor. A great grand niece of the saint, Marie Nabal Cohen married the influential scientist and Pulitzer Prizewinner Jared Diamond, a native of Boston.

But many never made it. This area, says Kalinowski, was an 'immense cemetery' for thousands of deported Poles. So also was the town of Perm, now a large city, with typhus rampant in the hospital where the sick were piled on one another without help, consideration or consolation.

Kalinowski's brother Jerzy wrote about him on one occasion: "His only happiness was the Holy Eucharist and nothing worried him more than being deprived of it." This was in the context of his time spent in Perm, where Kalinowski was indeed deprived of the Eucharist. The Catholic Church in this place had been taken over by the Orthodox and in order to receive Holy Communion one would have to travel some distance which he was unable to do. This regular loss of Eucharist here caused him great distress.

Towards the Ural Mountains and into the unknown

The military supervisor Colonel Borodziez who was a good Catholic, tried to obtain better conditions from the Governor General, but received this reply: "They lived like dogs, let them die like dogs." [p. 115]. But soon after, that he was overruled. An inspector sent by the Czar toured Perm and was briefed by the Colonel. He visited the hospital with the Governor-General and when he saw the situation ordered the Governor to send immediately for a priest. They were able to arrange a little chapel amid the trees and foliage in the courtyard of the prison and the priest, named Szostakowski from the diocese of Mohilev, distributed Holy Communion to the prisoners every day. Kalinowski noted that this was the origin of the Catholic Church in Perm. Like the Irish dispersed to so many countries after the Great Famine, the Poles took their religion to almost every country in the Eastern bloc – and beyond – to which they were exiled. The suffering of an individual or a people has never been in vain, because it participates in the suffering of Christ himself, "Very truly, I tell you, unless a grain of wheat falls into the earth and dies, it remains just a single grain; but if it dies it bears much fruit" (Jn 12:24).

Kalinowski became aware of the weak faith and dismal knowledge of their religion on the part of many of his fellow exiles, especially the young, and he determined to do something about it. He knew he was initially destined for a short stay in Tobolsk so he wrote to his stepmother asking her to send on some of his books; various religious treatises, including the theology of Giovanni Perrone,[61] the *Imitation of Christ* (he had given his away to someone who needed it!) He also asked for his Latin grammar, his dictionaries, Latin-Polish by Bobowski, German-English as well as his mechanical, architectural and engineering textbooks.

So the sad pilgrimage proceeded on its way to Tobolsk.[62] Kalinowski informs us that in former times the Cossacks had forced men, women and children to march on foot before them and he noted with sympathy that these poor people were sometimes unable to eat their bread, which froze in their hands and became as hard as ice. Many died on the way from cold and hunger. In recent times a more humane mode of transport had been adopted and Kalinowski was fortunate to travel in the same carriage as his brother Gabriel who looked after his needs. Night time accommodation was usually spent at stations on the way, narrow, nasty rooms, without ventilation and full of vermin. On the other hand he observed that some rich people were kidnapped by a station manager named Kalusyn, in an effort to extort money from them. He also had anecdotal evidence that surgeons killed their patients for the same reason.

At the beginning of September 1864 they were leaving European Russia behind and advancing into the Ural Mountains, with the immense plains of Siberia stretching out before them. In spite of his circumstances Kalinowski could find it in himself to admire

---

[61]   Perrone was a conservative Italian theologian, active at the time of Vatican I on the Ultramontane side. Perrone set out to answer the problems of the day and entered the lists against unbelief and error.

[62]   Tobolsk was formerly known as Sibir.

this panorama. When they reached Ekaterinaburg on the approach
to the Urals, he was separated from Gabriel who was destined for
Szadrynsk. Before taking leave of Gabriel they exchanged items
of clothing – Gabriel received a military cloak while Kalinowski
was glad to get a good fur coat which would stand him in good
stead in the Siberian climate ahead. Up to now the weather was
unseasonably mild, a fact which amazed the locals. One of them
remarked: "Someone must be praying for you seeing the weather is
so good." [p. 123]. This remark resonated with Kalinowski, knowing
as he did that his mother prayed for her family every day before the
Blessed Sacrament. The prisoners set about organizing themselves
and appointed a prefect named Morgalec from Ruthenia, to oversee
affairs. They started a fund to which each contributed a tenth of
what he possessed. In this way they could also acquire assistance
for sick travelers and so on. When they reached the ancient town
of Tiumen, one of the prisoners was so ill that they had to leave
him in the hospital. Kalinowski gave him 30 roubles, not from the
common fund, but from his own meagre resources. The impression
Kalinowski created on his companions both before and after
conversion should be noted. A Russian officer who had supervised
them along a stage of the journey broke down in tears when he said
goodbye to Kalinowski. The same thing had happened to a Sergeant
Ulups when Kalinowski was imprisoned in Vilnius, though in that
case the sergeant thought he was about to be executed. It is obvious
that Kalinowski never harbored prejudices against either Russians
themselves or people of other nationalities, even when they appeared
under the guise of oppressor.

As they progressed on their journey the prisoners were greeted by
autumnal northern winds, glacial in the extreme. Kalinowski admits
in a letter to his stepmother that he somewhat reluctantly returned
to a smoking habit which was thought necessary in Siberia to ward
off the scurvy. The journey from Tiumen to Tobolsk took fifteen
days and just outside Tobolsk they were faced with a difficult ferry
crossing of the Irtys River now in full spate. The prisoners stood

around awaiting their turn to cross in freezing conditions. Having negotiated it successfully they headed for Tobolsk, the next stopping place – the most ancient town in Siberia. Siberia has the unenviable reputation of being the coldest country on the face of the earth – sometimes the temperature plummets to -50 Celsius or more. Here he was delighted to meet up with his friend Felix Zienkowicz, with whom he would correspond all his life. Kalinowski was disappointed to find that the Blessed Sacrament was not reserved in the Catholic church, as there was no resident priest.[63] Here he did have the consolation of finding some letters from home awaiting him. It would have been necessary to await heavy falls of snow before they could use sledges as modes of transport. In the absence of snow they were compelled to ride on horseback which was more tiring. At this stage carriages were out of the question because the terrain was extremely boggy. Reflecting back on this nightmare journey Kalinowski writes:

> We were impeded by the ice that the river was carrying and it was impossible to proceed. Our journey was fatiguing: we travelled on horses supplied by the peasants and the route was really bad. The jolting was such that often the carriage or the axles broke and sometimes the horses refused to budge. We arrived at a station quite late and then we had to find lodging, which was not always easy; the peasants were not very cooperative especially on the Baraba steppes which stretch from the Irtys to the Orb. The Lord however, preserved our health and the diversity of places and peoples was so interesting that it made us forget our trials... The general impression which stayed with me from this journey is that people are much the same everywhere. Under a thick skin the people of Siberia conceal similar sentiments as those

---

[63] A priest did take up residence however, in 1866, but that was two years later.

of so-called civilization. This is a known fact, but it does not sufficiently account for the business of life. [*Memoirs*, ch. 4].

Kalinowski also gives an example of another characteristic of people out there in the wilds. It was known of course that some people, including freed exiles, were eventually able to make money in Siberia from trading and business. One of Kalinowski's close friends Casimir Laudyn engaged in the skin trade after release. In the example he gives, what intrigued Kalinowski was that one of the hired carters was very obviously quite wealthy but was not ashamed to involve himself in this humble occupation and still preserved his dignity. His wealth, however, didn't inhibit him from demanding money for a supply of vodka or the equivalent from the poverty-stricken prisoners. However, when they pointed out their wretched state he relented.

Kalinowski observes that on the whole it wasn't an easy life for the native people of the Baraba steppes. He wrote home: "We felt the population of the steppes was especially unfortunate as regards material and moral welfare; it's quite true the countryside is not favorable for development; there were lakes and mud and scattered villages. The beasts were often sick, there were frequent fires on the steppes, and rivers and lakes often flooded the harvest and sometimes the houses. During this voyage, as always, I am close to you and sometimes I have the illusion that I am journeying along the roads of Lithuania."[p. 134].

This letter was written from the town of Dubrovna *(in present day Belarus)*. It had a population of about 8,000 of whom half were Jewish. They specialized in making woollen garments called Tallits or Jewish prayer shawls. Kalinowski lodged here with a poor Christian family and shared their meager resources. He hadn't had a decent meal for two weeks. He availed himself of the time at his disposal to do what he liked doing best – teaching young people. His host, however, felt that education was somewhat lost on them in such a place. He was content just to teach the boy to make the sign of the cross. The absence of effective religious practice here reminded Kalinowski of his own indifference in the past. As they were detained in Dubrovna for an indefinite period, his friends came looking for him and invited him to join them where they were staying. He made the change, missing his solitude indeed for the noisier if cheerful company of his friends. Here again he began teaching some of the prisoners – to one boy teaching mechanics and also working with a Kiev university student from Ukraine, to whom he taught English. Kalinowski deplored the fact that these young people were being deprived of a good education because of the troubles in their homeland; also enforced idleness on this long trek was not good for the soul.

Tomsk to Irkutsk

From Tobolsk at the end of October, the sad procession pressed on to the next stop, a place called Tomsk.[64] At one of the staging points he struck up what turned out to be a lasting friendship, with Casimir Laudyn, the young man mentioned above. Apparently in these places prisoners were restrained by heavy plank beds being placed on top of them, and this young man was trying to pray in this position. Kalinowski engaged him in conversation and found out that, like himself, he had attended an Agricultural College. This is an example of how Kalinowski tried to help and befriend his companions in misery. By this stage he had given away most of his money to those in need. Prisoners were given 10–15 *kopecks* per day, the equivalent of 50 cents. With this they were expected to provide themselves with food and whatever else they needed. On the way to Tomsk, Kalinowski had the unexpected joy of meeting up with a relative, who like him, had been sent into exile. This man, Jan Rychlewicz, had been a fellow student at the Institute of Nobles. In

---

[64] The revolutionary figure Mikhail Bakunin was born in Tomsk. He was a friend of the young Hermann Cohen in Paris. Present day population is about 500,000.

1862 he married Caroline Puttkamer, sister of Joseph's stepmother and Kalinowski had been godfather to the couple's child, named Joseph. Rychlewicz had already been exiled and would not see his son for ten years.

It was not altogether a surprise to meet his friend there as Kalinowski had noticed his name scrawled on the window of the first staging post they reached in Siberia. In this ancient town of Tomsk he had searched for him but to no avail. Great was his joy when he looked around his lodgings before finally lying down to sleep and there was Rychlewicz right before him! "Seeing him," wrote Kalinowski, "I forgot all about my fatigue. I was given permission to spend all my time with him while we stayed in Tomsk; I only returned to the barracks for the night." [p. 141].

It was also a great joy for him to be able to attend Mass for the first time since leaving Vilnius. In fact this encounter with the Lord in the Eucharist was a most moving experience for him – he admits to have cried like a child. All resentful emotions from his past in Vilnius flooded his soul. He would frequent the Eucharist as often as possible during his time there. Another heavy cross awaited him just as the group was due to depart – Kalinowski was unable to join them. Suddenly his body rebelled, and he woke up one morning with severe rheumatism which meant he was unable to continue the journey. This enforced stay in Tomsk, while allowing him silence and prayer time, nevertheless also depressed him; not so much for himself, but because of the misery, both physical and moral, that he witnessed all around him. Kalinowski accused himself of being guilty of sin in looking at things this way, and tormenting himself from a purely subjective point of view in wishing the world to be otherwise than it was; people were not as perfect as he would have liked them to be. Moreover his impotence to provide any solutions was a cause of greater stress. This time he muses in a more theological way: "It was God who created the world and he knows better than me how to govern it. Moreover human frailty is a fact of life! But I have noticed that some cruel disappointment and subsequent downfall for some people, causes me more sorrow than simply looking at my own misery." [p. 141].

In these circumstances Kalinowski would turn to prayer, which he hoped would put things right. Indeed he immersed himself more and more in prayer. He grew in detachment as he reflected that he had lost everything – loss of all rights and property had of course been part of the penalty imposed by unrelenting Russia. "O my God," he prayed, "what a treasure you give to those who put all their trust in you." [p. 144]. As always, Kalinowski worried about how his family were coping. He had heard that things were not going well for his older brother Victor who was managing the estate of "Studzionki" near Minsk, that place referred to by the poet Mickiewiez as an "Earthly Paradise". He wrote an encouraging letter to Victor which he hoped would steady his resolve to win through. Victor was his only full brother, the rest of the family were step siblings. He worried about the next brother, Karol, finishing his studies at the University of Kiev, where Kalinowski felt his faith would take second place in his life. He complained that Karol, like his father, wrote too infrequently. Kalinowski wrote letters to his father begging for money, not for himself, but in order to address the miserable plight of those around him. In spite of his courage in advocating the needs of the poor, it still pained him to plead for money with his father. He even wondered if his insistence was a factor in his father rarely writing to his son. But he still made the point that it was easier to find money in Lithuania than Siberia![65] In a follow-up letter to his father when his first request went unanswered, the son seems to chide him gently: "God, in his mercy will not abandon those who have confidence in him. In the depths of my heart I possess the treasure of hope which no one can take from me, and neither can material things add anything to me; remember one thing, I am ready

[65] Andrew Kalinowski resigned from his directorship of the Institute after the 1863 Insurrection and the arrest of his sons. However, he was honored by the Russians on his retirement with the title *Councilor of State* and *Gentleman*

for all annoyances, but there are some people whose material poverty leads to moral failure, and it is of these that I am always thinking when I ask for money." [pp. 146-147].

There is no doubt that in these exchanges, Kalinowski's altruistic nature is predominant and we can easily see how he gained a reputation for holiness among his fellow prisoners. In addition to sharing his paltry resources with whoever was in need, he also insisted on keeping church fast days which were severe in those days – but of course should only have applied to normal life, not an abnormal one in a captive setting. It was now nearing Christmas and the Advent season required fasting on Wednesdays and Fridays; this he insisted on for both himself and his companions, to their great annoyance.

Kalinowski's letters and *Memoirs* are a rich source of information on conditions among Sybiraks as they were called, just as Solzhenitsyn would inform us about the Russian Gulags in the following century. Writing from Tomsk he tells us: "Here we have painters, musicians, sculptors who by using their talents earn their daily bread. Artisans can also find work; other people however, only with difficulty, there is nothing available in business places." [p. 147].

Always the spiritual advantage of his friends and people around him was foremost in his mind. For this purpose he asked his mother to send on two more devotional books and include also some popular almanacs!

On December 26, 1864 the travel writer again tells us: "Tomsk is an amusing place: sledging courses, magnificent horses, perfect runs, Siberian cold, glacial air, not a cloud in the sky. All that's missing is the Pospieszki walk in Vilna. But these distractions don't make any impression on me, but John admires the horses, he's the great amateur." [pp. 148-149].[66]

Kalinowski's interests of course were in reading and study; he was learning Latin at that point. He was reading the works of the

---

[66] John was a relative by marriage.

Italian moral theologian Peter Scavini, whose three-volume work was standard in the seminaries of the 19th century. Much of his time was spent in the church though no regular Mass was possible. However, Christmas Day provided a spiritual bonanza and he was able to attend six Masses, three for himself and three for his friend Laudyn who had contracted typhus and had also grown somewhat indifferent in his faith – by Kalinowski's standards! That Christmas the temperature fell to minus 40 degrees and the mercury froze in the thermometer.

It is also touching to note that our saint in the making had a truly human side to him, though in this case the experiment in self-indulgence went badly wrong. One day he met up with an old acquaintance from home with whom he smoked a really strong cigar which did his head in! Result – sick all day. Needless to say the victim drew a salutary lesson from the experience: "What a fragile creature a human being is! Just a little smoke and one is reduced to helplessness!" [p. 150].

Later in his *Memoirs* Kalinowski recalled an incident during his stay here. He was suddenly summoned to the Exhibitions Hall and was given an opportunity to go and live in the Tomsk surroundings as part of a drive to colonize the area. This at first sight might appear to be a softening of his sentence but Kalinowski's good sense made him decline. He suspected in fact it might be worse than going through with his sentence of forced labor. He could foresee himself being thrown into an alien environment without friends, who at least could be companions in misery. Happily the authorities didn't insist and after a two-month stopover in Tomsk had expired it was time to move on, which they did on January 1, 1865.

We must remember that they were traveling in the depths of a Siberian winter. He and his friends Korzun and Mitiewiez and the other prisoners continued their march on the way to Irkutsk. His friend Laudyn was forced to remain in Tomsk recovering from typhus.

The journey was particularly trying. Sometimes it was a question of going from one extreme to another: looking after horses in the freezing open air or being stifled in a room. He and another friend named Korzun purchased a sleigh at a reasonable cost and they made progress. At one of the stops he would study his Latin grammar. This part of Siberia differed somewhat from the Tobolsk region as it had been colonized much earlier.

On January 14 Kalinowski reported on a difficult stage of the journey when they had to make do without horses. He found himself lodging in a spacious house where the woman was jealous and treated her husband badly. This was normal, it seems, and nothing was done about it. He thought the women generally were good managers, but at times greedy and avaricious. He wrote: "I was amazed to see the men idle all day; though today I excuse them, there is nothing they can do in this cold and they sleep in an attic the whole day. I'm distracted by the young conscripts who are singing, in spite of the cold, but under the inspiration of Bacchus not of Mars. It's a swan song. Many sell their sons for 400 to 700 roubles. Today we witnessed the farewells of a mother and her son. What tears, what grief! The poor mother expressed her sorrow in a curious lament from which poetry was not lacking." [p. 152]. The next staging post they reached was the town of Krysnoyarsk situated on the River Yenesei.[67]

Kalinowski would appear to have been developing a strong spirituality and a deep prayer life on this arduous march. When they arrived at Krasnoyarsk he tells us they were housed in an immense barracks which reminded him of his former College of Engineering. The conditions were extremely uncomfortable. He had no interest in

---

[67] This was the area where the notorious Josef Stalin spent his third and final stint in exile. Though a small town at that time it was still an important center and has grown in importance, with a population today of almost a million. It is a place rich in minerals – gold, silver, copper, together with coal mines, all found in the region. There were also about 30,000 Catholics there, even in those days.

exploring the town but instead: "I was able to find a solitary corner where today I console myself with God and now I struggle with my thoughts." [p. 154].

Kalinowski was a faithful and prolific correspondent as we know, writing letters to his family every week, sometimes more often.[68] He wrote to his parents and also separately to his father. At this point too we can notice how he was going through a time of darkness and deprivation. One reason for this was his father's silence. Writing to his mother Sophie he complains bitterly: "I was sad earlier; today I am more sad at not having received any letter – and in a situation as unhappy as mine is. I was hoping to find at Krasnoyarsk some explanation of this cruel enigma in response to my letter mentioned earlier, but there was nothing and I have to plod on again dragging a heavy weight of sorrow. I am obsessed with a thousand anxieties. Perhaps I have taken a wrong turn and my past conduct has alienated my father's heart." [p. 154].

He follows this up with a letter to his father: "My very dear father, I cannot explain your silence; it weighs on me like a heavy burden. If my past conduct or something in my letters had turned you against me, well and good dear father, tell me frankly. I humbly acknowledge my fault. I know I have greatly transgressed, especially in regard to yourself. I have not been sincere with you. Bloated pride and self-confidence prevented me from offering the submission of a son, and God has punished me." [pp. 154-155].

In the same vein he wrote again to his stepmother Sophie: "How have I alienated my father's heart? At the same time I can say my conscience is pure and I ask only that God will forgive me for the sins and carelessness of my youth, caused by human weakness. I am a man and I searched for earthly consolation. But I always had regard for and still do, those whom I love most in the world." [p. 155].

---

[68]   Between the years 1978-1986, 1,723 of Kalinowski's letters and notes were published, but this is not the complete number. (Teresianum, Czeslaw H. Gil, Rome 1989.)

But in a way Kalinowski is probably too severe on himself on this issue. In fact he deferred to his father in agreeing to go to the Agronomy Institute in Horki when his own preference would have taken him elsewhere. What perhaps did upset his father was the fact that he had joined the insurrection and taken a position in the national government (of Resistance) without having consulted him. In this sense his conscience though was pure – he had acted out of love for his country. He also wondered if pestering his father for money had got to him; but the money he begged was not for himself but in order to alleviate the distress of the poor he encountered on this cruel journey.

On a more objective note, writing to his father again, Kalinowski shows his powers of observation and his talent for social comment:

> The towns of Siberia differ only slightly from those of Russia. For the most part they are inhabited by government officials and those who work in the gold mines. The gold mines are the chief sources of revenue. The rural population is composed chiefly of deportees and the second generations take the name of Siberians and lose the traditions of their native country. Those who live along the route to Siberia are wagoners; the Ostiaques and the Toungouse live in their caravans. The peasants are sufficiently comfortable. In distributing flour they serve it from sieves made from women's hair. Bread is well baked and good value. I needed to pay only ten cents for my maintenance. My chief nourishment is milk. The morals of these people leave a lot to be desired. Paternal authority is misunderstood and when their parents become old, sometimes attempts are made on their lives. Slothful men lose a lot of money on the cabaret. The women are economical but nasty. They often poison their husbands and are cruel to their children. The men regard their women as *dishcloths*, which is in fact the name they give them. And if they have any regard for their

children it is because of what they hope to gain from them later in the domestic scene...[p. 157].

The older generation seemed to have more heart than their children; it seems the bitter and wild nature of the landscape exercises some influence on the inhabitants. In spite of this as always there were some exceptions to the general rule. They also encountered some good families where peace reigned and who were hospitable to the travelers. Kalinowski attributed this to government initiatives of starting schools to improve the lives and moral fiber of the people who were essentially religiously orientated. Kalinowski makes the astute comment that there were too few people who work for the advancement of the population on the pretext that they are a simple class who are better off without education, which is the privilege of the few who can use it – and do use it to the detriment of the people.[69]

Looking back on this journey in his *Memoirs*, Kalinowski recalled other interesting details. Instead of having cause for annoyance from the natives, it was sometimes the other way round. There were a number of sects along the way such as the Starowiercy whom we have encountered already; there were Sabbath observers and other such who never smoked cigars and who strongly objected to the travellers doing so in their homes. When their host's objections were ignored, as happened all too often, there was an outcry – their homes had been profaned.

However, much of the journey was sheer drudgery and worse. They were frozen stiff at times; twice he sustained a frozen nose which was very painful. If a man of Kalinowski's faith and moral character was becoming depressed, we can imagine what the rest of the company was feeling. He gave vent to his feelings once in this outburst: "Humankind is meant for society, but there is no society

---

[69] It was this attitude which provided a fertile soil for revolution when the masses in fact rose up against the few.

around us. Our convoy is like a body without a soul. At Perm we lodged in a former hospital and some people were billeted in the mortuary. Someone scrawled on the wall, *Hotel for the Dead.*" [p. 160]. But even in these dire circumstances his faith was coming to the fore. He writes: "It's only by a special grace of divine providence that we are able to withstand the fatigue and journey in such cold conditions for whole days and sometimes for the night." [p. 160]. They had traversed a huge frozen expanse of tundra, called *taiga* in Russia. Kalinowski thought the inhabitants looked uncivilized. It happened to be Mardi-Gras and there was a lot of singing and carry-on. Both men and women appeared inebriated. Back home he recalled that it was the time for the Forty Hours devotion, and this made him feel a bond with his family. "Our convoy," he tells us, "is made up of 28 people, three of whom are accompanied by their wives and children." [p. 61.

Change for the better was on the way and at the beginning of February 1865 they reached the province of Irkutsk though they were still hundreds of kilometres from the city. Here the countryside was beginning to look totally different.

"We arrived in Irkutsk at the beginning of spring, during the Lenten season, and then we celebrated the Feast of Easter." [*Memoirs*, ch. 4]. Irkutsk was the most important town in Siberia at that time with a population of over 50,000 people of whom about 4,000 were Catholics. It became known as the 'Paris of Siberia.' (The population is now over half a million.)

Here again there would be a break-up of the group, some marked out for forced labor in various destinations. Kalinowski had the joy of attending Mass in Irkutsk but was tearful and apprehensive about his own future. He begged the Lord after Holy Communion to help him. Soon after this he felt that his prayer was answered; an agent approached him and told him to get into a carriage with the Governor General Szalasnikof. Presently Szalasnikof addressed him, "I have a letter from your family. What can I do for you? Where would you like to be sent?" [Memors, ch. 4]. On the spur of the moment he mentioned the iron works at Piotrowsk of which he had heard good reports, but the Governor said: "I will give you better advice. Go to Usolye where you will find good company."[70] Kalinowski agreed to go along with this. While he was heartbroken to leave his friends, especially Korsun his soul mate all the way from Vilnius, he saw in this development an answer to prayer.

---

[70] In recent years the Teresian Carmelites, both men and women have made foundations in Usolye. Kalinowski had prepared the way for them there.

Chapter Five

Saltmaking in Usolye 1865-1868

$\int$o it was soon off again on another gruelling journey, in wet, windy and freezing weather conditions, taking the muddy and boggy road to Usolye.[71] At the end of the day they hobbled in, frozen, famished and fatigued to another prison that awaited them. However, they would normally have some hot cereal when they got there. It was a real wrench for Kalinowski to have to part with friends again.

Now, having reached Usolye, he was reunited with a friend from his time on the rebel National Government, Felix Zienkowicz, who had already got there before him. In a way he took the place of Bruno Korzun and they would stick together for the duration of their stay in Siberia. In addition Kalinowski was able to meet another friend from Lithuania, Aleksander Oskierko,[72] who had

[71] Now known as Usolye-Sibirskoye. Appropriately the word *Usolye* denotes salt. The Trans-Siberian railway passes through the town. It was also a Gulag under the Soviets.

[72] Aleksander Osierko was a member of one of the richest families in Lithuania and he and Kalinowski became lifelong friends. After an amnesty when they were free to leave Usolye, Aleksander's fiancée Miss Grabowska courageously left her family and joined him in Siberia. They were married by Christopher Szwermicki at Irkutsk in the summer of

also been one of the leaders of the insurrection. Due to influential friends Osierko's death sentence had been commuted in spite of Muravyov's determination to hang him; Osierko was the person who would eventually arrange for Kalinowski to become tutor to Auguste Czartoryski. Here in Usolye, Oskierko assumed a leadership role, being named *Staroste* or Prefect by his fellow prisoners, a position he held during their time in Usolye.

In the small and impoverished town of Usolye they found in place the huge boilers which were used for evaporating the water in order to make salt. These were situated on a spacious island formed by two branches of the river Angara. It would also be the site of their prison which consisted of a large chamber designed to hold 60 to 80 people. Families, however, were billeted in homes in the town along the banks of the river.

The day after their arrival they were presented with heavy chains which had to be worn whenever they left the island. These had to be adjusted to each one's feet in the local blacksmith's forge. The chains were so well polished that they appeared to be made of silver, which provided a point of wry humor for the wearers. Their job on the island was to extract the salt crystals from the boilers after evaporation. They also had to collect various deposits of lime, marl and other minerals from the containers and dispose of them. This was an extremely difficult job as the deposits strongly adhered to the inside of the boilers. If you were unable to accomplish this task then you would have to pay someone 40 kopecks a day to do it for you. Later on the prisoners were allowed to leave the island and live in houses previously used by government employees. The work too was diversified and some were ordered to create a kitchen garden

---

1866. After their return from exile Osierko got a job in an insurance company in Warsaw and later in Vilnius. They had four children, the eldest Hedwig, born in Siberia. He survived his wife and died on February 11, 1911, four years after Kalinowski. Osierko was related by marriage to Sophie Kalinowski. Kalinowski speaks high of him and pays him a glowing tribute, praising his rare qualities and transparent piety.

by clearing the nearby forest. Kalinowski didn't have the energy for this heavy work and was helped by the local priest, a stalwart from Samogitia named Stulginski. Other work involved tending the hospital garden or clearing out the stables of the beasts kept for work in the fields. For their pains they were given three kopecks per day and some inferior flour once a month. Inevitably the bread produced from this was also inferior and bad for one's health. While the prisoners were allowed to receive gifts of money from home, this was limited to 25 roubles per month.

Things eased off for a while and there was some degree of freedom, but when this was abused, Kalinowski's friend Osierko, as 'prefect' of the group had to take the punishment, which meant being confined to a room in the police barracks all day once a week. The abuse of the freedom culminated to the extent, that ironically, some in the group had obtained guns in order to hunt in the forest.

An escort drawn from the local indigenous tribe of Bouriates accompanied them everywhere and Kalinowski had nothing but praise for them.[73] They were Buddhist and moreover honest, temperate and good living. But it was not the same with the Russian Cossacks who went through the pockets of overcoats left in an antechamber, helping themselves to the contents.

Walks through the island were permitted and Kalinowski found these refreshing, especially in spring. The island itself was not wooded, but the limpid waters of the Angara gave an air of life to the scene. However, by contrast the nearby mountains emitted cheerful echoes, and the larch woods extending as far as the eye could see were the chief ornaments of this area. Kalinowski observed that a lot of damage was done to this forest, with some trees up to 400 years old being chopped down to feed the boilers. Here we have a lover of nature and an early environmentalist speaking.

---

[73] In addition to speaking Russian, Kalinowski also began to learn the difficult Bouriate language so as to be able to communicate with this indigenous people.

Life in the Prison Camp

The prisoners tried to organize themselves well so as to maintain order and harmony among the group. As noted they elected a prefect, in this case Aleksander Osierko, with councillors and judges. A fund was established and 10 per cent of gifts received was put aside for the future and for communal expenses. Dining facilities were arranged even though food was not all that plentiful. There were plenty of priests in the area and they led morning and evening prayer. The authorities suppressed Mass and religious ceremonies as such, with the exception of some feasts and Easter, though there was a small church in Usolye built in a simple style, but that was kept locked. When one prisoner wrote home for some religious items, of course letters were censored, it was assumed by the authorities that religious services were being held. A search was immediately made and though nothing was found, all the priests except Stulginski were sent elsewhere. For Kalinowski this again was Providence taking care of them, as Stulginski continued quietly with his ministry, especially to the sick.

However, the prisoners were able to get on with their lives, such as they were, doing the usual chores to keep things ticking over, fetching wood for the boilers, sweeping, preparing vegetables for the kitchen and so on. In the depth of winter, because the river was frozen over, no work was possible and so every activity ceased. That meant there was some freedom to pursue personal tastes and they were even able to educate their children.

They managed to acquire a stock of books for spiritual and literary enrichment. On their shelves they numbered the following: *History of the Church* in four volumes, by Darras.[74] (Kalinowski

---

[74] The early theological studies of Darras did not include a good foundation in ecclesiastical history; this defect he sought to make good by private studies. Darras' *Histoire Générale de l'Église* in four volumes appeared in Paris in 1854 (14th ed., 1890). It follows the reigns of the popes, but betrays in the author a lack of methodical training and critical skill, defects noticeable also in his other works. (Catholic Encyclopedia).

wrote a summary of these in 250 pages). They had 6–8 volumes of the works of the great Frederick Ozanam – now Blessed – founder of the St. Vincent de Paul Society. Also there were the Conferences of Fr. Felix,[75] *Sermons on the Passion* by P. Ventura as well as his *Women of the Gospel* and *The Catholic Woman*. On the bookshelf too was the work *Jerusalem Delivered* by Tasso,[76] plus Dante's *Divine Comedy*, the Catechisms of Guillore[77] and of De Gaume,[78] and *Theology* written by Perrone.

In the evenings those who wished could play games of checkers or chess. In summer you could walk along the island taking in the fresh air with a book in hand. They indulged in discussions of a political or religious nature. They talked about the plight of their exiled friends in other places. Occasionally they discussed certain questions of Church history but tried to avoid controversial issues that could disrupt the community. However, Kalinowski reports that unpleasant incidents occurred on two or three occasions when the group were deprived of some normal benefits because of the behavior of a stranger among them named Ornani (who, Kalinowski thought, had come from Italy or France).

Kalinowski also relates that they were privileged to have a visit to the island of Angara from Governor-General Korsakof of Eastern Siberia who came and spoke to them in French. They took the opportunity of making a complaint to him that they had not received some monetary gifts in the post. He assured them that justice would be done and soon afterwards it was discovered an employee had siphoned off 6,000 roubles. The money was returned to the prisoners.

---

[75] In a speech he gave in Malines (Mechlen), Belgium, Hermann Cohen refers to the influence of the Felix talks in Paris.

[76] An epic poem by the Italian poet Torquato Tasso on the First Crusade.

[77] Francis Guillore S.J. (1615-1684), a noted preacher.

[78] Père Jean de Gaume was Superior of the Paris Carmel and was known to Hermann Cohen.

At one stage the group was allowed to reside in a big block in the town and they lodged according to home areas – Lithuanians, Ruthenians and Poles clubbing together. Later, however, they were ordered back on the island to another prison and here they suffered some privations. Soon afterwards – Kalinowski doesn't say how long – they were allowed back to the town after an amnesty had been proclaimed.

Writing to Jean-Baptiste Bouchaud the year after Kalinowski's death, Osierko gave him a detailed account of Kalinowski's life in Usolye: "In 1865 and 1866 the number of convicts kept on being added to, so that in 1867 and 1868 there were about 500 in all." [p. 177]. He referred to the meagre allowances of food – at the beginning only bread and meal were provided. This improved when they were allowed to grow vegetables and some meat was available for making soup.

Osierko observed that "The most difficult thing was the continual movement in the camp and the noise in the dormitory. It was impossible to find a silent and tranquil corner where one could give free rein to one's thoughts. This got on one's nerves and kept one in an abnormal state." [p. 179]. Osierko continues in words that again remind us of the Gulag Archipelago in the twentieth century:

> In the course of daily life the dominant note of the moral state of our soul was a kind of languor caused by the thought of, and the desire for, our former life in our native land. To this you could add the tragic implosion of all our hopes, caused by a great misfortune, by the ruin of all our aspirations and the destruction of all we had done in our lives, or at least all that made us what we were. The complete absence, at least in the first two years of exile, of all hope of ever seeing our country again, or our families or the places we had loved, all this kept us in a state of lassitude and inertia – all aggravated again by our powerlessness to leave Usolye, as also the lack of news from home and from Europe. [p. 180].

As the outgoing mails were monitored by the government employees in Irkutsk, even a mail from St. Petersburg took weeks to reach its recipients. Also the prisoners were allowed to write home every three months only. So it was really like living in a desert, isolated in one's thoughts and feelings, and at the same time surrounded by a group of friends sharing the same conditions, and noisily going about their daily business. Like Kalinowski, Osierko was a deeply religious man who drew salutary lessons from his predicament. He wrote:

> In this hard and deprived state one's thoughts were naturally raised to heaven and kept one habitually in God's presence. Here below you had to be occupied with the duties imposed by love of humanity in general and of neighbor in particular. You mustn't forget that a man condemned to forced labor or the *katorga,* is also generally deprived of all human rights. Russian laws and administrative ordinances are geared to ensure subjection and peace in the prison and the workplace, clamping down on the turbulent nature of criminals and maniacs, permitting the authorities and supervisors to beat and even kill a convict with impunity in any instance of disobedience. Naturally these laws didn't apply to us, but at the same time our supervisors, even the good ones, made a point of informing us of these iniquitous laws, no doubt perhaps to prevent some unfortunate accident. The feeling that we were deprived of everything that could guarantee human dignity was one of the most trying torments. [p. 180].

Osierko also found that the younger exiles, especially those who had received an inadequate education, seemed to take things less to heart, and even looked forward to a change of circumstances, thinking that freedom was round the corner and they would return home. They sang stirring rebel songs every day. They were able to get away with this because the police didn't know the language. It was necessary for Osierko as Prefect to impose some moral restraint on them so as to calm down boisterous temperaments, and so avoid collisions with the authorities or other greater evils. This was a full time job for him. Osierko also said that Kalinowski was a great help in this matter, confronting troublemakers and giving them good advice, in his typically low profile way, using few words that no one heard except those to whom they were addressed. Osierko further states:

> The amount of good Joseph did in that regard is known only to God. He didn't speak about it to anyone, not even his friends. He also tried to involve the youth in some occupation, so that their intelligence and their wills could be applied to work which would curb dangerous outbursts. Joseph himself worked without any let up. He tried to encourage those who were less well instructed to study languages and mathematics; because he had no manual, this was difficult and tiring for him. But he gave himself to this task with unlimited dedication. Those of us who had received a better education made a point of exercising a ministry of care over the young, in the event of our freedom being restored, so that we could return to our country healthy in mind and body and fit to face up to the obligations Providence might place upon us. And in the case where we might be able to mix with the local population, we might give them a useful understanding of affairs, and so contribute to their development. Joseph, who quite certainly felt called to the service of God, worked more consciously in this area than most others, and contributed not a little, during our stay in Usolye, so that we might be able to live in peace, without hazard or persecution. In 1866 the first amnesty was made which reduced the duration of the term of our penalty. This was for us the first breath of a favorable wind like a spring breeze imparting life around us. The manager of the

Works was an intelligent man who harbored no hard feelings against us. As the number of deportees grew from day to day, and as the prisons were unable to cope, those who so wished and were able to, were permitted to move to lodgings in the village without surveillance and without chains. A big number took this opportunity, and Joseph also lost no time in leaving the island. So gradually our harsh life became more tolerable and everyone could find his own space where he was free to relax and look for some employment. But of course this meant that we were split up and only saw each other at certain times. I know that Joseph didn't remain idle, but took in hand the education of the children in a family, as there were several in our colony. [pp. 180-181].

However, though they were close friends Osierko didn't feel he knew much about Kalinowski's interior life, but was able to conclude from what he saw externally, what his interior dispositions and moral strength were like. Osierko relates how after a further amnesty in 1868, many were freed from forced labor and were now simply deportees. Some were given a choice of where to go, and Kalinowski and Osierko opted for Irkutsk. However, Osierko later left for the province of Perm while Kalinowski remained behind in Irkutsk, and they didn't meet again until 1874 or 1875 in Warsaw. Osierko notes that they kept in touch only occasionally by letter and he had no details about his friend's life as a Carmelite. Osierko ends his letter: "Forgive the imperfection of my style and my writing, as well as any mix-up in the details. My age (78) explains all that. My eyes are weak and I can only write with great difficulty. Narowla-on-Prypec, 21 January 1908. Aleksander Osierko." [p. 183].

There is a slightly new situation in December 1865. The convicts were allowed to live in the village of Usolye away from the oppressive surroundings of their island work place and the large and noisy dormitory they shared. This period of his exile seems to have gone well, given the expected privations, and, to use his own word,

Kalinowski found life tranquil. There were curative spa waters also in the area and he had access to these, which he would frequent at 5 am. They reminded him of similar bathing facilities at Ciechocinek in his native Lithuania. That first Christmas then outside the island itself, where the prisoners enjoyed more freedom, was a big affair and a memorable one. There were 200 convicts in the village who followed traditional Polish-Lithuanian customs; they decorated the dining area and fasted on Christmas Eve. They had a light meal at midday and in the evening exchanged Christmas greetings, breaking off pieces of a special bread and passing it round according to Polish tradition. Quaintly the seating arrangements consisted of three tables, one for the men who made up the biggest number, one for the forty women there and the third for the five priests present. The priests proceeded to recite the grace in Latin, broke the bread and chanted vigorously. The priests declined to accept traditional kissing of their hands and preferred to show solidarity with their companions. Many of these women had shown great heroism by going into exile voluntarily to support their husbands. At the end of the meal they all sang some patriotic songs, something that inevitably evokes thoughts of home and feelings of sadness.

Kalinowski would also read theology when the opportunity arose, and he would balance this by continuing his studies in his own profession of engineering. The prisoners took a meal in common and were allowed tea twice daily. Kalinowski himself says he abstained from sugar in his tea because it was expensive, but he used milk generously!

Kalinowski's tastes were simple and his needs few. He insisted he didn't want for anything and asked his parents not to send anything further, as he was also doing some work for which he was being paid. If life proved hard at times then he felt it was no more than he deserved in view of his past sins. Obviously the call to religious consecration when the opportunity eventually presented itself was now growing stronger within.

Both his mother and his sister Mary suspected he was living too austerely, given his precarious health and surroundings, and they counselled moderation. He admitted that he tended to go to extremes, driven by a certain impetuosity in his character, but still protested that though austerity might be the case in insignificant matters, in more important things he would take advice from his spiritual director. In fact he received some advice from the priest simultaneously with the letter from home. In it his director counselled him not to neglect studies in his profession of engineering which might still be necessary later on. Kalinowski accepted this advice and replied: "My personal attraction is for spirituality but I fear that in this attraction there could well be laziness or even laxity…I try to reconcile the two and offer to God the suffering caused me by this interior struggle between two opposed elements." [p. 189].

On one occasion, while washing his clothes, Kalinowski scalded his foot with boiling water and the wound tended to cause an attack of scurvy. Scurvy was often the bane of a convict's life as it was for sailors also in those days. His good doctor friends who shared his exile, treated the wound and he resolved to avoid similar encounters with boiling water in future. He was forced to keep to his room for some time and this gave him the opportunity to do some extra spiritual reading. He was particularly interested in a section of the *Conferences of Fr. Felix* where the author spoke about education, which was of course one of Kalinowski's own concerns. Here he was confirmed in the conclusions he had reached when first imprisoned in Vilnius. He felt that: "Youth, abandoned prematurely to themselves and exiled from their families, had gradually become indifferent to the refined joys of family life, looking for happiness in tainted areas – all this to the detriment of our country. When father spoke to me about our little boy Aleksander, I begged him to keep him under his wing, so that his spirit and body might not be pushed in that direction, and so that the world could not do to him what it had done to so many others among us." [p. 190].

In providing encouragement to his mother, Kalinowski's spiritual convictions clearly emerge at this time. "I know that nothing," he assured her, "can happen either to you or with you that is not the will of God, and that thought, even if it doesn't console me, at least it gives me a sense of peace." [p. 191].

Jean-Baptiste Bouchaud emphasises Kalinowski's devout life, dedicated to the needs of his neighbor, and he tells us that in spite of the restrictions imposed on him, he found a way to converse with God 'all evening.' He would also engage in prolonged periods of prayer in the early morning before any of his companions awoke, thus ensuring a time of complete quiet. Alternatively he would pray late at night when they were asleep. He usually read the life of a saint in the evenings. Indeed his reputation as a person of prayer was so well known that some wag made an addition to one of the litanies: *By the prayers of Kalinowski, deliver us O Lord!* [p. 194].

One difficulty weighed heavily on Kalinowski and that was the lack of solitude for serious study and prayer. It was this intense life of prayer that sustained him amid the rigors of exile, and indeed he maintained an uninterrupted communion with God. Kalinowski at all times pursued his interest in a life of prayer, expressing the wish, with St. Paul, "to be dissolved and to be with Christ." [p. 201]. Around this time Christopher Szwermicki, curate at Irkutsk, was able to visit Usolye and Kalinowski took the opportunity to share with him and seek spiritual advice.

Kalinowski describes for us a momentous event that occurred during his exile, namely a revolt by a large group of Poles. The occasion of the uprising was when these convicts were being transported in steamships across the immense Lake Baikal on the way to Irkutsk from remote parts of Siberia. The lake was subject to thick fog which made the journey even more dangerous. In the course of the journey 700 prisoners mutinied. They overpowered the small group of Cossacks who were escorting them. However, the gesture was hopeless; reinforcements arrived from Irkutsk and they were arrested. The leaders were later executed. Among the remainder was Karol, the brother of the future Capuchin Fr. Wenceslaus, who was a friend of Kalinowski in Usolye. Many of these contracted typhus and died including Karol. Wenceslaus was transferred to Tunka where other priests were interned, simply because of his relationship with one of the rebels. Kalinowski mused on the futility of such actions, though he understood the motivation behind them. Apparently some of the rebels had hoped to escape to China.

Kalinowski filled an additional role in the group as *procurator:* he had to ensure there were sufficient provisions available for the community from day to day. With this in view also he requested his family to send some seed to grow vegetables – carrots, salads, peas, parsley etc, as well as seed for growing flowers. He was moreover able to make a modest profit from such activity.

Kalinowski also looked after the accounts at the end of the month and if there was a shortfall, which there usually was, he would try to balance it from his own limited resources. The group was also expected to do manual work, such as clearing bush for development, and though this was strenuous for so many of them, unaccustomed as the nobility were to such work, and to which many of them belonged, they found it good for their health.

When Kalinowski was relieved of his procuratorial duties he devoted more time to visiting the sick in the local hospital. The appalling conditions of the sick and dying took their toll on him, and he reflected that he was not as strong as some of his companions in this regard. Often they would keep vigil during the night for one of their dying comrades.

Kalinowski now had some changes in his accommodation arrangements. At first he stayed with Boleslas Osierko, a cousin of his friend Aleksander. Later he moved from there and with his friend Felix Zienkowicz went to the house where the Smolenski family lived. Here also the 12-year-old son of Joseph Lagowski lived, and Zienkowicz prepared him for entry into the school at Irkutsk. Kalinowski took over the education of other children in the village and when the priest was away, as he often was to cover his vast parish, Kalinowski taught them the catechism.

This was Kalinowski's typical daily program during this time: "I rise between 6 and 7 in the morning. Having finished prayer I boil water for tea while my companions tidy the apartment. At 9 am I am ready to give lessons in French[79] and Mathematics. At 11 am I'm back and work until noon, which is lunchtime. From 3-4 pm I give lessons in religion and at 4 pm when I am alone, I pray. After evening tea I study or visit our friends." [p. 207].

Kalinowski meanwhile kept up his study of mathematics, using the books sent by family friend Louise Młocka. She also sent him a copy of the Spiritual Exercises of St. Ignatius which he carried out. He notes in his *Memoirs*:

> It was at Usolye that I first did the Exercises of St. Ignatius which had been sent to me by Mlle Młocka This book helped me to know myself better. Reading of the *Compendium of the Catechism* made me understand better the beauty of the truths of faith, this true gift from heaven, which God himself in order to unite us with himself, has given to the church. *The Life of the Saints* by P. Skarga flooded my horizon with new lights. One day I found in this book details about the Order of Our Lady of Mount Carmel, about its beginning in the East and then in the West. This then, I thought, was the Order destined to bring back to the church those who had separated from her. I always desired from the bottom of my heart, to see Russia return to the fold of St. Peter. By a

---

[79] Kalinowski had been giving lessons in French at that time to a student at the *Normal School* and also to a former pontifical officer of Zouaves; this for him was a pleasant relaxation, as well as being productive. He admits, however, that the 'professor' had somewhat neglected his homework and was becoming rusty in French.

special act of divine Providence I was able to join that Order ten years later. [*Memoirs*, ch. 4].[80]

This book became a source of inspiration for him, as he considered the Carmelite Order well placed to promote unity in Russia and its surroundings. Writing to a benefactor at the beginning of spring 1867 he says:

We now have real spring sunshine but the ground is completely denuded of verdure. The nightingale cannot be heard here – the country is too glacial for its delicate throat. We do make a little music. We have one damaged piano but it follows its owner into forest areas as he tries to soften the mores of a primitive population. The fine arts don't flourish here as the emphasis is on the useful rather than on the pleasing. No artists either, but we have a few poets. I continue as usual and I put my energy into the company of the children I teach, which is my only relaxation. The Lord wills that I can be of some use in an activity which gives me more pleasure than pain. [p. 208].

The way in which Kalinowski endured and even welcomed the suffering entailed in exile, reminds us of the example of St. John of the Cross. John of course is the doctor of the *nada* or detachment from all that doesn't lead us to God. Sometimes the saints seemed to have deprived themselves of things which we would otherwise regard as good and legitimate. We have enough evidence that Kalinowski

---

[80] Peter Skarga Paweski (1536-1612) influenced Karol Wojtyła, who based one of his plays on a theme of his. He was quoted as saying that Poland would fall if it did not put its house in order. (Michael Walsh, *John Paul II, A Biography*, Harper Collins, 1994). He was a renowned Polish preacher and very influential even in the politics of his day. He became the Court Preacher of King Sigismund II and was known as *The Polish Chrysostom*. He was eulogized by the great Polish poet Adam Mickiewitz.

loved his family, prayed for them constantly and always worked for their happiness. He looked forward to receiving letters from his family and was bitterly disappointed when his father failed to write to him for a long period. He had met up with his brother Gabriel as we saw, but then they were separated later and Gabriel was exiled to the town of Shadrinsk in another part of Siberia. Kalinowski later complained: "Gabriel writes to me rarely and always the same tune, "I keep well and I embrace you!" [p. 208]. Kalinowski admitted that he needed this earthly consolation, news from his family, which gave meaning to his life. But he also began to see that the Lord was slowly making him understand that "He alone suffices." These words from the *Bookmark* of St. Teresa would be sent to him later by a Carmelite nun after his return from exile.

In June of the year 1867 there was talk of an amnesty and Kalinowski began to prepare for such a development by revising his geometry, geography, mechanics and architecture. There were journals available but the only one he read was the French *Revue de Deux Mondes*; he found an article on the Church and the First Empire 'very interesting.' Czar Aleksander II proclaimed a kind of amnesty in July 1868, which was a half-way house between full freedom and hard labor. Kalinowski shared the good news with his family: "My dear parents, yesterday an amnesty was proclaimed which means that Gabriel and myself are freed from hard labor. I now pass to the state of *deportee*, and I will ask permission to settle in Irkutsk, which I am certain will happen." [p. 212].

Though now free to leave, Kalinowski's next move, or rather failure to move, that demonstrates such a noble and generous side to his character, surprised no one who knew him. He voluntarily extended his stay in Usolye because of his commitment to the children whom he had been preparing for First Eucharist. Naturally, all wished to leave as soon as possible as a first step to full freedom, but Kalinowski refused to join them and stayed on until a Marian priest, Christopher Szwernicki, came along and completed their instruction and presided at their First Communion. Here was a case of Kalinowski sacrificing his freedom for the good of others. He showed by his example, not with words only, what living by the Eucharist really means. These virtues of Kalinowski's altruism and charity to others continued to manifest in circumstances, even when doing so left him in a kind of dilemma. Once he procured a bottle of green tea at a bargain price, a favourite of his father's; but just as he was about to send it as a gift home, a poor person presented himself at his door. He promptly sold the tea and gave the money to the man. He hoped the Lord would recompense his deprived father in better ways!

It was not until July 19 of the following year 1868 that the *ukase* or decree arrived declaring both himself and his brother Gabriel dispensed from forced labor. Kalinowski then decided to ask permission to move to Irkutsk. This joyful news was quickly followed by a fresh blow and one that struck closer than the death of his friend – a letter on the 27th July announcing the death of his young stepsister Monica. He received this news in a spirit of Christian hope, convinced that she was now praying for them all. He felt closer to her in death than he had been in life.

Chapter Six

Goodbye to Siberia

Now we have a change of scene and status for Kalinowski – the hard laborer becomes a deportee. His great friend Felix Zienkowicz with whom he stayed, preceded him to Irkutsk and so Kalinowski was on the lookout for new accommodation, and also for a job. However, as we saw at the end of the previous chapter, he was not in a hurry to leave, though he could have done so, as he felt obliged to look after the little church until the priest returned from one of his missions. He also wanted to help the community prepare the children for First Communion.

Only when the priest arrived back in Usolye did Kalinowski make the necessary preparations for departure. Then he set off and when he reached the city his friend Casimir Laudyn who had suffered from typhoid fever early on, offered him a room as well as financial help. So he shared his meals with Laudyn and other great friends Jan Giejsztor and Miecislaus Siesicki.

Soon after arriving there Kalinowski informed his parents on August 8, 1868: "I have been in Irkutsk for six days. I was not able to write immediately. I wanted to investigate the town and work at settling in. I cannot write any more just now as the post is departing." [p. 212].

Irkutsk had a fine church with a high spire and Kalinowski reported that it was a great joy for him to attend Mass every morning.[81]

Again he would come back in his letters to the passing of his dear sister Monica. He tried to console his parents though he himself also needed consolation: "Death is for me a passing over to a better life, and this thought is the only consolation I can give you. I pray that God will do the rest." And he quoted a passage from St. Paul from the Mass for the Dead, "Do not be sad like those who have no hope." In the same letter he thanks his parents for the money they sent and said he was able to reimburse Casimir and what was left over was sufficient for his needs.

Though the government made it difficult for deportees to find work, Kalinowski felt that Providence had intervened. He was able to do some teaching of youth, though that was frowned upon by the authorities, and that together with another part-time job, procured him more than fifteen roubles a month, with a prospect of adding to that another hour and half of work later. Local head teachers were happy to avail themselves of new staff in their schools and turned a blind eye on government prohibitions, as did the Police Commissioner. They were particularly happy to use the services of Polish people and especially those of doctors. Kalinowski goes into detail about the sad case of one such very popular man, Dr. Lagowski, another great friend whom he dearly missed. He was an excellent and most charitable man, much sought-after in Irkutsk. He died a painful death from stomach cancer and in his last days his only nourishment was some morsels of ice from the river Angara. Dr. Lagowski's funeral took place at Easter and the whole of Irkutsk accompanied his remains from the church to the cemetery.

---

[81] This church was Polish built in 1840 and Kalinowski was pleased to discover the name Clement Polonski among the founders who was possibly his mother's uncle. The pastor enlarged and renovated it in 1869 but it was burnt down in a town fire in 1879. After appealing for help all over Poland he was able to rebuild it.

Kalinowski had tutored the doctor's children and in a letter to his brother Victor asked his sister-in-law Marie to send him some textbooks suitable for their age – if the books were still in the family home. He further asked for additional books adapted to their age, especially books in French. The boy Michael was twelve and he had two younger sisters, Mary and Constance. Before that Kalinowski had written to his young sister Mary, asking her to send on a course in education which had been used in France for young people and which he had seen in the family home. He followed this up with a direct request to his father to send on the teaching course of literature which he now specifies, i.e., *Course of St-Denys,* as well as his copy of Shakespeare if it was still in the house!

Kalinowski's comments on the education of the young one hundred and fifty years ago might well be relevant for today's educators. Aside from classical works, he wished to give the children books which would tend to recreate, develop and enrich their faculties. He was against over-stimulation of the imagination and the sensibility and would prefer to focus on useful and suitable knowledge. He also wanted to instil values of the heart and a solid religious outlook. In his view, formation of the heart was crucial to all good education.

With a surprisingly modern approach he wrote to family friend Louise Młocka: "In so far as I know the temperament of young people in our century there is no point in giving them books promoting sentimentality which can only distract them, but rather we should give them books that treat of the findings of the natural sciences, modern discoveries and recent inventions. My young students are very much attracted to this kind of reading that has a practical bent, and it is in this area that they can develop their talents. A dutiful spirit, carefully maintained, will form their heart." [p. 217].

Kalinowski was opposed to stimulating young people's minds artificially before they were mature enough to cope. He wrote: "Feverish activity, so characteristic of our century, is also reflected in modern education. We want to turn these poor children into intellectuals before their spirits and bodies are mature enough for mental exercises. And what do we see? Weakened organisms with enfeebled spirits that cannot nourish the organism; they are alive, no doubt, but bruised, and need to look to the hospital for help." [p. 217]. Local Russian doctors seemed to agree with him, and one in particular, Dr. Persyn, thanked him for his advice on the education of his children.

Up to this point Kalinowski had lodged with his friend Laudyn on a busy street and after that another friend, Stanislaus Olendzki offered him hospitality. However, he needed more solitude for study and prayer life, so he rented a ground floor apartment from a friend and companion in exile, Count Romain Bninski from Ukraine. Another friend, Mieclaus Siesicki, lodged in an adjoining room. On May 18, 1869 Kalinowski wrote to his stepmother Sophie on her feast day. He admitted that he worked extremely hard from early morning until late at night. One teenage student he tutored was Marian Kwiatowski whose parents were working a great distance away. This was in addition to his ordinary occupations. Returning home from work one evening he found the boy struggling and embarrassed trying to translate some fables from German. Kalinowski helped him with the work until 11 pm. Like all those who can throw off the oppressive yoke of being under constant surveillance, Kalinowski enjoyed his newfound freedom. Sensibly he saw the need for some degree of recreation to relax taut nerves. Once a week he went for a walk with Marian and perhaps Michael, the late doctor's son, along the banks of the Angara. Speaking of one such walk with his students he remarked:

> It's great to relax once a week from work and rejoice, as we did today in the charms and freedom of rest! I went for a walk this morning with Marian and his friend along the other bank of the Angara. It is just before spring and the weather was good. The flowers were not yet plentiful. The shrubs and plants had not yet budded but the vegetation

charmed the eye and the air was perfumed with the scent of larches which abound in this country. ... The appearance of the vegetation, the pleasant scent of the fields, the creek with its silver waters that runs along the field – all this carries me away in thought to a better world more in harmony with the beauty of nature. [p. 219].

Kalinowski's concern for the success of his pupil who was sitting an examination to enable him to pass into Fourth Grade, reminded him of the anxieties parents have for their children: urging them to work, preventing them from failing, preserving them from danger and a thousand other such like. He wrote: "I have been slow to realize how thankful children ought to be to their parents for all the trouble and difficulty they cause them! Today I can strike my breast and ought to admit that it took some time for me to be convinced that whatever is good in me I have received at the paternal hearth; and the good education I received in my home is a real treasure." [p. 220].

There are eyewitness accounts of Kalnowski's dedicated lifestyle when he moved to Irkutsk. A lady called Casimira Czekatowska testified that he was completely taken up with the education of the children and loved to share the treasures of the knowledge he possessed with them. She also gave testimony to his ardent piety and devotion in attending the Eucharist each day. She tells us he would attend early Mass, taking up a position on his knees just inside the door or kneeling in a side chapel, head bowed and hands joined in profound prayer. "He fasted often," she tells us, "he did penance and did good unknown to anyone, and lived in that manner until the hour struck for his return to his home. Later he spent some time in Smolensk where he met an old companion and friend Dr. Czekatowski." [p. 222].[82]

---

[82]   Casimira was the wife of this doctor.

There are other glowing tributes from eyewitnesses who observed how Kalinowski was a man of great integrity and piety and an excellent teacher of the young. And he did all this so quietly and unobtrusively that he managed to escape the attention of most people.

From a personal devotional standpoint, Kalinowski was delighted to find a quite spacious church in Irkutsk where the Blessed Sacrament was reserved. It was served by the Marian priest Christopher Szwermicki.[83] He had been a longstanding thorn in the side of the Russians, having taken part in the 1831 insurrection and suspected of being involved in another attempt in 1846. He was in charge of the largest parish in the world!

Another friend, Marian Dubiecki, is on record to affirm the same qualities in Kalinowski in very similar words, saying he spoke little but always acted and preached by example. It seems Kalinowski came back from his lessons one evening and left his cloak, warm headgear and a cup with silver spoon in the hall. An opportunist thief grabbed the lot and made off. He was soon caught by the police in the market square, trying to sell the stolen goods. He duly received a jail term and later Kalinowski was observed going to the prison at night taking with him packets of tea, sugar and cigarettes for the vagabond.

When Marian, and the doctor's children graduated and were allowed to attend a school in the Russian town of Zhytomyr in the Ukraine, Kalinowski continued to show interest in their wellbeing, sending them good books, etc. This was reciprocated and a lovely letter is extant to him from Constance, the doctor's daughter, only 12 years of age; she wrote to her teacher when she and her family

---

[83] Szwermicki was a priest in the diocese of Seyny in the Kingdom of Poland. He was born in 1812 and died in 1893. After the 1846 attempted insurrection he was imprisoned for five years in Warsaw. Even though his innocence was recognized he was exiled to Siberia in 1850 and was given the immense parish of Irkutsk. To visit the whole parish involved a journey of 10,000 km.

left the area: "Most revered Sir, Now that I'm far away from you surrounded by my parents and friends, my thoughts and my heart often take me back to those people who, like you, have given me so many tokens of affection…. In the midst of all our undertakings, we often think of you and very much miss Irkutsk. We are sad when we don't have news of you, and you must surely believe in the sincerity of our affection for you…. I would like to write a longer letter but I'm afraid I'd miss some lessons…. Today, revered and excellent Sir, I greet you with the sincere affection I have for you." [p. 227].

Constance's mother had a high opinion of Kalinowski, saying she was always happy when her children were under his care. She echoes the fine sentiments of her daughter: "Today I cannot be at ease. I've been advised to send them to the gymnasium but cannot make a decision. There I find only cold egoism and I burst into tears when I think of you." [p. 228]. The Lagowskis were not Catholics, which in a sense gives their witness added weight.[84]

Irkutsk – Paris of Siberia

Kalinowski was a keen observer and he has left very complete descriptions of places he knew. His account of Irkutsk would do justice to a good travel writer. The city was situated on the banks of the Angara, a river that reminded him of the Wileika of his native Vilnius. Though large and quite beautiful, the streets were without lighting and were not paved. Summer conditions entailed wading

---

[84] Michael Lagowski later was absorbed by the *Russification* programs in the schools and broke off all contacts with his former friends. He qualified in medicine at the University of Kiev and died soon afterwards while ministering to military victims of typhoid. Another pious boy, Fiodor Gomello, whom Kalinowski also taught at Irkutsk and praised highly, studied at Kiev with Michael. Though he tried, his mentors made it impossible for him to write to Kalinowski. Later in his *Memoirs* Kalinowski tells us he married Constance Lagowska there but he also died at an early age.

through mud and dust; in winter the streets were frozen over. But Irkutsk had plenty of gardens and was blessed with pure air. He tells us that there were 20,000 volumes in the Orthodox seminary and 27,000 in the town library! There was one daily journal and several weekly ones, etc. There were five hospitals, two refuges for poor children, elementary and high schools for boys and girls, a military school, a medical school, a school of music, a mining school, a school of commerce, a Department of the Imperial Society of Geography of St. Petersburg, an Ethnographical and Archaeological museum, and a theatre. Again he informs us:

> Towards the month of October, the town disappears under a blanket of snow which protects it from the winter ice until spring. During the months of December and January the cold is dry and glacial and the thermometer drops as far as 30-40 degrees below zero. For almost eight months nature is as good as dead and the spirit is affected as much as the body. Sledging rides are the principal diversion. During Carnival time you will see long processions of people decked out in colourful damask parading the streets. [p. 237].

In his correspondence, too, Kalinowski tells us that what he found hardest was not the cold itself, but the length of the winter. However, he acknowledged that summer could be very agreeable in Irkutsk. Writing to his father in October 1869, he mentions the constant threat of earthquakes in the region due, he thinks, to a build-up of snow and ice in the whole region as far as the Chinese frontier. He relates how a superstitious pagan population in the Lake Baikal region call it the 'Holy Sea,' and the pagan priests prophesy dire calamities to come.

He described how the Irkutsk area was rich in minerals of various kinds. Because of the unusual climatic conditions, the countryside was a haven for naturalists and Kalinowski tells us the city possessed a magnificent collection of minerals and a mineralogical exhibition was being arranged. He was happy to meet up with the famous Doctor Benedict Dybowski, like himself exiled to Siberia for his part in the 1863 insurrection. [*Memoirs*, ch. 4].[85] He was the leading naturalist and zoologist of his time. A member of the Russian Geographical Society he was awarded a gold medal by it. He was also a medical doctor and tended the sick and opened hospitals in various areas. Kalinowski liked to share with this likeminded scholar, and was given the opportunity of spending some weeks exploring with him in Kultuk in the great Lake Baikal region. Kalinowski said that Dybowski's studies of the fauna of the region were already well known in the academic world. He recommended that anyone who was passing through this area should call on the genial and jovial Dybowski and view his laboratory. Kalinowski himself was invited to contribute articles on meteorology to the *Imperial Society of Geography* which he did. [p. 242]. His friend Zienkowicz accompanied Dyboski on one of his expeditions and painted tiny crayfish unknown to naturalists up to that time. Fish in fact were found at the bottom of Lake Baikal at a depth of 1,242 metres.

Kalinowski also accompanied Dybowski to the Kultuk area on July 3 and remained there for some weeks of his holidays. As he was unable to follow Dybowski on his researches further afield, he settled down to observing barometric variations, and to drawing and painting the seals – as a service for the naturalist. He admits that he had discovered in himself this latent talent for painting. As game was plentiful in the area he took a gun with him on his walks. However, he laments not having a dog, because whenever he managed to shoot a bird it was lost in the undergrowth.

Kalinowski remained in Kultuk for a short while and wondered how the people could survive in such an isolated area. He shows his

---

[85] An account of his research on sponges in Lake Baikal at this time was published by the *Proceedings* of the Academy of Natural Sciences (Part II, April-August, 1887). His brother was also a scientist.

keen powers of observation of a local ethnic minority of Mongolian origin known as Bouriates whom we met earlier, and were originally Buddhist. He was amazed at their cheerfulness and smiling faces. But even though always cheerful, Kalinowski noted that most of the menfolk were subject to drunkenness. He had to admit that the "women were more reasonable than their husbands," and mothers by some means or other, had to find ways of extracting from them the money necessary to feed their numerous offspring. When an Orthodox missionary was asked if he had made any converts during his twenty years in Siberia he replied: "Not one. My secretary writes down their names in a register, but for myself I don't bother. In my opinion it is better to be a pagan than a drinker!"[86]

Before leaving Kultuk Kalinowski made one final expedition by horse with Dybowski into the Chamar-Daban Mountains. They then parted company but maintained a correspondence with one another. During that expedition he drank in the exhilarating beauty of nature as befitted a future son of St. John of the Cross. The mountain range, covered in sombre woods had a wild but picturesque aspect that charmed the eye. On the highest plateau he culled a tiny flower that had pushed through the snow and sent this back home as a memento for his parents.

Kalinowski returned to Irkutsk at the beginning of August 1869. He kept up a correspondence with the doctor and it was through Kalinowski's good offices that Dybowski's observations on natural science were communicated to the Inspector of Schools. When, after his release, Dybowski was a professor in the University of Lembeck (Leopoli) or Lviv, he wrote a tribute to his friend Kalinowski: "I was united with Fr. Raphael, Joseph Kalinowski, by the bonds of a most cordial friendship. Whenever I was in Irkutsk I went to visit him and when he was in Kultuk he came to see me. He also helped me in my work and painted some anatomical details about the seals in Lake Baikal." [p. 246]. He also refers to the fact that their friendship

---

[86]   Buddhism forbade alcohol among other things.

stemmed from a mutual friend named Jean Czerki who studied in the *Institute of Nobles*, when Kalinowski's father Andrew was Director of that Institute. Czerki had also been deported to Siberia and later came to Irkutsk to study under Dybowski. In the meantime he had joined the Orthodox Church and in spite of Kalinowski's efforts to change him, remained firm. Dowbowski's cousin Emilia also wrote a tribute to Kalinowski:

> Peace is a great gift of God. Surely it is the result of a very powerful faith. For me Joseph Kalinowski was the personification of that Christian peace. Referring to the death of his sister he said, I am not sad, her purity will lead her to heaven. Joseph's life was admirable, wholly dedicated to prayer and works of charity. He was called *a saint* and even the most irreligious were forced to admit his true greatness concealed beneath a veil of rare modesty. If he found a child abandoned anywhere, Joseph would undertake to teach it. If he found a sick person he would help them as also he would help out a neighbor in need. Joseph was always first whether to the church or the confessional. Moreover, thanks to his virtue, many people have obtained grace. [p. 246].

How remarkably prescient was this good lady, a contemporary of his, as we now venerate him as a saint, over a hundred years later!

The case of Joseph Wasilewski, whom we hear about later in Kalinowski's life, is a good example of what all of those who knew him testified regarding Kalinowsksi's great charity and his attention to the needs of those around him. In 1872 his friend Brother Wenceslaus, a Capuchin who had been exiled even from Usolye to a remoter place named Tunka, came to visit Kalinowski. He wanted to confer with him about the mental illness of his nephew Joseph, a young man who had been helping Kalinowski in teaching the children. Two years earlier on June 22, 1870, the young Joseph's mother wrote to the priest at Irkutsk, describing her anguish about her son's illness:

> My Reverend Father, my son Joseph has told me more than once that he has received from you paternal marks of affection. Now he is alienated, so to say, and I don't know what will become of him. I am verging on despair when I think of the misfortune that weighs me down. My poor child, the most virtuous, the most noble, is today declining badly, without help or support. I've been told that gloom and languor have caused him to do foolish things. If my presence out there were necessary, I would sell all I have and go immediately. But I ought first to write a letter to you. Please, good father of poor children, give me news without delay and look after him so that he doesn't succumb. Have pity on me, dear Father! Joseph tells me in his letters about an engineer full of goodness and nobility, J.K. [Kalinowski]. ... I am sending clothes for my son and my brother. Dispose of them as you think best without consulting anyone. [p. 247].

In fact we know that in May of the preceding year, Kalinowski had already lent them the princely sum of 150 roubles, and this delayed his release from Siberia for another year, as this would have constituted his travel expenses. Another revealing aspect of this sad case can be noticed in Kalinowski's engagement with those in need. It seems he had been teaching a young lady, Michalina Siesielska, for six months. Writing again to the boy's mother he told her the story of this girl's sacrifice. "One day when I was weeping at my inability to help you, in order to dry my tears, she arranged for me to have the sum of 100 roubles which her father wished to give her to buy a fur coat of which she had need. And with what sensitivity she made this offering to me! She didn't give me the money herself but asked her father to send it to me." [p. 248].

Another insight into Kalinowski's personality and one which hinted at his later success as a tutor and restorer of Carmel in Poland, was the fact that he never shrank from doing what he thought was necessary in a given situation. The boy Joseph's mother admits that, "he warned the sick boy, he encouraged him, he threatened him in turn. He was always charitable towards him, but also severe when needed and always inflexible. He stood in for him when he was unable to give his lessons, so that he wouldn't miss out on his remuneration. Eventually he confided him to a renowned doctor who restored him to health." [p. 248].

In June 1872 uncle and nephew returned to Russia. They took a steamship to Tomsk and from the boat Joseph Wasilewski wrote to his benefactor: "I am far from you but I feel you are watching over me. I have always looked on you as my protector, my intercessor before God and a constant qualm of conscience – when I do something good I can look you in the face, and when I do something wrong I'm afraid and I want to hide. Now your memory is present to mine and most certainly I will never forget you. I know that the only way to acknowledge my gratitude is to become better, to submit sincerely to my uncle's direction and to follow good advice..." [p. 249]. A little later he wrote an even longer letter spelling out his indebtedness to the person who had done so much to rehabilitate him. Wasilewski himself took up teaching in Ekaterinasburg in 1874 and on May 13 that year he joined the Jesuits and eventually did great work in reforming the Basilian Order in Galicia and working for the reform of the clergy in Romania.

In November 1870, the pastor departed on a prolonged four-month visit of his vast Siberian parish. His vicar then moved into his room, while Kalinowski moved into the Vicar's room. Commenting on his new accommodation, he was happy to report first about his proximity to the Blessed Sacrament, just an antechamber separating him from the sacristy. Kalinowski wrote: "I can be with my Savior night and day before the altar. I am in need of this consolation, far away as I am from all I love." [p. 250]. Here of course was another anticipation of his future life as a Carmelite. Christmas was approaching and this year he was busy looking after the practical side of things, so as to celebrate Christmas Eve in true Polish fashion. He arranged for a supply of wafers seasoned with poppy seed. Then after the evening meal there was a break until it was time to prepare for Midnight Mass. After Christmas and into January the Poles would gather in the evening to sing the *Kolenda*, beautiful and devotional carols in honor of the Divine Infant.

The following Christmas, when the pastor left for a similar visit, Kalinowski was invited to move into his room, and after initial hesitation he did so – and it was a warm and lofty chamber. The pastor entrusted him with the administration of the house. We know from a letter the pastor sent Kalinowski how highly he regarded him: "How indebted I am to you, dear Joseph. Your prayers, your good example are good for a sinner like me. I'm not trying to flatter or spoil you – humility is always necessary, but allow me to remain convinced that knowing you has made me a better person. Continue then to pray for me." [p. 252]. Christopher Szwermicki continues in the same vein in another letter. "I emphasize, dear Joseph," he wrote, "that the more I got to know you the better I have become. I can't explain this, but surely it's a result of the divine mercy. The example of your devotion and detachment, and particularly, I think, your good prayers, have brought about a great change in me, which I find so good." [p. 252].

It should be noted that we also have witnesses to the fact that Szwermicki himself was a good and heroic priest. Marian Dubiecki described what that pastoral visit entailed: "The journey ... was made in the midst of a thousand privations, sacrifices and numerous difficulties through temperatures between minus 40-50 degrees. What devotion, what apostolic fervor, what energy and what health he needed to endure such work without faltering over a period of 42 years! M Szwermicki did endure them and never weakened." [pp. 251-252].[87]

Generally the Polish exiles kept to themselves and only medical doctors mixed with the local population, whom they would know by virtue of their profession. This was true of Kalinowski, though he tells us he did get to know some Russian people. One such was mathematician Aleksander Orlof, of whom he had a high opinion. He met him later in the town of Perm where Orlof had gone to teach mathematics. He also knew a history teacher who lived near Orlof in Irkutsk, to whom he gave lessons in mathematics. He filled the same role for the local Police Commandant, with whom he had a good relationship. He also got to know the Persyn family and taught the children. In addition to these he got to know the Curator of the Science Museum who specialized in meteorology, a subject in which Kalinowski was also an expert. He knew some of the prospectors in gold and many of them had become very rich. He was familiar with a family from the nobility; he had shared a room with the man's brother in St. Petersburg. They used to invite him to visit but he felt somewhat embarrassed by his status as a prisoner and liked to confine his relationship with them to ceremonial visits.

---

[87] Certainly the good seed scattered by a dedicated Polish pastor in the frozen wastes of Siberia bore good fruit. His parish was greater in size than the whole of Europe but some years later there were ten new parishes and six subsidiary chapels in existence. Catholicism in Siberia has emerged from the suffering and persecution of the Soviet era stronger than ever. In the year 2000 a new Catholic cathedral was blessed and opened in Irkutsk.

Chapter Seven

Life in Irkutsk

$\mathcal{D}$uring his stay in Irkutsk Joseph Kalinowski worked hard, not only for the children but for the the sick whom he visited in hospitals. He had established these charitable habits in Usolye. He would distribute food, money and clothes as these became available to him, keeping a bare minimum for himself.

But instances of death and misery surrounding him depressed him greatly. He writes to his parents telling them that one poor man had died leaving his wife and a child of fourteen years. Sadly, the woman then took refuge in drink and passed on the habit to her young son. Kalinowski thought of finding a family to look after the child but the mother would have none of it. To give an idea of Kalinowski's dedication, he interrupted his letter in order to put into action a sudden solution that occurred to him though it was quite late in the day. The effort failed. He comes back to this case in subsequent letters.

Kalinowski would give special care to anyone in need, drawing on his own immense resources of faith. The weather of course was a heavy cross. Even in September 1869, he reflected: "Winter is approaching and we will be locked again in a prison of ice, and externally there is as little comfort as ever. God is the only support for my poor soul and the light of faith in divine providence shines out. The words of the Gospel, *seek you first the kingdom of God*, afford me peace and hope amid the harsh conditions of life." [p. 259].[88]

A month later he wrote: "Six years have passed since the day of my civil death, six years in a veritable tomb. Still I have to admit that sometimes it has its good side, not lacking in charm. In our personal impotence, we are able to triumph over the difficulties of our environment, and in subduing our will we submit so completely to God, so that each moment is a prayer and an act of homage to his divine providence." [pp. 258-259]. Such strong faith did not mean that he was free from the pangs of loneliness and feelings of isolation over so many years. But when his sister Mary offered to come out and share his exile, he would not hear of it. He replied to her letter: "Don't trouble yourself much on my account. If the external circumstances of my life are difficult, internally I am filled with light and peace: and then, suffering here below is the lot of mortals, that is why I can willingly put up with my misery. And then again, a ray of joy comes to scatter the darkness that surrounds me." [p. 259].

But light was quite intermittent, as he wrote to her again in April 1870: "Nothing has gone well this year, but don't they say that God is good to those who carry the cross? That's why I offer up my troubles and especially I do so with joy, when I think of you and my dear parents who are concerned so intimately with all that afflicts me." [p. 260].

Kalinowski prepared assiduously for his Easter confession by going on retreat for some days. On these occasions he would withdraw into solitude and would tend to overlook everyday affairs. Before one such retreat he noted: "How can I thank God for the

---

[88] Since the start of the millennium the Irkutsk climate has altered somewhat and now enjoys a more continental style climate and the 'prison of ice' does not last as long as in Kalinowski's time.

ongoing benefit of this time of renewal? Without Him where would we find rest in the midst of the incessant struggles of life? I recall the words of the Apostle: *Lord, to whom shall we go, you have the words of eternal life.*" [p. 260].

Before leaving Siberia he wrote: "I lead a simple and tranquil life before the altar of the Lord. For some time now the pastor has counselled me to receive Holy Communion every day, something I do with great happiness. The Lord helps me on occasion to be useful to my neighbor and if my usual poverty-stricken state, or some sickness from time to time, the remoteness of my family, or some other upset looms on the horizon, I still have every reason to be grateful to God for his numerous benefits." [p. 262].

But for all his piety Kalinowski was never stiff or starchy. He would take part in parties given by his friend Bninski for the children exiled in Siberia. On another occasion when attending a wedding there was a ball and Kalinowski was invited to dance which he did with good grace – presumably taking part in traditional Polish dances!

But his inclination was always to return to his room for meditation and prayer. Writing again to his parents in December 1871 he said: "I have been distracted by lessons all day, but now I'm a little more recollected by reading the beautiful meditations of P. Chaignon, and now I'm about to retire." [89] It is at this point that Kalinowski reveals a secret to his parents, a dream he had been harboring in exile. The letter runs:

> You know, dear parents, about the project that I formed at Vilnius about leaving the world so as to consecrate myself to the service of God. Not only has time not changed that intention, but it has confirmed me in my resolve and I intend to put it into effect as soon as possible. Only one thing might

---

[89]   Pierre Chaignon SJ. It's interesting that one of his best known books was called *Priestly Meditations*, which seems to be the one Kalinowski was reading.

cause me to hesitate – if you couldn't do without me. In that case my work for you would be the path by which divine providence would want me to reach the port of salvation. That's how I see things at the moment, and I beg God to enrol me in the number of his faithful servants. In serving the Master I will be better able to obtain the gifts of grace and intercede more efficaciously for you. [p. 263].

Kalinowski was embarrassed by the reports that reached his parents about his exemplary Christian behavior in exile. He turns the praise back on his mother by quoting from a book, *L'Homme comme il faut* [man as he ought to be], sent him by his friend Louise Młocka: "In the world it is rare to find a firm affection, always fixed on the same object. What an incomparable benefit for me is that affection of my father and of you also my dear mother, so caring and so strong! I recognise that so well today and it is a great satisfaction to write to you. The constancy and strength of your affection is a gift and at the same time a lesson for me: it shows me how I should behave in regard to others." [p. 264].

Like many other Polish exiles Kalinowski kept up his reading and study at all times. By now he was proficient in many languages, though he felt he was getting rusty at French and English. With his friend Zienkowicz he was revising geography through the medium of French and they also revised differential calculus. A professor in Irkutsk asked him to translate a German book on Mathematics into Russian. He read French periodicals such as the *Revue Catholique*, in a Polish version. In 1870 this magazine kept him informed of the disastrous war between France and Prussia in which Hermann Cohen also got caught up. His Latin studies stood him in good stead also, and in the evening he would read Caesar's *De Bello Gallico*. That elicited from him the comment in a letter to his parents: "The cruelties committed in past times, can make one forget those committed today." [p. 265]. He was asked by the Imperial Society of Geography to take part in their sessions, and was invited to submit papers on metereology for their journal. He was pleased to engage in this work and was happy to mix with the professionals. But while happy to engage also with members of the press, Kalinowski's growing spiritual outlook on the things of this world began to manifest itself. He complained that his young colleagues did not really know the *Master of Science* and didn't follow his leading. He wrote to his friend Jan Giejsztor:

> It seems to me that those who, in our days, dedicate themselves to journalism, prematurely take it on themselves to teach and to critique; and again they contribute a lot to the confusion of ideas which promotes error. You know what results flow from troubled water. They wish to popularize science and in reality all they do is transport into the domain of science a kind of conversational gossip. What good can result from that? [The letter is interrupted by the ringing of the bell for May devotions, and afterwards he resumes where he left off]. I return to my subject and I can say without taking sides, that all this superficial writing – it is difficult to call it anything else – is remarkable for its lack of personal and serious thought. Moreover it's a bad omen for the future. What profit can all this confused and ill-digested mass of knowledge, evaluated precipitously, bring us? What deleterious effects can it produce on society? Assuredly they don't lack goodwill, but they are returning, and wish others to return, to a barbarian state. And I don't choose the word in a metaphorical sense but in its real sense. [He returned to the attack in another letter to his friend a month later]. As I see, in your last letter, we are both of the same mind in how we view society as it is. People work (I work) to reconcile faith with science and the arts. Only God alone is able to make this work fruitful and will counterbalance the blindness of a great number of people. They may be in good faith but have an astonishing superficiality, blinkered

by the darkness of the present time and incapable of reading or dealing with the future. [p. 266].

In December 1872 the Geographical Society invited him to take part in an expedition the following summer, with the aim of exploring the rivers Angara and Yenissey, as they wished to establish a steamboat service there. However, this didn't materialise. But Kalinowski's friend, renowned naturalist Benedict Dybowski, together with a geologist named Godlewski, were commissioned by the Society to explore the whole area between Lake Baikal and the Pacific at the expense of the Russian government. This they did in 1872.

A number of exiled Polish scholars made pioneering expeditions into this uncharted territory and made marvellous contributions to science as a result. Even more important perhaps was the contribution made by Polish teachers like Kalinowski and the service given by doctors and other experts to Siberian society. In an article in *The Siberian* in 1883, the Russians themselves acknowledged that the Poles had a salutary influence on the moral life of the people. The people of Siberia themselves were very aware of this and showed themselves grateful to the Polish people.

Homeward Bound

In 1869 Kalinowski's parents submitted a request to the Russian authorities to obtain his return from exile. Kalinowski's one reservation on this move was that it would mean abandoning the children he felt were at risk in Russian schools. In any case deportees like Kalinowski were required to spend two further years in Russia before being allowed home. Many of Kalinowski's close friends had been dispersed in the general area of Perm, including Bishop Adam-Stanislaus Krasinski of Vilnius. Krasinski had refused to bow to Muravyov's demands and had been exiled to Wiatka. He spent his time compiling a large dictionary of Polish synonyms that illustrated the great flexibility and richness of the Polish language. Kalinowski's friend Siesicki lived with Archbishop Felinski of Warsaw who had also been deported to Siberia in 1863. Bishop Paul Rzewuski, his co-adjutor and successor was soon forced to follow him into exile to Astrachan for a period of twenty years.[90]

In February 1870 the Police Commandant in Irkutsk received a letter from St. Petersburg asking that he expedite Kalinowski's departure from Siberia. This prompted Kalinowski to write to his parents: "I thank you for your requests on my behalf. Nothing on earth can take the place of the heart of a father, and to think there are people who protest against the existence and necessity of the family." [p. 276].

So here were the first official indications, thanks to the intervention of his parents, that Kalinowski would soon be allowed to leave Siberia. At the beginning of May a medical report had been sent from Irkutsk to St. Petersburg. Though the report was not flattering to his health, as Kalinowski observes, still it had the positive effect of hastening his transfer. He would be allowed to stay in a Russian town or return to the Kingdom of Poland, but not home to Vilnius or anywhere else in Lithuania. He sent his family a photograph in case they might be scared on seeing him without prior warning!

The journey would be daunting – about 4,000 miles – and Kalinowski hoped he could make it under government expenses via the postal courier, rather than through the more fatiguing State arrangements consisting of travelling by stagecoach. However, his request was refused and his father suggested he ask to be allowed to make his way to Perm instead. This was not a great improvement because he would still have to live with the Siberian climate, and the reports coming from Perm were not encouraging.

---

[90] This area is famous for the production of caviar from local sturgeon but there was an unpleasant fishy smell everywhere. The Bishop was eventually able to return to Poland and died in Kraków in .1893. Archbishop Krasinski also returned home and would later visit Kalinowski in Czerna.

Kalinowski himself was inclined to take up a position that would involve quite difficult work in the Kama region. Some of Kalinowski's best friends like Osierko and Giejsztor were serving out their sentences in the region. Osierko was resident in the town of Solikamsk over 300 kilometers from Perm, and Giejsztor was in Slobodzk about 500 kilometers west of Perm. Others were dispersed to various other regions.

To make matters worse, it was impossible for the priest to offer services in the Perm area on a regular basis as his parish was more than twice the size of France! In addition to the rigors of the climate, the exiles were extremely isolated.

Writing to his brother Victor in March 1870 Kalinowski conceded that: "The lack of religious help and being deprived of agreeable company, contributed to debilitating the spirit and corrupting morals. Many of our number, condemned to this kind of life, little by little have lost their reserves of nobility which they had carried with them from their native land. These people inspire fear and compassion. Let us pray for them and ask God to send others into better conditions where they are allowed to praise their Creator. May he have pity on us." [p. 275].

Kalinowski's father sent him some money in October in anticipation of his journey, but winter travel was out of the question and it would have to be June at the earliest. The money was returned to his father's residence in Hrozow, near Minsk. Another preoccupation for the Kalinowski family was that the younger son Aleksander was studying at the University of Moscow but the family would prefer him to attend the University of Warsaw. As his studies in Moscow would be free, but not so Warsaw, this would be a financial burden on them.

For a number of reasons, such as the lack of opportunity for religious practice and the unlikelihood of getting a job in the Perm region, Kalinowski decided to ask to be allowed to stay in Irkutsk for one year; permission was granted in August 1871. His plan was then to return to Warsaw or nearby and get a lucrative job. This period was a trying time for Kalinowski, a real dark night of the soul. He would miss friends who were leaving, and felt that without them he would be living in a kind of twilight world. The weight of the cross was heavy and he understood the Lord was detaching him from much that he held dear. The year passed quickly enough and on July 10 he informed his parents: "I have applied for my ticket for the journey and I will go and pick it up at the chancellery today. The day after tomorrow, God willing, I will leave Irkutsk. When I reach Perm, I will wait there until I get complete clearance. I will be happy to meet up with my good friends from Irkutsk in Perm." [p. 280].

Finally then, the reverse journey was under way and he headed first to the town of Perm. Looking back in his *Memoirs* later on he reflected: "It was with great heart-wrenching that I departed, not only from the town of Irkutsk but also from a number of friends to whom I had become sincerely attached and who had to remain there. I missed especially my little corner in the presbytery where I had passed my final years of exile peacefully. My greatest sorrow was to have been parted from the priest Szwermicki, whose fatherly heart and wise direction had put me so much in his debt. Young Gomello came with me and that gave me courage." [*Memoirs*, ch. 4].

Kalinowski was happy to learn also that there was a church in Perm tended by an exiled Polish pastor. He and his companion, 18-year-old Russian Fiodor Gomello took the postal transport, and though it was July 12 the weather was appropriately melancholy and misty. He had been provided with a revolver by his good friend Zienkowicz as it was not unusual to encounter brigands on such a perilous journey. "Without resting by day or night," Kalinowski tells us, "we made our way from Irkutsk to Tomsk and passed through Krasnojarsk, altogether a journey of about 1,500 kilometres ..."[p. 281].

They reached Tomsk without incident, and then took a steamer, cruising down the river Tom. Kalinowski again draws attention to the majestic scenery he had remembered from the outward journey. The scenery was indescribable, though he makes a tolerable attempt to do so. Here again the future Carmelite echoes nature-loving St. John of the Cross. The wide waters of the Orb were in flood and commanded a sweeping view over an area which had not known a similar inundation in living memory. The boat floated above the tops of submerged trees and Kalinowski commends the expertise of the captain who ensured that they reached Tiumen safely. Kalinowski's companion Gomello had to hurry so as not to miss the last steamer which would conduct the young man from Perm via the Kama and the Volga as far as Nizhny-Novgorod. From here Gomello would continue his journey to his destination – Kiev. They reached Perm on August 6 and Fiodor's boat was due to leave the same day. Here he parted from the young man with a heavy heart for he had developed a high regard for him. He was now alone, friendless and forlorn.

Kalinowski's first port of call in Perm was the Catholic chapel, (after a false alarm when the coachman took him to the Protestant one) where he had the joy of meeting up with Sigismond Czechowiez, a college companion from Vilnius. The chapel was in fact just a room in a private house. This old friend was able to arrange some accommodation for him. However, the accommodation was in the midst of a poverty-stricken family – a mother and five children. Kalinowski thought her husband had neglected his family. He was soon able to help them financially and he tried to instil some religion into the household, something that was sadly lacking.

In spite of everything, Kalinowski had indeed happy memories of Perm. It was here he had been reunited with his young brother Gabriel, like himself exiled to Siberia. From Perm he was able to write to his parents and friends and receive a generous gift of money from them by post.

Here Kalinowski had to bide his time and wait for directions from the authorities. He could still have been ordered to go elsewhere. His determination to frequent the sacraments met with some raised eyebrows in Perm, not just among the faithful, but also among the two priests there. However, they soon got used to it. The priest allowed him to rent a room near the chapel as the family with whom he lodged was far from satisfactory.

Kalinowski informs us that Bishop Borowski of Zhytomar was also in exile here. The bishop had a little chapel in his house where he could say Mass assisted by two priests. Kalinowski relates that at this time plans were underway for building a Catholic church in Perm, but he is silent on his own part in promoting the project. The necessary funds were collected and the foundation stone duly blessed. A similar church was being planned in Ekaterinasburg. This was the pattern in Siberia where Polish people in exile were responsible for the establishment of Catholic Churches, as also in other parts of Russia.

As time went by he encountered many exiles of Polish background here, some like himself, from Lithuania. Kalinowski, never one to remain idle, accepted a post as tutor obtained for him by his friend Orloff, Inspector of Schools, whom he had known in Usolye. He was engaged to instruct three children from the Diageleff family who belonged to the Orthodox Church and he duly applied himself to the task. He was engaged in teaching other children as well.

Kalinowski reproaches himself for having reduced his seven-year-old pupil to tears after giving him an unsatisfactory note about his French lessons. "I should have given it to his mother" he mused, "How can you expect too much from a seven-year-old," he asked himself. The same boy once piped up when Kalinowski was late for his lesson: "Sir, I'm annoyed with you!" [p. 288]. But as a tutor he was in fact loved and appreciated by parents and children alike. Kalinowski endeared himself greatly to this family and when he was about to leave Perm, Diagelleff offered him 12,000 francs per annum to stay and teach his children. But this was not possible.

All in all Kalinowski was very happy in Perm. Arriving there in August the town was looking its best; the fields and the trees in the woods were covered in verdure which presented an attractive aspect.

Chapter Eight

Those Who Instruct Others in Justice

$\mathcal{A}$s in Irkutsk, so in Perm, Kalinowski continued to involve himself in the education of the young and not so young. He taught the children of the Pozniack family and pastor Fiszer himself approached him for lessons in French language which he willingly gave. The sons of the Director of the College came to him to resolve their mathematical problems. Kalinowski was armed with recommendations from Irkutsk to the Police Chief in Perm and to the Minister for the Interior, so he was able to stay put in Perm.

He informed his parents on November 10 that he had secured accommodation in a street near the chapel and could even see the altar from his room. The pastor came a few times for French lessons and they would read the *Meditations* of Chaignon together. For his part Kalinowski would often consult Bishop Borowski, exiled bishop of Luck and Zhytomar in Ukraine, regarding problems he encountered in his study of theology. This was obviously with an eye to the future. Kalinowski continued to write short theological essays for his friends as he had done in Irkutsk. For instance he wrote one on the obligation to pray for members of the Orthodox Church who had died in good faith. Another was devoted to the appropriateness of the Immaculate Conception and a third on the commandment to love God, one's parents and one's neighbor.

Borowski was a doctor of theology and had been professor of Sacred Scripture and History of the Church in the Academy of Vilnius. The bishop received the *Revue du Monde Catholique* through the post and Kalinowski too read it regularly. The bishop had translated extracts from the Apostolic Fathers, Ignatius of Antioch, Polycarp and St. Gregory of Nazianzen. Kalinowski tells us that in addition to his own diocese he had been Apostolic Administrator of Kamieniec-Podolski until its suppression after 1864. The famous Carmelite foundation of Berdichev was situated in his diocese.[91] The bishop's assistant Fiszer had experienced the wrath of the Russian authorities, having been shunted around various areas in Siberia and eventually assigned to Perm. It was here he made the acquaintance of Kalinowski praying in the church, and they struck up a lasting

---

[91]   The Carmelite shrine at Berdichev was an impressive edifice with towers and cupola. It possessed a miraculous image of Our Lady. The church had been founded by Jan Tishkevich, who was descended from Tyszko, Prince of Kiev. In connection with this an interesting anecdote is associated with one of Tyszko's sons, Theodore. He had been imprisoned by the Tartars and had promised, if he regained his freedom, to build a religious house in his territory. He had a vision of a religious who consoled him. On gaining his freedom, he came to Lublin and visited the Carmelite church there where he immediately recognised St. Teresa of Avila in a painting in the church, the image that figured in his vision. Soon afterwards he met the Fr. General of the Carmelites and made his offer, which was accepted. This was the origin of the Carmelite house of Berdichev in 1642. Tyszko had given the church an image of Our Lady venerated in his family. This became the source of many miracles and she was called *The Protectress of the Ukraine*. The loftily situated foundation became known as *The Fortress of the Blessed Virgin Mary* – and it literally was a fortress, with shops and commercial centres within the walls of the monastery. Due to the vicissitudes of history the Carmelite community came and went and returned again where they still minister. The local bishop has declared it the *National Shrine of Our Lady* for Latin Rite Catholics in the Ukraine. The original icon was destroyed in a fire during World War II.

friendship. Kalinowski was often invited to join the bishop and Fiszer and another friend Maurice Mierzejewski for meals and discussion. Kalinowski notes that on Pentecost Sunday 1873 they visited the bishop and were not disappointed in receiving an additional "dose of spirituality." Bishop Borowski's informed theological conversations reminded Kalinowski of the Allocutions of Pope Pius IX which they read in the Catholic journals they received from Poland.

At Christmas Kalinowski served three Masses, a tiring exercise in those days. He would not accept any invitations on that day, but would invite some young people for a meal on the Vigil. They would celebrate in true Polish style which went some way to compensate for their absence from home. We have a valuable witness to Kalinowski's developing spiritual life at this point from his friend Fiszer: "When I lived in Perm with Bishop Borowski, Joseph visited us often and the fatherly conversation of His Excellency alleviated for us the hardship of exile. Joseph rarely went out: but you would often see him in the public chapel, where he was always in adoration before the Blessed Sacrament or in the bishop's chapel when he came for Mass. Every evening when I came to visit I found him in prayer in the chapel with a rosary in his hand." [p. 294].

Over thirty years later Kalinowski recalled: "Thanks to your wise direction, dear Father, what benefits I received in Perm from the divine mercy! How happy I was in your esteemed company and so close to Jesus!" [p. 294].

Early in the new year Kalinowski was distressed to hear that his younger brothers Aleksander and Jerzy were ill. He tried to console his parents and pointed out the fact that they were good boys and devoted to their religious duties. He thought he might have an opportunity to return home to help even if he had to return to Perm. Moreover he offered to make a monthly contribution of 10 roubles which might enable them to be sent to Southern Russia to improve their health.[92] Such a gesture if carried out would obviously leave him short if not impoverished considering his circumstances. He was known to have to borrow suitable attire from a friend if invited to a special occasion. Certainly for up to a year at this time he had no bed linen but managed with substitutes. Any superfluous items were always given to the poor. We need to bear in mind that winter temperature in Perm could be from minus 30 to 40 Celsius. He remarked: "My little room resembles a cottage in the Alps. Someone came to sweep away the snow from one side of his dwelling which had disappeared in snow up to the eaves." [p. 295]. We can pick up clues in his *Memoirs* as to where some of his money (and clothes) went:

> Before my departure from Irkutsk, when I lived at the presbytery with Zienkowicz and Gomello, a peasant originally from the Kingdom of Poland showed up at the parish house. He had received an amnesty and wished to return to his family. He didn't have the money for the journey but he was so anxious to see his family that he was prepared to leave at any cost. We gave him what we could and he set off on foot, and would not be detained either by the distance or the dangers of the journey. Some weeks after my arrival at Perm he turned up there also and appeared suddenly before me. He had joined up with a transport carrying tea from Irkutsk to Perm... Now he wished to take the steamboat from Perm to Nizhny-Novgorod and from there he would set out on foot again to Smolensk and on home. His money was gone and the boat was leaving next day. I asked him to let me see his papers to assure myself that all was in order and that he deserved to be helped. Next day a torrential shower inundated the town and the poor traveller arrived

---

[92]   Kalinowski probably has in mind the health resorts on the Black Sea in the Crimea area.

in the early morning thoroughly drenched. No doubt divine Providence had taken a hand: for I would not have been so willing to give him money and clothes had he turned up on a fine day! [*Memoirs*, ch. 4]. His papers were in order and I gave him a letter of recommendation to Stanislaus Slavinski still interned in Smolensk. (Slavinski) was so impressed with this courageous and indefatigable traveller that he even gave him a railway ticket, and a few days later our exile fell into the arms of his wife and children. I still recall this man so full of nobility and humility who shone with the seal of chosen souls full of love for country and family combined with a sincere devotion – true children of holy Church and homeland. [pp. 296-297].

Kalinowski was just as profligate with his books as he was with his clothing and resources. His family and particularly Louise Młocka occasionally sent him books and when he had read them they found their way to those who he thought might benefit from them and be a source of moral help to them and even contribute to their eternal salvation.

It is instructive to look in on Kalinowski's correspondence with his long-term friends and colleagues, especially those who had fallen foul of the Russian authorities during the insurrection of 1863. Several of these shared his exile. First among these was Jan Giejsztor. Kalinowski frequently tried to communicate his own sense of Christian commitment to people like these. He would comment on the value of suffering which frees us from earthly concerns and unites us with God. He would urge works of charity and he spoke about the happiness of approaching the Holy Table daily: "I tremble at the thought that some day I would be deprived of this happiness." [p. 297].

Kalinowski could be quite direct and unambiguous towards his friends when he felt like it! Another of them, Jan Czerski found the horn of a rhinoceros and wrote a detailed description of it which he wished to publicize. But Kalinowski wrote to Zienkowicz: "Can you tell Czerski that I don't have the aptitude for the propagation of his study on the horn of a rhinoceros." In fact he would prefer if Czerski would devote his talents to what he considered more useful occupations such as his own hobby of meteorology. Czerski took the hint and took up the study of geology in which subject he would become renowned. He made valuable studies of the Lake Baikal coast with another friend of Kalinowski's, Benedict Dybowski. [p. 298].[93]

Another loyal friend was Felix Zienkowicz. Towards the end of 1872, Zienkowicz wrote him two lengthy letters. The first was four folio pages, the second a dozen, all in closely packed writing! The letters ranged over a variety of topics and included scientific accounts of findings made by Kalinowski's friends as well as plenty of chit-chat. But Kalinowski took exception to the fact that in all this wealth of material there was no mention of God! It is interesting then to read Kalinowski's reaction:

> I have numerous mementoes on my table that testify to your friendship for me and bring your memory back to me. But something is nagging me and disturbs me a lot. Obviously I don't have sufficient love for God or I would have succeeded in lighting a tiny spark in your soul. What is simpler then or more natural than to love Him from whom we hold all that we are – our spiritual faculties and those of the heart which enable us to do some good. But this sometimes suggests thoughts of vainglory to us as if we ourselves were responsible for the good.[94] Suppose, dear Felix, that a person unknown renders you or one of yours some outstanding

---

[93] Several areas of Siberia were named in honor of Czerski including the Czerski Mountain Range.

[94] Zienkowicz had informed Kalinowski how he had tried to help an unfortunate woman abandoned by her husband and he was engaged in teaching her children as an act of charity.

service; wouldn't you like to know his name in order to thank him? But when it's a question of Him who has given us existence, you don't enquire who it is, you don't wish to know his name, you don't have a moment to spare in order to ask his assistance. Loaded by him with exceptional gifts, don't you have more of an obligation towards him than a simple villager? All these thoughts, dear Felix, came to me after I read your letter and felt close to you: I bring them before you because it is you who have given rise to them. [p. 299].

Then he relates an anecdote about an orphan named Ignatius whom the Pastor was taking care of in Irkutsk and with whom Kalinowski corresponded. He tells his friend:

This is the third letter I have had from him and it is more badly written than the first ones. It is of course the fault of Ignatius who could do better if he put his mind to it, but he needs to be supervised. After returning from school he should be carefully supervised in the house. If we are not concerned all the time about the education of our own children then certainly it will be in vain that we will care for those of others. It is necessary to put oneself out a bit for them. In the first letter you appear to find a contradiction between the teaching of the church and that of Jesus Christ. Tell me then isn't this precisely the case we're talking about, the fact that the church recommends us to look after our family, both spiritually and physically – doesn't this flow directly from the teaching of Jesus Christ: Whatever you do for the least of these little ones, you do for me? It seems to me that he is not talking about simply *training* the child, the expression you use, but of something else more important, especially with Ignatius, an orphan and such an orphan! Your heart will dictate the rest. [p. 300].

Felix certainly took this rebuke meekly for he replied eight days later:

> You have shown me great tokens of affection! Your last
> letter is something new and more eloquent. It is a faithful
> echo of all the years we have passed in exile, of that mutual
> love which has softened our sufferings. Now as always, you
> have the tenderness of a sister for me; you have drawn my
> attention to things like an elder brother. When you made
> that observation, my proud and mutinous mind bridled
> before you, but you lanced the wounds that they caused you.
> Soon, indeed, with a little reflection, I recognized that you
> had good reason for what you said. I was humiliated, and
> even if I had not done all that you implied, I resolved to go
> in the direction you indicated... You have said much. You
> have put your finger on the wound and who knows if that
> word has had the effect of a surgical operation? Your letter,
> dear Joseph, came to the point; I take it then on reflection
> and it can be said, I take it to heart and I thank you. [p. 301].

Pursuing his thoughts on the education of youth, Kalinowski goes on: "Illustrations drawn from animal life are often attractive for children, but they also involve a degree of danger. There are movements of cruelty and egoism in the behavior of animals which can make a fascinating impression on the delicate mind of a child, if an informed person is not on hand to clarify the matter. The same thing holds when history is being taught to children and when you put a book in their hands for them to read. The deceitfulness in the story of Dido[95] appeals a lot to them and won't easily be effaced from memory, while at the same time they will easily forget serious

---

[95]   Virgil tells the story of Dido, Queen of Carthage and Aeneas in the Aeneid.
It's not clear what deception Kalinowski had in mind concerning Dido.
Aeneas himself might have been a better candidate for deceitfulness. Here
again Kalinowski shows the breath of his reading and classical culture.

and useful traits." [p. 304]. Similarly writing to his youngest brother
Jerzy from Irkutsk he notes:

> Here we have some children who sing in church, badly it's
> true, but devoutly and piously; almost all orphans for whom
> God alone holds the place of father and mother, plucked
> from misery and corruption and gathered at the foot of
> the altar to serve God. Their bad habits sometimes resist
> the care they are given, but they are always charming in
> my eyes because of their unhappiness and distress, as well
> as the perfume of innocence, which render these children
> and consequently you yourself, my dear little brother, so
> precious to God and others. When you are praying, my
> dear, see to it that you think from time to time of these poor
> little children deprived of the supervision and love of their
> father and their mother and condemned from the cradle to
> drag out an unhappy existence in a foreign land. When you
> suffer some inconvenience just think of the misery of these
> poor children and surely your troubles will appear sweet and
> delicious. [p. 304].

Writing again to Jerzy on the feast of his patron the soldier saint
he exhorts him: "And you also, my dear little brother, you ought to
become an intrepid soldier in the army of Christ, prince of peace."
[p. 305]. In fact at this time Kalinowski had requested his brother
to procure a document for him, attesting the fact that he belonged
to Lithuanian nobility which would recall for him the glory of
his ancestors and how it was incumbent on him to follow in their
footsteps.

Speaking about other members of his family, Kalinowski had
a special place for his young sister Mary whom he considered to
have been instrumental in his return to God. He visualized her also
training children and communicating to them her own sterling
qualities. He shared with her his own insights in the matter. "The

mother of my pupils would wish me to be a little severe with them, not feeling she could act in this way herself, but really I can't imitate the lion! I'm sometimes impatient, but I try to make amends by redoubling my gentleness. Truly, in order to direct these little creatures, no less skill is needed than to direct adults. For children discipline is not enough – they also need the help of religion. If these are lacking, education will be no use. Here I advise you to be prudent lest we fall into unfaithful territory." [p. 305]. Kalinowski found it a handicap when teaching the children of members of the Orthodox Church that he could not instruct them in their faith.

Going back to additional points he raised in the earlier letter in which he took his friend Felix to task, Kalinowski draws on his own experience as a student in St. Petersburg to reinforce the need for a strong spiritual and religious foundation in the life of youth. It was the absence of this that caused him to stray at that time. He outlines his reasons:

> The mental illness of three of my students and my reflection on what caused this spiritual alienation gave me food for thought. They all originated in the conscience and the heart, or at least in the emotions, and so it was not long before their minds became disturbed. And what good can contemporary medicine provide for this bad state? Leaving aside as they do, or at least treating with indifference the remedies that religion can provide for moral evil, medical science without taking into account the way in which this evil develops, doesn't seek to assuage or cure these unhappy people except by material and crude means. Or sometimes they try an altogether artificial approach through the use of physical exercises to build up the body, forgetting to strengthen the faculties of the spirit. [p. 305].

To strengthen his position Kalinowski cites the example of Joseph Wasilewski, a troubled young man who recovered and later became a Jesuit priest. He writes: "The cure of Wasilewsksi undeniably proves this – it's not in a course prescribed by doctors but in religious practice that you should seek a remedy for this illness. It's true that for it to succeed you need charity and dedication, something never lacking in the Catholic Church as witnessed by the establishments of the Order of St. John of God. Today everything is in the hands of seculars and if the hospitals have won out that's only in number and extent." [p. 306].

Reflecting on several letters he received on March 18 in time for his feast day, Kalinowski muses in thoughts reminiscent of spiritual writers of the period: "Vain thoughts strike me when I see myself the object of so much solicitude, but they vanish quickly in face of another thought – that of the last judgement. In the presence of those who give me so much affirmation today I shall be very embarrassed when the great book is opened before me containing the material on which I shall be judged; everything veiled today will then be revealed and avenged." [p. 307]. On a similar note he writes to his father:

> There was a time when youthful vanity attributed to myself a little knowledge and assurance which I noticed within myself; God, however, has blown away such feelings of pride. I realize my own incapacity and I'm convinced I possess no real knowledge except what I have received from you, my dear father, at a time when you watched over me with such solicitude and took so much trouble over the formation of my heart and spirit. When I look over the little good I may have done, God, in order to impress humility on me, has made me aware that thanks is more due to you for whatever is good rather than to me. God has given increase to what you have sown and cultivated with such care which I acknowledge. Today I place at your feet, my very dear father, with humility and with love, the homage of my gratitude. [p. 307].

Kalinowski was always willing to help and excuse young people who got into trouble with the authorities. He would personally encourage them and contact their families back home, or enlist his own family to contact them. He would usually shift the blame to negligence or indifference on the part of those responsible for the young people in question. This further prompted him to reflect: "In the face of this indifference, of which I have much experience in Siberia, I esteem as a great prize, my very dear parents, your continual vigilance in teaching the members of our family, scattered on all sides, that unbreakable bond of reciprocal love of which your heart is the center." [p. 309].

On Leave at Last – Visits to Family

Kalinowski's great friends Aleksander Osierko and Jan Giejsztor, already in Warsaw, wrote urging him to join them there. They lobbied the authorities for his definitive release. As we saw Osierko had made provisional arrangements for him to tutor the children of Prince Lubomirski,[96] which he declined. A gentleman named Diagieleff, whose grandchildren Kalinowski had tutored in Irkutsk, also lobbied General Ogareff, a friend of his in St. Petersburg, for Kalinowski's release. His release ticket was scheduled to arrive in six months, not the four months he had hoped for.

On a heart warming note, Kalinowski's stepmother Sophie wrote to him on May 15: "This night your father, Mary and I had the same dream; it seemed to us that we saw you arrive at Hrozow safe and sound. That was indeed a consolation which God sent us. We then carried out the Rogation devotions together as well as those for the month of Mary, whom I ask to take you, my angel, under her protection. During this time you no doubt are praying for us. It is in your prayers and those of our dear departed that I place all my trust." [p. 309].

---

[96]   These were related to the Czartoryski family.

When this letter reached him Kalinowski was still in Perm and in fact was struggling with a bout of illness due to the cold weather and heavy falls of snow. He was anxious to remain there for some time as the children he had been tutoring came to Perm on June 15 to complete their studies. In his last letter from Perm he had written: "I depart in a few days."

So after all the letter-writing and pleading on the part of his family with friends in high places, Kalinowski was given his 'ticket of leave.' This arrived in the spring of 1873, and permission also came for Kalinowski to spend six months with his family. He said goodbye to the local priest Michael Fiszer whom he would not see again for ten years – when they were reunited back in Kraków. He took a steamer and made his way along the Kama and the Volga as far as Nizhny-Novgorod, and after that took the train to Moscow and on to visit his family. Kalinowski referred to a curious but disagreeable experience on the way back. Sharing his cabin was a young Orthodox cleric and a young man who looked like a merchant. The pair started playing a game of cards and from time to time took a swig from a bottle of spirits. Then, thought Kalinowski, under the influence, an altercation arose and they kicked up quite a fuss, freely insulting one another. Kalinowski continues:

> I don't know for what reason, they turned to me and then this priest in his drunken state latched on to me with his impetuous nature and I was unable to shake him off. Initially he couldn't identify my nationality and interrogated me suspiciously, and finally his persistence broke all bounds. He was the leader of a village on the banks of the Kama. When we arrived at a station he invited me to descend from the carriage and follow him. This I refused to do and his insistence was such that I had no little trouble in evading him. A sad thought struck me, seeing this priest, fundamentally good, mixing with such company and addicted like him to the vice of drunkenness. [*Memoirs*, ch. 4].

This was not the only Orthodox cleric he encountered in similar circumstances – he met another near St. Petersburg, of higher rank indeed but on the same slippery slope. This led Kalinowski to moralize somewhat on the failings of the Orthodox church.

Kalinowski made his way through Russian territory and on June 20, 1873 reached the charming rural château, 'Les Studzionki,'[97] near Minsk, where his brother Victor was manager, and where he was welcomed with outstretched arms. A few days of much-needed recuperation followed. With the keen eye for the beauties of nature that we have noted, Kalinowski drank in the splendor of these grounds. On one side of the house there were two vast lakes united by a little river. From the south to the west there was a magnificent park as far as the eye could see, planted with all kinds of trees – oaks, linden, larches, charming pines; elsewhere there were weeping willows, elderberry trees, jasmine and rose bushes spread out on an immense carpet of verdure. Near the two lakes, reflecting an azure sky, a little river meandered like a snake across the park and under two pretty bridges linking the two rivers.

Victor's wife Marie had been ill and had gone abroad to recuperate, so she didn't meet him at this time. Kalinowski wrote to tell her about his visit and how well he had been received. He noted how Victor had changed a little and was somewhat feeble, but still keeping very active. Kalinowski ends the letter by paying her a compliment in regard to the house: "The chapel and halls are just as they were ten years ago and replete with memories of the past: at present the ornamentation continues and I recognize the hand of a conservationist." [p. 313]. He admires the fact that she cares so much for things that are so well loved.

---

[97] This imposing house originally belonged to the Radziwill family. It then passed to General Count Rozwadowski who first married a sister of Prince Karol Radziwill and later married Wegrowska. There were six children from this marriage and of these Sophie married Aleksander Gruszecki. The eldest of the children of this new marriage was Marie Gruszecka who in turn married Victor Kalinowski.

After these few days' rest he proceeded to the château of Hrozów[98] where the rest of the family eagerly awaited him. This was also a beautiful mansion with extensive parks and lakes, and an English garden. The warmth of this reunion after almost ten years of exile, with his stepmother Sophie, his father Andrew and his sisters Emilia and Mary, together with his grandmother Madame Polanska, can scarcely be imagined. His brother Jerzy, future priest, was only twelve years old. It was a case of tears all round. Jerzy commented:

> Ten years of suffering had not failed to leave their mark on the beloved face of our brother, but the change that had taken place in his soul was very remarkable. During his imprisonment he had promised God to consecrate himself to his service if he survived. From that day he had worked earnestly and perseveringly to do everything God's will required of him. His look was modest and in his face you could read recollection and constant union with God. There was much restraint and prudence in his words. When we questioned him he carefully avoided any query which might lead to criticism of neighbor, even of enemies. During his time at Hrozow he either studied or read but nothing worldly. He didn't like large crowds which might dissipate him. His life was like a lovely summer's evening when the sun goes down and nature is brought into shadow and repose. [p. 313].

---

[98]   This house with Portico in the province of Minsk originally belonged to Mierzejewski family. Valentine Mierzejewski had taken part in the insurrection and was exiled. He was ordered to sell his property, but as there was no time to arrange this, he was forced to auction it. It was bought for a nominal sum by Prince Leon Wittgenstein, son of Princess Radziwill. Karol Kalinowski married Martine Mierzejewska and he decided to lease the house. Karol later gave the house to his father and moved to a more modest place at Hrozówzek, some kilometers away.

From Hrozow he visited his grandparents' home 'Musicze' with its linden and hazelnut groves where he and his siblings had spent idyllic summer holidays, sweetened by a budding friendship with Celina Gruszewska. It must have been a supremely nostalgic visit.

Kalinowski later reflected in a letter to his friend Louise Młocka his bitter-sweet feelings on returning home. Sweet, because of the immense joy of being reunited with his family after such a long absence; bitter, when he surveyed the total ruin of his country. The Russians, as always, had taken vicious revenge for the rising of 1863. In a letter to his old and staunch friend Zienkowicz he uses the graphic image of the dead loved one. He visualized his country as a corpse which can now only repulse one. Deeply cultured man that he was, Kalinowski now recalls some lines from the Romantic English poet Lord Byron writing about stricken Greece, from whom he seems to have taken this image, though he adapts it somewhat. In his poem 'The Giaour,' Byron had written:

> Before Decay's effacing fingers
> Have swept the lines where beauty lingers.

Kalinowski quotes the following from the poem:

> 'Tis Greece, but living Greece, no more!

Then he omits several lines and continues:

> Shrine of the mighty, can it be
> That this is all remains of thee? [p. 316].[99]

Finally, Kalinowski wryly continues: "Greece ... is this all that remains of you?"

---

[99]   In Byron's poem, after the lines *'Tis Greece, but living Greece, no more!* there follows: *So coldly sweet, so deadly fair, We start, for soul is wanting there.*

Turning to a reflection on his family, he continues: "I found my father much changed by age and sickness, but the rest of the family are well and spritely, thank God…"[p. 319]. Then, somewhat moralistically, he reflects on the good old days:

> I understand that society today is a little superficial and that mutual relationships, even among members of the same family, are not what they ought to be, and that heralds danger for the future. To promote union it is necessary to have a common hearth, where the members of a family can be reunited and revive their mutual affection. The confusion of religious ideas introduced by the Reformation in our country has, in many places, already produced these results in politics, in social interaction, even in the bosom of the family. The novelties flooding in from the West, have found a fertile ground in our demoralized provinces. These are replicated with such ease that our provinces are deprived of the support of a strong society, and especially that of religion, united for the common good. [p. 319].

Kalinowski lamented the fact that even in exile he had free access to a church, but now, though he could see the spire of the local church in Hrozow from his window, it had been closed for many years, and he had only been able to go once to the nearest church, which was four miles away.

Kalinowski described the changed circumstances in the area following the insurrection of 1830 and the apostasy of Siemasko.[100] Things deteriorated further after the insurrection of 1863. From the first floor of Hrozow he could see the parochial church, now closed and serving as a base for the Siemasko sect. There was no Catholic church within reasonable distance and in the nearest

---

[100] Siemasko, mentioned in the Introduction, was a Ukrainian Catholic priest who later joined the Russian Orthodox Church and became a leader of a sect Kalinowski often refers to.

Catholic Church the pastor veered towards the Schism: he followed the Russian Ritual and processed before the schismatic bishop when he came to visit. In his *Memoirs* Kalinowski mused: "I found conditions in my own country worse than in Irkutsk or Perm, where I could receive Holy Communion every day and where I found more friendship and goodwill among the people than I found among the Ukrainians bowed down under the yoke of police agents and Orthodox leaders. There was also a Basilian monastery at Hrozow which had been suppressed and as far as I remember now occupied by Orthodox monks." [p. 318]. For years the established line of the authorities was to withdraw the peasants from the influence of the Catholic clergy and the nobility. In these circumstances, Sophie Kalinowska used to assemble the peasants on Sundays and feast days and give them religious instruction which was unavailable in the local church.

In addition to these woes in a religious context, Kalinowski was also saddened by his father's failing health. Andrew had developed a liver complaint which was not yielding to treatment. Neither did the external circumstances described help his aging parent. Sophie too was adversely affected by all this and it was real torment for her not to be able to approach the sacraments. At the beginning of September his brother Aleksander had left Hrozow together with his sister Mary and had gone to his brother Victor's home at Studzionki. From there he went on to Moscow to take up his University course again. As we know Kalinowski was opposed to studying abroad in these circumstances, citing his own failure, as a young man, to adhere to his faith in similar circumstances. His father Andrew had retired some time previously as Director of the Institute of Nobles but had taken another job for a private establishment. When he retired from there, in turn he took a post as tutor to the children of some friends. Now his failing health prevented him from working and supporting members of his family who were still without work themselves. But he continued to give instruction to members of his own family especially his grandchildren and the children of other

133

family friends. By the time his son returned from exile in 1873 he seems to have retired from these occupations. Kalinowski himself had no work at this time and so was not in a position to offer any assistance to his parents.

Though Kalinowski had quit Siberia he was not forgotten by his friends. The priest Fiszer wrote at this time: "After your departure I am sad and I experience a great void around me. I found it so pleasing to pray with you, to chat and to take a walk with you! – I love you sincerely and I press you to my heart, like the good Catholic and my brother in Jesus Christ." [p. 320]. Later on he wrote in similar vein: "If you remember I was so happy to pray and meditate with you! It was a joy for me to unite myself with you in thought and heart before Our Lord. I wish I could read with you again so as to stimulate myself by your example to make progress in perfection!" [p. 320]. Fiszer even regarded him as a mentor. He wrote: "There is a question of me transferring to another diocese, what is your opinion? I rely entirely on you. Everyone wants you back in Perm, including the bishop." [p. 321]. Even the Governor General of Perm esteemed him highly and provided him with necessary references.

Kalinowski shared his concerns about the situation back home with his other good clerical friend, the pastor of Irkutsk Christopher Szwermicki who wrote him an encouraging letter: "Your letters are sad, my dear Joseph! I understand your distress and share your pain. First of all, to be without church, far from the Blessed Sacrament, that's very hard for a devout person, a desolation. Also the uncertainty on the subject of your future is unsettling. But, my dear Joseph, patience wins out in the end. Trust in Jesus and he will not abandon you. And then, you know, we ought always tell ourselves: it is not my will but that of Our Lord Jesus Christ that should be done." Then aware of Kalinowski's financial worries the priest added delicately: "My finances are good, whenever you wish you can approach me as a brother. I'm indebted to you for all the good you have done me." [p. 321].

Fiszer also wrote to say Bishop Borowski would welcome him to the seminary at Zhytomyr in Ukraine without financial commitment. But Kalinowski was concerned about staying on to help his father in need. But he did accept the loan of 200 roubles from Szwermicki.

In September Victor's wife Marie returned home to "Les Studzionski" and came to visit her brother-in-law at Hrozow. She was concerned about his health which left a lot to be desired, and proposed to write to St. Petersburg to get an extension of his leave. However, Kalinowski demurred at this and said he would be satisfied to return to Perm or go to Smolensk until the required two years had elapsed. Marie went along with this and offered to go to St. Petersburg herself to obtain this favor. And she was as good as her word. In fact two weeks before his leave had expired he was able to make his farewells to his family and head for Smolensk.

Chapter Nine

Transition Period

*O*n October 2, 1873, Kalinowski wrote his first letter from Smolensk to his father:

> Only today I have obtained an answer to my request and it was favorable: tomorrow I will submit the medical evidence and wait for the result of Marie's intervention. I am asked to leave. It is true that Count Szuwalow is in southern Russia, but at least the preliminaries can be done. I foresaw that Marie would have to remain in the capital a little longer than was thought, as she will have to oversee, as far as possible, the drawing up of documents and telegrams, without which my stay at Smolensk can only jeopardize my chances. [p. 323].

He relates other news to his father – the nearby church where he was able to attend 7.00 a.m Mass each morning, the presence of friends such as Doctor Czekatowski who had shared his exile, and Stanislaus Slavinski who had been a student under his father and colleague of his own at the Institute of Nobles in Vilnius and a colleague also in St. Petersburg.

Kalinowski looks back on this period in his *Memoirs:* "Divine Providence sent me a savior in the person of Father Cyprian Bielikowitz. He asked the pastor of Smolensk Father Denisewitz to give me at his expense a little room which was available." Kalinowski writes: "The little church which has now been greatly enlarged, is situated on a hill behind the cemetery and it shines like a star on the dark sky of the town. My heart was drawn there constantly, and the sight of that sanctuary where Our Lord will dwell with us in this valley of tears, was for me a source of strength and consolation." [*Memoirs*, ch. 4].

He also wrote a long letter to his good friend Felix Zienkowicz with additional details. He tells us that Smolensk was one of the most ancient cities of Lithuania, which Napoleon had laid siege to in August 1812 and almost completely destroyed it by fire. Kalinowski was not overly impressed by the people here, and stories had reached him that robbery was rife in the town. Again, as elsewhere all the Catholic churches had been transformed into Orthodox or breakaway ones. Here also, as in all his previous locations, Kalinowski occupied himself with the education of youth – and some indeed were the same children he taught in Perm, now also relocated to Smolensk with their families.

Kalinowski enjoyed opportunities for reading religious books in the presbytery, and he translated articles from the *Revue du Monde Catholique* which he sent to a Catholic journal in Warsaw. He appreciated being able to read the latter magazine because it treated in-depth questions of a social, historical and religious nature. He revised his book on architecture hoping he could make something from the sale to support his family. His favored study however, was theology.

Writing to his mother soon after his departure, he mused on his inability to provide his parents with much support, and like St. Paul, tried to glory in his weakness: "God gives us a lesson in humility and we understand that we are nothing. Let us take hold of life as it comes, renewing our energies and pressing ahead, using the awareness of our feebleness. That is indeed a sort of martyrdom, but the martyrs suffered with joy. Let us do the same." [p. 327]. His mother replied: "I suffer martyrdom because of the state of our finances, but you, my angel, you are my comfort, my only hope is in your prayers. You occupy the first place in my heart." [p. 327].

Wherever he was, in his letters Kalinowski continued to dispense sound advice. In a letter to his sister Mary at this time we find this passage: "The person who is unoccupied is like sterile ground, or more exactly uncultivated ground which produces only bad growth. On the contrary, work reinforces activity and allows salutary fruits to grow." [p. 327]. As if to illustrate what he had said, he informed her that he himself was at that moment occupied in translating an article on the Grand Chartreuse, because he recognized his debt to St. Bruno for many a good inspiration, and that this work only confirmed him in his resolution of consecrating himself to God. And it appears he desired the same grace for his little sister. He writes to her again: "In commerce, in industry, in the arts, people work with the diligence of ants, but what do they do for Holy Church? Pray to God for me and I will ask God to give you a way of life by which you can be securely united with Him, for this is the one thing necessary." [p. 327]. To his friend Felix he would add similar sentiments: "My wish for you is that you carry in your soul the fullness of life, paying no attention to either location or time, or to yourself, but only to God. *If the Lord does not build the house, in vain do the builders labor* (Ps. 126)." [p. 328].

In the meantime the matter of his definitive release was rapidly moving forward. His sister-in-law Marie Kalinowska, who had stayed on in St. Petersburg, requested him to send on a medical certificate. Another friend collected information in Smolensk and in Minsk. Marie wrote again expressing the hope that he would shortly reach port. She had made contact with Balthasar Kalinowski, another influential friend. On December 9 Kalinowski wrote to his mother: "M. Bielikowicz came to give me a letter from Marie which shows the final results of our efforts. The favor asked is given and signed by the Czar. Now I can be regarded as finally settled in Smolensk and will wait here for my full deliverance." [p. 329].

Amid the crisis of the exile and return of a favored elder son, life with its ensuing pains and pressures continued on an uneven keel for the Kalinowski family. Like all mothers Sophie was now concerned about the future of her youngest son Jerzy. Due to bad health her husband could no longer work and he had communicated this (as well as his wife's concerns) to his son now living in the halfway house in Smolensk. Kalinowski wrote to his mother emphasizing the need for a spiritual approach to such worries and urged, "that our own wills should be guided under the eye of Providence." Regarding young Jerzy, he too ought to bring his will into line with the will of God, whether studying at Riga or elsewhere and be a man of duty. Moreover his parents had lovingly encouraged him to pray and resort to the sacraments. For that reason vain fears on their part ought to be put aside, fears which would only undermine his mother's health. "Your prayers" he tells his parents, "have delivered me from great distress. Why, then do we fear today for Jerzy's temporal wellbeing? And then the future is not known to us, why do we paint it in colors which may, perhaps never materialize?" [p. 329].

Kalinowski then encourages them to say his favorite prayer mentioned above, that he had already given to his friend Felix. It is his prayer for the Church and he tells them it has the recommendation of the Pope; it is to be directed to Jerzy's temporal and spiritual wellbeing. He tells them: "Said well these vain thoughts will no longer trouble you and you will feel strong, no longer beset by imaginary needs, but with the real needs of the here and now, rather than those of an unknown future." [p. 329].

He then admits that he cannot help them financially just now, but that all his prayers and good works are directed for the good of his parents, sisters and brothers and their families. And he also wished to provide a spark of joy and consolation for his brother Karol as his wife Martine was ill at this time. In the latter case it was soon not just a matter of family health issues but real pain and loss.

After the birth of her third child Martine fell gravely ill. It was near Christmas and on December 18 Kalinowski received the sad news that Martine had died. The news threw a dark cloud over Christmas for the family. Kalinowski was so numb with grief that he didn't have the energy to write to his brother. All he could say was "Poor Karol!" Even more sadly, their eldest daughter Angelique soon followed her mother to the grave. One year later Karol imitated what his father had done years earlier, by marrying Martine's sister Sabine and so also providing a mother for the two young children. Like Sophie Kalinowski she too would prove a good stepmother.

Immediately after Christmas Andrew Kalinowski went to visit his son in Smolensk, while leading his younger son Jerzy to the Polytechnic in Riga. Jerzy later reported what they observed there. His brother had two small rooms in the presbytery, near the church where he would visit every day. He would pray on his knees, hidden behind a pillar all during the Mass. He also received Holy Communion every day (which was not usual at the time). He was greatly esteemed by all the priests. Jerzy also noted, with some amazement, that Kalinowski had no domestic help. He had a little stove which he lit, fetched water and made tea for them himself. Obviously a family of Kalinowski's status would have a servant to do such chores.

On New Years' Day, Kalinowski got in touch with his father again, offering seasonal greetings accompanied by the blessing: "May God give you peace and eternal life." Soon after this the priest from Irkutsk sent Kalinowski 300 roubles and he immediately sent 200 to his family. With the gift he included some unsolicited advice of a spiritual kind for his mother. St. Teresa of Avila tells us that good people in the early stages of a serious spiritual life sometimes lecture their families and friends in this fashion! He admonishes her: "If you had no bread, no clothes, no roof, I could understand your disquiet, but it is not like this with you. Think of the poverty of the home of Nazareth and do like the Holy Virgin. Pray to her with your whole family. She will inspire good thoughts in you and give you peace!" [p. 333].

Kalinowski was already living a quasi-Carmelite life before he had even decided to join the Carmelites. Even his language is a giveaway. For example when his brother Victor came to see him, they went to visit some friends and Kalinowski put it this way in a letter: "During the two days he spent with me I violated my cloister!" However, it was not all contemplation and he did in fact lecture on a different topic – mathematics – at the military college. He also pursued young Jerzy by letter to make sure he kept to the path of virtue. He emphasized the need for self-control and that his brother should allow himself to be guided by right reason and faith – the duty of everyone. "When you use a little violence on yourself during your youth, it will prove easier later on." As a priest himself later in life, Jerzy recalled that his brother had often sent him pious books, and one in particular on the life of St. Aloysius Gonzaga which he treasured.

Again, writing to his friend Felix Zienkowicz in February 1874, Kalinowski was toying with the idea of religious vocation, not only for himself but also for his friend. He begins by making these interesting observations regarding a marriage ceremony he attended:

> I don't have a great liking for mingling with crowds but I do have a weakness for church ceremonies, especially solemn ones. What deep thoughts spring up in one's heart when two people come to the church asking God to bless their union! When I think of family life, the source of so much devotion and self-denial, how can you not prefer the life of celibates, so often egotistic, focused on themselves and aimed at their own interests? And if in that way of life a person does something good for family or neighbor it is considered almost heroic, but the domestic scene is regarded as commonplace. In truth however, I can see that only lack of health or the more sublime vocation to a life of devotion

for the glory of God and with the blessing of Holy Church, can dispense us from the duty of founding a new family. [p. 338].

While waiting or discerning what to do, Kalinowski advised his friend Zienkowicz to give himself to works of charity. Zienkowicz assisted the pastor in the education of orphans in Irkutsk. It wasn't easy. Kalinowksi tried to encourage him: "Though the state of these unfortunate children is far from satisfactory, it is preferable to where they were previously. And when we reflect on ourselves, don't we discover similar faults in our own youth, in spite of the best efforts of our parents in the work of our education. So then it's not an attitude of indifference that these poor little creatures need, but lots of affection and compassion. And by treating them with love, perhaps we can motivate them sufficiently so as to make the bad things disappear." [p. 339]. Then he continues in a more spiritual vein, appealing to the example of Jesus in the gospel as well as the certainty of us ourselves being judged by God.

Kalinowski had written to the pastor of Perm (Fiszer) who had been his spiritual director, apparently sounding him out on the possibility of vocation. And in mid March he received a reply. The priest advised him to consult his conscience and do what that dictated:

Those who triumph over the flesh, the world and the spirit of the century, will receive a beautiful reward as they await a glorious crown from the Father of Lights. The fact that you have remained firm in your resolution over so many years is a certain sign that God wishes you to consecrate yourself in a special manner to himself. Dear Joseph, the sacrifice that you wish to make, will certainly be pleasing to God and useful for holy Church. I have known you for so many years already, it is with special joy that I read in your letter about your firm resolution to embrace an ecclesiastical state.

I am sure you will be an ornament and model for evangelical works. And don't believe, dear Joseph, that this testimony which I'm giving you is an empty formula proceeding from politeness or flattery: no it is a conviction of my conscience. [p. 339].[101]

Fiszer rounded off his letter on a very personal note, which is further evidence of the quality of the friendship between the two men. "Whatever path you take continue to write to me, for even though we ought to guard our heart and all its affection for our dearest Savior, it nevertheless seems to me, that our correspondence will unite us to him more profitably. So I beg you, don't refuse me this pleasure. And indeed I must tell you, that I have become better myself during the time I have known you and I have been better able to integrate my misery. Don't forget me in your prayers. Your humble servant..." [p. 340].

The priest appended a letter from little Francis, one of Kalinowski's pupils. It is a charming letter, the child admitting that his studies weren't going all that well and that Greek was getting him down and taking up an undue amount of time: "I have made most progress in French, for which I have given you so much trouble to teach me." [p. 340].

From the foregoing details we see a clear image emerging of Kalinowski gravitating towards a consecrated form of life in a religious Order, though he was not sure what Order that might be. At the same time, as we noted in letters to his friends, he was under no illusions about the hazards of religious life if it was not lived with generosity. At this time, during his stay in Smolensk, Kalinowski teased out the ramifications and advantages of this state in a letter to his father:

---

[101] How prophetic these words of his director proved to be! Fiszer was 60 years of age at this time and had spent 30 of these serving in Siberia, covering tremendous distances.

I long for a regulated life, because nothing disturbs interior harmony so much as the absence of exterior peace – and how destructive that is! I'm beginning to convince myself that the worst thing in this world is to spend your time being torn apart inside. I aspire after one thing: to maintain purity of heart, because a conscience free from all sin allows the soul to lift itself up to God and helps it sustain the burden of life with a good heart. Also I am very stressed and today I started to look for an occupation which could engage all the hours of my day. Unemployment, in effect, is most injurious to an interior life, because it opens the door of our soul to the devil. [p. 341].[102]

Earlier in March, Kalinowski had begun a novena to his patron St. Joseph and this reminded him to write to his parents and thank them, especially his mother, for inculcating in him a devotion to St. Joseph. Kalinowski wrote to his spiritual director in Irkutsk (Fiszer) and included in it a letter for the exiled Bishop Borowski. In replying to this letter Fiszer remarked: "I read your letter aloud to His Excellency. The good old man listened benevolently and in regard to your desire to consecrate yourself to the service of God, he gave me this message: go to a warm country and put it into effect. His Excellency is quite sure that the sacrifice of your life will be of benefit to humanity and will redound to God's glory and that you will find immense good. I advise you to write to him directly, that will give him much pleasure. Your memory is always dear to him and he showed much benevolence in your regard." [p. 342].

The Bishop was almost blind at this time, but the pastor read his letters and articles from journals to him as well as assisting him to say Mass and recite the Breviary. The old man was conscious of his approaching death and would say, "Gaspar, offer each moment of your life to God, because death is at the door!"[103]

---

[102] *The devil finds work for idle hands.* Proverb.

[103] In fact Bishop Borowski lived for several more years. He was released from exile and returned home in 1882 and was nominated bishop of Plock, a position he filled for three years until his death. He was accompanied to

Kalinowski's friends, Giejzstor, and especially Oskierko, already back in Warsaw, were trying to arrange a position for Kalinowski that he could take up when eventually, definitively released. For instance, in March 1873 Oskierko lined up a job teaching the children of Prince Eugene Lubomirski. This Kalinowski declined, obviously because he was thinking of a priestly vocation. Oskierko knew that this would be difficult in Poland so suggested that by continuing to teach children and say a *Sursum Corda* to them, would be the nearest thing to priesthood! He didn't seem to suspect that Kalinowski would be prepared to go anywhere to achieve his goal – even facing another kind of exile – which is exactly what he eventually did. He also received letters of support at this time from his great friend Giejsztor and that gave him a lot of encouragement.

But the months dragged on and the Czar made no move to issue a certificate of final freedom. This did not materialize until January 25, 1874. That was exactly nine and a half years since he was forced to take the lonely road into exile from his home in Vilnius; only now was he given a passport and allowed to go wherever he wished. However, that was qualified to the extent that he would not be allowed to return to Lithuania or Ruthenia (Ukraine). He would only be permitted to reside within the confines of the Kingdom of Poland.

Not surprisingly it was not a question of hurrah for freedom as Kalinowski didn't have sufficient money to travel anywhere. This delayed his departure for several months. He wrote to his good friend the pastor of Irkutsk who sent him the necessary fare. He thought first of making his way to Livadia[104] to work in architecture. Kalinowski had a twofold aim – earn some money to support his

---

Plock by Canon Fiszer. Like his mentor, Fiszer was almost blind by 1892 and retired to the house of a clerical friend in the region of Piotrkow in Poland. Kalinowski's succinct opinion of his spiritual director Fiszer was this: "He was a holy priest."

[104]   Livadia boasted one of the Czar's favorite palaces.

family and pay off some debts that had mounted up as well as benefit from the pleasant climate in the Crimea.

However, when he weighed up the pros and cons, the ties of friends and friendship in Warsaw saw him opt for the capital of Poland. He told his family he would join them for the Easter holidays, after devoting an Easter retreat and the Easter festivity to God. Then, as it happened, after nine and a half years of exile in Siberia, (apart from the less than six weeks sick leave he had been previously granted) his family would only enjoy his company for a mere eight days. Sadly he would never get the opportunity of spending time with them again.

The Way to Warsaw

Kalinowski wrote in his *Memoirs*:

> After ten years in exile, at last I received permission to return to my country, or rather to the Kingdom of Poland, because Lithuania and Ruthenia (Ukraine) were forbidden me in the amnesty decree. I was indebted for the favor of my release, in part to General Niepokoiczycki, Governor of Petrograd, with whom we had some family links and whom my brother Victor's wife had personally asked to intercede with General Szuwalof, chief of the secret section; in part also, as I later understood, to Prince Eugene Lumomirski who spoke to me himself during my stay in Kraków. In May or April 1874 I left Smolensk and went to Warsaw, where my brother Gabriel, after his return from exile, had definitively settled. Cyprian Bielikowicz had replaced me as tutor for M. Czarnecki's children; the Pozniak family had already left for Petrograd, where one of their relatives was working. I then had to part from Fr. Denisewicz, to whom I was so indebted, and say goodbye to the priests in Smolensk. Firstly

I was grateful for their generous hospitality and secondly for the good example they had shown me. [*Memoirs*, ch. 4].

So Kalinowski first made his way to Warsaw on April 11, 1874, there to be reunited with his brother Gabriel. He wrote to his father: "It was 6 am, and Bunio (Gabriel) was still asleep. I went to share his room though it's very tiny, but I shall at least have the advantage of talking to him for an hour morning and evening, without counting the visits I shall make with him to the store.[105] Yesterday we spent the evening with the Weryho family,[106] where we were treated in true Lithuanian style, that is with perfect hospitality." [p. 347].

Kalinowski made it a priority to call on his friends Aleksander Oskierko, Louise Młocko, Jan Giejsztor and others. He had made up his mind to take the lucrative Paris position which had materialized at this stage, and about which we will hear much more. He would receive 4,000 francs per annum with all expenses paid for board and lodging. But first he had to establish himself in the city in order to be registered as a stable resident and take an oath of fidelity.

Kalinowski had to admit he was a little unnerved by the number of friends he would be expected to call upon in Warsaw. He considered himself blessed that his new residence was close to St. Joseph's church where he could receive the sacraments and attend Mass.

Writing to his father on May 2, Kalinowski admitted that he could get a job as a Professor of Engineering in Warsaw, but that he had his eye on the job abroad where he would have the opportunity to grow in new areas of knowledge – presumably he meant theology. There remained, however, the little matter of acquiring a passport out of Poland and that involved further red tape plus a delay of several months. It's interesting that during his period of waiting Kalinowski started to write an account of family friend Louise

---

[105] Gabriel had opened a shop in Warsaw.
[106] Gabriel's future in-laws.

Młocka. She was a cousin of his brother Victor's wife Mary; her niece Wanda Drewnowska married another brother, Aleksander. This biography is now lost. Jerzy Kalinowski however, does give us some details on this admirable woman's life. A most charitable person, she answered calls for help from far and wide. She spent all her resources on charitable works, being involved in the ministry too of the St. Vincent de Paul Society. Frugal in her habits she always dressed simply. She kept a container in her home and would ask visitors to donate something for the poor. Młocka had known Kalinowski since 1862. When he went into exile she wrote to him regularly and sent out anything he needed. She also secured a job for Kalinowski's brother Gabriel as manager in Rosenblum's tobacco factory in Kraków.

In the events, small and large that he lived through, we notice a characteristic of Kalinowski's future spirituality – his readiness to see the hand of Providence in everything that happened to him. For instance a relative recommended Fr. Borzewski, a priest in Warsaw, as a suitable confessor. Then when he eventually got to Warsaw, Kalinowski went as usual to a church for confession. It was the chapel of the Visitation Sisters, and who should he find in the confessional but Fr. Borzewski who was chaplain to the Sisters! The latter became his regular confessor and Kalinowski attended the talks that he gave; these he found engaging and illuminating. This for him was "an admirable disposition of divine Providence."

Kalinowski also went occasionally to confess to Father Henry Kossowski and felt honored that the distinguished priest and future bishop agreed to be his spiritual director. The church at Lezno served by this priest had been formerly attached to the Carmelite Reform of Blessed John Soreth. Kossowski, who later became Bishop of Wroclawek,[107] published a Polish edition of the works of St. Teresa

---

[107] This was the first town where a sizable Jewish population were required to wear the yellow star by the Nazis. Blessed Jerzy Popieluszki was martyred near here in 1984. Cardinal Wyszynski attended the seminary here.

of Avila. Surely this must be a further example of small providences accompanying him everywhere. Kossowski had initiated a discussion group between the Jewish community at Lezno and church and civil authorities to deal with literary and religious questions. Kalinowski was very interested in this initiative and wished to become part of the group.

Kalinowski continued to do useful work, translating articles for religious and secular magazines. The secular magazine was devoted to a subject he had studied – Agronomy, and Kalinowski was disappointed to see it carried an article on Darwin's theory of evolution. He tells us that he had a discussion with the Editor-in-Chief on this matter and apparently succeeded in having Darwinian theories in the magazine banned![108] While he thought the periodical good, he told his brother Karol that the somewhat materialistic tendency of the magazine made him a little uneasy. However, he felt this was partly the fault of subscribers who ought to write in and put across what for him was the correct point of view. And in what sounds like a modern touch, he concludes his letter to Karol: "The inhabitants of Warsaw don't pay any attention to the defects of materialist science. They are more occupied with their work,

---

[108]   We ought not blame Joseph Kalinowski or Hermann Cohen for the limitations of their views on theological or scientific topics of the day. Many of their contemporaries, including church leaders like Cardinal Manning in England thought likewise. Bishop Wilberforce, an Anglican, had a famous debate with Aldous Huxley on the matter. When Wilberforce challenged, "Are you saying Sir that your ancestor was an ape?" Huxley replied, "I would prefer to have an ape as an ancestor than a benighted bishop!" It would take great minds like that of Blessed John Henry Newman not to be rattled by the discoveries of science. Just a few years before Kalinowski made this remark on Darwin, Newman had been asked about evolution and replied: "It does not seem to follow that creation is denied because the creator, millions of years ago, gave laws to matter. He first created matter and then he created laws for it ..." (Quoted in *Newman's Unquiet Grave*, John Cornwell, Continuum: London, New York, 2010).

commerce, walks, recreations, prayers; only the youth in the schools show any inclination for scientific debates." [p. 353].

At this time then Kalinowski made up his mind to take up the offer from the Czartoryski family, undertaking to become the official tutor in their Paris residence of the sickly Prince Auguste Francis Czartoryski, affectionately known as Gucio who was heir to the Polish throne. He was the son of Hermann Cohen's deceased friend Princess Maria Amparo. This would further Kalinowski's aim of eventually becoming a priest – something not possible in Poland at that time.

A cloud on Kalinowski's horizon, however, was his father's weakening health. He admitted in a letter to his friend Louise Młocka that it caused him a real martyrdom to dwell on his family's troubles. His decision to leave was a decisive blow to his family – an ailing father and a devoted stepmother. Sophie considered him her "consoling angel and, after God, her better hope," and she was about to lose him for good this time. She was particularly upset and blamed his friends for arranging the post for him. Kalinowski tried to respond as best he could, pointing out that it seemed to be God's will for him and it wasn't fair to blame his friends Osierko and Giejsztor. Kalinowski had heard that Prince Czartoryski had trawled the universities of Kraków and Paris for an ideal tutor for his son, and he had been chosen. He also reminded Sophie that it was her good example that instilled in him the strong Christian principles and faith that appealed to Czartoryski. And to cap it all he stated he had the approval of his confessor and in addition that of Bishop Borowski. The latter was a kind of *ex cathedra* endorsement from which there was no appeal! Kalinowski also tells her, as he had told his father, that though he could have got an engineering job in the railways, it would not promote his ultimate aim – "the state I am resolved to embrace." Here he obviously meant religious life though he doesn't spell it out for Sophie.

Kalinowski had gone to great lengths to pacify his family, but in this situation there was no easy way, or even any way for them to come to terms with his decision. Here they were, having supported him in every way throughout almost ten years of exile – and why? Because their favorite and most talented son had joined a hopeless rebellion against impossible odds, and in that scenario there could only have been one outcome. We can readily sympathize with Andrew and Sophie Kalinowski. Dedicated Catholics though they were, that scarcely softened the blow. But it still remained true that Kalinowski understood this was what the gospel demanded of him in order to follow Jesus; it meant in practice that family would have to take second place. At the same time he continued to show the utmost concern for them. He expressed the hope that his younger sister Mary might embrace religious life and suggested that his other sister Emilia might take up a position in the Lubomirski household in Warsaw – a position he himself had declined. Should this eventuate, he suggested, his parents might be able to move to Warsaw too, and there would be the additional benefit of being near their other son Gabriel. In fact this did eventually happen and Emilia worked for the prince. And finally he proposed that he and Emilia could undertake the maintenance of the youngest son Jerzy.

When Kalinowski applied for his passport, he discovered that his papers were not in Perm (where he had spent some time). Neither could they be found in Smolensk, his previous base. After various bureaucratic mix-ups his papers were eventually found in Astrakhan. He informed his father of developments and expressed the hope of leaving Poland in a matter of weeks.

Finally Kalinowski's passport arrived on September 3, 1874. He had just turned 39. Naturally he wrote a farewell letter to his parents. As always filial sentiments abounded. He told them how he wished to make a farewell visit, but had to hurry to make a first acquaintance with Prince Auguste Czartoryski. He stated how the last letter from his mother had touched him profoundly and how his heart was sorrowful in having to leave, but it was too late to turn back. He was happy with his decision and only wished he could cut his links with a world which had proved only burdensome. He was at ease about the fact that his siblings didn't need him any longer and in any case they themselves had given them a completely satisfactory formation. But in spite of that he did in fact have some final advice for his sister Emilia, recommending her to read methodically the *Meditations* of the French priest Chaignon, which had stood him in good stead in exile. He ended this farewell letter to his parents on an upbeat note: "I beg you, my dear parents, to write me joyful letters. For really there is nothing which should make us sad. It's true we can't avoid the cross, but a person united to God and free from mortal sin can benefit from trials. I ask your blessing and commend myself to your prayers and happy memory. I regret that I cannot kiss your hands today. May the Lord cast a benevolent glance on this sorrow. May my elderly aunt give me her blessing and pray for me. I press Karol, Emilia, Mary, Gabriel and Jerzy to my heart." [p. 359].

(His other brothers, Victor and Aleksander were not at home).

Kalinowski set out on his journey on September 8, 1874, Feast of the Nativity of Our Lady. He spent the whole of the following day on a devout visit to the famous shrine of Our Lady of Częstochowa, the Lourdes of Poland. He had previously promised himself after a bout of illness, that he would make this pilgrimage. There was a huge crowd around which meant that a sense of recollection was not easy.

On the same day Kalinowski left for the ancient Polish capital of Kraków to keep an appointment with Prince Ladislaus Czartoryski. He was met at the station by his young friend, Marian Kwiatkowski, returned from exile in Irkutsk. That same evening he was also thrilled to be taken to the home of Count Bninski, his other friend from exile whose children he had taught and who had given Marian a home.

Kalinowski reported on his journey to his parents, referring back to Chęstochowa and amusingly telling them that it was almost "at the peril of my life that I was able to get as far as the altar of the holy Virgin to render homage to our revered protector who, according to a pious tradition, had covered the roof with her mantle." [p. 362].

It was a joy for Kalinowski to walk in the footsteps of Saint Stanislaus, Patron of Poland, when he visited the Cathedral of Wawel to pray at his tomb. He also toured the churches of Saint Hyacinthe and Saint John Kenty. In the morning he first attended Mass at the church of Our Lady and then went to see the Sukiennice Museum, set in the Merchant's Square, dominated by the magnificent market building. In addition he saw numerous other monuments in the city during those days, but found himself becoming unmoved with tourism, as his heart was elsewhere. He only glanced at some of these landmarks and then, in a thought very reminiscent of Hermann Cohen whose memory would later inspire him, wrote: "Since the day I believed in Jesus Christ, present in the Eucharist, my whole being has been drawn to the altar, where he wishes to be present for us." [p. 364].

Kalinowski had to admit that the presence of such numerous friends in Kraków was becoming a burden, interfering as they did on his contemplative habits. Even a surprise meeting with Balthasar Kalinowski, who was not related to him but had done so much for him, also weighed somewhat on him. Though he loved him as a brother, he felt that deep down he did not share the same aspirations, the same convictions, or the same way of life.

Chapter Ten

Menton and The Riviera

*I*n a letter to his father on February 28, 1875 Kalinowski referred to the plan he had in mind to leave shortly for Menton on the French Riviera. This was a disappointment to him as it meant Gucio's studies had to be put on hold, as also his own plans to avail himself of educational opportunities in Paris with an eye to priesthood in the future. However, the thought, "man proposes, God disposes," was not far from his mind. That 19th century killer tuberculosis, or consumption, now manifested itself and was undermining his health, as it would the health of the young Thérèse of Lisieux some years later.

So for health reasons a change of direction for Prince Auguste became necessary. At this point doctors advised that Gucio move to a more salubrious climate. The place chosen was Menton on the border between France and the Principality of Monaco. Prince Ladislaus and his son, together with Kalinowski, arrived in Menton in early March. He gives us a most informative and poetic commentary on his new abode: "The little town is truly enchanting. The villa in which we live is situated in a garden planted with olive, orange and lemon trees. I was surprised to discover such a pleasant climate here. The surroundings display the same kind of beauty as Vilna itself – I say this because it is my home and I can compare the two. The disposition of the inhabitants is most agreeable and, what is even better, they are sincere Catholics. In church the singing and other ceremonies remind me of our Lithuanian churches." [p. 401]. Adding to his account eight days later he wrote:

> Thanks to the mildness of the climate the flora here is very beautiful: violets flourish all year and all year too plants and trees are covered in blossoms and fruit. Orange and lemon trees, olives and myrtles, palm tree and gigantic cacti are the adornment of nature, but all this perhaps seems less beautiful than the forests and fields of Lithuania. At the moment we experience hot conditions but this is tempered by the proximity of the sea. The devotion and fervor of the inhabitants give this area an added charm. [p. 402].

On the other hand, in a letter to his brother Jerzy, Kalinowski notes the town is not all that cheerful due to the number of sick people there:

> There are sick people from all over, especially England, but I have seen Russians and even Poles. You hardly hear any language except English. The native idiom is a patois, a mixed bag of Italian, French, Provençal and Arabic; for during medieval times this area was the abode of Saracens and Moors, and even today you can see the ruins of their fortresses suspended like eagles' nests on the high summits. In Menton, at the citadel location you can see a cemetery. The site is most picturesque; it is planted with cypresses and dominates the whole town ascending little by little to the summit of the mountain. [p. 402].

Kalinowski was touched to notice a monument to a lady named Paszczensko who died in the spring of the previous year. Continuing this informative letter to Jerzy he writes:

> The population occupies itself above all in the cultivation of olive and lemon trees: agriculture is impossible because of the sheerness of the terrain. For the production of oil the olives are pressed in mills which remind me of those of our old establishments in Lithuania. You can also find perfumeries in Menton because it gives the area an unbelievable quality of scented flowers. Another group of people work on building steam boats which are becoming popular. Another speciality of Menton (and each village has one) is that of making beautiful objects from citrus wood. The old village streets are so narrow and steep that it's difficult to walk on them or even travel with donkeys or mules. The new town is made up mainly and indeed uniquely of hotels, boutiques and villas here and there. The main diversion for the sick who have come here to improve their health is their habit of going for a walk along the promenade or cruising in canoes on the sea or taking a carriage to Monte Carlo or Monaco, and also to travel up the mountains on donkeys. I don't do any of this. I accompany Gucio, true, on all his excursions, but nature, breathtaking as it is, has no attraction for me. My thoughts rise towards God on high and I like to rest in him, the source of all beauty. I wrote to you on Holy Saturday. You remember perhaps, that I liked to take part in the ceremony of the Resurrection, as it was celebrated back home and liked to sing the Alleluia with the Italians and the French – but they don't have those processions here. [p. 402].[109] And you must admire that religious spirit,

---

[109]   In Poland a procession in honor of the Resurrection would be held on Holy Saturday or early on Easter Sunday.

so prominent at home, which had introduced such sublime ceremonies into divine worship. That spirit had been handed down to us by our fathers and we ought to preserve it. If we cannot do much in regard to others at least by the sacrifice of ourselves and by prayer, we can obtain from God the grace of perseverance for ourselves and the light of salvation for our neighbor. [p. 404].

Writing to his mother, Kalinowski fills us in with additional details of life in Menton:

The climate exercises a happy influence, it seems to me, on the health of the young prince. True, our life is a continual distraction: we pass the time walking and pampering our bodies; our spiritual exercises from time to time only bring a little color to this scene. I rise at 6 am and go to the church which is a distance of a quarter of an hour from our villa. I return at 8 am and rouse Gucio. When he is ready we recite morning prayer together and at 9 am we take our first breakfast which consists of a glass of chocolate and water. After first breakfast we work on until the second breakfast about 11. Then we take a walk by the sea or in the mountains. On returning to the house we have an instruction and then wait for dinner which takes place between 6 and 7. At 9 we retire to our rooms. We will remain at Menton until May and will spend the summer, I'm not quite sure, either in the mountains or at the spas. There's talk of spending the next winter in Algeria or Egypt. In that case I would be obliged to cancel my employment with the prince; Gucio needs a doctor and a priest and not my humble self. Besides, our present mode of life does not fit in with my inclinations. I go along with it for the moment quite willingly because Prince Auguste is a good and lovable child. While I have known this boy, a little frail but highly intelligent, a bit capricious but frank and open, I wouldn't wish to abandon him. [p. 404].

Writing to his father later he said:

> We are lucky to have all the advantages of country and seaside. Gucio is much the same as when I first made his acquaintance. He is tall for his age, taller than I, which contributes to his weakness. It is an additional worry for us that his mother died of lung disease. There are three of us here, Prince Ladislaus, Gucio and myself. The prince is leaving soon and then our companion will be his former tutor called Blotnicki, a lovable old man of eighty-four. He it was who gave me my first lessons in Greek and will continue his work here which is an agreeable occupation for me. [p. 403].

In a letter to his sister Mary on April 18 Kalinowski shares further impressions of the Menton locality and the devotional habits of its occupants:

> The congregation crowds round the altar and seems to have a great devotion to the Blessed Sacrament. Communions are frequent and when holy viaticum is taken to the sick, the faithful accompany it singing the *Miserere* and on the way back the *Te Deum*. When the priest is near the sick they sing the litany of the Blessed Virgin on the street. The clergy are constantly taken up with a ministry to souls. The pastor, who was my confessor, died last week. He gave beautiful sermons in Italian and there was a palpable sadness when you saw his chair draped in black on the day of his funeral. [p. 405].

At Irkutsk I knew a young man who had fallen into a similar state and the doctors held out no hope for him. We were able to heal him, however, by means of confession and manual work. He worked every day and went to confession every week: that young man who was the worst case among all our companions in exile, is now in Galicia, in the novitiate of the Jesuit fathers preparing himself for the sublime mission of bringing healing to souls and being a mediator between God and humankind. I know of no other remedy for such a malady. But nevertheless we must use it with charity, firmness and perseverance. [pp. 405-406].[110]

Then he encouraged his sister to pray constantly about her work and commend herself to his patron St. Joseph. His sister was competent in Latin so he sent her the Latin text of a 'prayer of Holy Church,' that he advised her to translate into Polish and recite every day, *ad utilitatem tuam et tyronum tuorum, (for the benefit of yourself and your students).* The ending of the letter is reminiscent of the letters exchanged between St. Thérèse of Lisieux and her family, including the ubiquitous 'petite':

> My dear little Mary, when you write don't imitate this bad example I'm setting you today! Don't let yourself be carried away with the impetuosity of your thoughts or by the first movements of your heart; learn from my faults and act like a prudent and wise woman. I will finish now to go to work

---

[110] This was Joseph Wasilewski. Afterwards he became a Jesuit priest. He attended Kalinowski's ordination and helped spread devotion to the Scapular in Romania. Kalinowski's solution to depression seems very Teresian. It is important not to think this is pious claptrap. Some of the greatest physicians and psychologists both past and present have indicated the same thing. For example, the famous contemporaries of Kalinowski, Fulgence Raymond and Pierre Janet were experts in neurology and neurasthenics, writing eight acclaimed works on these topics. In *Les Obsessions et les Neurasthenies* they stated: "Regular confession seems to have been invented by a doctor of genius."

with Gucio. Keep well, very dear little sister and may God bless the seed which you scatter in the souls of the children entrusted to you, and may your work in the world produce a delicious fruit, *ad majorem Dei gloriam* (*for the greater glory of God*). Work then, *in loco pascuae, ubi Deus collocavit.* (*In that place of pasture where God has placed you*).

P.S. "Do you say morning and evening prayers with the children? Nothing is as strong as the union we enter into in God's sight." [p. 408].

Kalinowski was somewhat harder on his dear brother Jerzy (who later became a priest), using a somewhat lecturing tone (which he denies using, however). Jerzy's mother had gone to visit him in Riga, in present-day Latvia. So in writing to his younger brother there, he delivered this advice: "I think you ought to moderate the liveliness of your character a little in the presence of your mother. This is not a rebuke, I'm just expressing a thought that came to me when reflecting on the actual dispositions of your heart and spirit. Write to me, dear Jerzy, about any of your needs. Perhaps I may be useful to you in some things." [p. 408].

Kalinowski's father worried about his son's health and about his reported absences from meals to pray before the Blessed Sacrament. (Kalinowski himself suffered some respiratory problems – ten years' hard labor in Siberia, often in hugely sub-zero temperatures did nothing for his health!) However, his son set out to put his mind at rest on this issue:

Very dear Father, I want to answer your last two letters: I am much touched by your love, full of concern for me which promoted your help and counsels... I ought first of all to put you at ease as regards my fasting. I am writing on Easter Sunday. My health is good, my spirit is tranquil ... I owe you an explanation regarding your deep concern about my temperance. Compared to those who love God more than me I seem to live a life of luxury. So that my very dear old father may really believe that I don't exaggerate – in the houses of the high and mighty it is excess you must watch out for rather than fasting. It's true that I sometimes disappear at meal times and my dear father is convinced that this is a huge mortification. I'm of the same opinion myself, but on the other hand in this little struggle with myself, God seems to me like a good father who wishes to give me a few moments of rest, paying homage through this spiritual relaxation to the Blessed Sacrament exposed in the churches for the Forty Hours' Adoration: that's where I spend my moments of free time, giving Our Lord the gift of myself. [p. 409].

As an additional reflection on his life he tells his father that he is easily irritated particularly if hungry and needs to watch that. He adds: "If I insist on observing the commandments of the Church, I do so in the firm conviction that it is for us the voice of the Holy Spirit, which governs holy Church. Moreover, in neglecting to obey that voice, so clearly expressed, on the pretext that I am mortified enough, I would be departing from a sure way in order to follow my own feelings." [p. 409].

Kalinowski thinks it necessary to supply further reasons to explain his absences from meals. Because Princess Margaret's health was not good and her husband Ladislaus was frequently away, Gucio really had nobody but himself to turn to, so he had to take whatever opportunities arose in order to be alone. He was in full-time attendance with the prince, including hours of recreation. "So that's the reason," he could say "that when I get a chance I tend to disappear, and I chose fast days so as to cause least disruption." He had made his point.

Kalinowski keeps his family informed on his frequent traveling with young Gucio. He tells his father at the beginning of May that they will be returning to Paris, taking in health spas on the way.

Gucio's health was so precarious that it hindered his intellectual formation, and Kalinowski was obliged to accept things as they were and not ask the impossible. They spent a few weeks in the little village of Neuilly, a place which nestles on the right bank of the Seine near the Bois de Boulogne. It reminded Kalinowski of his brother Victor's residence, 'Les Studzionki,' which, he held, yielded nothing to it in beauty. In fact he had just received a letter from his sister-in-law telling him of embellishments Victor had carried out on the estate.

He also writes to his father, who was alone just then in the estate at Hrozow, about the famous places they stopped off at on their various journeys. An epidemic, however, meant they had to avoid Marseilles; but they visited Toulon, Avignon, Lyons and Dijon.[111] Again he noticed the hard work the French were putting into rebuilding their country after the disaster of the recent Franco-Prussian war: "At Lyons we visited the church of Our Lady of Fourviére, renowned for its miraculous image of the Holy Virgin. There are still many devoted people in France who by their prayers and good works are saving this nation." [p. 410].

Gucio's health was in such a parlous state at this point that his tutor had to ease off on serious study and decided he would try to impart instruction in a recreational way. So they visited also the *Jardin d'Acclimatation* near the *Bois du Boulogne*. The gardens were an experiment in propagating useful plants and animals. Kalinowski did not see much merit in this institution.[112] He was not overly impressed by the paintings in the *Salon* which they visited. He

---

[111]   The Carmelite Elizabeth of the Trinity would spend her short life in the convent here some years after Kalinowski's visit and she would die in the same month as he, but one year earlier, in November 1906.

[112]   These were Zoological Gardens founded in 1860. About a year later the Director exhibited humans, such as Nubians and Inuits as curiosities. These would be taken on tour of other cities – London, New York, Milan, Barcelona, Warsaw, etc. They drew enormous crowds of sightseers. These displays were glorified with the name *Ethnological Exhibitions*!

felt they lacked beauty and inspiration and really were an eclectic mix of Christianity and paganism. He made an exception for the painting *La Prière* depicting a woman at prayer.[113] In his comments on various situations, Kalinowski gives the impression of a shrewd judge of human nature. Speaking about the travel entailed in his work, he remarked:

> I believe at the same time, that these journeys are doing him no good: they simply keep him in a permanent state of dissipation. Youth has need, besides the practice of religion, of a certain discipline in mental activity. It is true that his religious formation is capable of impinging on and regulating his life, but I'm unhappy to see the dissipation of his faculties. And I even feel anxiety at the sight of this helplessness or I would like to inspire some personal effort in a frail and shaky spirit that could save and make him more useful to society. [p. 412].

The example of his young brother comes to mind. In hearing that Jerzy is struggling with such courage against his sickness and not giving up his studies, he rejoiced in this victory of the spirit.

Again he informs his father that they went to visit the Dominican College of St. Albert the Great in Arcueil, near Paris, only newly built at the time. They noticed an enormous cannon ball which was called the 'Prussians visiting card.' It was here that shortly afterwards the Dominican priests were murdered by the Communards. A priest called Captier encouraged them saying: "Let us go, my brothers, for the good God." Some years later the words of the Rector, Fr. Henri Didon's address to his students, prompted his friend Pierre de Coubertin to adopt them as the Olympic motto: "*Citius, altius, fortius,*" "faster, higher, stronger." These words were also inscribed over the door of the college.

---

[113] This could be *Femmes en prière* by Alphonse Legros, now in the Tate Gallery, London.

Kalinowski had ascertained that in Paris there were 45,000 people, popularly known as *La Gouape*, either held in prisons or being monitored by the police who were on standby for all kinds of crimes and easy targets for fomenters of trouble. Kalinowski has an incisive comment to make in this context. He asked himself why a band of rascals, so few in number by comparison with the population at large, were able to hold the city to ransom. His answer? There weren't enough either bad people or good people with sufficient initiative to do something! Lukewarm people and those without solid convictions, in spite of the fact that they have a numerical advantage, either put up with it or move somewhere else. How aptly do these remarks fit modern suburbia, when the elderly and vulnerable are assaulted, not just on the streets, but in their own homes.

Kalinowski ends his letters to his family telling them that Gucio and his father were going to visit Queen Christina of Spain, the boy's grandmother. Princess Margaret and Princess Blanche would accompany them. He himself would attend a procession of the Blessed Sacrament in the parish. He also had to attend another procession on the octave of Corpus Christi at the military camp in Meudon. Here there was a chaplain from the Samogitian region of Lithuania who worked hard for the conversion of French soldiers.

Finally, Kalinowski announces that soon he is due to leave with Gucio, for the curative waters of Eaux-Bonnes in the south of France.

Eaux-Bonnes

The end of the previous chapter saw Kalinowski prepare for the next move, but as we found he had no great enthusiasm for shuttling from one health spa to another. But he didn't want to let the family down at this point. So they headed for a place called Eaux-Bonnes, in the lower Pyrenees, a name suggesting that the curative properties of the waters would benefit Gucio's tuberculosis. They reached their destination on June 20, 1875. From June to October or for the

Season, as it was called, it was popular with the sick, those suffering from various maladies, catarrh, bronchitis, laryngitis, etc.

Reporting soon after to his father, he writes: "The baths complex are hidden in a ravine and on one side they touch the flank of the mountain. I began to drink the water, I took some baths and I hope it will do me some good. The rains which at this time inundate the west are not lacking here. The melting snow is rushing down in impetuous torrents and joining up with the waters, it blocks our way and causes the local people no end of trouble. After passing the winter at Menton, now we have a cold spell here at the beginning of summer." [p. 420].

This letter was interrupted by a visit from the doctor. Kalinowski was pleased when the doctor informed him that his lungs were sound. It was if, he thought, someone had given him something that he didn't have! His next thought was how to place his health at the service of God – "All I lack now is the Call!" News from home cheered him also. His family had all come together to share the holiday season. His mother had returned from Riga with youngest son Jerzy. Aleksander had just qualified as a lawyer, which was a cause for celebration. Kalinowski was delighted for him and for the satisfaction his ailing father would have in seeing his family around him.

So here was Kalinowski, in the Pyrenees, a long way from Menton, still surrounded by sick people wherever they went. However, the locality was charming and commanded beautiful views. In this case, Kalinowski seemed to appreciate the majesty of the Pyrenees:

> Above our heads, all the summits of the Pyrenees are covered with snow; at our feet lies a beautiful valley at the base of the mountains, with torrents gushing down to form the river Oloron. Eaux Bonnes is forty kilometers south of Pau near Lourdes. The church, which is near our hotel, overlooks the ravine, but it is beside a rocky outcrop which pours out a

huge quantity of water at the base, which renders the ground soft and threatens to undermine it. There are numerous Masses here because there are many priests, especially preachers and religious who are obliged to recite the divine office. The thermal waters, the repose and the good air are a great help. [p. 421].

He was preparing to go with Gucio on a riding trip in the mountains for the first time. This caused memories to stir in his heart: "How much water has flowed by since I first went on similar rides with my brothers across the fields of Lithuania!" [p. 421]. We hear no more at this point for several weeks and then we find Kalinowski writing from Lourdes on July 23. He reported having been thrown from his horse, though not badly, on the outing with Gucio. The young prince had returned to Paris and his mentor stayed on for a few more days. "I departed from Lourdes more quickly than I would have liked. It is definitely a very attractive place and a profound feeling of joy filled my heart when visiting the grotto where the Blessed Virgin manifested herself." [p. 422].[114] Kalinowski would also visit the shrine of Our Lady of the Sacred Heart at Issoudun in order to renew his spiritual energies, of which he felt greatly in need. He then returned to Paris.

In spite of getting a clean bill of health from the doctor, Kalinowski was not feeling well at this time. He writes again trying to reassure his family who had noticed of course that his last letter had been written with a shaky hand:

The weakness and dizziness which I feel again, don't allow me much concentration. I dwell on one thought that occurs

---

[114] Hermann Cohen, who would be one of the sources of inspiration for Kalinowski in pursuing his vocation, had experienced similar feelings at Lourdes over ten years previously. Zélie Martin, mother of Saint Thérèse, would come here also just two years later with her daughters, hoping and praying for a cure for her cancer.

to me: happiness is not our lot here below. If the burdens that weigh us down are the result of our work, or the duties of our state in life, or independent circumstances of our will, let us place them at the feet of the Savior. But if our troubles proceed from our temperaments or our passions, then we should strive against these because in fact we can't overcome them. Only God, in his goodness can pour peace into our hearts and allow our trials to serve our own sanctification and the spiritual good of those who are dear to us. [p. 422].

Meanwhile Gucio had returned to Paris alone and was due to visit the family seat at Sieniawa in Galicia with his father. Kalinowski was ordered by the doctor to rest up for a while before undertaking his own journey to Kraków. In fact from May to September that year Kalinowski had covered 7,000 kilometers. Back in Poland he rejoined Gucio and his aunt, Princess Iza, at their magnificent turreted castle of Goluchow, seat of the Grand Duchy of Poznan.[115] From here they set out for Paris by way of Breslau.[116] On the way they took in various cities, such as Gniezno and Berlin. Berlin impressed Kalinowski for its cleanliness and sense of order, but he felt that the buildings and monuments were not distinguished for their beauty or style.

Kalinowski kept in constant touch with his family and their needs, helping them financially when he could. Their spiritual welfare also was paramount for him.

---

[115] Princess Isabella had the castle restored in French Renaissance style and assembled a magnificent collection of art. In this she was following in the steps of her grandmother, also Princess Isabella. Poznan was called Posen by the Germans when they ruled there. Hermann Cohen would also preach in the city.

[116] Breslau or Wroclaw was the capital of Silesia. Formerly Polish territory, it had been conquered by Prussia but after World War II it reverted to Poland. The Carmelite martyr Edith Stein (St. Teresa Benedicta) was born here in 1891.

He was now in a position to pay off some debts that had accumulated. Working for the wealthy aristocratic family of Czartoryskis enabled him to save. So he was also ready to give financial support to needy members of his family. In this case, youngest brother Aleksander, newly graduated as a lawyer, intending to work in Moscow, became the object of his solicitude. He suggested to Aleksander that he should ask Gabriel for some money which he himself would later repay, and Gabriel was happy to do so. Kalinowski advised his young brother "to work conscientiously, but when you are in need, approach your brother with confidence. Above all write to me at length and tell me sincerely all your financial and spiritual worries." [p. 427]. Enquiring discreetly about the young man's frequentation of the sacraments, he continues: "Do you avail yourself of this source of help of which you are in need?" [p. 425].

Again writing to his brother Jerzy, the future priest who had gone back to college in Riga he said: "When I think of you I recall your needs, both of body and soul. While we have all these faults and it's very difficult to overcome them by our own energies, we should seek the help of God in addition. I advise you to recite this little prayer during the day, *Jesus meek and humble of heart, make my heart like yours.* I emphasize this last point; on this subject your confessor will give you better advice than mine." [p. 424].

He then enquired about his godson Joseph. While studying in Riga Jerzy was staying with his aunt Caroline. The concerns of an educator of youth are obvious in what follows:

> Recently great changes have come about in France on the subject of education. They are not just catering for the intellectual formation of the child, they also try to import solid religious convictions. The [religious] congregations insist above all on this point and try hard to anchor youth in the heart of holy Church. I often see children in the churches singing the praises of God.

He then alludes to the fact that apart from the Brothers of Christian Schools, others dedicated to the education of youth like the Jesuits and the Dominicans also have colleges of higher education. He expresses the wish, now that religious education had been allowed, that Paris may soon have a Catholic university.[117]

After mid-October it was time to take Gucio back to sunnier climes, as the Paris weather was becoming very chilly, even for a Northerner like himself. As they depart he writes to his parents:

> I am delighted to hear that Mama has at last found interior peace, and by God's grace she is being comforted as before. My dear father tells me he is studying Hungarian literature; for myself since my arrival in France, I have read almost nothing, and I say to the Lord more often than ever: *give me your love and your grace and I shall be rich enough, I ask for nothing more.* Tomorrow we will spend the night in Lyon, then Marseille and after that the goal – Menton. Please give me your blessing. [p. 428].

Back in Monaco their accommodation was close to the sea, only a road and the side of the garden between them. This time round Kalinowski intended to mix more with the local people, as on the previous occasion he was confined to the house and taking walks, and only saw the inhabitants in church.

Kalinowski was happy to find a Conference of St. Vincent de Paul which he began to attend. It consisted of about twenty members and he was impressed by the genuine Christian charity he saw there.

---

[117] In fact the 'Institut Catholique de Paris,' on the site of the old Carmelite foundation, was founded the same year – 1875 – that Kalinowski was writing. During the September Massacres in the French Revolution, 150 Carmelites were murdered here. Famous past pupils have been actress Audrey Tatou (Da Vinci Code), Jean Vanier, Cardinal Lustiger, retired Archbishop and Cardinal Vingt-Trois. The controversial former American Dominican Matthew Fox also studied for his PhD here.

There were a couple of priests present and one man, who was English, had come to Menton for the benefit of his sick children. Kalinowski notes the fact that this gentleman was shortly to leave for Rome on an English-German pilgrimage which was being organized by a convert to the faith, a former Grand Master of French Freemasonry.

The party resided on the first floor of the villa 'Gena' and below them was the famous Prince Leon Sapieha of Galicia and his family, like the Czartoryskis, in exile in France and availing themselves of Menton's curative air.[118] While he liked to fill his lungs with the fresh Menton air, still he tended to hark back to Lithuania, or perhaps better, Siberia, where his preference would be to walk around wrapped in a good fur in more bracing air.

Kalinowski's old friend M. Blotnicki, known as Bobo, who later became a go-between with Mother Xavier to persuade him to join the Carmelites, arrived in Menton at the beginning of December after the departure of Prince Ladislaus. He had two students whom he taught Latin and Greek. He read Cicero to Gucio and Kalinowski as well as the New Testament Greek gospels and epistles for Sundays and feast days. Gucio also studied the history of the church and Christian doctrine under the direction of his own teacher. There were fixed times for prayer which were enforced. Recreational activities included whist drives and daily walks or otherwise carriage and boat trips or a railway rides which were most recreational. Kalinowski would take any opportunity to retire to his room in solitude for prayer and meditation.

Though Lithuanian born and with Polish ancestry, we might expect Joseph Kalinowski's spirituality to be somewhat different to 19 century West European models. However, this is not the case. Certainly his lifelong devotion to Our Lady was typically Polish and this was not essentially different from European and

---

[118]   A close relative of his was the Prince Cardinal Archbishop of Kraków who ordained Karol Woytyla a priest; he dissuaded the future John Paul II from joining the Carmelites!

French models, for instance those put forward by Luis Grinion de Montfort. However, as in the case of Hermann Cohen, there was a strong French flavor to much in his devotional approach. This is not altogether surprising as French authors were popular in Poland and elsewhere. I have noted earlier in our story that Kalinowski went to listen to the French Dominican Souaillard in St. Petersburg until he was banned from the country. Similarly as we have also seen, one of his favorite meditation books was from the work of another French priest named Chaignon. Kalinowski was influenced by St. Francis de Sales and his classic work, *Introduction to a Devout Life* which he recommended to his sister Mary. He also read French religious periodicals. Kalinowski's social conscience prompted him to take an interest in the work of the outstanding young Paris intellectual who founded the Society of St. Vincent de Paul – Frederick Ozanam. There were other influences. Kalinowski's time at the Hôtel Lambert in Paris exposed him to French spiritual concepts. He attended many sermons in French churches in the time immediately leading up to his entry into the Carmelite Order.

At Nice in France Kalinowski took an interest in the confraternity 'For a Happy Death' which emphasized the gaining of indulgences and promoted meditation on the sufferings of Jesus and his mother Mary on Calvary. We know that devotion to the Sacred Heart of Jesus gained great momentum from the revelation to St. Margaret Mary at Paray-le-Monial, culminating in the building of the great Basilica Sacré Coeur in Montmartre in 1871. Around the same time Kalinowski joined the Confraternity of the Sacred Heart in Paris; its aim was to render homage to the love of Our Savior Jesus Christ, attested in the suffering of his Passion and in the institution of the Eucharist, a love unrecognized and outraged by indifference and ingratitude; this was always emphasized in the devotional works and prayers of that period. Kalinowski also became a member of a confraternity in Warsaw for the propagation of devotion to the Sacred Heart. He would spend half an hour every Sunday in adoration before the Blessed Sacrament, again, in the language of the day, "to make reparation for the outrages to Jesus in the sacrament of his love."

From his letters we find Kalinowski, still a layman, fully committed to the ascetic life: "All three of us are accustomed to our solitude and it is a trial for us to respond to the invitations we receive. One family invited us to a meal one day. I went along but it was a mortification for me because we were into Lent and I felt I didn't have the right to eat the rich food permitted to the sick of the house. But I didn't take it at the risk of appearing to be a 'Holy Joe.'" [p. 437].[119]

In the same letter he mentions an encounter on the train with Bishop Gaspard Mermillod of Geneva, who was on his way to Rome. Kalinowski joined the throng who knelt to receive his blessing and took the opportunity to ask him to pray for his family. [pp. 437-438].[120]

There had been a very mild winter in Menton in 1875. Kalinowski told his parents he could write to them on January 3 with an open window to allow the hot rays of the sun to come through. They were able to take a long walk to the village of Saint Jean through a countryside decked out with greenery and flowers. However, later on it became unusually cold and he commented: "During the past few weeks there has been a cold, penetrating wind and even into April; such cold gusts that the old people could not remember ever

---

[119] He added another culinary note: "What I foresaw came about. We were served sardines, tea and an apple. This family entertained us in Slavic fashion because they were our own race. The French have different ceremonies."

[120] It was Bishop Mermillod who welcomed Hermann Cohen to Geneva when he was forced to leave France at the beginning of the Franco-Prussian war. The bishop asked Cohen to undertake the pastoral care of war refugees, which he did, opening a chapel for them on October 7. However, next month Bishop Mermillod asked him to minister to the French prisoners of war in Spandau, near Berlin because the Prussians would not allow them a French priest. Cohen died there, a martyr to charity five years before Kalinowski's journey through here.

having taken place and though it hadn't yet snowed, there had been snow at nearby St. Remo. None of this was good for Gucio's frail health of course, and with the onset of a sore throat, Kalinowski felt deeply concerned for him. Kalinowski never left his side and when his father returned to Menton soon after, he decided that they would all return to Poland, visiting Northern Italy on the way.

Chapter Eleven

One Journey Ends, Another Begins

*A*s a change for Gucio from the harsh weather in Menton, it was decided that he travel to Italy in early May, though they would not remain there very long. Their first stop was at Genés on the Riviera where they spent the day and then it was on to Milan. The weather was still cold and Gucio found the going tough. Kalinowski remarks that this part of Italy produced many saints; they visited the tomb of St. Ambrose, and that of St. Gervais and St. Protais as well as that of St. Charles Borromeo where he attended Mass in the Cathedral dedicated to him.

On May 17 the party reached Venice and stayed in the Hotel Europe. He noted the splendid buildings and masterpieces of art, as well as the precious relics venerated by the people. He was particularly impressed by the devotion of the people who filled the churches, honoring Our Lady during her month of May. They visited the house of the Armenian Fathers on the island of Saint-Lazare, an extremely interesting place and here they enjoyed the requisite ride in a gondola. They spent a week in Venice, covering the palace of the Doges. Of course they toured St. Mark's and venerated the saint's body there; they saw the relics of St. Athanasius and those of St. Francis of Assisi, St. Catherine of Siena, etc. At the chapel of the Visitation they viewed the heart of St. Francis de Sales. This part of Northern Italy, he thought, was choc-a-block with centuries of culture.

Then on May 26 Kalinowski and his protégé made their way to Vienna and from there to Kraków, where they reached two days later. By June 1 they had reached home, the Czartoryski ancestral mansion of Sieniawa, near Prezemysl. Kalinowski continued to provide constant care for the sickly Auguste but he also had the joy of family reunions. His brothers Aleksander and Jerzy came to see him there and later his sister Mary. They remained during June, July and part of August. Kalinowski returned to Kraków early, and Mary, who was not at all well, stayed on with the Czartoryskis. However, she joined him in Kraków on July 16.

France may have its spa waters in the Pyrenees, but Poland boasts similar health resorts at the foot of the Carpathians in Galicia. One such area is the beautiful scenic setting in Szczawnica, a major tourist area and popular in Kalinowski's time. The Szalaya family had built it up in the 19th century and, like the south of France, it attracted large crowds hoping to improve their health, particularly those with respiratory problems. Though Kalinowski found the place 'charming' the weather was quite bad. They only allowed themselves a brief visit of three days – less if you factor in travel; he was back in Kraków on the 18, and his sister Mary returned to the Czartoryski residence. From Kraków he wrote her this very intimate letter: "Here I am at Kraków. The journey was fast but fatiguing. Have you made all your arrangements? Are you happy with your lodging? Look after your health, dear little sister and particularly when you feel tired, make sure you rest before the open window of your room. Write to me from Sieniawa and let me know what your program is each day. Write without delay and do tell me about everything you need. I insist! And I will remember you in my prayers." [p. 441].

It appears that Mary was going through a bout of ill health and her vacation was meant to help her recover. She had a hand in

Kalinowski recovering his faith about ten years earlier – something he had never forgotten. Her devoted brother writes to her again:

> You, little angel, to whom I owe my return to God and the church, how I wish you now to recover the energy you need to serve God! In the Kraków library I looked through many books, trying to decide what would suit you, but I found nothing suitable. Write to me yourself and tell me what you would like to read and I will send them immediately. For the moment I'm sending the *Philothea* of St. Francis de Sales. You should find there abundant nourishment for your soul." [p. 442].[121]

Later he would recommend that Mary do a retreat with the Visitation Sisters in the solitude of the cloister. Sadly his 'little angel' only lived for a few years afterwards and was never to don the habit of a Sister of Charity which her brother had envisioned for her.

On August 1 the Czartoryski party, again with Gucio's overall interests in view, decided to set out for Davos, second-most-important town in Switzerland. It lies high in the Alps, 1600 meters, and the idea was to remain there for some months if the climate proved favorable. The valley of Davos is surrounded by mountains, the peaks of which are covered with snow and ice all the year round. Today the snow covered the mountains nearest to us that soared thousands of feet above our heads. The air was certainly bracing and one day they had to light fires in their rooms, something he never did before in the month of August, not even in Siberia. Generally, however, the weather was good and they intended to spend the winter there.

Kalinowski worried constantly about Gucio's lungs and hoped the pure mountain air would do them good. He felt he was idling his time away, something that never sat well with him, but such was

---

[121] The book *Philothea* of St. Francis de Sales is better known as 'Introduction to a Devout Life.'

their isolation, there was nothing he could do about it. Kalinowski observes that Davos was a Protestant area but that the people were well disposed to Catholics. There was no church but he was hoping that a priest who had come to recuperate might celebrate the Eucharist for them. Sharing his impressions of his Alpine surroundings and other places with his family, Kalinowsksi observes:

> The countryside provides us only with milk and butter, everything else comes in from elsewhere. At a height of 1,600 meters beyond the mountains, pasture grounds, firs and larches, what can you see? The Davos peasants are honest and hardworking, but they are foreign, not only in nationality but also in religion. Never, I believe, have I felt the pulse of life to be so weak as in the area where we now dwell. And yet here we have a splendid landscape with nature at its best. The valley of Davos has a little river bed which receives the waters pouring down from the mountains and it serves to stabilize the banks. On one of the banks there are a dozen hotels for invalids. Here too there is a Protestant church with a tower made of beams resembling a stockade. From time to time a goods wagon, a stage coach or a carriage with tourists would pass by. During the day the inhabitants, that is the sick, walk through the gardens or along special trails set out for them along the mountains. From 9.30 in the evening music starts up and shrill sounding waltzes are the usual fare. You can work out for yourself how Gucio and I pass like shadows through this earthly purgatory. [p. 448].[122]

---

[122]   Kalinowski is probably referring here to the tradition of accordion music that was gaining momentum in Switzerland in the 19 Century. And of course yodeling was an ancient tradition of communication and music used by herders and shepherds in the Swiss Alps.

While they were in this area Andrew Kalinowski enquired from his book-lover son if he had a sufficient supply up there and what books were they? He replied in the affirmative and lists some of their reading material. Gucio was in fact reading works by contemporary authors who were friends of Kalinowski senior, Fredro and Ignatius Chodzko and these they were enjoying immensely. They were also reading the letters of Romantic writer Antoni Odyniec, a kind of lesser Mickiewicz, and also a friend of Andrew Kalinowski from Vilnius University days. They had finished reading Volume One and had begun the *Letters from Rome,* but these didn't appeal to either of them. Kalinowski found himself becoming annoyed with Odyniec's near idolatry of Mickiewicz. We don't know how Kalinowski senior took this verdict on his friend.

Kalinowski had worked out a program of study for his protégé: an hour in the morning was devoted either to a treatise on Elementary Physics by Adolphe Ganot which had been recently released (1868), or a book on Philosophy by Bishop Bouvier.[123] From mid morning they studied the lives of Polish St. Stanislaus or St. Aloysius Gonzaga. Later on, time was devoted either to letter writing or to a study of geography. Kalinowski tells us he read aloud an account of journeys and expeditions from a publication called *Le Tour du Monde*.[124] They also studied Polish classics and Kalinowski waxes nostalgic when he mentions he had bought the Polish Tales of *Ramoty and Ramotki* for Gucio which he himself had read as a boy.

Carmel Beckons

It was during the time of their sojourn in Davos that Kalinowski began to broach the subject of his religious vocation with his parents. He told them he wished to leave the world and live in a little religious cell. He constantly asked his family and friends to pray for him,

---

[123] He had been a professor at the famous seminary of St. Sulpice in Paris about 1842.

[124] This was the forerunner of *National Geographic* magazine.

reminding them that it was the prayers of his family that saved him the first time; now he needed them again for his new life! Writing to them on August 25, 1876 he stated:

> Here is a new token of the mercy and goodness of God which brought new consolation and hope to me through people I love. The revered Sr. Mary Xavier of Jesus, aunt of my Gucio, former princess and a powerful lady, is today a religious in the convent of Discalced Carmelites; I met her only once at the *grille* and she barely knows me. But she was kind enough to send me recently a quotation from the seraphic St. Teresa, and especially when I didn't deserve the attention of this holy person, but at the same time it was something I really needed – here they are:
>
> > Let nothing trouble you,
> > let nothing frighten you.
> > All things are passing;
> > God never changes.
> > Patience obtains all things.
> > He who possesses God lacks nothing:
> > God alone suffices. [*St. Teresa's Bookmark*]

These words are in perfect accord with those which I found, very dear parents, in your last letters and they arrived at the same time brought to Davos by M. Blotnicki...[p. 452].

Around this time the Czartoryska women, Marcelina and Mother Mary Xavier were on the lookout for a potential reformer and restorer of the Carmelite Friars in Poland. It didn't seem to matter that Kalinowski was not yet a member of the Order or even a postulant for that matter. Another member of the family, Princess Iza set the ball rolling – she had already made contact with Kalinowski.

We have a letter on subsequent developments written by Mother Mary Xavier. (She is referring to news regarding developments from

Princess Iza. Though lengthy, it is worth quoting in fiull.)) In the beginning of the letter she talks about the great impression made on her and the whole household in Paris when Hermann Cohen visited the Hôtel Lambert. He was the first Teresian Carmelite they had met. She then goes on to talk about her own vocation to Carmel and the eventual vocation of Kalinowski also:

> It is easy to imagine what happened at Wesoła when this letter was received – unlimited gratitude to God and continual prayer that what had miraculously begun would be brought to completion. Gucio Czartoryski, the pupil of Joseph Kalinowski, and son of Prince Ladislaus and Princess Amparo, went from Sieniawa to Davos, where they were to spend the winter, and they passed through Kraków with the boy's mentor. They came to say goodbye. But I was so timid that I didn't dare talk to them in the parlor about our projects. When they had gone I was mad with myself for not having availed myself of such a favorable opportunity, and when I got to recreation all the mothers and sisters got stuck into me! Some time later, M. Hippolyte Blotnocki also came to say goodbye. I began to breathe freely again; he is a great friend of our family. Before the revolution of 1831, he had already been secretary to Prince Adam Czartoryski. After that he became the teacher of his two sons, and later of his grandson, Prince Auguste (Gucio); so I was able to confide everything to him. After we had exchanged most cordial greetings, I begged him earnestly, to get involved, to pray, to ask M. Kalinowski to kindly help us with the reform of our Order in Poland, which without him would come to grief. Good M. Blotnicki was so profoundly touched by my ardent prayer, that he promised to tell him [Kalinowski] everything, and he regretted that he was no longer young (he was nearly 80) in order to take to the Discalced Carmelite arena himself and help us realize our

project. He returned next day to inform us of his efforts. With what anticipation and what impatience we awaited his arrival!... Well, Sir, I said after greeting him, did he refuse you? To which he responded: I told everything to M. Kalinowski, I told him absolutely everything. And what did he say? He said nothing, he just continued to pack his bag for his departure. That's a good sign, Sir, and it shows that he wishes to reflect and take the matter seriously. Our whole community started to pray and to offer penance and holy communions to God. Immediately our Mother Sub-Prioress, Mother Teresa of Jesus, attached a note on the choir door of the intentions for which we were to pray: 'Our Holy Order and Poland – M. Kalinowski.' And I myself, writing to Gucio at Davos, always added on some words to my letter: We are praying to God for him (Kalinowski) to let us know God's will, for the Holy Spirit to communicate his light to him; we are offering communions and making novenas for these intentions. And in every reply of Gucio we always recognized a few words written under the dictation of M. Kalinowski which filled us with tokens of joy. [p. 453].[125]

At this time also (August 25, 1876) Princess Marcelina visited Davos and suggested that Kalinowski join the Carmelites. She herself was involved in establishing the Third or Secular Order in Poland. Though he had given nothing away initially it was obvious to everyone that Kalinowski had taken time to reflect and pray about the possibility of joining the Carmelite Order. Even while still in exile Kalinowski had given hints to his parents that he would not

---

[125] We see clearly from the first paragraph something of the role or at least the indirect influence exerted by Hermann Cohen in the renewal of Carmel in Poland. Without him Mary Xavier would probably have entered the Paris Carmel which had no contact, nor did they wish to have any, with the Discalced Friars. Having met Hermann Cohen, Mary Xavier could not accept the attitude of the Paris Carmelite nuns.

be returning to the engineering profession when he came home. His heart was already set on religious life.

Kalinowski continued to press home the point to his parents that he was anxious to embrace religious life. The person who had spent time in the fortress at Kronstadt was now thinking of living in a holy fortress of religious life where he would be safe from attack by his spiritual enemies and be enabled to "persevere in an indissoluble union with our divine Savior."

Soon after this Kalinowski began to plan his future as a Carmelite. He was not abandoning Gucio in this situation. He could see that the boy had made considerable spiritual progress under his tutelage and he felt he had taken him as far as he could. He was now convinced that a priest would be the right person to continue to guide him. He made this proposal to Gucio's father who found it acceptable and consequently would soon release him from his contract.

Before severing his links with the world, Kalinowski was keenly intent on doing everything he could for his family both materially and spiritually, realising he would not be able to help them financially from Carmel. He first turned his attention to his sister Emilia showing his concern for her welfare. He told her he had traveled through the Pyrenees and the Carpathians, as well as the Alps. But he tells her he won't be writing about these locations; such sights no longer held great interest for him. Neither will he be concerned with the French he met in Paris, the Italians at Menton or the Swiss at Davos. "So why am I writing?" he asks himself: "It's about yourself!" He will not talk about himself – that would be too sad a story – for himself he just needs her prayers. At this point Kalinowski's heart is heavy as he requests final news about his family. "Write to me with all the details," he tells her, "about yourself, about our family and about each one in particular, and tell me about Hrozow, Hrozowek, Musicze. Don't forget Aleksander, Jerzy, or Karol's growing children. If you have already got as far as Warsaw give me news also of Gabriel." [p. 460].

When writing to his father, Kalinowski alluded to some funds he had sent home and asserted that this was not just an act of generosity but really only repayment of the debt he owed his father – for all he had given him over the years. He then tells his father he wishes to support Aleksander and will make representations for him with some of his old contacts who may be able to direct him in the way of some employment. One concern he had was that Aleksander might be forced to work in an area where the carrying out of his religious obligations would be difficult. He was anxious also to provide his younger brothers with suitable uplifting literature and wonders if Gabriel would be able to help in this – though in what way is not specified. Presumably he meant Gabriel could distribute the books. In any case he assures his father that he himself wishes to pay for the books and that he would reimburse Gabriel for expenses incurred. In the same letter he asks his father to send the priest in Perm, Michael Fiszer, the works of Denys the Areopagite, in a French translation by Archbishop Darboy of Paris. "I am so indebted," he writes, "to this true friend, that I earnestly request Gabriel to search out this work and send it to Perm. I will remit the cost." [p. 464].

Finally, reviewing all that he and all the family owed his esteemed father, he made arrangements to acquire for him a Papal Blessing as a fitting seal on an exemplary life.

On April 6 Kalinowski reported home from the first stop on their journey which was the town of Coire or Chur. For him it was a re-entry into the world after the seclusion he experienced in Davos. He was glad to be within reach of a Catholic cathedral and a chapel attached to the seminary. Other churches had been taken over at the time of the Reformation. The cathedral possessed many religious artefacts – they viewed the relics of what he understood to be those of the somewhat legendary St. Lucius from England and those of many Irish saints who are known to have evangelized the area. The countryside was looking beautiful in spring and the priest was very hospitable to them. Kalinowski wasn't looking forward to the next stop, Lucerne, where he didn't think it would be the same. And in a rather nice touch Kalinowski enclosed with his letter a spring flower for his father which he had culled in the mountains.

On April 13 they arrived in Paris. From Paris he again outlined his plans to his parents indicating that he would leave soon to enter the Carmelite novitiate. Kalinowski, ever anxious about the spiritual wellbeing of his family, then sent his sisters Emilia and Mary the biography of Sophie Barat, who founded the Sacred Heart Sisters, and that of Blessed Margaret Mary.

Pentecost was spent in Paris where he and Gucio attended Mass in the church of the Jesuits. There followed, however, an enforced interruption as Gucio had a relapse in the hot Paris atmosphere and it was decided to take him to the seaside at Trouville for a few days.[126] They returned to Paris via Le Havre and Kalinowski discovered that his plans to leave 'soon' had to remain on hold as the priest who was meant to replace him as guide for Gucio still hadn't turned up. This delay was understandably unsettling for Kalinowski, being as it was, a completely unforseen obstacle.

---

[126] It was at Trouville that the young Thérèse Martin had her first impression of the sea, whose immensity moved her deeply.

Part Two

Chapter One

Answering the Call

*A*t the end of Part One, we left Joseph Kalinowski waiting impatiently for a clerical replacement to take over his role as tutor to Prince Auguste Czartoryski. Finally, the obstacle of the delayed arrival of his replacement was resolved, and tutor and tutored took their farewells of one another.

Leaving forever those he loved, Kalinowski wished to emphasize his ongoing commitment to them, remembering them all: parents, brothers, sisters, friends from the neighborhood, friends from further afield – Warsaw, Smolensk, St. Petersburg and far-off Siberia. He particularly recalled the memory of his benefactor Christopher Szwermicki, pastor of Irkutsk, and another good friend, Felix Zienkowicz, who still lived in the rectory there. "I want to write to the Reverend Father Szwermicki," he told his father, "to tell him that I received his last letter on August 26; and I ask God to give him all necessary graces in return for all the goodness that I witnessed in the venerable father." Then he mentions a set of books on the History of England by Macaulay[127] that Christopher Szwermicki was expecting to collect from his friend Felix:

---

[127] Englishman Thomas Babington Macaulay wrote a multi-volume work by this name. Certainly he would have regarded Popery as a superstitious

The books that I intended to give Felix, include opinions unfavorable to our Holy Church, so I destroyed them. Don't say anything about this to Felix. I'll try and get him (Szwermicki) a better gift. This command is for me a matter of conscience. [He finishes the letter]: So that's what is going on, my dear Father, and after so many efforts made on my behalf in the past, you now have more chores to do on my account. I am hurrying now to make a visit to the Blessed Sacrament and will pray to Jesus Christ for you, Father, and for all of yours and mine, despite my unworthiness. With paternal love, I kiss your hands and I recommend myself to your inexhaustible kindness. Give me your blessing, my dear parents, and lovingly embrace for me Karol and his children, and Aleksander, Emily and Mary. Your unworthy and respectful son, Joseph. All the best to Sabine.[128]

This was a farewell letter to his parents at the time of leaving them. The parting was a painful experience for the entire family, especially for his father, whom he particularly loved. Following the Carmelite custom of the day there would be no holidays with his family in the future. To soften the sadness, his son included in his letter to his father the following passage from a letter of Sr. Mary Xavier Czartoryska:

religion but funnily enough he saw advantages in the way Catholicism broke down class barriers, i.e., Beneficial Operation of the Roman Catholic Religion, Volume 1. Kalinowski shows himself somewhat intolerant here, though understandable in the context of the times.

[128] Père Jean-Baptist Bouchaud OCD, Miłość za Miłość (Kraków: Wydawnictwo Karmelitow Bosych, 2006) p 32. Karol had remarried by this time – to deceased Martine's sister Sabine. [In the second part of this biography most of the references are to the above book by Bouchaud. The references will be cited in the text with its page number/s].

There is no happiness in the world equal to that afforded by religious life. Please read the autobiography of St. Teresa. We ask God before the Blessed Sacrament, to fulfil his will on earth as in heaven. Every day during the octave (of St. Teresa), our Prioress offers her Holy Communion intention for you, for herself and for the community.

He goes on: When I rewrite these words, my dear parents, I am aware of the great benefits I have received from God, which help lift me out of my misery, and I cannot refrain from saying, "Forever I will sing the mercies of the Lord,"– *Misericordias Domini in aeternum cantabo.* [p. 31].[129]

Kalinowski Becomes a Carmelite Novice

On July 5, 1877, Kalinowski left the Czartoryski household and headed for the Carmelite house of Linz in Austria for an interview with the Provincial. He was 42 years of age, quite a late vocation by the customs of those days. The Provincial accepted his request for admittance; he was shown to a little cell in the house and immediately felt he had reached home. The imminent celebration of the Feast of Our Lady of Mt. Carmel would be very special for him that year. Next day, he had to leave for the Novitiate House of the Austro-Hungarian semi-province of Teresian Carmelites in Graz, also in Austria, where he was required to spend the next few months as a postulant.

On November 26, 1877 Kalinowski was clothed in the brown habit of a Carmelite novice and was given the name Raphael of St. Joseph, the name by which he would henceforth be known.

Kalinowski, we can ascertain from his letters, didn't become a religious to inaugurate a renewal of Carmel in Poland, but merely to repent of his sins. The Prior of the house was Gabriel Gadi,

---

[129]   This verse from Psalm 89 was a favorite with St. Teresa.

while the Master of Novices was Teresius Jung. It was the latter – well-educated and experienced, if exacting – who undertook the spiritual guidance and religious formation of the new novice. The background of candidates to the Order was strictly investigated before they were accepted, so as to discern their suitability for the life. The investigation is primarily about the candidate himself and his past life, but also about his family. Kalinowski wrote at that time: "God bless the hand which directed me under the roof of the sons of the Holy Spirit." He was resolved to commit himself to Our Lady's Order and continue in "allegiance to Jesus Christ" as the Carmelite Rule urges, for the rest of his days.

Regarding the candidate's background we can say that Kalinowski's pedigree was impeccable, as his family belonged to one of the most respected in Lithuania.

But church affiliation checks were not so easy to come by. Kalinowski had travelled a lot and lived in various dioceses in Europe and Northern Asia. And we know 10 of these years away from home were not of his own volition. Sometimes a bishop would have to respond that the candidate was unknown and therefore no information could be provided about him. In this case, he may receive the habit after a three-month trial. Consequently, Kalinowski was only admitted to the novitiate at the end of November 1877.

Though restricted in letter writing during the novitiate, Kalinowski was allowed to write to his parents monthly or for some serious reason. So when family tragedy struck, we find the novice writing to his father: "We need the protection of Divine Providence, so that in every situation a person can benefit from the goodness and mercy that God gives each of us. Pray for my intentions, my dear parents and my very dear brothers and sisters." [p. 31]. In the same letter he sent his grieving family words of comfort and sympathy on the death of 7 year-old Angela, his brother Karol's daughter: "I can imagine the grief of Karol and all those in Hrozow, Hrozowek and Musicz." A greater personal double loss was soon to follow.

Kalinowski's younger brother Aleksander lived in St. Petersburg, where Balthazar Kalinowski, a family friend, was glad to welcome him. The novice thought of his loved ones, and wished to share with them the good things that had become his through prayer and Eucharist. Kalinowski wrote to his father: "So Aleksander leaves Hrozow to settle in St. Petersburg, enjoying the hospitality of Balthazar, whose noble and grateful heart does not cease to show you true filial love. No, all we can do is ask God to reward him with his blessings, enriching the gift of religion and virtue in him, by granting him the favor of using the treasures found in the heart of our Holy Mother the Church. This is the only way to reach God through worship, and drawing on God's grace in the sacraments flowing from the Passion of our Redeemer." [p. 31].

Kalinowski's life during the novitiate year would have been uneventful by secular standards. He had finally and forever broken with the world. He could be all alone for long periods in a tiny cell, something he had dreamed of for 13 years, that is, since his conversion. He was happy and thanked the Lord that he had come through so many storms and had now reached port. "Who can tell," writes his colleague Diaz de Cerio, "what a zealous novice he was? He had a high opinion of religious life. He didn't take in everything at first, it was all new and difficult. Of course, the beginnings are always difficult, but his strong love for God made him view this new life gladly, and nothing in the world could give him as much happiness." [p. 38].

It is safe to say that Kalinowski didn't find the Carmelite novitiate as tough as the run-of-the-mill postulant found it, strict as it was in those days! Years of hard labor had inured him to hardship and the solitude, penance and prayer were, as far as he was concerned, part of the course. He was already a full-blown contemplative. In the context of novitiate life Kalinowski wrote: "My dear Parents, I want to mention that my correspondence will be very moderate and very seldom. Do not give in to anxiety and entrust me to the mercy of God, and give me dear Father, your paternal blessing." [p. 43].

Kalinowski asked his father to write to Michael Fiszer in his name and to Bishop Kasper Borowski in Perm, and also to Prince Auguste in Davos, to inform them about his joining the Carmelites; and to recommend him to their prayers. "Our life is a life of prayer, contemplation and study," he wrote, "our acts of love for God and love of neighbor is a prayer, which – from rising until retiring – accompanies all our actions, prayer for the intentions of the Church, for our benefactors, etc., as well as for us poor sinners! Many times during the day I recommend you and all our family to the mercy and goodness of God." [p. 43].

Kalinowski also sent greetings to his older brother Victor and sister Mary. Victor was still unwell, so he wrote him some words of consolation and encouragement. "I extend sincere wishes for your health that God will give you the necessary strength to endure the hardships of our mortal life." [p. 43]. He prayed for their intentions every day, and earnestly asked prayers for himself, confident they wouldn't refuse.

The next day he asked the Novice Master for permission to write to his family again as his father's health was deteriorating.

> Dearest Father! I take my pen; I was impressed by your letter of February 7. I ask God to be pleased to relieve your suffering, and if the intentions of Providence are that God will not hear this prayer, I won't stop begging him to help you use these sufferings in union with the merits of the Precious Blood that Jesus Christ shed for us in agony on the cross, the source of merit for you, my beloved Father. It is far from my thoughts to extend your sufferings, but at least with the help of grace I wish to bring you comfort. [Referring to St. Teresa of Avila, he continues] … the saint seeing her own father subject to severe bodily pain, and unable to assist him, urged him to help Christ carry the cross to Calvary. May the intercession of this saint with Jesus and Mary in her Immaculate Conception, and St. Joseph,

whose feast is celebrated today, help me in my prayers to God for his grace and mercy. [p. 45].

This was his last letter to his father. When he wrote these words, unknown to him his beloved and generous-hearted sister Mary had been dead for two weeks, and in a matter of five days later, her father followed her to the grave; we might suspect this was partly due to heartbreak. They were buried side by side in the little Catholic cemetery at Hrozow, although the church itself had been taken over by the Orthodox. Surely this was a baptism of fire for Kalinowski during his novitiate year, involving as it did, a heavier cross than any incurred in 10 years in Siberia. We have the following details from his brother Jerzy:

My sister Mary, born in 1847, died in Hrozow on March 3, 1878, three weeks before her father, and she rests in the cemetery next to him. Mary received a thorough education at home; she had a lovely voice, and liked to play the piano. In 1874, the Rymszow family, our relatives, put her in charge of their children and that is where she contracted tuberculosis, which she fought bravely for four years. She died the death of the just, yielding her soul to God whom she loved above all else. Her face in the coffin was charmingly beautiful. My father suffered a lot before his death. One of his friends at the university named Cypryński, during a visit wept at his bedside. The patient said to him: "I feel sorry for some people dear to me, I pity you: my turn today, yours tomorrow." Father confessed and received Holy Communion and Extreme Unction from the hands of Albert Rubszy, a Carmelite from Vilnius. In 1876 this priest was pastor in Kopylu, a small village, about 14 kilometers from Hrozow. Hrozow belonged to the parish of Slutsk, (or Sluck) in Belarus but the local priest at the time had been excommunicated for disobeying the Holy See, like many others in the province of Minsk. My father was buried next to Mary in the cemetery, which overlooks Hrozow ... News of the death of Andrew Kalinowski was received with deep regret in Lithuania, Belarus and Samogitia, where former high school students of Vilnius and the Institute of Nobility knew and loved him as a father. The poet Antony Odyniec composed an epitaph for the tombstone of his friend: "He won honor and love for his goodness, learning, work, and love for life; we grieve for the death of a compatriot." [p. 47].

While grieving the death of a father and sister, Joseph's deep faith helped him to endure this painful experience, so that he could say, as he did after the death of young sister Monica some years earlier: "I feel closer to my sister now, than I did during her life on earth."

Every month, one of the novices had the duty of practicing a special devotion to the Blessed Sacrament and spending a specified amount of time in adoration before the tabernacle. This practice was particularly dear to Kalinowski. It was for him a rich source of strength and consolation, and he was never happier than when praying before the Blessed Sacrament. In this he resembles his hero Hermann Cohen.

Why did he join a religious Order? In a letter to Sr. Mary Xavier from Paris on July 9, 1877, Kalinowski himself gives us the answer to this question raised briefly earlier: "The thought of repentance alone leads me to Carmel, and I reject any other idea. What I now write is the literal truth, and not just an expression of humility. As I write this now God reads my heart and sees that I am a sinner." [p. 47].

It seems that Kalinowski had considered a vocation to the Capuchins like his friend Wenceslaus, and apparently other friends had urged him to join the Resurrectionist Congregation in Paris, founded there by Polish émigrés, but he declined both.

After completing his novitiate in Graz, Kalinowski made his first profession on November 26, 1878 and was then sent to Gyor, also known as Raab, in Hungary, to continue his formation and begin his studies for the priesthood. It was not so much a question of taking up theological studies, as of complementing what he had already studied over the years. For instance, during his stay in Siberia as noted earlier in this book, he had summarized four volumes of church history by Darras. Later, he studied Bishop Bouvier's philosophy and the moral theology of Scavini, based on St. Alphonsus Liguori, and recommended by Pope Pius IX. He spent three years in Gyor and was under Fr. Jerome, Master of Students, a model religious and professor there. Jerome remarked that Kalinowski was an exemplary religious, very attached to the Rule and loved by his fellow students.

The Carmelite Rule is imbued with a spirit of solitude, meditation and prayer. That meant writing few letters, unless friars were required to do so by obedience, necessity or charity. Kalinowski filled in the time performing the acts of community life and by prayer and study.

Background to Carmelite Renewal in Poland

In the late 19th century a liberal regime came to power in France and gradually carried out a secularization of the country. By 1880, 161 monasteries had been closed, many of which had been run by the Jesuits. Some of the Carmelites migrated abroad – to Italy, Belgium, England or Spain. During the Kulturkampf period initiated by Iron Chancellor Bismarck, as it affected the Carmel in Poznan, religious personnel were exiled and the Carmelite sisters from there sought refuge in Wesoła Carmel in Kraków.

There were already 20 sisters there, but the group in Poznan numbered 18, and the Constitutions of St. Teresa didn't allow more than 20 sisters in any one convent, so they had to proceed immediately to establish a new convent. Looking for a suitable place in the city, they found a house with quite a large garden on the outskirts of Kraków. It was in the suburb of Łobzów, at the end of Ulika Łobzówska, and this property was duly purchased. A convent was quickly built there, together with a tiny chapel. The community moved there in 1875. The foundation at Poznan had originally come from Belgium in 1867 and numbered five sisters. Mary Xavier Czartoryska, whom we meet so often in this story (1833–1928), came from her home in Paris in 1873 and joined the Discalced Carmelites in Poznan. She was one of the first five sisters to be professed in the new convent in Kraków, making her vows on April 14, 1875. In the years 1898–1901 and 1904–1907 she was Prioress at Łobzów. She had a profound impact on the development of the Order in Poland.

The Carmelite sisters had always wished to be under the jurisdiction of the fathers of the Order, but the only house of the Discalced Carmelites in Poland was at Czerna and it had no one available to fill the role of Superior for the new convent. To rectify this, the sisters decided to pray and also have recourse to the General of the Order. To this end they wrote a letter to the General, Luke Ranise; he replied that first of all they needed to pray and ask God for vocations. One of the General Councillors was Serapion Wenzel, the first provincial of the Austro–Hungarian Province set up in 1872.

The Lord would eventually answer the sisters' prayers in full by giving them Raphael Kalinowski. First, however, there was a promising pioneer in the pipeline, namely Ferdinand Drescher, who later received the religious name Francis Xavier. Drescher belonged to the Carmelites of the Ancient Observance, or Calced Carmelites as they were sometimes known, based at Leszno in Warsaw. A second candidate, Bruno Rybka, who would be known as Casimir, was a member of the Carmelite Third Order from Galicia, and was now in the Carmelite priory of the Virgin Mary 'Na Piasky' (The Sands) in Kraków. This community also belonged to the Ancient Observance. In April 1879 Rybka was in Czerna, where he waited for a response from the General of the Order regarding his application. On April 4 he wrote to the Prioress at Łobzów: "The Lord blessed the request sent to Rome. The Provincial informed the prior of Czerna that the case is complete and that an indult will arrive before Easter. So expect to see me in Graz before Pentecost … We must thank God, and Jesus and Mary, and you Reverend Sister in Christ." [p. 55].

However, Holy Saturday arrived but permission didn't come as quickly as expected, and so on May 2 we find Rybka writing again: "When I was in trouble, I cried to the Lord and He heard me (Ps. 119.1). Finally, I received the indult on the first day of the month. I thank Our Lady for the longed for fulfilment of my desires. Imagine what thanks I owe to Jesus, to Mary, our holy Patrons, and the Superior for their concern and prayers. May God reward you handsomely for your kindness, care and prayers Mother … I send warmest greetings. God bless you! I leave for Vienna on Monday morning. But please continue to remember me in your prayers, and thanks also to all the Sisters. May the Virgin have the sisters in her care." [p. 56].

On 12 May, Rybka arrived at the novitiate at Graz and received the Carmelite habit taking the name Casimir, patron of Poland.

Regarding the important role Drescher would play in the future, we note that he returned from a pilgrimage to Jerusalem in 1879, and went to Kraków to visit his friend Vincent Smoczyński (1842–1903), doctor of Canon Law, who was pastor of St. Florian's Church in Kraków.[130] Drescher confided in him that he did not feel happy in Warsaw, because the observance generally was not followed there. Vincent, knowing the desires and intentions of many people for the Teresian Carmelite reform in Poland, went to the sisters and told them the good news of this possible vocation. The community was delighted, responding: "Please tell this good father that we wish to speak to him and invite him to visit us." This wish was complied with, and he went and had a long conversation with the Carmelite sisters.

---

[130] A Collegiate church of Kraków university. Pope John Paul II was chaplain here from August 1949 – September 1951.

Meanwhile, Bertold Schormann, Vicar Provincial of the Discalced Carmelites of Austria-Hungary and Poland lived in Linz. He wished to reform the Czerna house and asked God to send him some talented Polish friars. For now there were Kalinowski, Drescher and Rybka, and when he discovered the good intentions of the latter two, Bertold was very pleased, and received them warmly. As mentioned they first needed to inform the General and obtain his permission to join the Order. Schormann immediately sent a request to Rome and Drescher returned to his priory in Warsaw, where he awaited a response. As we saw in the case of Casimir, the answer was a rejection. Drescher's Warsaw community had made every effort to obstruct him, because he had worked very successfully in the church in Leszno, and they didn't want to lose him. There was a moment when, under pressure, Drescher doubted his vocation and wrote to the Carmelites in Kraków, informing them of the negative response from Rome and didn't hide his feelings about the matter. The sisters immediately wrote, encouraging him to persevere. He replied: "I will repeat my request once again, and if that is not enough, I will go myself to Rome to seek the permission I need." [p. 58].

When permission eventually came through he wrote on July 19 from the novitiate in Graz: "I cannot, dear Sisters, describe the joy and the peace that fills my heart at the thought that in a few days I will join the Discalced Order of the Blessed Virgin Mary of Mount Carmel. Casimir (Rybka) was really good, too, it seems that his disposition is quite consistent and that we will be happy with him." [p. 58].

Drescher received the Carmelite habit on August 2, 1879, with the religious name Francis Xavier. Together with him, Br. Dominic, a young candidate from the novitiate in Linz, also received the habit.

Luke Ranise from the Province of Rome was the current General of the Order since 1872. He had been a reformer of the Austro-Hungarian province. In the autumn of 1879, in fulfilment of the Carmelite sisters' wishes, he agreed to travel to Poland. So, accompanied by Serapion Wenzel and a Br. Joachim, he came to visit the sisters in Kraków in October 1879 and they greeted him enthusiastically. He held a canonical visitation, met with the sisters in the parlor, and they used all their powers of persuasion to bring about the desired renewal of the priory in Czerna. Ranise countered that he had no friars available for the job, but the sisters replied that God has already sent them three religious, and other provinces would probably provide more.

They also presented him with an Address signed by dignatories in Kraków, notably Czartoryskis, Lubormiskis and Potockis.[131] [p. 60] They were supported by the Archbishop of Kraków and others. Fr. General took all this into account, and before leaving promised to do everything possible to satisfy the wishes of the sisters and such highly placed people and friends of Carmel in Poland.

Ranise returned to Rome, and in December the General Council asked the French and Belgian provinces to volunteer some friars for Czerna. These were made up of Bertold Schormann (First Prior), Brocard Losert (both were former secular priests), Andrew Gatzweiler, Fulgenty Zalduegui (one of many Spaniards, who had contributed to the renewal of the Order in France), and Jean-Baptiste Bouchaud, Kalinowski's biographer, from the province of Aquitaine. The two latter friars intended to go to Mesopotamia,

---

[131] The Address: "We, the undersigned residents of Kraków, want the old Order of the Blessed Virgin of Carmel, once so flourishing in Poland, and now newly revived in our country, which is in so much need of spiritual renewal and of zealous people souls in the service of God, we turn to the Superior General of that Order with our humble request. Knowing that the Austrian province, to which all the three existing priories in Poland belong, is quite large and big enough to manage on its own, we would like to submit a plan to Father General pointing out that several people are interested in this project and that we could find sufficient support to achieve our objective. So we hope to get a few friars from other provinces to come to Poland and lead us with a faithful observance of the life of the Order. Therefore, we most humbly ask Father General, to graciously consider our request and possibly bring about this plan in honor of God and the Blessed Virgin Mary of Mount Carmel, Queen of Poland."

where French Carmelites started a mission in Baghdad in the 17ᵗʰ
century. Zalduegui and Bouchaud came to Kraków on May 21,
1880. In addition there were two lay brothers – Avertan Schindler
and Thomas Wagner. These all joined an existing community of
four in Czerna, including Joseph Tyszkiewiczówna and Gabriel
Tyrka. Kalinowski was then engaged in his theological studies at
Gyor in Hungary where he later made solemn profession.

Kalinowski's friend Mary Xavier Czartoryska wrote to him
while he was still a student in Gyor, giving a full account of the
great new beginning in Czerna. She described how the local bishop
presided over the proceedings. She informed him that members of
her own family were there to welcome the friars. Mary Xavier gave a
minute description of the scene in the priory – walls were festooned
in greenery and an image of the Sacred Heart to whom the Province
was dedicated was displayed, together with the Promises made to
St. Margaret Mary. On another wall hung an image of St. Teresa
of Avila, surrounded by stars, on which the name of each friar was
written. Next day the Provincial celebrated Mass for the sisters in
Kraków, while Andrew Gatzweiler did the same in the Convent at
Łobzów.

So it happened that in 1880, with the help of friars from
other provinces, Carmelite life at Czerna was restored, with a full
community of friars. Schormann was appointed prior and gave them
a short but stirring address in June, the month dedicated to the
Sacred Heart, to whom he was greatly devoted. He mentioned how
the establishment of a Novitiate to foster native vocations was now
paramount. This came about on June 11 and Brocard Losert was
appointed Novice Master. Austrian by birth, Schormann arranged
for candidates of Polish descent to enlist, wishing as he did, to work
for the renewal of religious life and attract native vocations. He
hoped that this would lead to the rebirth of the Order in Poland
and the renewal of the Polish Province. Despite the assurances they
were given, all the Poles he had recruited left the Czerna Novitiate
and Schormann had to start again from scratch.

Later on, two other friars also came from the Province of Aquitaine, responding to the call of the Superior General: they were Adrien Dubourdieu, a Frenchman and Bartholomew Díaz de Cerio, a Spaniard. Dubourdieu left Czerna after a few years, while two other aspirants joined the Polish underground. Mary Xavier Czartoryska described the Frenchman as being: "very young and blond, gentle, with St. Gonzaga looks, always courteous and sensitive with French suavity and a willingness to work, with love of neighbor which flows from the love of God." [p. 103].

In the spring of 1882 Schormann, seeing that the reform of Czerna was developing successfully, decided that his presence in Poland was superfluous and he returned to Austria. On April 24 a new prior was elected – Andrew Gatzweiler.

The Austrian Carmel now had four communities where religious observance flourished, namely, Graz, Linz, Gyor (Raab) and Czerna. In November 1882, the new Carmelite General Jerome-Mary Gotti established the Austro-Hungarian Province and appointed Serapion Wenzel as Provincial.[132]

A Goal Attained

Raphael Kalinowski made his Solemn Profession as a Carmelite into the hands of the new General of the Order, Jerome-Mary Gotti – later created cardinal – in Gyor, Hungary, on November 27, 1881.[133] Kalinowski was ordained a priest on January 15, 1882 at

---

[132] In later years, thanks to an influx of candidates, another house was opened in Kraków (1909). Young friars then came to the conclusion that they should become independent of the Austrian Province and create a Polish Semi-Province. Officials of the Generalate of the Order agreed to this (1911). At the time of setting up, the Semi-Province had 56 friars, including 25 priests.

[133] Jerome-Mary Gotti, General of the Order favored the Polish Carmel which he visited twice, and worked hard on the development of the priory in Wadowice. Soon afterwards the Pope made him an Archbishop and appointed him Nuncio in Brazil. After fulfilling his task he returned

the age of 46 by Albin Dunajewski, Archbishop of Kraków. Present at his ordination were his brother Gabriel, Count Romain Bninski, the Capuchin Wenceslaus Nowackowski and Joseph Wasilewski, the former troubled young man now a successful Jesuit priest. All had been his companions in exile. Princess Marcelina Czaroryska provided a dinner to celebrate the occasion.

Dunajewski suffered for the cause of faith and fatherland, and that fact formed a deep and genuine friendship between him and Kalinowski. They supported each other with prayer and counsel. Dunajewski undertook the task of the reorganization of the archdiocese of Kraków. To cope with this, he needed the help of a willing and educated clergy. He worked on this all his life, prayed for this intention and asked the prayers of others, especially the prayer of Carmel. His concerns included not only his archdiocese of Kraków, but the whole of Poland, especially beyond Galicia, still persecuted by the enemies of the Catholic faith.

Kalinowski's ability and worth were quickly recognized. On May 6 the Definitory General appointed him assistant Novice Master. This duty exempted him from work in the church and allowed him to dedicate himself totally to prayer and penitential exercises, something he greatly welcomed. Kalinowski had a special gift for discerning the qualities of young people entrusted to him and if he didn't see in someone either knowledge or virtue, or the qualities required by the Constitution, would let his views be known to the student director and the young man would have to leave the novitiate. He expressed his opinion on the matter: "Do not allow those without the required qualities to be professed, because they will cause many annoyances to superiors." On the other hand he

to Rome where Pope Leo XIII, in recognition of his services, made him a Cardinal. The Pope admired him very much and in his opinion was worthy to be his successor. Pope St. Pius X succeeded instead and appointed Gotti prefect of the Congregation for the Propagation of the Faith. He was honored too by the Beatification of the Carmelite martyrs Dionysius and Redemptus by Pope Leo XIII on June 10, 1900.

would encourage those who seemed to possess the right qualities to stay. When tempted to leave he would tell them: "Stay a few months, just think of it as penance for your sins."

Further promotion followed for Kalinowski. In December 1882 he was appointed Prior at Czerna for the first time. It was a tremendous expression of confidence in him by his superiors. He proceeded to enrich the work of reform already begun there by helping to keep it viable. He did not, of course, carry out the reform of religious life in Czerna himself – this had been done before his arrival – but his subsequent work in fact led to the redevelopment of the Order in Poland. "The basic problem of reviving the Order was the lack of good native vocations." Częslaus Gil Losert would succeed him as Prior of Czerna in 1885 and Drescher in turn would succeed the latter after less than a year. Drescher only completed two years of office before being succeeded again by Kalinowski.

Andrew Gatzweiler became second Definitor Provincial and Master of Novices. At the same time, Rybka returned to Graz in Austria, to help in the church there, together with Drescher who had also returned home previously.

The new prior in Czerna commented, some time after his appointment: "My vocation to Carmel was the happy ending of my initial struggle, which ended in victory for the glory of the Divine Master – I mean the grace of my religious profession and ordination. I owe it all to the intercession of people whose sharing and other good deeds brought to birth in me remarkable Christian love and an awareness of how much the Savior sacrificed for me. The names of these good deeds are written in the hearts of Jesus and Mary, and when we get to heaven you will see them." [p. 104].

A month after becoming prior in Czerna, Kalinowski wrote to the Prioress of the Convent on Łobzów: "Because of the office which recently fell to me, a new link has been forged in the chain and it has made me a prisoner for life. People who put this chain on me should really help me carry it, so please Mother, accept my deep respect and gratitude for all the good providences that God has given me through your community." [p. 104].

In the first chapter of the old Carmelite Constitutions it was stated that in correspondence, unless otherwise required by the dignity of the person to whom you were writing, or the importance of the case, you should only use a half sheet of paper! This was just an insignificant detail in Carmelite houses but Kalinowski didn't neglect it. There are many letters written by him from the time he entered Carmel, and some of them are written even on quarter pages.

Carmelites were, in his eyes, the suffering members of the mystical body of Jesus Christ. He would say: "Our Divine Savior spoke to people and completed his mission among them, speaking even as a victim from the pulpit of the Cross. And also over the centuries Jesus teaches people and involves them in his ministry by means of the expiation made by his suffering members. The good thief was drawn to him, and there are many other witnesses to the final completion of the work of redemption. In this way the Church, the body of Christ complements the divine mission of Jesus." [p. 106].

These words of Kalinowski are a summary of his whole life, and of all the teachings he gave the community in conferences each week. He himself lived the interior life, completely detached from the affairs of the world, in solitude and silence, in union with Christ and fully devoted to the service of God and neighbor.

"Raphael highly valued the inner life," wrote his colleague Diaz de Cerio, "and practiced it. To the very end his life was one of prayer, silence, solitude, meditation, mortification and penance." Diaz de Cerio lived in Poland for 40 years and helped Kalinowski very effectively in his work of reform.

When Kalinowski finally found his happy solitude, which he had sought for so long, he devoted himself entirely to the practice of the interior life. Reading the works of Teresa and John of the Cross, he knew the route to be followed from the beginning of conversion – in St. Benedict's phrase, *conversio mores* (Conversion of life). He was happy to meet the challenge and, strengthened and encouraged by his new zeal, proceeded to meet further challenges. These would extend even to the observance of minutiae, as noted above in regard to his observance of poverty.[134]

Here are a few examples of his zeal even if we think it misplaced. The chapel of the Discalced Carmelite Convent in Przemyśl[135] was painted with murals by famous artist Tadeusz Popiel (1902). As the Prioress Anna Kalkstein puts it: "Fr. Kalinowski came to us in passing, I knew beforehand that he didn't want to go and watch the work of Mr. Popiel, but one of our priests asked him to come and view it but he refused with the comment, 'I'm afraid to commit imperfections by viewing it.'" [p. 111].[136]

Kalinowski loved the Czerna priory where he spent the greater part of his religious life. His confessor wrote: "There, far from the world, he enjoyed his solitude, and could repeat with St. Bernard, 'O happy solitude, sole happiness.'" [p. 111].[137]

In another letter the same person – his confessor – wrote: "I cannot describe his love for contemplation and solitude. His poor cell seemed to him to be a heaven, where he enjoyed a foretaste of the happiness of the saints. The feeling of peace, which he experienced there, pervaded everything in his life... While engaged in meditation there the Lord spoke to him, his faithful servant, and he in turn spoke in prayer to the Heart of God."[138]

---

[134] In Czerna and Kraków it was noted that he never used a mirror, even when shaving.

[135] An ancient town in south-eastern Poland on the border with Ukraine.

[136] It is not clear what troubled Kalinowski's conscience in this matter. From this distance we are entitled to think that this was somewhat narrow-minded behavior, as in the case of avoiding the use of a shaving mirror.

[137] The Latin is more expressive and rhythmic: "O Beata Solitudo, O Sola Beatitudo." The phrase is attributed to Roman philosopher Seneca and was taken up by St. Bernard of Clairvaux. It was part of an inscription over the entrance to Czerna priory.

[138] "The sweetness of the religious life!" – We read in his notes and memos – "to work for one's own salvation and for that of others, to assist in saving

In his biography of St. John of the Cross, Fr. Chrisogono OCD tells us that on one occasion John was asked, and expected by his community, to visit the city authorities and thank them for various services rendered to the community. He refused. But after some pressure he agreed to meet the councillors; after apologizing to them for his lapse he discovered that they were happy simply knowing that he was praying for them. That was all they expected.[139] John was able to use this outcome to justify his stance! Kalinowski took the same approach: "Let us put an end, to the desire to conduct correspondence, except in cases where the good of souls and the duty of love is involved." [p. 114]. And what Kalinowski advised others, he observed as strictly as possible himself. He wrote letters only when there was a need to raise the spirits of colleagues and friends, some of whom were still exiled under Russian rule and deprived of spiritual comfort.

Silence predisposes the person to become aware of God and adds strength to the quest for God. St. John of the Cross advised silence, and the Rule of Carmel, with its goal of union with God, places strong emphasis on silence and the avoidance of unnecessary conversation during the day. Kalinowski affords an example in this respect, though it sounds somewhat affected to our modern sensibilities. When his youngest brother Jerzy visited him and asked for advice on his future, Kalinowski counselled him to first of all do an eight-day retreat. He naturally turned to his brother asking for a directed retreat. When the conference had taken place, it was time for the Great Silence. [p. 114].[140] "Joseph," Jerzy said, "I want you to talk to me." But his older brother put his finger to his lips as a sign that he was no longer allowed to speak, and the spiritual conversation

---

souls for Jesus." The Carmelite Rule stipulates: "Each one should remain in his cell or near it, meditating day and night on the law of the Lord."

[139] Chrisogono De Jesus, *The Life of St. John of the Cross* [Translated by Kathleen Pond] (Longman: Green and Co, 1958).

[140] In monasteries and religious houses, this ran from after Night Prayer until after Morning Prayer the following day.

had to be postponed until next day! Then he immediately got up and left, without saying a word.

Kalinowski read with interest and with pencil in hand the conferences of Carmelite Ferdinand Wuillaume, given in Paris on the inner life and prayer. He seems to have completely assimilated these, to the extent of making Wuillaume's thoughts his own and he would share them in his own conferences. Certainly they mirror exactly Kalinowski's own reflections as found elsewhere in his writings. Here are some thoughts from Wuillaume as outlined by Kalinowski: "Search for God, try to get to know Him, and think only of Him, love Him with all my heart – that's really the best way to live; work to deepen those feelings; the inner life grows strong ... so that we will never grow weary, and each day brings a new store of consolations."

I will now paraphrase rest of Wuillaume's spiritual advice. The first step in the inner life is the awareness of the presence of God within us in every circumstance. We are then close to God and His work is easy, we fight bravely and suffer with peace and submission. We work for such a good and loving Father, and if He allows us to experience suffering, God does so for our own good. With God! That thought is firmly etched in our hearts, a sweet and comforting word; it brings peace, strength and hope.

The second step in the inner life is listening to the voice of God, Father and Friend, who wishes to converse with us. The life of the saints is a continual conversation of God, with the soul and the soul with God, a continuous exchange of thoughts and feelings, without noise of words. Sometimes God gives someone a conviction of his love, draws and attracts her to once again speak confidentially to her heart: "My child," He says, "come to me and I will come to you, and you will respond to me; you will speak to me, and I will respond."

But to pray in such a way as to be aware of God and hear God's words, you need to maintain reverent silence and recollection.

Prayer is primarily a matter of the heart and an exchange of thoughts and feelings between God and ourselves. Filial confidence is absolutely essential for the person who wishes to converse with God.

In order to speak to God, do not seek out beautiful thoughts, or calculated words. Speak to God just as the heart feels. God does not need your flattery or promises, nor forced assurances, God just wants your heart.

If your imagination wanders, try to rest in the presence of God. The freedom of filial love will not allow you to offend against the reverence we owe to God.

Even living in the world, you can experience the intimate presence of God. You just need a little solitude and time to focus every day. [p. 116-119].

In that final maxim it is obvious that Kalinowski wanted not only to see Carmelites practice the inner life of prayer; he knew from personal experience that this great benefit can be enjoyed by the laity. And the rest of our story proves that he never neglected anything that would make it easier for those he directed to experience the joy of the Divine Indwelling.

Chapter Two

Renewal at Czerna 1885–1889

*T*he Carmelite friars in the communities at Graz and Gyor, in the Austrian-Hungarian Province, knew and appreciated Kalinowski's unique qualities. They wished the whole Province could benefit from the experience he had acquired in Siberia over a period of 10 years of unswerving fidelity to grace through suffering and prayer. The Carmelite sisters in Kraków were also waiting for the day when he could become their confessor. At the Provincial Chapter in 1885, Kalinowski was elected Councillor and it would be his duty to meet with the Provincial and the three other Councillors two or three times a year. He would participate in those meetings in Linz, Austria, where they discussed all matters temporal and spiritual affecting the life of the Province.

Since 1883, after the death of Andrew Gatzweiler, Kalinowski was *extraordinary confessor*[141] to Kraków Carmelite sisters and this entailed going to visit them four times a year, making the arduous journey from Czerna to Kraków. Around this time Serapion Wenzel, the Provincial, sent Kalinowski to expedite matters regarding a projected foundation of sisters in the nearby city of Przemyśl.

---

[141]   This was a the name for a confessor who heard nuns confessions on a few occasions in the year so as to provide a choice for the community.

Although he had only been ordained a priest since January 1882, Kalinowski had already proved his worth, prepared for this by long years of suffering, and a life of steadfast fidelity to prayer and religious exercises.

Naturally gifted as he was and having acquired a sound all-round education, Kalinowski had the gift of discernment, which made him capable of directing anyone. But he was especially adept at directing religious, and particularly those of his own Order. He became their father, brother, and devoted friend. The needier the person was, the more his kindness and compassion showed. Częslaus Gil comments: "Those who knew Fr. Raphael emphasized that although he could be very accommodating to lay people, he was very demanding of nuns and friars."[142] Some sisters regarded him as authoritarian but others sought him out.

Needless to say, St. John of the Cross was also a great inspiration for the Carmelite sisters at the beginning of St. Teresa's Reform. He was always concerned about their spiritual growth and Kalinowski certainly followed him in this; we might say he was a director after John's heart. Sometimes it was thought that John was a bit too harsh and that he directed the sisters through fear, rather than love. St. Teresa, however, disagreed with this verdict, holding that fear and love should not be separated.

When Kalinowski seemed to be somewhat harsh on some of the nuns, the apparent severity was simply prudence and indeed charity on his part. He knew that one unnecessary word can disturb the equilibrium of a person and prevent her rising to God. To use an image from St. John of the Cross, even the smallest thread can prevent the bird rising above the ground and flying away, and if it tries to fly without having broken the thread it will be unsuccessful.[143]

---

[142] Częslaus Gil OCD, Father Raphael Kalinowski (Kraków: Carmelite Fathers, 1979).

[143] St. John Of the Cross, 'Ascent of Mount Carmel,' Ch.11.

211

St. Teresa wrote of one of her confessors that despite his wide theological knowledge, he did great harm, because of shortcomings in his knowledge of the Carmelite spirit. Several sisters from the Convent in Łobzów experienced the same problem, and even more so than in Teresa's time; they had been deprived of priests of their own Order who could share the Carmelite spirit with them. Despite the exhortations of Kalinowski, it was difficult for them to get back on track. Teresa Steinmetz who was Prioress on no less than five occasions in Łobzów illustrates this:

> I have not written yet about Fr. Raphael as a confessor. It is true that soon we were fortunate to have him and the memory of that year and what I owe the good Father, remains with me always. You can really say that I was progressing one step at a time, according to his own expression, and that he guided me like a guardian angel, looking out for where one stumbled and fell. Not a word or thought escaped his vigilance, and amazingly he was able to correctly guess my needs in many cases. The Lord gave us an ideal Father, not suited perhaps to all the community but ideal for those who were happy with him. It was a very difficult time for our community, something I had not encountered up to then. I think I would have taken a wrong turn without this angel guide and I was so happy under his direction. The result was a deeper union of hearts and minds in our community, which, by the grace of God, still continues. We had the opportunity to observe closely the charity and humility of our good Father. At that time, the senior sisters were not impressed with him. They gave him to understand that he was not their choice, but those who were most opposed to him, afterwards became his keenest followers. ... May God be blessed who enlightened us and helped us understand the benefit of spiritual guidance from our dear fathers. I was happy that I was directed by him from early on,

and please God, I can continue like this to the end... One event especially helped to finally convince us of the value of Fr. Raphael's direction. One of the sisters in Łobzów initially wished to make a retreat under his guidance. She was endowed with extraordinary gifts of nature and grace. Here's what she wrote about the retreat: With a very stern expression Father gave me a book called: "The Lord Blasts the Cedars of Lebanon."[144] By giving me this book, he assured me that it would clip my wings and make me walk on the ground. I admit that during these spiritual exercises I not only walked, but sometimes had to crawl, so demanding was he! One needs to add that Father Raphael, who came from Czerna, devoted a lot of time to some sisters, but sometimes he left without even seeing me. I only heard his reports on my situation a little later. [p. 123].

In addition to the demands of religious life, Kalinowski's strength was exhausted from ministry in Czerna, with only two other colleagues, Rybka and Drescher to help him. There was also moral suffering. Several of the friars at first failed to recognize his good qualities which he tended to conceal. But over time this changed also, just as with the nuns in Kraków, and the friars became more appreciative of him. When Kalinowski tried to carry through a reform in Czerna, he soon found that some of the friars were not prepared to live according to its requirements and asked for secularization. This was a new and painful blow to him as it was for Hermann Cohen in similar circumstances in France.

Kalinowski worked not only in Czerna and Łobzów, but the Convent at Wesoła also owed its renewal and development to him. One of the sisters at the latter Convent left a testimony to the great

---

[144] Martin Rubczyński O. Carm, *The Lord Blasts the Cedars of Lebanon* (Berdychev: 1768).

work Kalinowski carried out for her community, and she said, that thanks to him it was able to "rise like a phoenix from the ashes."

It's interesting to note that when in 1882 Kalinowski was ordained a priest, the novitiate doors of the Carmelite Convents in Kraków had been closed for some time – in Łobzów for two years, in Wesoła for 12 years, but both were opened again shortly afterwards and some excellent candidates were admitted to profession. These became the future of Carmel in Poland – in Kraków and Przemyśl and in Lviv in Ukraine. The same year, 1882, the Archbishop of Kraków, Albin Dunajewski who worked with great zeal to reform his diocese, and gave great support to the Carmelites, suggested founding a new convent, under his own jurisdiction. One of the sisters of the Convent at Łobzow, Mary Angel Trzmielewska agreed to this and a new convent was opened the same year in Wieliczka, a small town near Kraków.[145]

We do not know exactly what happened in that house, but things didn't go so well and in 1888, a report was filed: "By order of the public authority, the former monastery, which was threatened with ruin because of damp, was razed to its foundations and the sisters are going to settle in another city." When in 1885 the Carmelite General Jerome-Mary Gotti visited the Province, the Archbishop told him about this convent and pleaded: "Please release me from this ball and chain around me like a galley slave." [p. 127]. Soon after this meeting the convent came under the jurisdiction of the Order, and in 1888 the community settled in Lviv or Leopoli as it was also known.[146]

New Foundation at Przemyśl

On the eve of St. Teresa's feast, October 14, 1883, the Provincial Wenzel came to the Convent of Łobzów to discuss with the sisters

---

[145] This is the site of the famous Salt Cathedral. It is a most impressive sight, visited by 1.2 million visitors annually.

[146] There seems to have been internal dissension in the convent and Sr. Mary Angel left the Order in 1891.

214

the matter of a new foundation in Przemyśl. Kalinowski was still prior in Czerna and soon had to travel to Linz and submit plans for the project to the Provincial Definitory. He faithfully fulfilled his task with the referral of plans and the foundation was duly approved. Anne Kalstein, the third to be professed in the Poznan community, was appointed Prioress and the following year she moved to Przemyśl in the company of Kalinowski and Canon Stanislaus Spis, together with four other sisters from Mieczysław.[147] The hardship involved in bringing about this successful foundation took its toll on Andrew Gatzweiler who died of pneumonia a few weeks after his return from the Provincial Council.

The clergy of Przemyśl were hard-working, and some, like Bishop Pelczar, became quite renowned in the Polish Church.[148] St. Teresa would be happy perhaps with the choice of venue for the foundation. Though the house was quite small it was simple in design and situated on a hill above the town. Sr. Anne, the founder of the new Convent, commented: "Fr. Raphael brought us to Przemyśl (February 29, 1884) accompanied by Canon Spis, our confessor. He stayed two days and apparently was sorry to depart without finalizing the enclosure and having to leave us in such great poverty. He was with us again in the summer and was happy that the enclosure had been settled in this small residence. I always enjoyed it despite the great constraints of the building." [p. 128].

Kalinowski, in fact, was always proud of this Convent and its community. There was really something special about Przemyśl, and when, a few years after the house had been set up, Gotti, the

---

[147] Canon Spis who belonged to the Diocese of Przemyśl was weekly confessor. He was a professor and later rector of the Jagiellonian University in Kraków and for many years confessor to the Carmelites. He was very dedicated to them and wrote a commentary on the liturgical Mass of St. Teresa.

[148] He was canonized by Pope John Paul II on May 18, 2003. Canonized with him were three others including Ursula Ledochowska who was beatified on the same day as Raphael Kalinowski.

General of the Order, came in 1885 for the canonical visitation already mentioned, he rejoiced to see so much zeal and dedication despite great poverty. Kalinowski accompanied Gotti everywhere and provided for his needs. The General relied on him and benefited from his advice, turning to him in all matters pertaining to the Carmelites in Poland. The Prioress of Łobzów, Sr. Teresa, spoke about Kalinowski's humility and charity, two virtues that were indeed the basis of his character. Kalinowski also asked God for the gift of humility in a prayer which he composed during his exile in Smolensk: "God, grant me humble simplicity, let me not regard myself greater than I am and don't let me appear exteriorly to others any different to what I am before you, who penetrates the secrets of my heart! Let people judge our work, talent and virtue, without either flattery or jealousy, but in a spirit of truth, personal dignity and love."[149]

"He never tried to impose his opinion or viewpoint on someone," writes Jerzy about his brother, "and he once said to me: 'don't give advice to anyone who doesn't ask for it,' and he always respected that principle."

Humility was the source of Kalinowski's affableness and patience. In his own eyes he was a great sinner, and he felt he deserved all the suffering that befell him and any humiliation he received. Kalinowski admitted to weaknesses; he always found a way to praise the virtues of his neighbor, and effaced himself. He even feared for his salvation, for persevering to the end, and often commended himself to the prayers of others. His colleague de Cerio, who lived in community with him for many years, said that he only once saw Kalinowski tetchy and that was because of the attitude of a businessman who disregarded the rights of the community. But when circumstances required it Kalinowski could be strong and unwavering and he demonstrated this in 1884.

---

[149] From Kalinowski's book, *Be Holy.*

Czernenskie Hill on the Carmelite property in Czerna was rich in iron ore and in the early 19th century, after the decline of observance in the priory, the community paid little attention to their rights and privileges, or were perhaps quite unaware of them. When a local company planned to extract iron ore in the area, a new road was constructed on the Carmelite property without the knowledge of the friars, and it had been marked on the map as public. In 1881, a Jewish businessman named Gustave Bresaluer had received permission from the government for exploration of the old wells, and to carry out new drilling inside and outside the walls of the Carmelite enclosure. The land beyond the walls of the property belonged to Count Andrew Potocki. Kalinowski was still a student in Hungary when the problem arose. The Czerna community, almost all the members from other countries, made a contract allowing Breslauer to convey the ore mined from the wells on Count Potocki's land along the road leading through the enclosure. This license was renewed annually. The contract meant this was very disruptive to the priory, which was a novitiate needing quiet and silence. There were loud conversations in the area, together with singing and shouting from the workers who gathered after meals at their leisure time.

When Kalinowski became Prior he understood, better than anyone else, the inconvenience to the community and when the ore deposits within the enclosure had been exhausted, he forbade the transportation of the ore by the road leading through the Carmelite property. There was a public road nearby equally convenient, but somewhat longer, and the carters would not use it, urged on as they were by the clerk of works and by a neighbour, as well as the Jewish businessman. Kalinowski, however, refused to give in. He studied the matter carefully and was confident of the rights of the community. The process came before the court in Krzeszowice, which agreed with him. The opponents appealed to the court of Kraków, who carefully examined the matter and confirmed the judgment of the first court. The local prefect ordered the map to be amended and the road within the enclosure to be re-entered as belonging exclusively to the Carmelites. Henceforth no one was allowed to use this road without permission from the community, so through the efforts of Kalinowski they were assured of a peaceful environment.

Just before this, the local parish, which included the village of Czerna, decided to build a new church, and collect the necessary money for it. The landlord, Count Andrew Potocki, agreed to cover most of the costs and the parishioners, if possible, would make up the rest. The Committee also earmarked the Carmelite priory to contribute a certain sum, namely 6,000 francs. Prior Schormann left it to Kalinowski, his First Councillor, to reach a settlement on the matter. Kalinowski told the local pastor that the friars were exempt from the jurisdiction, not only of the pastor, but even the bishop. Moreover, the Carmelites would not benefit from any ministries in the parish church; they had their own church that they themselves had built and maintained, and so could not be considered as parishioners and ought not pay this sum. A process was started and the Carmelites lost the case before the local court in Krzeszowice. An appeal was made to the Ministry in Vienna, where their opponents had powerful protectors and they lost the appeal there also. Kalinowski then went to great lengths to successfully address the problem. He studied the law for Austrian Galicia, and got competent advice, because he was fully convinced he had a good case. Not discouraged by the ruling of the minister for religious affairs, he appealed to the Supreme Court, which reconsidered the matter and ruled that the priory in Czerna was free from any burden proceeding from the parish, as it maintained its own church. "The process was carried out," writes Diaz de Cerio, "with great tenacity by both sides, but with fairness and the pastor, Jan Polowiec in fact remained a friend of the Carmelites." [p. 137].

For Kalinowski love of God and neighbor meant making sacrifices for both. He would say: "The first duty of love is towards our own, next we love those for whom we are able to do good, in other words – we should pay our debts first and then give alms to others. It's the same with the law of God: first, love God, through whom we exist, then my family, those who belong to me, after that those with whom I live – parents, one's neighbor. And again: God made me, for himself, so I should live for God, justice requires it, and my happiness depends on it. I have often repeated this truth, to instil it deep into my memory." [p. 137].

Kalinowski's Idea of Meaningful Suffering Leads Him to Join the 'Association for a Happy Death'

Kalinowski never ceased reminding people of the value of suffering in their lives. He comforted them and gave them courage, pointing to the need for and the benefits to be derived from suffering. What he taught by word of mouth, he backed up by example: his whole life was like a school of suffering, which he endured with remarkable patience. In 1890, Kalinowski received a new stimulus to his zeal. A certain man, who experienced an incurable disease, was worried that he was not utilizing his suffering to best advantage as a Christian. And seeing many other people around him in similar circumstances, he came to the conclusion that Divine Providence would want to use such suffering for the good of people.

The idea of the 'Association for a Happy Death' emerged and first circulated in England on October 13, 1884. This Association was widespread at the time in Scotland, Ireland, France, America and Africa, and received the approval of many bishops and cardinals, and was praised by many hospitals and superiors of religious congregations. About 12 years after its inauguration, the Bishop of Shrewsbury in England asked the Pope's permission for the establishment of the Association worldwide and the appointment of directors to propagate it. This was done on March 28, 1886. At the request of Lord Thomas Longueville, founder and first Guardian of the Association, it was entrusted to the care of Our Lady, Health of the Sick, St. Camillus de Lellis and St. John of God, and aggregated to the Congregation of Canons Regular of St. Augustine. It would thus come under the patronage of the General of the Congregation.

In 1890, a pamphlet printed in Tournai described the setting up of the Association with its rules and privileges. This pamphlet fell into the hands of Kalinowski, who immediately felt that much good could be achieved by such an Association. He reached an agreement with Lord Longueville, promoter of the Association and began to spread this apostolate. An Association for the incurably sick was started in Galicia, in the Kingdom of Poland and in Lithuania.

In October, there was a lot of work to be done in Czerna to cope with the big influx of people on the feast of St. Teresa, but due to illness Kalinowski had to remain in his room. He offered his suffering to the Lord thinking of those who suffered like him, but may not have known how to use their suffering in a positive way. He wrote to his friend in Warsaw, Louise Młocka sending her two cards with a letter from the Association for the terminally ill. One was for a sick friend and the other for a sick sister Carolina Nowowiejska. A little later, with the help of Teresa Moruzi, the first member of the Association in Poland, he had produced some information in Polish about it and made membership cards of the Association available. This would facilitate the dissemination of a group that brought consolation to the sick, giving them the means to sanctify their suffering.

Kalinowski as a Spiritual Guide

The compassion, kindness and dedication of Kalinowski attracted a great variety of people to him: small and great, rich and poor, saints and sinners, and he became all things to all in order to win all for Christ. Diaz de Cerio, who had lived with him in the same house, wrote of him:

> Father Raphael was only in Czerna for a few months, when people of the area already knew what a treasure they

possessed. They came to him in distress, in suffering and in all their deepest needs and not for anything did they come. He always received them with great kindness, compassion, throwing light in time of doubt and gaining the hearts of all by his goodness... He liked to talk to the village people... I loved him as a father, and sought his advice. In particular, he gave advice in sensitive family issues, especially to those troubled in conscience; and everyone went away enlightened, comforted and ready to withstand the troubles of life, if not with joy, at least with patience and resignation. This Christian charity that people sometimes so desperately needed was never refused, and for that purpose he never hesitated to sacrifice his rest and health. [p. 165].

Kalinowski also carefully searched out and cultivated religious vocations among his penitents. In the early years at Czerna a girl came for the Sacrament of Penance. She received her First Holy Communion from her uncle who was a priest. The girl had been well brought up and from what she later wrote one could see that she had been a beautiful person. It occurred to Kalinowski to recommend her to join a convent. He tried to develop good qualities in her, and especially the spirit of sacrifice, that can so readily take root in young hearts. Ten years later she entered Carmel.

In regard to the religious call of his brother Jerzy, he wrote: "You need to persevere – imitate our Savior, who was obedient unto death, even death on a cross. In the virtue of obedience, you will find all treasures." [p. 170]. Kalinowski held that if God calls a person to his service, they should respond promptly to this call. But if you don't see signs of a true vocation, if the person is guided by purely human considerations, or if unstable, sullen, or had been expelled from another religious congregation, he was adamant that that person should be refused permission to join. In that case no amount of pleading would sway him. As a spiritual director in Kraków he enjoyed general respect. Here's what one of the Polish Carmelites wrote; "My cousin, being in great uncertainty and anxiety about choice of career, told me that in Kraków she was advised to go and see Fr. Kalinowski (she did not know that I knew him), because he is a holy priest and has a very enlightened and impartial manner and whose opinion can be completely relied on." [p. 171].

Surely a fitting endorsement of a reliable spiritual guide!

Chapter Three

Carmel is All Mary's

In the previous chapter I touched on topics that epitomize St. Raphael Kalinowski – themes like love of Christ and the Church, Eucharist and Priesthood. In the present chapter we turn to an all-encompassing theme that permeates Kalinowski's life; that is his relationship with Mary the mother of the Lord. Here we encounter the one whom Kalinowski regards as his and his country's Queen. As we reflect on this central aspect of his faith from our present-day vantage point, we look to the teaching of Vatican Council II, 50 years on. There we find Chapter 8 of the Constitution *Lumen Gentium* treating of Mary's role in the Church. In Par. 65 we read:

> We turn our eyes to Mary who shines forth on the whole community of believers as a model of virtues. Faithfully meditating on her and contemplating her in light of the Word made man, the church enters more intimately into the great mystery of the Incarnation... For Mary unites in herself the great teachings of faith... and so she calls believers to her Son and his sacrifice and to the love of the Father. Seeking the glory of Christ, the church becomes more like her and

Timothy Tierney

progresses in faith, hope and love, seeking and doing the will of God in all things.

And again in Par. 68:

Just as the Mother of Jesus, glorified in body and soul in heaven, is the image and beginning of the church as it is to be perfected in the world to come, so too, does she shine forth on earth, until the day the Lord comes, as a sign of sure hope and solace to the People of God during its sojourn on earth.

These Council statements were subsequently echoed by Pope Paul VI in his Encyclical *Marialis Cultus*. But in the context of Raphael Kalinowski, it makes sense to refer to the great Encyclical of the Polish Pope John Paul II on the same subject – *Redemptoris Mater*. There the Pope wrote:

This presence of Mary finds many different expressions in our day, just as it did throughout the Church's history. It also has a wide field of action. Through the faith and piety of individual believers; through the traditions of Christian families or 'domestic churches,' of parish and missionary communities, religious institutes and dioceses; through the radiance and attraction of the great shrines where not only individuals or local groups, but sometimes whole nations and societies, even whole continents, seek to meet the Mother of the Lord, the one who is blessed because she believed, is the first among believers and therefore became the Mother of Emmanuel. This is the message of the Land of Palestine, the spiritual homeland of all Christians because it was the homeland of the Savior of the world and of his Mother.

And having mentioned the well-known shrines of Mary in Lourdes, Fatima and Guadalupe, the Polish Pope says he cannot omit a reference to Jasna Gora in his native land. We can only imagine how Raphael Kalinowski would have rejoiced had he lived to read this Encyclical from the man born in Wadowice only 13 years after he himself had died there.

All the evidence points to the fact that Raphael Kalinowski was a devoted servant of Mary.[150] She has been long regarded by Carmelites as the inspiration of their Order, and moreover, for Kalinowski, was Queen of Poland and Duchess of Lithuania! He tells us how from childhood his parents taught him to love Mary. I mentioned earlier how, when working as an engineer in St. Petersburg, a simple recitation of the Ave Maria brought him great peace in the midst of danger. Again in his notes, written while exiled in Siberia, he cites her beautiful privileges of Immaculate Conception and glorious Assumption. On the day of his religious profession he promised God and Our Lady of Mount Carmel to try to persevere until death in a life of obedience, chastity and poverty. He understood what this promise entailed and we can safely say his life was one long act of devoted love for God and Mary.

In a booklet he wrote to mark the Marian Congress at Leopoli (Lwov or Lviv) in 1905, at which he was invited to give a Conference, Kalinowski stated: "Carmelites are the first-born of Mary." Then he tells us that, following the tradition of their Father Elijah, they were the first to build a chapel to Mary on Mt. Carmel. Here Kalinowski

---

[150] On this subject see the excellent article in Italian by Szecepan T. Praskiewicz, "Maria sempre e in tutto," in Teresianum, Rome, XLI 1990/1. This phrase means, Mary always and in all things which was a motto of Kalinowsksi. As he rightly points out Kalinowski's intuitions on Mary's role in the church is echoed by the Lumen Gentium and the Decree on Ecumenism of Vatican II: the cult of Mary is one of the factors that makes for common ground between the Eastern Orthodox Church and the Roman Catholic Church. The same thought can be found in Redemptoris Mater (Par 31) of John Paul II.

exploits a pious tradition about the little cloud mentioned in the Book of Kings being a figure of Mary. For him she could be regarded as the Founder of the Order. He continues: "It is she who, according to the expression of Pope Gregory VIII, has spiritually engendered them and nourished them with her milk." He further holds that it was the Virgin Mary who gave the strength to the Polish church to withstand attacks from all sides. And so as a true Pole he was happy to install her as "Queen of the Kingdom of Poland."[151]

In Kalinowski's own words, redolent of an earlier era – and now perhaps somewhat dated, at least in regard to religious affiliation – he asked: "To whom does it fall to reign over this nation situated on the borders of Christianity, unless it be the most holy mother of God? Who better to give us the strength to defend the sacred truths of faith against the unbeliever, the schismatic and the heretic? Who else could so ardently desire the propagation of the faith, unless she the most pure Mother of God, the immaculate Virgin Mary? During her earthly life she had the mission of watching over the child Jesus and protecting the infant Church, the holy and unique source of the true faith."[152]

Similar sentiments had a longstanding tradition in Poland both before and after Kalinowski's time and – minus the anti-ecumenical overtones – have been echoed in our own time by Saint John Paul II. Kalinowski found the prospect of writing for the Congress somewhat daunting and remarked at the beginning: "When we read about the

---

[151] The title of the booklet in English would be "The cult of the Mother of God in the Polish Carmel" (Leopoli-Warsaw, 1905). A Pre-Conciliar Preface for Our Lady of Mt. Carmel states the tradition thus: 'Who through a little cloud ascending from the sea wonderfully foreshadowed the Immaculate Virgin Mary to the blessed Prophet Elijah, and you willed that her cult should be followed by the sons of the prophet' (Carmelite Missal, 1922).

[152] In spite of the strong words employed here Kalinowski was in reality quite sensitive to the Orthodox and in his Memoirs asserts that he has "no intention of offending any member of the Orthodox clergy."

lives of the saints, and in general regarding the holiness of famous people, we sometimes feel a certain diffidence, but in reality they turned out to be easy to approach." [p. 174]. Before beginning this pamphlet he resorted to the sacrament of reconciliation, in order to be better prepared to write it, and to feel spiritually close to the luminous beauty of Mary, the Lord's chosen one about whom he wished to treat. In the same booklet Kalinowski wrote, among other things:

> The Marian tradition of Carmel is the heritage that has been passed on to us and that we have accepted in coming to Carmel. We ought to preserve it by our activity where possible, and by our penance and prayer where that isn't possible... Believe me, our devotion to Mary is not sufficiently alive. It's a point of the greatest importance for both Carmelite friars and sisters, to honor the most holy Virgin. We show our love when we try to imitate her virtues, her humility, her pondering in prayer, when we work to correct our faults in order to be pleasing to her. We ought to fix our gaze constantly on her and give her all our affection; we ought to remember her gifts to us and always be faithful to her. [p. 174].

Ever practical, Kalinowski translated and had printed a little booklet which he entitled, "Mary always and in all things," which promoted devotion to Mary such as we find in the writings of Julian Grignon de Montfort.

Brown Scapular of Our Lady of Mt. Carmel

Of a piece with his devotion to the Queen of Carmel, Kalinowski was also a great believer in the efficaciousness of the brown scapular of Our Lady of Mt. Carmel, and promoted the scapular everywhere. A young man called Joseph Wasilewski, mentioned already in the course of our story, and who became a Jesuit priest, later helped him spread devotion to the Scapular in Romania. Again, in the booklet of Kalinowski 'Mary Always in All Things,' we read:

> If the statement *All things through Mary* covers all the needs of humanity, then it applies particularly in our own case. Who is to motivate the Order to grow, if not the founder? Special graces received in the churches of Our Lady of Mount Carmel and numerous miracles cheer the heart and lead us to celebrate Our Lady, Founder of Carmel. By accepting the scapular, a sign of salvation, which honors her as the Blessed Mother, Mary increased the number of her servants. Thus, there grew confidence in her mediation and a desire to erect shrines throughout her Order especially in Poland. [p. 175].

In the 17th century, the Carmelite Order had 80 monasteries in Poland, where Carmelites prayed and worked for the Church. Among these, Teresian Carmelites had 27 monasteries, and of those, 15 were along the border from Kamenets Podolski to Vilnius and from Glebokie to Polotsk in Belarus. There, especially together with members of St. Josaphat's Basilians, the Carmelites struggled against the spread of disunity.

Kalinowski holds that the Virgin Mary intervened at that point in the growth of the Order. "The Mother house of the Carmelite family in Poland," he writes, "that belonged to the Carmelites of the ancient observance, still exists in Kraków, known as Na Peskau" (on the sands). J. Dlugosz tells us in his *Liber beneficiorum*, that Ladislaus II, Polish king, and Queen Jadwiga, his wife, "wishing to celebrate in a special way the Virgin Mary Mother of God, and celebrate Mary's Visitation of Elizabeth, built the church and priory, and so introduced a new Order into Poland which up to that time was unknown there. This was for the greater glory of God, and to affirm the growth of the Kingdom of Poland, in the year of Our

Lord 1397." [p. 175]. Devotion quickly developed in the country in honor of the Blessed Virgin Mary of Mount Carmel, and with the development of this devotion in the nation came a desire to build new churches everywhere.

Some Discalced Carmelites were travelling through Kraków in 1604 on their way to Persia to set up a mission there. Ladislaus IV, who was very young at the time, together with some nobility, was enrolled in the scapular by Paul Simon Rivarola, and this made Ladislaus well-disposed to the Order. A year later the first priory of Discalced Carmelite nuns was founded at Wesoła on the outskirts of Kraków and was dedicated to the Immaculate Conception of the Blessed Mary. When travelling through Antwerp, Ladislaus IV met the famous Carmelites Dominic of Jesus and Mary and Blessed Anne of St. Bartholomew, and spent a long and enjoyable time with them.[153]

The prince was accompanied by Stefan Pac, who would later become vice-chancellor of the Grand Duchy of Lithuania. Stefan Pac was a cheerful young man and while he was initially amused by being kept waiting at the Convent grille, was soon peeved by the delay. A holy picture given to the prince by Blessed Anne was revered by the royal family. Years later it came into the possession of Stefan Pac's wife. Her devotion to this picture was derided by her husband. To encourage him to change his ways, she gave him the life of St. Teresa to read. It worked. Stefan Pac became a devout man. He built the Carmelite Church at the Gate of Dawn known as Ostra Brama. Together with his wife he founded the Discalced Carmelite Priory in Vilnius.

---

[153] Spanish-born Dominic Ruzola (1559-1630), miracle worker and papal diplomat, he was famous for his involvement in the 'Battle of the White Mountain, in 1620. Blessed Anne Garcia, (1549–1620), was nurse and secretary to St. Teresa of Jesus and her collaborator in the reform of the Order. She participated in the first foundations in France and Belgium. She was beatified in 1917.

Kalinowski also mentioned the benefits that later Carmelite houses in the Polish provinces derived from devotion to the Mother of God, and what the Carmelites achieved there. He speaks at length about Our Lady of Ostra Brama and Our Lady of Berdychev, which became for Lithuania and Ukraine respectively, what Our Lady of Lourdes meant to France. He maintains that the Carmelite priories were beacons from which the light of faith and devotion radiated far and wide across the country.

Carmelites helped to promote veneration of Mary and the Carmelite spirit, the spirit of penance and prayer, by means of the Scapular Confraternity. Members of the Confraternity were urged to do penance; Kalinowski gives examples taken from the Carmelite Annals. Then he adds some comments himself: "Prayer unites us with God, allowing God to flow into our lives, and it obtains the grace we need from heaven." [p. 175]. He recommended the recital of the Chaplet of Mount Carmel by the Confraternity throughout Poland, which contained a meditation on the sevenfold shedding of the Precious Blood. Kalinowski comments:

> In addition to the ordinary Confraternity there is the Third (or Secular) Order whereby people living in the world who wish to attain spiritual growth are given the opportunity of progressing on the path of Christian perfection under the protection of Mary, thereby promoting her honor. The Scapular Confraternity also promotes communion with the Church together with the opportunity for spiritual exercises, and ensures that the Blessed Mother and Queen doesn't preside over a kingdom without subjects... Looking at the ruins of ancient Carmelite houses, where Mary was venerated as Queen, we must pause and shed tears of regret that after terrible storms only a few light breezes remain indicating her presence; these shrines were lost, leaving only a few survivors, but are slowly coming back to life. But who will restore them if not the same Immaculate Mother... Let

not a profound reverence for her mediation, however, as well as gratitude for her maternal help, vanish from the hearts of the people. In these sanctuaries Mary was hailed as Queen. [p. 180].

Kalinowski encouraged all whom he directed to cultivate the same devotion which he himself had for the Blessed Virgin. Here's the advice which he left the Carmelite family, the Brown Scapular Confraternity and all the faithful on this matter:

We should praise and venerate the one who is the refuge of sinners here on earth and in heaven. We should love the Blessed Virgin, because she is the mother of us all: "Here is your mother." She is a loving mother, because she not only carries us in her bosom, but with Jesus loves us as her children, and helps us in all our needs. She is a gracious and merciful mother for all sinners who draw near to her, a powerful mother because God gave his riches into her keeping. She wants to be loved as mother and says to us: "My son, give me your heart, a heart that is loving, grace filled, focused on my Son; this is what I expect from you first of all." ... Come, Mary, rule over us and direct us. As breathing is not only a sign of life, but also its cause, so the name of Mary should be constantly on the lips of the servants of God, it is a sign that the person is alive. [p. 181].[154]

In these brief remarks gathered from his notes, we see Kalinowski's touching devotion for Mary and his desire to see her loved and revered in Poland, and especially in Carmel.

---

[154] The final thought appears to have come from Herman of Reichenau known as St. Herman the Cripple. He flourished in the eleventh century. The Salve Regina is thought nowadays to have originated with him rather than St. Bernard. The Alma Redemptoris Mater is also attributed to him.

Kalinowski taught with great insistence that devotion to Mary is the way to salvation: "If you want to go to heaven," he said, "call on Mary, because she is the gateway there. The easiest way to achieve salvation is to approach her pure heart, and ask her to intercede with God for us and beg his mercy. I don't need to worry about the person who flees to her and trusts in her, for she speaks to God for us as a mother and obtains for us the grace of forgiveness." And again: "The Queen of heaven and earth serves God and if we serve her well, we shall rule over the world and our enemies for to serve Mary is to reign." [p. 181].

To a Carmelite who complained that she felt like an orphan on earth, Kalinowski retorted, "You say that you are an orphan, and yet you have Mary as your mother!" [p. 182].

When his brother Jerzy asked him for a guideline to help bear the burden of life, he gave this response without hesitation: "The guideline is the grace of our Lord Jesus Christ and we should always ask for it for ourselves and for others, but always through the intercession of the Comforter of the Afflicted, Our Lady and Queen." Again:

> Our Order is proud of the fact that it bears her name, and so we should act more from love than from obligation and work to augment the honor of our mother. ... For some time I feel the interior need to do something that will redound to the glory of Mary. I cannot find anything better than to translate Fr. Maucourant's book, entitled: *Living in union with the Savior*. In this way we find guidelines that we ought to follow, so that we can live in an intimate union with our Savior and follow His Blessed Mother in union with her divine Son, our highest model, and so promote her glory.[155]

---

[155] François Maucourant, *La Vie d'intimate avec le bon Sauveur* (Nevers: 1890).

It was not enough for Kalinowski that he himself labored for Mary; he wanted to enlist others to her standard. In 1892, his brother Jerzy sent him a photograph of Our Lady of Ostra Brama in Vilnius. The sight of it brought to his mind his visits there as a child and revived in him the heartfelt devotion that he always had for her. It recalled the grace he received from the Mother of Mercy, as he admitted. He immediately ordered 20 copies of the image and distributed them to the Carmelite priories in Poland as well as to his friends.

His friend the Capuchin Wenceslaus urged him to write the history of this picture which he did. He later wrote a history of the miraculous image of Our Lady of Berdychev, a town situated in his friend Wenceslas' Ukrainian homeland. He devoted the last years of his life to writing up the story of all the images of Mary revered in Poland and in countries that formerly belonged to it. This work consists of three large volumes. By carefully gathering together all that Mary had meant to Poland and what she had done for the country during times of conflict with the Turks, Tatars and separated Christians, Kalinowski encouraged his friend and helped him in his own good work. He also distributed pictures of beautiful Carmelite churches, such as those of the nuns in Lublin, and of the friars in Lviv, Wisniowiec and several other places.

Kalinowski had a special affection for those dedicated to Our Lady and willing to witness to what she had done for them. He read a book entitled *Annus Marianus* (Marian Year) in which there was a short biography of one or other devotee of Mary for every day of the year, with a description of what he or she had done in her honor. Kalinowski saw this as an effective means of expanding devotion to Mary and so he translated it into Polish.

Many people believed Mary had given the scapular to the Order of Mount Carmel, through the English Carmelite and early General of the Order, St. Simon Stock. From as early as the 13th century the brown scapular made its way through Western nations. While reading the old Carmelite Convent chronicles, Kalinowski saw the

value of the scapular as evidenced there. He attributed to it great
achievements in regard to conversions and in helping good people
persevere and progress on the path of virtue, and so he had a special
respect for this gift of the Mother of God. He duly tried to respond
to Mary's request, recommending the scapular to people whom
he directed and to his penitents. The friars at Czerna followed his
example and soon the brown scapular devotion spread far and wide,
not only in the neighboring parishes, but also around Upper Silesia
and in many parts of the Polish Kingdom under Russian rule. On
Sundays, especially and on solemn feasts of Our Lady, the altar was
besieged by the faithful, requesting the scapular.

Princess Teresa Moruzi, who was attracted by Kalinowski's fame
for holiness in Czerna, was present when crowds of the faithful
received the scapular on one occasion. Then she thought of Romania,
where so many good and well-meaning people sadly spent their
lives in the cold atmosphere of religious indifference, coupled with
the lack of encouragement and comfort that comes from faith and
Christian hope. The princess herself described the situation:

> This small country has had autonomy for only 20 years, it is
> only beginning to develop and grow, organize the military,
> industry, commerce, etc. Religion is always pushed to the
> periphery and no one cares about it. People believe what
> they please, and religious indifference is so great that even
> Catholics baptize their children in schismatic churches.
> They don't do this from malice, but only because it is a
> matter of indifference to them. The Greek schism is the state
> religion. There are a lot of Catholics in Romania but few
> priests to minister to them; and those are mostly engaged
> in the schools. There have never been religious associations

or any confraternities in this country, and no one thought about initiating them. [p. 186].[156]

Kalinowski was spiritual director to the princess for several years, and she usually spent her holidays in the vicinity of Czerna or Wadowice. So he was thoroughly informed about everything that happened in Romania. The Princess knew of his concern and zeal to work for the spiritual good of people deprived of care in that country. Unable as he was to personally come to their aid, Kalinowski used the all-powerful means which is prayer, and prayed so fervently, writes Teresa Moruzi, that he achieved unexpected results.

In May 1893, after a lengthy stay in Wadowice Teresa Moruzi returned to Sulina, Romania; Wenceslaus Nowakowski tells us: "Teresa Moruzi told her pastor in Sulina, Michael Wirwoll, about all she had seen in Czerna and Wadowice, and praised the work of the Carmelites and their devotion to the Mother of God, their austere lives, their night vigils before the Blessed Sacrament, their dedication to the faithful who besiege the confessionals all day and receive the scapular at the hands of the fathers. She said that Fr. Kalinowski, the Prior, is one of the most famous people in the Church in Poland." [p. 186].

There is a letter from the Pastor Wirwoll, who originated from Silesia, saying he had just received a letter from Father Raphael, in which he recommended himself to the Princess. Wirwoll replied: "The Princess and I thank you. On Wednesday we began a novena for your return to health, just before Corpus Christi. It was a wonderful time, the procession was very peaceful. Everything went well and we owe it to you, Father. Apparently you are blest in the eyes of God the Father. ... Thank you very much Father for the pictures and scapulars, and for the authorization for enrolment into the Confraternity." [p. 186].

---

[156] Romania only adopted this name for the area in 1863. It declared independence from the Ottoman Empire in 1877.

For two years, Kalinowski was primarily engaged in promoting the spiritual progress of those who wished to deepen their devotion to the Mother of God in Sulina, Romania. First, he recognized their potential, and then he helped them perform whatever good works of which they were capable. At the Provincial Chapter in 1894, he was again elected Prior of Czerna and the following year their wishes were fulfilled: Teresa Moruzi received canonical permission from the Archbishop in Bucharest to establish the brown scapular Confraternity in Sulina. Kalinowski, encouraged by this first success, wrote to Canon Joseph Baud, Rector of the cathedral in Bucharest and Vicar General, recommending the Confraternity to his care and asking help spread veneration of Our Lady of Mount Carmel in Romania. The Vicar General's reply was friendly and encouraging: "From childhood," he wrote, "I belonged to Carmel, and always wore the scapular, and believe me I would be very happy if you want to bring such a salutary devotion to our communities. In the area I come from there was a Carmelite monastery, next to the big church, which belonged to them. On the many occasions I visited my family home, I always made a visit to this church. I tell you this to assure you that I will do all in my power to carry out your wishes." [p. 189].

In another letter Baud wrote that the church he referred to was that of Laghetto. "When I was a student in the Jesuit College in Monaco, I went to this church every Thursday; my first visit there was in preparation for First Communion. And then I used to have a chat with these good fathers." [p. 189].

At the time when the Vicar General wrote the letter quoted above, Michael Wirwoll, the pastor of Sulina had already received from the General of the Order of Discalced Carmelites the necessary document to set up a Scapular Confraternity in his parish, and Kalinowski sent Baud instructions for organizing and running the group. On July 17, the pastor wrote:

Yesterday we had a great Feast in Sulina. We laid the foundations for the Confraternity of Our Lady of Mount Carmel, and we owe this to the prayers of Father and Princess Moruzi. ... Last Sunday I preached about the Confraternity and the obligations it imposes, encouraging everyone to join. On Monday afternoon, I ordered all the children from school to come to confession. Because of the great heat I announced that Mass would be held tomorrow at 9:30 am and from 5 am I sat in the confessional. ... More people have been to confession than on Maundy Thursday. I celebrated a quiet Mass before the altar of Our Lady, and the church was full. ... Father, there were tears in my eyes looking at these innocent little children, and I recommended them to the care of Our Lady of Mount Carmel. After Mass I gave a lengthy talk on their duties and on the life of St. Simon Stock. At the end, I told them about the original miracle, and then enrolled them in the Scapular. Last Saturday I got a registered letter from Kraków with the pictures which you sent me. Thank you very much. Pray for me and for my Confraternity. [p. 189].

In 1895, before the feast of Our Lady of Mount Carmel, Kalinowski had written to Vicar General Baud in Bucharest and sent some scapulars with permission to enrol the faithful. He gave him instructions as a lead-in to the canonical setting up of the Confraternity. In his reply Baud wrote on August 2: "I am writing to Fr. General with a request to give me permission to set up the Confraternity in our parishes. I'm writing in Italian to ask permission to cover 14 parishes. I'm sure that other priests will be willing to promote the devotion at home."

On August 21 the Pastor of Sulina wrote again, saying he had received 24 people into the Confraternity, among them a separated Christian who had converted to Catholicism in order to have the joy of wearing the scapular. Her name was Elizabeth Mrak. She was the first fruit of the new Confraternity which Kalinowski intended to be an instrument of salvation for Romania. ... The conversion of Elizabeth Mrak was the first but not the last result of their dedication. [p. 189].

Kalinowski also eagerly propagated devotion to the scapular in Poland itself and tried to encourage priests in the surrounding territories to join the Scapular Confraternity. He wrote to a certain Irena Balatowska: "Do try hard to establish the Holy Scapular Confraternity in your parish and become a promoter of devotion to the Blessed Virgin."

In his letters he insisted on how people should pray in relation to wearing the scapular, so that wearing it didn't tend to become routine or border on the superstitious. He translated various spiritual books such as a guide for daily meditations on the Virgin Mary with the intention of publishing them.

In his ministry in the different churches in which he served, Kalinowski transformed them into sanctuaries of Mary of the scapular; Czerna itself became a great pilgrimage center as also St. Joseph's in Wadowice, a house he himself had founded. During his stay in Czerna, group pilgrimages from the Prussian sector of Silesia came to seek spiritual direction from him. Here they would also buy Polish religious books available in the priory.

Though the Carmelite Secular Order and the Scapular Confraternity are distinct they are interrelated. Part of the ceremonial for induction into the Secular Order (as indeed for the other two Orders) is the conferring of the scapular. From the point of view of the Church's formal worship, a scapular, in connection with whatever Order, is called a sacramental, just like holy water or a religious medal. It is called a sacramental because though it is related to the Church's sacraments, it is not part of the seven. A sacramental can prepare and lead up to a fruitful participation in the life of the sacraments, and it can help people prolong this fruitfulness by having a blessed object on their person or in the home. The value of the sacramental does not reside in the object itself but in the rite of blessing carried out by an approved minister of the Church. The rite for the blessing and enrolment in the scapular was approved by a Decree from the Congregation for Divine Worship on January 27, 1989 and signed by Cardinal Martinez. Formal membership of a Confraternity of the brown scapular is not required in order for a person to be enrolled. In the enrolment ceremony the cloth scapular is always used but subsequently a medal can be substituted for this, especially in warmer countries, and according to individual preferences.

Kalinowski also encouraged Jesuits working in Iassy in Romania[157] to propagate devotion to the Scapular. For eight years the Polish Jesuits led seminars in Iassy, but not in the parish church. They heard confessions and preached in three languages. One of the Jesuits was Joseph Wasilewski, nephew of Kalinowski's friend Wenceslas; we remember Wasilewski was looked after by Kalinowski with great solicitude during their stay in Siberia. Kalinowski believed he could call in some favors from a man whose life he once saved! So he wrote to Wasilewski in July 1895, hoping that the Third Order of Our Lady of Mount Carmel could flourish in Romania under the direction of the Jesuit community. Wasilewski wrote on July 5: "Thank you very much for your letter, which after so long a silence, I was not expecting and I know it proceeds from your zeal for the glory of Mary."

The Rector of the Jesuit House, missionary Felix Wiercinski, added that the only Catholic Church in Lassey didn't belong to them. The scapular could be given to those who requested it but they had no Confraternity in place. A very religious young person had already joined the Third Order, and was observing the month-long exercises of St. Ignatius. She preferred to give up the idea of marriage rather than marry an Orthodox Christian who would not agree to the conditions required by the Catholic Church.

---

[157] The second most populous city in Romania, also known as Lassey and Lasi. It is an important cultural centre.

In late July, the Rector went on vacation together with 17 seminarians to the home of one of his colleagues named Andrew Czarnota, pastor of Husi or Husz in Moldova. On July 16, the feast of Our Lady of Mt. Carmel, the scapular was given to 21 people, whose names were sent to Czerna. Czarnota had asked permission for them to be accepted into the Confraternity. "The local population," he wrote, "did not even know what a scapular was; we gave them only to the most devout people. The ceremony was held with great solemnity, and their joy knew no bounds, because – as they say – 'they made a covenant with the Mother of God.'" [p. 191].

Those who received the scapular were surrounded by a crowd of eager people and after the ceremony the people naturally wanted to know what a scapular was. There were about 3,000 people living there and Czarnota was anxious to build a church for the Confraternity.

In a letter written in September Wiercinski gives new names to be included in the Confraternity Register and thanks Kalinowski for pictures, scapulars, and a book received. In February 1896, Wiercinski wrote to Czerna saying the scapular was responsible for many moral miracles in Husi.

"The population is transformed," he said, "They don't over-drink or blaspheme, and since wearing it everyone has changed." A little later Fr. Przembel, Rector of Dunaburger requested Kalinowski for authority to enrol people in the Confraternity and also asked the same faculty for other pastors, Szydłowski, Bondi and Lipski, missionaries in Romania, and he adds: "The scapular produces wonderful effects: improvement of morals, frequenting the sacraments." Kalinowski showed his gratitude to those priests, sending material assistance, as the Catholic people there were very poor.

In September 1896, the Pastor of Sulina wrote: "I have received the scapulars through the instrumentality of Fr. Raphael. Fr. Arndt, a Jesuit priest from Kraków, came here and gave us a learned retreat; we all benefited a lot from it. May God give us that happiness each year. We feel abandoned, and if we're not sinking, it is thanks to a special grace given to us by God because of the merits of a holy person who prays for us as Father prays for me." A few months later, on February 7, 1897 he wrote:

> You're really good and I'm pleased with the news I received in a letter that you are praying for poor Father Michael Wirwoll of Sulina. May God the Father preserve you for years to come for the good of people. When I manage to convert anyone, I say to myself, I owe it to the merits of Fr. Raphael and his prayers. We are few in Sulina and it is difficult to work here. Despite this, Father, I am now sending the names of thirty persons who requested the scapular and among them are Orthodox and Protestants. The latter belong to the family Schnell, who originate from Austria. Four of their children went to our school; one of the daughters was even baptized by me. The oldest of these is the assistant agent on English ships and earns a lot of money, but he went astray frequenting the casino with officers from these ships. The whole family was ashamed of his bad conduct, and his mother came crying to me to confide her worries. I comforted her and told the boy to go to you. He told me that he felt an irresistible attraction to evil, and he asked what he could do about it. I plucked up courage and told him to wear the scapular, and he willingly agreed to do so. I loaned him a book and recommended him to read it. Today he is happy, devout and unwavering in his convictions. His mother came to thank me and brought candles for the church. "Please do not thank me," I told her, "but thank the Mother of God and Father Raphael of Czerna." Three of her daughters are already enrolled in the Confraternity of Our Lady of Mount Carmel. Some time ago I performed the marriage for two people who have been living together for a long time. Everyone, bride, bridegroom and witnesses went to confession and received the Holy Scapular. [p. 192].

The good news delighted Kalinowski and stirred up his zeal. For two years he had been in touch with Franz Jelinek, the Austrian Consul in Romania and his family, who lived in the town of Braila and who were friends of the Moruzi family. Fanny, the Consul's eldest daughter, an intelligent and devout girl, often signed her letters: Child of Mary or Servant of the Sacred Heart. Kalinowski was eager for her to join a convent, and dedicate herself wholly to the service of God, and he used the Scapular Confraternity to realize his plans. He suggested to Fanny, that she could help him start the Scapular Confraternity in Braila and gave her the necessary information with a request for the parish priest to enrol people. The letter was sent in early February (1897) and the answer came at the end of March:

> Reverend Father, after all the proofs of kindness which I received from you, my thanks is overdue. This is because of my mother's illness. It was hard work and, apart from this I had to stand in for our housekeeper and carry out her duties, so I could not write sooner. With the help of your good prayers my mother is almost completely better but not home yet. Father speaks of you with great esteem and recommends himself and the family to your prayers. I did what you asked and gave the necessary papers for the Scapular Confraternity of Our Lady of Mount Carmel to our Pastor Father John Knossala. He wrote to Bucharest and recently received the required authorization. We have all joined the association, but Lili, my youngest sister, will receive the scapular tomorrow with several other girls in the English chapel. Signed "Fanny Jelinek, Child of Mary" – P.S. Princess Moruzi also sends compliments to you. [pp. 193-194].

In a letter to Kalinowski dated June 14 of that year, the pastor of Braila thanked him:

Father, I'm sending a list of people who wear the scapular. Reverend Father, I am happy that I could start the Scapular Confraternity in my parish in Braila and I trust that our heavenly Mother will pour out blessings on her children. On the great feast of Ascension Day the Archbishop himself enrolled the people in the scapular. He had promised that he would visit Braila during his pastoral trip to Dobrogea, and I then asked him to enrol those who wished in the scapular which he agreed to do. The ceremony was wonderful, and his sermon on the scapular inspiring. Father, I would be very grateful if you could find us a popular book on the scapular in Hungarian. Please accept my respect and gratitude. [p. 194].

Teresa Moruzi, who was the initiator and an instrument in spreading devotion to the Mother of God in Romania, summed it all up: "Morally," she writes, "Romania is very weak. The public is not religious and retains only some outward forms. Religion is not understood, people know nothing about it and what's worse, don't feel the need for it. ... I can only think how pleasing in the eyes of God must be the prayer of Father Raphael, asking for the protection of Mary for this poor country." [p. 194].

Kalinowski expected a successful development of the renewed Carmel in Poland through Mary's prayers, and on one of the canonical visits he wrote: "God gave us the beloved Mother, to help us to follow in the footsteps of our ancestors and restore the glory of the past." On December 5, 1904, he wrote: "St. Francis Xavier worked with all his strength for this – that everywhere the Immaculate Conception of Mary would be honored. Great apostle of India, martyr and prophet, St. Francis Xavier, you who have been enriched with so many graces through Mary, pray for us, intercede for me; I promise to pray often your own favorite prayer: Mother of God, remember me."

Chapter Four

Third or Secular Order of Carmel

$\mathscr{T}$he aim of the Carmelite Secular Order[158] is to direct people along the Way of Perfection to use the title of St. Teresa's classic book on prayer. The Carmelite Secular Order came into being in the 14th century in Western Europe but did not have any permanent institutions or legal norms at that time. The Carmelite Secular Order may be defined as a group of lay people dedicated to the Carmelite spirit or *charism* of St. Teresa and who, in an organized way, recite the Prayer of the Church and take part in the Eucharist on a regular basis. Members would usually meet monthly at a given location. All lay people belonging to the Carmelite Secular Order belong to the Carmelite family; to a lesser extent people who wear the scapular as members of the Brown Scapular Confraternity of Our Lady of Mt. Carmel also belong to the Carmelite family.

So also members of other Carmelite Confraternities, such as those of St. Joseph, the Infant Jesus, contemporary Carmelite mission groups, Secular Carmelite Institutes, or Carmelite Missionaries. Two

---

[158] The Carmelite Secular Order is formerly known as the Third Order. In our book we use the title 'the Secular Order' meaning same. I am indebted to unpublished notes by Szczepan T. Praskiewicz OCD for much of the information in this chapter.

groups of the latter were founded by the Spanish Carmelite, Blessed Francis Palau.[159] Others such as the Elianum, the Institute of Notre Dame de Vie founded by Fr. Marie-Eugene OCD, or various other Teresian groups also belong to the Carmelite family.

There have always been numerous people living in the world who devoted themselves to prayer, penance, and other spiritual exercises, as family responsibilities permitted. In the early years the number of brothers and sisters of the Secular Order soon equalled that of friars and nuns. The Carmelite Secular Order was approved by Popes Nicholas V and Sixtus IV, who gave its members the same rights and privileges as those enjoyed by others such as the Third Orders of Franciscans, Dominicans and Hermits of St. Augustine. A Bull of Sixtus IV also gives them all the privileges and indulgences that up to that time had been or, in the future, will be given to Carmelites. It also gives the power to the General of the Order to admit to the Secular Order people of both sexes who possess the requisite qualities, clothe them in the scapular and allow them to commit themselves to keeping the rules of the Secular Order of Carmel.

Increasing interest in the Carmelite Secular Order has resulted from a rapidly growing devotion to Mary based on the brown scapular of Our Lady of Mt. Carmel. This trend embraces a great number of contemporary Christians. For example the original Carmelite Rule of Life, the Rule of St. Albert has been lived out for centuries by the Carmelite family, including lay associates, throughout Europe. Many people, in addition, shared in the Carmelite spirit, through a devout wearing of the brown scapular as a sign of dedication to Our Lady. This fact also ensured a welcome for Carmelites when they returned to a specific area, after decades of suppression in various countries throughout Europe. Thomas Walmesley, a layman, wrote to the public in 1863 asking them to support Hermann Cohen's

---

[159] A community of Palau Sisters known as Carmelite Missionaries work with Carmelite friars, based in Varroville near Sydney.

work in restoring the Carmelite Friars to England. The brown scapular was already popular in England. He wrote: "I appeal to all who have any devotion to Our Blessed Lady, but especially to those who wear her scapular, to assist her sons."[160]

It is true of course that the Carmelite Order would have been known through the presence of the sisters in England in the preceding centuries, but inevitably their hidden contemplative life would have placed limitations on how well the Order was known.

Interest in the scapular also derives from a former religious culture itself, and the desire people traditionally have had, to identify with the spirit or *charism* of a particular Order: to that extent people wished to be closely connected with religious Orders which were – in their opinion – the most certain way to salvation. People often wished to wear a symbol of the particular Order such as a medal or scapular, and follow the Order's spiritual practices, as well as be buried in the habit of the Order. The latter was quite common in countries like Ireland up to relatively recent times.

Communities of Carmelite friars spread rapidly in Europe in the 13th century after their expulsion from the Holy Land. Women imitated the men and created communities that adopted the contemplative life of the convent in order the better to serve God. People of both sexes remained in the world bound by family ties and wished to live a spiritual life in their homes, if possible, and practice religious exercises. Thus, in religious families three branches emerged: the first order – men, the second – women, and the third – a Secular Order open to both women and men. All were united with the Carmelite Family so as to share in its spiritual benefits.

Teresian Carmelites also developed a rule for its Secular Order members, consistent with the spirit of St. Teresa's Reform. The first edition of the rule originated in Liège, Belgium in 1699, the

---

[160] Letter of Thomas Walmesly in Carmelite Archives in Kensington, London.

second in France in 1708. The same rule, repeatedly adapted to the changing conditions of life, is today that of Secular Order.

There was moreover a widespread revival of the wish to find support and guidance for a life of prayer on the part of many people towards the end of the 19th century. This development led to a growth in the Carmelite Secular Order in modern times.

Raphael Kalinowski took a leading role in renewing the Third or Secular Order of Carmel. Long before Vatican II encouraged lay holiness, Kalinowski was sensitive to the needs of the faithful and devoted himself fully to them, spending a lot of time celebrating the Sacrament of Penance and opening to them the treasures of Carmelite spirituality. He could be said to have brought Carmelite spirituality closer to lay people in many different ways – publishing various leaflets, books, giving talks, promoting the brown scapular, writing letters to people in a number of surrounding countries, such as Russia, Hungary and Romania.

On December 8, 1873, the Secular Order was established in Poznan at the Discalced Carmelite convent, by the Belgian Discalced Carmelite Andrew Gatzweiler, an esteemed confessor, who on that day received the first person into the Secular Order. This was a certain Fr. Wladyslaw Meszczynski, secretary to the Cardinal and a Papal Chamberlain of Pope Pius IX. When the Discalced Carmelite nuns left Poznan in 1875 and moved to Kraków, they took with them the books of the Secular Order. In the years 1875–1910, 46 people were admitted to this community. Many people from aristocratic families and members of the clergy belonged to it, among them clergy from Poznan, e.g., Bishop Chrysostom Janiszewski, and many from the ranks of the ordinary clergy.

Raphael Kalinowski was the founder of the Carmelite Secular Order in Czerna and Wadowice. Even before that, immediately after ordination, he was appointed by the Provincial as Director of the existing Secular Order, set up and led by Princess Marcelina Czartoryska, at the Discalced Carmelite Convent in Łobzów, Kraków. Secular Order meetings took place in the Carmelite chapel on the first Friday of each month. Kalinowski took part in those meetings, directing and preaching conferences and hearing confessions.[161]

Secular Carmelite members certainly were very devoted to Kalinowski as their Director. They went to him for the Sacrament of Reconciliation, he carried out the usual ceremonies for them, gave them inspiring talks and received what are now called their Promises. He tried to give them spiritual consolation such as arranging a meeting with Fr. Gotti, General of the Order when the opportunity arose. Jean Baptiste Bouchaud describes how Kalinowski encouraged the members in Kraków to engage in charitable activities such as helping poor people, etc. It should be mentioned that Bouchaud himself made a great contribution to the Secular Order when the new house was established in Wadowice, but in his book he modestly omits any mention of this.

The Secular Order as we saw had been in existence in Poland before Kalinowski's time but it was he who gave it a new impetus and established new communities. There are additional aspects concerning the Secular Order in Poland and its relationship with Raphael Kalinowski that may be noted. Central to these was the role of a remarkable woman, whom we have met before but about whom much more needs to be said.

---

[161] When Kalinowski sought advice from Fr. Jerome Gotti, General of the Order, (later made a Cardinal) during his visitation in Poland, on how to run the Secular Order community, he received this reply: "As far as teaching the community members is concerned, I would advise you to make it as simple as possible. If The Secular Order has its own chapel, it would be different, but since you gather in the nuns' chapel, I would like the teachings to be edifying but simple. Don't introduce any changes in the community's usual agenda. In my opinion it would be too much to expose the Blessed Sacrament. Instead, you could put out the relic of the Virgin Mary after giving your teaching, then decide on a virtue for the month, recite the rosary and litany of the Blessed Virgin Mary. Then bless the group with the relic and allow them to venerate it."

Princess Marcelina Czartoryska

In 1840 Marcelina Radzivill married Prince Aleksander Czartoryski, nephew of Prince Adam, and she spent 18 years in the family mansion in Paris until the death of her husband. Her house was open to all who loved Poland, and its literature and art. Distinguished guests included her former tutor Frederic Chopin and other household names.[162] The main feature of the Princess's character was her sheer goodness – one can confidently say her whole life was devoted to works of mercy. After leaving Paris she spent the rest of her life in 'Wola Justowska' in Kraków, where she dedicated herself to the support of the poor. If she gave a concert, it was to help her people condemned to exile for attachment to religion and homeland. In Vienna, she supported young Poles who went to school there; in Paris, she used to visit veterans of the 1831 insurrection; she took care of the poor with such maternal solicitude that they called her Mother Princess, or our Princess. One day in the hospital she had to admit to who she was but one patient, seeing her so austerely dressed didn't recognize her and said curtly: our Princess! You're not even worthy to be her servant." She wasn't angry at him for saying this, and visited him in the days following.

Marcelina returned to Kraków in 1874. At that time, her cousin, Princess Mary, the widow of Prince Witold Czartoryski, had entered the Carmelite Convent in Poznan and received the name Sister Mary Xavier of Jesus. Marcelina was certainly deeply moved by this event. She would have been happy to follow in the footsteps of her cousin, but family ties detained her in the world and then she settled for the Secular Order. This opened up a new field of work for her. For nearly twenty years she directed the group, encouraging the members by her example, to walk the way of Christian perfection.

---

[162] These included; Montalembert, Berger, Villemain, Fr. Gratry, Horace Vernet, Ingres, Jules Janin, Dudley Stuart, Klaczko, Kalinka, Krasinski, Maurice Mann, Kwiatkowski, Matejko, etc., a veritable *Who's Who* of the celebrities of the day.

Her home 'Wola Justowska' at number 10 Ulika Basztowa, was a place where students and young artists were always welcome. When one of them fell ill, she would visit him, and when he left the area, she wrote him encouraging letters. In Kraków, as well as in Paris, her home was open to all who practiced the fine arts, or devoted themselves to helping the poor. She had words of encouragement for all. "I was deeply moved," wrote one of them, "when that star student of Chopin, played his seventh prelude and polonaise about the capture of Warsaw." [p. 206].

In Kraków, Marcelina lived modestly, almost in poverty: there were so many poor people to support. In the hospital of St. Louis, which owes its existence to her, she waited on the poor, took part in the work of the Society of St. Vincent de Paul which met at St Hedwig's Hall, and also in the work of the Daughters of Charity in Kazimierz. She would visit the poor in their homes, bringing them, together with material aid, encouragement and comfort. She did all this without fanfare and she shunned praise. One of her friends said once in her presence: "What will happen to us when we no longer have our Princess?" She responded quickly: "There are always people ready to support and defend the poor." [p. 206].

Marcelina completed her formation in the Secular Order in 1874 and was received by Andrew Gatzweiler at the Carmel of Łobzów, where the community had taken refuge from Poznan after fleeing persecution. The Princess was the first member received in Kraków. She contributed much to the spread of the Secular Order there. She saw to it that meetings were held regularly on the first Friday of every month in the chapel of the Carmelites. She was responsible for admitting new members. Talks to the community were conducted by priests who had joined the community. Marcelina did a tremendous amount of good for Carmel in Poland. Marcelina herself never hesitated to nurse the sick, whether rich or poor. She even begged for them and when the wealthy gave her something back for her personal needs, she would immediately share it with the poor. Neither did she hesitate for a moment to leave everything and rush to the help of the suffering members of Christ's Church.

Princess Moruzi couldn't fail to know about the good influence of the Secular Order in Kraków, and especially its founder, Princess Marcelina; this would have made her decide to follow in her footsteps. Together with another penitent of Kalinowski, and with the permission and encouragement of her confessor, Moruzi founded the Secular Order in Czerna. Many young people from Czerna, Nowa Gora and the surrounding parishes asked to join that group. A rule of life was published in Polish and the number of interested people continued to increase. Many people from Polish areas taken over by Germany and Russia, especially in Upper Silesia – Sosnowiec and the surrounding area – came several times a year to the Carmelites in Czerna to ask for prayer or the sacrament of reconciliation.

On the last day of May 1894, the eve of the Feast of the Sacred Heart, Princess Marcelina, then aged 77, wrote to the Carmelites at Łobzów informing them that she felt tired and could not come to the meeting the following day; she asked their prayers. At four o'clock in the morning she had a seizure and died five days later. Her confessor, Father Marszalkiewicz came to give her the last sacraments. The entire city was touched, and especially the poor and their caregivers. The Princess used to chair the meetings of the Sisters of Charity, so when they found out about her illness, they sent a telegram to the General asking for permission to take care of their benefactress. The Carmelite nuns being unable to visit her sent a relic of St. Teresa, which she joyfully received, saying, "I continue my journey, having St. Teresa on one side of me and St. Vincent de Paul on the other." Her son, Prince Marcel and his wife Princess Susanne came to see her. Deeply touched, she blessed them one last time and made known her last wishes: a funeral without any eulogies either in the church or the cemetery, her body to be buried in the cemetery in Kraków, and not in the family vault in Sieniawa. She died the following Tuesday, June 5 at 9:00 pm, seated in her chair. Prince Marcel had to notify her death to the Carmelite nuns at Łobzów who were gathered in the choir for matins; he asked them for a Carmelite habit for his mother.

The periodical *Cjas* (*Time*) published an article on June 7: "The mortal remains of Princess Marcelina Czartoryska are on view in her home at 10 Ulica Basztowa. Many people from all walks of life viewed the remains, especially the poor who loudly expressed their sorrow. The body of the Princess, dressed in the Carmelite habit reposed in a modest coffin." Prince Marcel observed: "A very sad medical student came in and stood by the coffin. Did you know my mother? I said. How would I not know her, she visited me when I had typhus and saved my life! A grandmother stops by sobbing: She was my comfort and support." [p. 208].

Before her death, the Princess collected 3,000 florins for the incurably sick. A Memorial service was held on Friday June 8 at the Church of Saint Mary, but there was no eulogy. She had done so much for the Board of the St. Louis Hospital that the funeral procession paused in front of the hospital, so that patients could pay their last respects to their benefactor. Kalinowski simply referred to her as a great benefactor.

Princess Marcelina was buried in the Carmelite habit in Rakowicki Cemetery in Kraków. Mother Xavier remarked of her, "Only God knows how much she did for the reform in Czerna." [p. 208].

The most rapid development of the Secular Order in Poland took place only after the renewal of the priory in Czerna. There followed a renewal in other parts of Poland especially at the instigation of the General of the Order Fr. Jerome-Mary Gotti, probably after his visit in 1885.

Kalinowski was the real restorer of the Carmel in Czerna. He became at that point spiritual director of the Secular Order there. The Register for the group in Czerna was begun in 1891. The first Register had begun with the group which, as we saw, was set up in Kraków at the Convent of the Discalced Carmelite nuns on Ulika Lobozowska. The group there was made up of members who came from neighboring towns (Krzeszowice, Nowa Gora, Paczoltowice) and later also from the Kingdom of Poland and from Silesia. The first name on the Register in Czerna was Princess Teresa Moruzi, Kalinowski's friend. The first one to make her commitment to the Secular Order in Czerna was Antonina Podolecka from Krzeszowice – which she did on December 9, 1894, taking the name Teresa of Jesus.

In 1892 the number of Secular Order members in Czerna amounted to fifteen. Teresa Moruzi (who lived in Sulina, Romania), Kalinowski's directee, and whose husband Dymitri was related to the Serbian Queen, was admitted that year. Though she lived in Romania she officially belonged to the Kraków community. By 1911 as many as 972 people had joined the Secular Order, but unfortunately the number of people making Promises was much lower.

When Kalinowski moved to Wadowice in 1893, he set up the Secular Carmelite community there also. He personally received the first candidates. On January 25, 1903 during a conference in Wadowice, Kalinowski quoted St. Teresa of Jesus from the first Polish edition of 'The Life of Saint Teresa of Avila by Herself.' He spoke about a good death, about the need for purification and of getting rid of one's faults. He also recommended the custom of choosing a monthly patron saint and writing down the name as well as practicing the virtue associated with the saint. During a conference on February 22, 1903 he spoke about faith, about good works and about prayer as a necessary means for tackling wrong tendencies. One month later, on March 29 he gave a talk, underlining a favourite topic, "The church is our home." This was on the occasion of the 25th anniversary of Pope Leo XIII's pontificate.[163]

Kalinowski would describe the essence of membership of the Carmelite Secular Order in three words: "Work, prayer and suffering." Elaborating on this he meant that one should draw

---

[163] Praskiewitz, Szczepan T, *St. Raphael Kalinowski*, p. 39.

blessings from work, one should pray in a peaceful way, and one should suffer willingly. To benefit from these we must preserve a pure heart and only Jesus Christ can purify our hearts and keep them free from sin. In addition it is the duty of a Secular Order member to practice virtue, and begin by striving against the opposite imperfections. This is the *agere contra* of traditional asceticism. He would also insist on faith in Christ's Eucharistic presence, on loyalty to the Church and to the Holy Father as a basis of a dedicated life.

Discalced Carmelites from Łobzów wrote about Kalinowski's work for the Secular Carmel: "Fr. Raphael never spoke too long but what he said was full of sense and communicated in a dignified way, and (according to people's comments) he urged them to concentrate on their inner lives." [p. 209].

Raphael Kalinowski didn't stint his penitents of his time but dedicated many hours to them, inculcating in them a genuine spiritual life. The experience of making a general confession to him was often the beginning of a new growth stage in their lives. For example, he treated the Princess Teresa Moruzi, who suffered from scruples, kindly but firmly. He didn't allow people to trawl over past sins but encouraged obedience and trust in a regular confessor.

Works of Mercy

Not only did Kalinowski look after people's spiritual needs, he also saw to their moral and material needs. In Wadowice he organised financial resources for the young women who worked in local night clubs and who were often driven to prostitution by poverty and need. In some cases he made arrangements for them to be cared for by the Institute of the Mercy Sisters who had a house for that purpose in a place called Lagiewniki, near Kraków.[164]

---

[164] This is the site of the famous and imposing new Basilica of Divine Mercy, promoted by Pope John Paul II who canonized Sr. Faustina, a member of this congregation, some years ago.

On his initiative, too, a Conference of the St. Vincent de Paul Society was set up and wealthy women from the town engaged in much charitable activity from here. Kalinowski's piety and devotion were noted by all and his influence over the friars, nuns, members of the Carmelite Family and on local priests was profound.

In 1898 a new Secular Order community was set up at the church of the Assumption in a place called Chorzow. More than ten years later Silesian communities of the Secular Carmel developed extremely quickly and their number reached a dozen or so, bringing together about a thousand members. They used to come on pilgrimage to Czerna and renew their faith at the shrine of the Virgin Mary and at the grave of Raphael. They also liked to collect water from the stream running by.

Later on the Secular Order was guided by Carmelite friars who had been friends and pupils of Raphael Kalinowski. The most prominent of these were Jean Baptist Bouchaud and the martyr Blessed Alphonsus Maria (Joseph Mazurek.) The heroic life of Alphonsus Mazurek and that of others must owe something to the inspiring example given by Kalinowski.

Chapter Five

Juniorate for Carmelite students in Wadowice

$\mathcal{R}$aphael Kalinowski endured long sessions in the confessional in the cold and damp church in Czerna. Perhaps it was not as severe as a Siberian winter, but as people grow older they become more vulnerable to cold. Kalinowski was involved in numerous ongoing activities that involved the administration of the Priory property and the spiritual guidance of his community. In addition he was called on to direct nuns in four convents of Carmelites. This meant undergoing tiring trips through Eastern Galicia. On March 25, 1891, he wrote to his brother Aleksander: "I am now declining toward old age and have no strength, especially for work in the confessional. If only the Lord had left me in my former post ... in the middle of April I finish my triennium [three years] and whether they leave me in Czerna or not, I do not know. – My health is very bad – colds, stomach problems and my lungs are affected with avian influenza." [p. 215].

The Provincial Chapter in fact left him free and advised him to take a complete rest and didn't appoint him to any office. But his mission was far from complete and soon his superiors entrusted him with a task that would greatly influence the future of Carmel in Poland.

The new Prior of Czerna was Casimir Rybka. He knew that his first endeavor should be to build up Kalinowski's strength. For this purpose he entrusted him with the office of bursar, which meant he could take long walks through the fields and woods that comprised the large Czerna property. Moreover, Rybka needed a wise counsellor like Kalinowski in a difficult and complicated job involving the administration of the goods of the Priory.

The Carmelite nuns continued to turn to Kalinowski in their concerns and he never refused advice and encouragement when needed. He took every opportunity to remind them of the need for continual prayer for the Church, as St. Teresa recommended. On May 13 he wrote to Sr. Teresa, Prioress in Przemyśl, telling her he had returned to Czerna and passed through Cieszyn. The visit to Cieszyn was in connection with a projected new foundation that the Carmelites of Czerna had long desired and was finally coming to fruition.

In July the Prioress asked him to come on an urgent visit. He answered in a few words, humbly suggesting he would prefer not to pre-empt the forthcoming visit of Fr. General: "I strongly doubt if it is feasible to come to Przemyśl before the arrival of Fr. General. I advise you to wait until you meet him, relying on the providence of God. Fr. General, according to a telegram received yesterday evening, should come to Vienna on Wednesday ... I do not know the program of our dear Father. Perhaps he will start with the convents of the nuns. The grace of God will work more for him than for me." [p. 217].

Kalinowski knew Fr. General well since his visit to Poland in 1885, when he acted as interpreter, and throughout August spent time with him in Kraków, Przemyśl and Lviv. In the latter city, Fr. General stayed on longer to oversee certain policies that needed to be put in place; Pope Leo XIII had entrusted him with the reform of the Carmelite community there. The nuns had originally come from Wieliczka near Kraków in 1889. But Mother Mary Angel, who founded that convent under the jurisdiction of the bishop, was unequal to the task of leading the community. In the intervening three years since the Carmelites from Wieliczka moved to Lviv, no novices had made profession. In 1891, when the canonical visitation was under way, the community consisted of only three nuns and four novices. In the directory for 1892 the names of the two oldest sisters are no longer listed nor are the names of three of the novices – they had obviously left. These were replaced by Carmelites from Kraków and Germany, led by Sr. Francesca, sister of Anne of Jesus, founder of the Convent in Przemyśll. After the canonical visit Fr. General gave the habit to two novices. When the time came for taking the veil the chapel was full, but the preacher hadn't arrived. They waited for some time to no avail, then Fr. General nodded to Kalinowski to go into the pulpit. This he did immediately without any preparation. He pointed out to the congregation, among other things, that the penitential aspect of Carmelite life, far from being burdensome is really the opposite – a source of happiness and peace.

In September, the Carmelite General was in Czerna and after the canonical visit he made an entry in Latin in the visitation book: "We need Polish novices and resolve with the help of God to find them and prepare them – so we will strive to achieve this goal." [p. 219]. In the Polish Carmel, as almost everywhere, it was difficult to find novices, and the friars in Czerna had long tried to do something about it. The Carmelite friars concluded that it would be best to follow the example of two houses in the Austro-Hungarian region – set up a Juniorate as many other provinces had done, as well as most religious orders. In a college of that kind the Carmelites could train boys who wished to serve God and teach them something about Carmelite life.

Father General and the Provincial Council urged the need for the establishment of a new priory in Poland, to serve as a Juniorate. The Council, after a careful reading of this proposal, adopted it at its first meeting. As the city where the new house was to be built had not yet been selected, Bonaventure Kirchstein instructed the Provincial Council to find a suitable place. This task, in turn, was laid at the door of the friars in Czerna: Rybka, Kalinowski and Diaz de Cerio.

In October the General took part in the meeting of the Provincial Council at the priory in Linz. This meeting was also attended by Diaz de Cerio from Czerna as third Provincial Councillor.

Since there were not sufficient friars available for teaching boys, they would be forced to start, much to their regret, by sending them to one of the gymnasiums in Galicia. So the new foundation was planned for a town which already had a secular high school. The friars visited Wadowice and Bochnia and reported to the Provincial on these two respective places. Their report was sent to Rome on January 11, 1892 and the General Council opted for the establishment of a new foundation in Wadowice.

Wadowice, birthplace of Karol Wojtyla as well as other famous Poles, lies in the diocese of Kraków, thirty-two kilometers from Czerna, in the foothills of the Carpathians and on the left bank of the river Skawa. It received municipal rights in the early 14th century, but in the 15th century the city was destroyed by fire. It was soon rebuilt, however, and Casimir, Duke of Auschwitz, restored its city rights in the year 1430.

We do not know when the first school was founded in Wadowice – it seems it was early in the 17th century when famed Martin Wadowita[165] taught theology at the University of Kraków for fifty years. In 1835 several people had collected a large sum of money and began efforts to establish a high school. In 1866, the city renewed its efforts and obtained permission from the state

---

[165] In 1567 Dr. Martin Wadowita, the son of a peasant was born in Wadowice. In the old chronicles he was called Campiusem or Vadoviusem (Martin from Wadowice). In the late 16th and early 17th century he was one of the most prominent defenders of the Catholic faith, revered even by Pope Sixtus V. He was also for a time Provost of Pope John Paul's parish of St. Florian.

authorities in 1882 to inaugurate a high school consisting of eight classes. The building housed a gymnasium built in 1875.

The good reputation of this school swayed the friars to make the foundation in that town. The residents were also behind the project. When the civil authorities, especially Governor Stanislas Dunajewski, nephew of the Cardinal Dunajewski, and Mayor Jan Iwanski learned that the Carmelites had plans to settle in their town, they supported the project and wished to see it realized. On April 22, Cardinal Albin Dunajewski, Bishop of Kraków, sent the necessary permission to Czerna as required by the Council of Trent.

Once everything was ready, the attorney for Czerna, Dr. Faustyn Jakubowski, a lawyer from Kraków instructed by the friars, went house hunting in Wadowice for a suitable place. He found one on June 3, situated on the road to Zator, less than a mile from the city. It belonged to Francis Foltin, a bookseller and one of the wealthiest and most respected property owners in Wadowice. The Provincial was on a visit at the time so he came to examine it. There were three rooms and a kitchen on the ground floor, and a spacious apartment on the first floor. Foltin, learning of the need for accommodation for four or five friars and a dormitory for the boys who would need to board, as well as a chapel, admitted that his house was too small. So he decided to build on two rooms, one of which could be used as a chapel. His proposal was accepted, and the enlarged house was rented for three years. Foltin instructed workers to begin construction immediately and prepare all that was needed for the friars.

In May 1892 the Polish Provincial, Kirchstein, visited the houses and in early June reached Wadowice. He was enthusiastic about the friars' choice for a new beginning. But the right person was needed to complete the project and this task was entrusted to Kalinowski. Before leaving Czerna, the provincial gave him the necessary authority and took him as interpreter during a canonical visit to the Carmelite Convents in Kraków, Przemyśl and Lviv.

At the end of July, following completion of the visit, Kalinowski returned to Czerna to make the final preparations. On August 1 he celebrated Mass in the early morning and with Br. Luigi Rossi proceeded on the journey to the new foundation. Just as they got to the car a violent storm broke out which lasted all the way to the train station in Krzeszowice.

The new house would be dedicated to St. Joseph, so in true Teresian fashion Kalinowski took with him the statue of St. Joseph which he had been given on his departure from Czerna. They arrived in Wadowice in the afternoon. Diaz de Cerio arrived the same day with a second Brother named Isidore Wojdarski, who remained in Wadowice until his death. There was not a stick of furniture in the house so they spread straw on the floor on which they slept. It didn't take much imagination to think about the stable of Bethlehem. An old chest served as the community dining table. This experience was very reminiscent of that of Hermann Cohen who, in similar circumstances as the founder of a new Carmelite priory in London, had to resort to flower pots as kitchen utensils in his first days there. Diaz de Cerio wrote home to his former prior in Czerna a few days later: "I am writing to you on my knees, not out of humility, but because we have neither chairs nor table. I am writing on an upturned box!" Two days later Kalinowski wrote (also on an upturned box): "Today we had the first decent meal: coffee and an omelette." [p. 233]. Earlier in the year, on behalf of the prior of Czerna, Kalinowski wrote to the Prioress in Przemyśl:

> We intend to establish a Juniorate in Wadowice. This is the custom in France, Belgium, Spain, Italy and partly in Linz and Raab (Gyor).[166] It's not easy in our country to find young men with a leaning towards contemplative life. There are plenty of boys ready to come to the Juniorate but then they quickly leave. Moreover, the formation of capable candidates also requires men who would be able

[166] Ireland also imitated this model and opened a Juniorate in Castlemartyr, Co. Cork in 1927. It was dedicated to St.Thérèse of Lisieux. Many Carmelites from the Anglo-Irish Province completed High School there.

to successfully engage in this work. Our Prior thought it would be desirable to look to the bishops for support. With this in mind he decided to ask the Prioress at Przemyśl to have a word with the local bishop which she agreed to do. The idea was that he would alert the priests to be on the lookout for possible vocations and direct them towards the Carmelites. [p. 234].

Kalinowski was diplomatic enough to suggest that this would not detract from the needs of the diocese but would redound to the benefit of all, young and old, and draw down God's blessings and the protection of Our Lady of Mount Carmel.[167]

At the opening ceremony for the new foundation all the students gathered in the gymnasium, from where the Rector and professors led the way to the parish church; there solemn Mass followed, combined with the singing of the hymn *Veni Creator*, to ask God's blessing for the new school year. Every morning, after prayers, the boys studied under the supervision and direction of the Prefect. After 7.00 am Mass they had breakfast and went to the High School until noon.

After dinner, evening leisure time was spent in the garden, adjacent to the house, under the guidance of the friars, and when school rules allowed it, they would go for a walk with the Prefect.

Because the friars didn't as yet have a chapel in the house, they received permission to celebrate Mass in the chapel of the military hospital nearby. Francis Foltin meanwhile tried to speed up construction work. The two rooms were soon ready and on October 15, feast of St. Teresa, one of them was furnished as a chapel. Everyone gathered there at half past seven in the morning, and Kalinowski celebrated the first Mass in this temporary chapel. Carmelites from Czerna and Kraków, Przemyśl and Lviv, Kalinowski's family and several people from the Secular Order supplied all that was needed for the liturgy.

167

The summer of 1892 was benign, which facilitated construction work. In late October, the new chapel was completed and the Cardinal of Kraków dedicated it. The main buildings in the city were illuminated and decorated with flags.

Kalinowski was given the honor of celebrating the first Mass on November 1 at 8 am. A bell weighing 25 kg was suspended in a small tower on top of the house. Kalinowski asked God to bless the work that was about to begin there. Typically there was a small statue of St. Joseph in place, with the inscription: *'Posuerunt custodem me'* – They placed me as a guardian (of this place). [p. 241].

On November 14 Kalinowski went to Czerna, passing through Kraków where he called on Cardinal Dunajewski. The Cardinal was very pleased when he heard how much good was being done in the chapel in Wadowice. During Lent 1893 the confessionals were besieged, penitents came not only from the neighboring parishes, but from further afield – 15 and 20 miles distant.

The task the Carmelites set themselves in the college at Wadowice was aimed at shaping young people according to the qualities required to become dedicated members of the Carmelite Order. In the early days the friars were guided only by their own experience; Kalinowski's many years working as a tutor stood him in good stead.

In October 1892 the Provincial Council discussed the matter of rules for the College. Diaz de Cerio, third Provincial Councillor, gave them a copy of the regulations in force at Gyor (Raab); these were adapted to Polish conditions, and given to the Superior for approval. Kalinowski read the document attentively, made a few changes and further clarified certain points. He insisted on his own system of discernment. The first sentence of his reflections is reminiscent of Cardinal Newman who was his contemporary in England:

We must not doubt that God in His mercy has allocated to each one a task that is to be completed in this world.

The same applies to the religious life, and if God chooses someone for this way of life He may include some early signs of this vocation. These signs can manifest themselves not only by good conduct, or some special talents, but mainly by an attraction towards spiritual exercises, by great modesty, tenderness of conscience, deference to colleagues, etc. If these characteristics, instead of developing over time, begin to slowly fade or even disappear completely, that must be attributed to negative external influences or the negligence of the people assigned to educate the boy... If a boy, as often happens in our day, lived some time in an unfavorable environment, it is quite a different matter, especially when at the age of twelve or thirteen he begins to think about another profession, or if the family is poor and without the resources to educate the boy, the parents may want to entrust him to us to ensure his future. This is often the case, although these boys should be accepted only by way of exception. [pp. 251-252].

Again Kalinowski speaks from experience:

First you have to give them an education suitable to their age, but a very thorough one, and you must be able to teach them good habits in living a deeper life. That is the touchstone, after which you can discern whether they are called to live as Carmelites or not. Only I, who went through hellish educational institutions, can attest to the truth of this assertion ... We have seen promising people who have just left the family home shaken in faith, and sometimes even lapsing badly soon after their first contact with peers." [p. 252].

Under the wise leadership of Kalinowski the junior seminary in Wadowice made rapid strides forward. The young people there gained the respect and affection of colleagues and professors. Other students from the local high school were influenced by them and wished to transfer to the Carmelite school.[168]

Helena Kalinowska, Gabriel's wife who had become a Catholic, was very supportive of the school. When she learned that Kalinowski had founded a new house in Wadowice that was struggling financially she weighed in to help. She and her children, together with her sister Wanda, who had also converted to Catholicism, came to Wadowice within a month of the setting up of the house. Helena's eldest daughter Mary had not yet made her First Holy Communion, so Helena knew her brother-in-law would be delighted to preside at this occasion. In fact Helena became a regular benefactor of the project and was there for them whenever some dire need presented itself. Helena's husband Gabriel, together with his business partner Edward Piorkowski, donated a ciborium for the chapel as well as seven hundred francs. Their generosity continued until Kalinowski's death so Helena and her friends were among the main benefactors of the Carmelites in Wadowice.

Additional benefactors of the friars were the Carmelites of Vilnius, as well as the Carmel in Wesoła. The latter gave the community the gift of a cross, a few meters high, with an image of Christ crucified, formerly venerated in their Convent. It was placed at the entrance to the church. The kindness of many was often quite touching. One poor woman came along, bent over with age, with a sack on her back. She walked past the chapel, passed by the choir and went to the sacristy door. When asked what she wanted by one of the friars she deposited the bag in front of him, kissed his feet and said: "I brought the peas, they are for you, and could I make a general confession please?" [p. 258].

---

[168] college of this kind was considered appropriate in a 19th century setting and for most of the 20th century, but not, at the present time, in many Western countries. The Juniorate in Castlemartyr closed some years ago.

The priory of Czerna also supplied anything that was needed. Princess Moruzi also showed her appreciation and gratitude to Kalinowski. The chapel, exposed to northern winds in winter was very cold, and despite his frail health Kalinowski spent so much of his day there that the princess told him to install a stove at her expense. She also donated the oak desk for the priory archives and the princely (or princessly) sum of 8,000 francs towards the upkeep of the seminary chapel.

As a spiritual director Kalinowski always tried to ensure people remained active and made good use of the gifts and talents they had been given. His devotion to them knew no bounds. What he did for Princess Teresa Moruzi in Kraków and Czerna, he continued to do for people in Wadowice. With Moruzi's help he founded the Secular Order of Our Lady of Mount Carmel there. The Princess came to visit in 1893 and spent her holiday time close to Kalinowski. As she had not yet made her commitment in the Secular Order, Kalinowski took the opportunity to prepare her for it which she did on November 14, the feast of All Saints of the Order of Carmel.

On November 24, former Feast of St. John of the Cross, kneeling before the altar of St. Joseph, together with another devout person, she received the scapular of the Secular Order and thus became its founding member. As patron and role model Kalinowski gave her the name Blessed Mary of the Incarnation, formerly Barbara Acarie, founder of the Carmelites in France. Her companion was given the name Teresa of Jesus. Her sister Marianna joined her as a Secular Order member on Christmas Day and two others were added shortly afterwards. Those two formed the nucleus of a flourishing group in the future. Kalinowski encouraged the group to go out and recruit more members. He preached the routine Carmelite asceticism to them that was promoted in Carmelite houses of formation. Kalinowski also directed people to live a Sacramental life, taking their cue from the saints. Reading a good book about the defect we want to uproot and its opposite virtue is also encouraged.

Some of his talks are extant and in one he tells the story of the blind man who asked the Savior to restore his sight. His prayer was heard and he was cured as a reward for his faith. Following the example of the blind man, a person should ask God for the gift of a living faith in the presence of Christ in the Blessed Sacrament on the altar, in the Church and in the person of the Holy Father, the Vicar of Christ on earth. A person should be noted for devotion to the Church, and to the Pope as its head. Because we possess in the Church the precious treasure of faith, the grace of the sacraments, the example of the saints and all the means for salvation, we should show gratitude and devotion to the Pope. So too should we pray for bishops and clergy, for the perseverance of the just and the conversion of sinners. To achieve this goal we need to avoid sin, and remember in prayer the goal we are aiming at. Members of the Secular Order should also devote their whole life to serving God and working for God's glory, turning even trifling things into sacrifices.[169] They should cultivate an apostolic spirit by considering what Christ suffered for their redemption and salvation. Great attention should be paid to the examination of conscience to review how daily duties are performed. These seemingly insignificant things have great value in the eyes of God. Saying one small 'no' to oneself can be an effective way to do great things, and one act of self-denial done for the love of God and neighbor can contribute to the growth of the Church. "Let us therefore strive to lead exemplary lives," he said, "let us remember that we belong to Our Lady's Order and wholeheartedly dedicate ourselves to the salvation of our sisters and brothers in a spirit of gentleness and humility. If these signs are present we know we are true children of the Church. We will

---

[169] Here and in the following paragraphs we see a distinct echo of the teaching of St. Thérèse of Lisieux with which Kalinowski had become familiar; he included aspects of it in his own spirituality.

267

constitute here on earth its vital members, and in heaven, with God's grace enjoy eternal happiness." [p. 258].[170]

Allied to ongoing ministry in the church in Wadowice and the privation that poverty entailed, was the burden of illness. In February 1893, after returning from Kraków, Kalinowski was ill and confined to bed for a month. He reflected: "Each of us must bear the cross." At this time he wrote to his brother Aleksander: "The cross is part and parcel of our life on earth and the whole value of our life consists in the faithful carrying of the cross. In it lies all our consolation on earth, and the hope of eternal happiness in the possession of God. Let us pray for one another, so that we can be ever united in the land of eternal joy. Oh, if only we could always pursue this joy through our daily work, under the protection of Our Lady and Queen." [p. 271].

In July and August of 1894 Kalinowski again accompanied the Provincial for the regular canonical visit of the Carmelite Convents in Kraków, Przemyśl and Lviv. Kalinowski found his long journey extremely tiring. In Lviv, the Prioress Teresa Francis Stolberg was confined to bed and could not take part in the community exercises. This worthy nun came from Germany to assist in the reform of the Convent in Lviv. According to the opinion of physicians she was not expected to survive much longer. She had been a great blessing for the community and had earned her heavenly reward. Around this time also Princess Margaret Czartoryska, a special friend of Kalinowski, died in Paris on October 24,1894; he was bound to her by ties of affection and gratitude. He heard the news on November 21 from the Carmelite nuns in Łobzów.[171]

There was no convent of religious women in Wadowice and Kalinowski wished to rectify this. At the beginning of 1894

---

[170]   Here we see a desire on Kalinowski's part to promote the holiness of the laity. In this he anticipated the teaching of Vatican II.

[171]   Princess Margaret Czartoryska was the second wife of Prince Ladislaus Czartoryski and it was she who first welcomed Kalinowski to the Hôtel Lambert in Paris.

Madeyski, the Minister of Education, visited his son-in-law Stanislaus Dunajewski, Mayor of Wadowice, and relative of the Archbishop. Kalinowski consulted him on January 26 and a project was approved by the Minister together with the Prefect of the school.[172] The Minister was favorably disposed to the friars; he inquired about the state of the community and its purpose. He concluded that the Carmelites had a big role to play in Wadowice, and expressed the hope that the Order would do much good there in the future through confessional ministry for families and individuals. The Minister approved the idea of a convent and promised that the government might help, but above all the city should do everything it could to facilitate such a project. Kalinowski also spoke about the project to Princess Moruzi. In due time the Sisters of Nazareth in Kraków opened a house in Wadowice and later on had two houses there.

The city wished to show its gratitude to the Sisters of Nazareth and a new hospital was built and the care of the patients assigned to these hard-working sisters. It opened before them a new and extensive field of action, because they provided not only physical but spiritual care as well.

Not only did ordinary people benefit from the advice and kindness of Kalinowski, but also people from the educated classes turned to the experienced confessor for direction. Inspired by him some women established a Conference of the St. Vincent de Paul Society which did much-needed charitable work in the town.

---

[172] This was Bouchaud himself. In the years 1892–1895 he was prefect of the seminary.

Chapter Six

Prior at Czerna (1894) and Wadowice (1897)

*A*t the provincial chapter held in Linz, Austria, from August 13 to 19, 1894, Kalinowski was again elected Superior of Czerna, while Rybka took his place in Wadowice. The news of Kalinowski's departure was a cause of general sorrow. The Director of the High School came to visit and thanked him for producing so many excellent students. Next day Mayor Iwanski and builder Foltin visited the priory, and on behalf of the City Council expressed their appreciation for Kalinowski and their regret at his departure. Wadowice was sorry to lose him but its loss was deemed Czerna's gain. People there had not forgotten all he did for them while he was Superior the first time round.

But the new Prior of Czerna had no illusions about his future: he knew that this office would be a heavy cross for the next three years. He recommended himself to God and Mary and took up this burden determined to carry it for the glory of God and Our Lady of Mount Carmel, as well as the good of the Order.

Meetings for spiritual direction, the fervor and fidelity with which exercises of the religious life were carried out, difficult and absorbing administration of house property – these cares gave him no time to relax. As soon as he arrived in Czerna, one of his first efforts was to provide material assistance for the new foundation from which he had just departed. Wadowice had no regular income and since donations were not sufficient, he had to seek help in the Czerna house, which in the early years contributed two thousand florins a year. When Kalinowski returned as Prior to Czerna, he noticed that some of the younger friars were reluctant to help the foundation in Wadowice. They complained that there were still no novices and the boys had not yet completed high school. Then they questioned if it would not be better to leave Wadowice altogether and open a new Carmelite house in Kraków which had been so long desired.

In May 1895 the Provincial Council considered the question of a new priory in Wadowice. New information was gathered and sent to Rome, where Austrian Provincial Benedict Herzog had been elected General Councilor. He was well disposed to the foundation in Wadowice, and in spite of the above-mentioned misgivings by some friars, it was not considered appropriate to leave Wadowice and the house there was given definitive approval.

A few months later Kirschstein, the new Provincial arrived for the canonical visitation and promptly put both the Czerna priory and the Wadowice house on a firm financial footing with generous allowances provided. A large sum was set aside to build a new church and monastery in Wadowice. On August 31, 1896 Church and State authorities gave the go-ahead for this.

New Priory at Wadowice

In June 1896, while Prior of Czerna, Kalinowski had been summoned to Wadowice, where he was given the job of making arrangements for the proposed new building. He found a suitable plot of land on a hill on the other side of town, commanding a view to the north. The property came to be known as Carmel Hill. A view of the Vistula valley stretched out almost as far as Czerna, while the southern Carpathian Mountains with their highest peaks could be seen in the distance. On August 10, 1896 permission came from the Provincial in Vienna to start work. Rybka, who was then Superior, with the help of Auguste Iwanski, the Mayor, bought the land necessary for the project, and during winter he ordered a supply of stone, lime and sand for the foundations of the church and priory. When Kalinowski came to Wadowice as Superior on June 16, 1897 everything was ready.

On August 31 the foundation stone of the new house was laid. The building was designed by Brother Hilarion Slowick together with T. Prauss and Adam Kozlowski, a builder from Wadowice. The design was reviewed and approved by another builder, Richard Jordan, and then sent to the Provincial in Vienna. Construction began at the end of autumn.

In spring, after the winter break, the work continued with redoubled energy. The materials had all been collected – people contributed building materials in abundance, thousands of bricks were donated. The foundations of the church were dug in April and throughout the summer, weather permitting, the work proceeded briskly. The priory was completed in late August, and the church a few months later.[173] On November 8 John Sikora of Wadowice placed a cross that he himself had made and donated on top of the bell tower. The church itself was a large three-nave Neo-Roman building. The main altar, the pulpit and the Stations of the Cross were made by the Austrian firm of Ferdinand Stuflesser.[174]

In July 1897 the Polish Provincial came to carry out a canonical visitation. Kalinowski, back to his old form, accompanied him, as usual, to Kraków, Lviv and Przemyśl. In August, the pair went

---

[173]   The present address is ul. Karmelicka 22. The plate near the entrance reads, 'Klastor Karmelitow Bosych' (Discalced Carmelite Monastery).

[174]   When the Carmelite church of St. Luke and St. Teresa was built in Wincanton, Somerset, England in 1907, the Lady Altar was carved in wood by the same firm of Stuflesser. This was the second foundation following on Hermann Cohen's pioneering work in London in 1863.

to Wadowice where the new church and new priory had been completed. They were present for the dedication of the church to St. Joseph, Guardian of Carmel. On August 26, feast of the Transverberation of St. Teresa's heart, they celebrated the last Mass in the 'temporary chapel.' The people of Wadowice worked all day on the decorations, festooning the scene with branches of spruce, wreaths, draperies, flowers and triumphal arches, as only Poles know how to do. These ran along three streets and three squares through which the procession of the Blessed Sacrament was to pass. The old chapel had been in use for nearly seven years and had endeared itself to the faithful. The procession, lasting two hours, was a triumphant march to the new church with the Blessed Sacrament carried in a monstrance by the Provincial. He was accompanied by the friars of Wadowice and Czerna, the City clergy and those of the surrounding parishes. Completing the grand array were the boys from the Carmelite school. There were also members of confraternities and various notables from the city and school children, followed by enormous crowds, who came from all over the city and nearby villages, singing as they went. We can imagine Kalinowski was in his element at this, knowing as we do, how devoted he was to the Eucharist. The beautiful melodies of Polish hymns were heard near and far.

Early next morning Cardinal Jan Puzyna,[175] Archbishop of Kraków, came to consecrate the church, and praised its beautiful simplicity. On the same day Kalinowski wrote to the sisters at Łobzów: "Bless the Lord, and rejoice in Him. Thanks to your prayers yesterday evening above all for the gracious weather we had for the procession and the celebrations. I will let other friars and John describe the scene – words fail me." [p. 301].

---

[175] At the Papal Conclave of 1902 Cardinal Puzyna colluded with Emperor Franz Joseph of Austria to oppose the election of Cardinal Rampolla as Pope. He was perceived to be pro-Russian as well as anti-Austrian. For this purpose the Emperor exercised his power of veto. This was later abolished by Pope St. Pius X who in the event succeeded Pope Leo XIII.

Notwithstanding, Kalinowski did decide to write more the same day. His friend and former fellow-exile Wenceslaus Nowakowski was invited to take part in the celebrations. After the consecration of the church, in the presence of the cardinal and the great crowds that filled all three aisles, Wenceslaus went into the pulpit. The people were happy to see this aging man again, whose face was beaming with kindness but also with the grief of a returned exile, his long white beard reminiscent of the venerable men of the Old Testament. After a moment's silence Nowakowski started a sermon with text from the prophet Joel, quoting the reading for Ash Wednesday. Living up to his appearance, Nowakowski's prophetic words became a terrible reality some years later:

> The biggest thing to notice, is that in these times all efforts and endeavors and extraordinary inventions have emerged to ensure more and more convenience and benefits in people's lives; many and various ways of relaxation and enjoyment, catering for the present life are available. Alas! Sadly, in reality children seem to be affected by the poison of increased poverty, misery and growing disillusionment. There is self-pity, increasing bitterness, sorrow, mutual hatred, great dishonesty and deceit, despair, crime and injustice crying out to heaven for vengeance, and even worse, everything seems to predict that in the near future, even more terrible catastrophies await us. [pp. 302-303].

Then he recommended prayer to St. Joseph, who, he said, "is the greatest of all the saints, his dignity is unequalled, it is all embracing. He was the guardian of the Blessed Virgin Mary and Child Jesus, of St. Teresa and her nuns, and your Pastor will work in the church dedicated to him. I go to him with confidence in all needs ... He obtains for you who serve him on earth, the solace and support that you need." [p. 303].

That day it was decided that Nowakowski's sermon should be printed, and Kalinowski wrote the preface. He recalled in his dedication the temporary chapel in 1892 on Ulika Zatorska, Wadowice, whose only ornaments were paintings of the Heart of Jesus, Our Lady and St. Joseph – the Blessed Mother as Queen of Carmel and St. Joseph as worker in this little house of God.

The celebrations lasted three days and on August 30 choir services were inaugurated together with other observances of religious life. On September 2 the memorial Mass of St. Brocard, the first prior of Mount Carmel was said, and Wadowice was given the dignity of a Vicariate, independent of Czerna, while a few days later it was opened as a Philosophical College.

The Lord seemed to bless the Carmelites at this time; the first two novices who came to join the Order in Wadowice were Czeslaw Jakubowski and John Kanty Osierda, soon followed by Albert Drobniak. Kalinowski's friend Nowakowski had originally alerted Drobniak to the presence of the Carmelites in Czerna.

Marian Goeschlberger was the first professor of philosophy, and the first two students of philosophy were John Wurm and Engelbert Deventer[176] who came from in *Györ* to Wadowice to complete their studies and join other Polish students for the Order. These were the first graduates of the new College in Wadowice.

But there were ongoing needs for more funds to sustain such a big new development and Kalinowski was a key figure in an effort to provide them. The friars in Czerna strongly recommended the financial needs of Wadowice to the numerous pilgrims who came there every year for spiritual guidance. Pilgrims from Silesia were especially known for their generosity. Money was sent to one of the

---

[176] Deventer went as a missionary to the U.S but later left the Order. John Wurm went back to Vienna. Osierda was a valuable member of the community at Czerna. He translated various works from German to Polish. Jakubowski became master of novices in Czerna and later a professor at the college. He made a collection of two books of Kalinowski's notes and was also the chronicler of the Polish Province.

friars, Edward Palka who came from Silesia, and was very popular with people from there. To facilitate fundraising Kalinowski wrote an appeal in which he clarified the purpose of the new foundation and the reasons for which it was undertaken. He went into detail about the history of persecuted Poland, and the Carmelite houses both there and in Ukraine that had once flourished, but had since been suppressed and forgotten. He recommended the whole project to the charity of the people. The appeal was sent to all and sundry, including family and friends. Contributions began to flow freely. The appeal outlined one of the Kalinowski's key motivations in all he did – his devotion to Mary.

Above all, Kalinowski ardently desired renewal in Poland, Lithuania and Russia. As we know, for more than a century prior to this, Poland, together with provinces belonging to it, had fallen under the blows of oppressors both internal and external.

Always on the lookout for an opportunity to avail himself of new evangelistic tools, one presented itself in 1895. The occasion was the biography of General de Sonis, written by Bishop Louis Baunard.[177] "That's it – I said to myself, reading it – he should be an apostle of Poland and Russia," Kalinowski mused. [p. 285]. And since that time he was constantly thinking about a Polish translation of the biography. The sisters of Łobzów came up with the answer: Madame Jerzmanowska, who had a cousin, a Carmelite, had just released a Polish translation of the life of Brother Francis of the Infant Jesus written in French.[178] When he learned about this Kalinowski proposed that she translate it. This idea was well

---

[177] Louis Baunard, Général de Sonis, d'après ses papiers et son correspondence, Paris 1890. De Sonis fought in the battle of Solferino in 1859. His sister was a Carmelite nun at Coutances and he himself became a member of the Carmelite Secular Order. This book can be found online Internet Archive.

[178] Ven. Francis Pascual Sanchez was a saintly Spanish Discalced Carmelite. He was two years younger than St. John of the Cross, being born in 1544. Even in his lifetime he was venerated as a saint and wonder-worker.

received, and with Baunard's permission, she undertook this work also. Baunard was pleased that his biography of de Sonis would be published in Polish;[179] it appeared in Kraków in the first months of 1899. Kalinowski, with the help of family and friends, covered part of the printing costs, and Mary Xavier Czartoryska covered the rest. She was known and loved by all landowners in Galicia and Ukraine, and distributed the biography of General de Sonis everywhere: in return she received the necessary funds from grateful donors. It was also well received in Poznan. The first edition was quickly sold out and as Mother Mary Xavier put it, "Galicia and the Grand Duchy of Posen (Poznan) were flooded with the General's biography." [p. 286] The Friars wished to issue a second edition in Warsaw and asked the editor of a magazine there, if he would undertake this work. The Editor willingly agreed and by his enthusiasm and his many contacts the biography was also distributed in Warsaw and parts of Russia.

In spite of his heavy workload it seems that these three years launching the new community in Wadowice were very happy ones. On July 26, 1902, three students from the college received priestly ordination in the church in Wadowice from Bishop Anatole Nowak, suffragan bishop of Kraków. One of the newly-ordained priests was Albert (Josaphat) Drobniack who died prematurely; all had been novices under Kalinowski and Diaz de Cerio at Czerna.

He was particularly devoted to the Infant Jesus. (Valentine Macca, carmelnet.org)

[179] Baunard was an admirer of Hermann Cohen and his music. Baunard, writing at the beginning of the 20th century, referred to Cohen's hymns in these words "... The artist (Hermann) was to sing the sweetest, the most mystical and penetrating melodies ever heard in our century." Baunard was a Professor at the University of Lille and later Bishop of Orleans and a prolific writer. St. Thérèse quotes the phrase grain of sand from one of the prayers he composed (Letters, ICS, Volume II). De Sonis fought the Prussians in 1871, serving in the army of the Loire, a conflict which Thérèse's mother Zélie Martin reports on at length in her correspondence. Baunard was a friend and correspondent of Frederick Ozanam founder of the St. Vincent de Paul Society.

On December 27 the same year Kalinowski wrote to one of the Carmelite convents: "What a loss for us, the unexpected death of Father Josaphat! It's a difficult time but he may help us from heaven." Three days later he wrote to Przemyśl Carmel: "We have suffered a great loss with the death of the late Father Josaphat. He ended his earthly life with a peaceful and happy death. We must trust that he has reached heaven." [p. 402]. He was just 36 years of age.

A few days later, Kalinowski described the details of Josaphat's death in a letter to the Carmel, written in the house of the Capuchins in Kraków, where in fact a new trial awaited him. His closest friend from Siberia, Wenceslaus Nowakowski, the Capuchin was dying, and asked him to come to visit him from Wadowice because he wanted to die in his arms. He remained with his friend during those last days of 1902 and the first week of 1903. On January 16 he reported the death of Wenceslaus to the Carmel of Przemyśl:

> I don't know what to write about Father Wenceslas. The most important thing was that he was fortified with the sacraments, and truly died on the cross in the way he suffered. These are the best signs of a good death: *Pretiosa in conspectu Domini mors sanctorum eius*! [Precious in the eyes of the Lord is the death of his saints]. But please pray for him – the best lives on this earth always show signs of human weakness... The moment of parting with the world for any one of us, and for myself perhaps it will come soon, as come it must. ... Accounts of posthumous praise or blame don't help much, but the main thing is how you die." [p. 407].

Provincial Councillor and Prior in Wadowice (1897–1900)

From a letter written by Kalinowski on March 13, 1897 to the Carmelite sisters at Łobzów, we know that Kalinowski was ill again, and that doctors could do nothing for him. But he merely turned to Our Lady of Perpetual Help and prayed for improvement. The time for the Provincial Chapter was approaching where he was elected second Provincial Councillor and again appointed Superior in Wadowice. This in fact was an improvement on his onerous duties in Czerna. In June and July 1898 he accompanied the Provincial, as he had done on former occasions, on a canonical visit of the Carmelite Convents in Kraków, Lviv and Przemyśl. After finishing the visit, he remained in Kraków to stand in for the Carmelite friars who had gone on vacation. On August 24, 1898 Kalinowski was in Czerna, where he participated in the profession of Czeslaw Jabukbowski and John Kanty Osierda.

On December 9, 1897, Kalinowski wrote: "In recent days, we are heavily under siege in the confessional; yesterday and the day before it lasted until 5 o'clock in the evening, and up to 450 people came for Holy Communion." [p. 291]. The community consisted of only three members, and as Prior he was responsible for everything; even the students came frequently to him for tutoring in mathematics, Russian and French. Not to mention the demands of the Carmelite sisters! The following year and again just before Christmas he was exhausted and on December 22, (1898), after returning to Wadowice, Kalinowski's letters betray a shaky hand with only a few clear words – evidence of his state of health, as he freely admits: "I don't have enough energy to write."

A few days later he had to stay in bed all week due to a cold. Nowakowski and several other friends came to visit him, and the Carmelite sisters on this occasion once again proved their loyalty. On January 4, 1898 Rybka wrote to thank them for all they did for their dear patient. In reassuring them, he attributes Kalinowski's recovery to the intercession of St. Joseph to whom the church was dedicated. On January 15 Kalinowski had already commented about how surprised he was that so much interest could be shown in him; he was almost sorry to have recovered!

"Often in times of sickness like this," he wrote, "when I was deluged with so many acts of charity, motivated by the virtues of faith, I was reminded of the reality of the Communion of Saints... Here I am on the way to recovery, it's amazing! – Sometimes I long for the days of fever: then you don't even feel human but now I'm starting to be myself again and you must re-direct your energies and set yourself to carry on with the hardships of earthly life. Prayer becomes even more necessary. My prison was softened by the fir-forest balsam, sent from Vienna. But I cannot take advantage of the things sent by the donor. Maybe you would be willing to give some hints on how to use it! At night, when weakness seized me, I woke up – and suddenly my gaze rested on the image of Our Lady of Perpetual Help before which burned a small night light. I felt as if I were in heaven! My current recovery is the hardest to bear, that is, my head feels alright but one has to stay stuck in creature comforts – like an animal in the mud. But such is the will of God, I must be humble and submit. My suffering is well worth it indeed as is the suffering of others.

He then tells them of a current news item, how a prisoner from Wadowice, who escaped from gaol and was found hiding in a damp and cold basement: "Jesus also died on the cross for this unhappy man. It is the grace of God that they were able to catch him – he can still repent. Pray for his conversion. So many people have already been converted by your prayers. Jesus, mercy!" [p. 293].

All the Carmels in Poland prayed fervently for Kalinowski's health and on January 19, 1899, he wrote to the Prioress in Łobzów: "Only today can I take a pen to thank your dear Sisters and for your prayers that brought me much help in a dangerous crisis, from which the Lord Jesus delivered me." [p. 293].

God delivered him from one cross, only to impose a different and heavier one still. He writes about it on March 3: "I beg you to pray for my brother [Gabriel] in Warsaw who wrote to me saying that the end had come for him." [p. 293].

In the absence of Kalinowski, Casimir Rybka and John Nepomuk had to redouble their work in the church in January and February. In March the celebrations in honor of St. Joseph were so busy that the Prior of Czerna had to replace him in the confessional. Kalinowski was so worried that the friars were overworked that he wished to leave Wadowice and make room for someone else as the house could only accommodate three people. After the canonical visitation in 1898 his Provincial allowed him to return to Czerna. In the meantime Diaz de Cerio took his place from November 27 and Chrysostom Lamos saw to the completion of the church and monastery in Wadowice, which was done with taste and expertise.

Earlier on in November Kalinowski had written from Czerna to the Carmelite nuns telling them how the Prior, the Brother cook and the infirmarian cared assiduously for him, and recommended them to their prayers. He ends the letter in typical fashion: "And my poor soul won't heal unless the Lord Jesus, the physician and the Blessed Mother wish it! ... So please recommend this great sinner to the merciful Mother and that I may receive medicine from the compassionate heart of Jesus!" [p. 294]. Five days later he wrote to his friend Nowakowski:

> My health is puzzling, for the past few days I have been quite bad. I have just been able to get up and I am finishing this note standing at the desk – your gift to me. I am not sure whether I will be able to travel to take part in the election (Prioress in Kraków). I am now reading the chronicle of our Sisters in Lublin, and translating it into French. After the introduction I will include a note about the siege of Berdichev, avoiding the various complexities in the story. For my instruction I'm reading and studying St. Josaphat. I am meditating on the *Vita D.N.J. Christi* by Ludolph of Saxony.[180] I am looking through the records of the old Polish Province and I would be glad to outline some notes about it. [p. 295].

---

[180] This was an influential four-volume book recommended by St. Teresa to her sisters.

Kalinowski enjoyed no rest on returning to Czerna. When the General or Provincial came on canonical visitations of the Carmelite houses, he always had to accompany them as interpreter. He would do research in the libraries of the houses they visited, especially that of Wesoła, where exiled sisters sought shelter during different periods of persecution. He would also examine records of the Carmelite priories of St. Martin (in Kraków), and Lviv, Warsaw and Vilnius, where he found very valuable manuscripts relating to the former Carmel in Poland. He made up his mind to share these accounts with his brothers and sisters in the newly-restored Carmel in Poland. He saw this as a vital and powerful means of consolidating the work that had begun. Reading these old manuscripts people get to know the spirit of the Order and the heroic qualities of those who went before them; this encourages new generations to follow in their footsteps. In a letter to Princess Cecilia Lubomirska in 1898 Kalinowski shows us what he is thinking: "Woe to the nation that does not try to preserve these records – they are courting a harsh judgement." [p. 296].

From the above-mentioned letter to Nowakowski, we learn that soon after arriving in Czerna Kalinowski began to read the manuscripts stored in the house archives and above all the Carmelite chronicles of Lublin. In the same letter to his friend he said he was soon going to Kraków for the election of a new Prioress. The new Prioress, Mary Xavier learned to have great respect for ancient documents, first in her family home in Ukraine, and from her brother Prince Ladislaus Czartoryski. She would look out for anything that might remind posterity of the qualities of those who went before them. Kalinowski was of course happy she was chosen as Prioress – knowing she would make a good collaborator. On November 29, after returning to Czerna, he wrote to her: "God bless you for all the consolation you gave me; I forgot to record yesterday the books you have allowed me to take – the manuscript journal of Vilnius, in one bound notebook, and the works of St. John of the [Cross] written in Polish, in two volumes, bound and unbound – this card may be used as evidence that I have borrowed them." [p. 296].

Kalinowski has searched for old manuscripts, and not only among the Carmelites. On December 9 he wrote again on this subject: "I am now reading the life of Marchocka (written at the request of her confessor Father Ignatius of St. John), formerly purchased by us from Warsaw." [p. 297]. He had already read the chronicle of Vilnius, since he adds in the same letter: "It was a regrettable thing that caused the deaths of our sisters in Vilnius, which can be read in the chronicle of Vilnius. ... How grateful we should be to Prioress Sr. Maury that these resources and the Vilnius archives are stored with you." [p. 297.

Kalinowski continued his research. "From 1898," the Prioress of Wesoła wrote, "he was very interested in our library. He asked me to gather all important documents, manuscripts and letters and after having read them he catalogued them all. He carried out the same work in the Convent at Łobzów, where he found real treasures." In his letter of December 9, he wrote to the Prioress: "Please do not forget the beautifully produced copy of the life of Bl. Marchocka (probably written by the same Father Ignatius, from a book by Antoinette M." [p. 297].

On January 2, 1899, he wrote to the sisters in Łobzów: "Please send me a list of what you have regarding the history of the Order here in Poland, or the lives of the sisters and brothers, or any chronicles you have." [p. 298]. A few weeks later: "We are missing only the chronicle of the Lviv sisters, we have all the others, some in Wesoła and some in Łobzów. I'm working on them and arranging them as a whole, but it's not an easy thing to do and requires a huge amount of work." [p. 298]. In the same letter he sent them the permission of the Provincial to publish the book.

Prioress Anna was already preparing a translation of the Autobiography of Sister Thérèse of the Child Jesus. The nuns were also working in Łobzów and soon completed an account of Venerable Thérèse of St. Augustine, formerly Louise Marie, Princess of France.

Following the example of Kalinowski they worked tirelessly for the spiritual good of their brothers and sisters in the new Carmel in Poland.

With the coming of spring, Kalinowski once again succumbed to illness, as we read in a letter dated April 17 to the Prioress of Łobzów: "As for health, the greatest problem is not being able to leave the cell, even to go to the altar, although my energy has already returned. Strong bouts of fever continue and my lungs are playing up. God grant that the weather will change, and free me from this. It would be good because it would then be more easy to commune with God – what with me being just a lifeless lump of clay!" [p. 298].

Chapter Seven

Heritage Recovery and Other Matters

Carmelite Chronicles

In the lead-up to the celebration of the Fifth Centenary of the birth of St. Teresa of Avila in 2015, the Carmelite leadership in Rome has proposed that all members of the Carmelite family should read and study the Book of the Foundations of St. Teresa. This is an invitation to look to the rock from which the Carmelites have sprung. It was this same idea that motivated Kalinowski to expend an enormous amount of energy in researching and writing up the stories of earlier Carmelites. In this he showed a true instinct for what is required to inspire a desire for renewal. In fact in a preface to his work he explicitly refers to St. Teresa's Foundations. Szezepan Praskiewicz notes: "In his desire to restore the Polish Carmel, Father Raphael was aware that it was not enough to assemble and form vocations and found new convents, but that it was also necessary to recover the heritage of the past."[181]

While most of the material concerned the convents of Carmelite nuns, he also added extracts from the Chronicles of the houses of Carmelite friars. In October 1899 Kalinowski attended a meeting

---

[181] Szezepan T. Praskiewicz, OCD, *Saint Raphael Kalinowski.*

of the Provincial Council in Linz, and from there he wrote to the Prioress in Przemyśl:

> I hope Sr. Joseph will be happy to take on the collecting of materials for the history of the Sisters of Vilnius from 1660 to 1667. Sister has a perceptive sense and has the skills needed to edit passages from the chronicle of Poznan and the chronicle of Lviv –Warsaw. But for this she will need the help of the sisters in bringing about the publication of the history of the Carmelite nuns in Poland. It will be called: *Convents of Discalced Carmelites in Poland, Lithuania and Ruthenia: Their origin, development and exile during the war which took place in the seventeenth century.* The material revolves around the chronicles of the Convent (Vols. 1-4), Kraków 1900-1904. [pp. 310-311].

Death prevented Kalinowski from completing this work, but he had published four volumes in quarto, of which Sr. Mary Xavier wrote: "The Chronicles: Vilnius, Lviv, Warsaw and Kraków have been produced by Fr. Raphael with great effort and with great care. A manuscript Chronicle of Vilnius, which is in our possession is written in his hand; other manuscripts, if the fathers don't have them, must be with the sisters in Łobzów or Lviv." [p. 311].

From September 1899 Kalinowski began to publish the Carmelite Chronicles of Vilnius, and he was most anxious to complete this work. We see this from what he wrote on September 9 to the Prioress in Przemyśl: "Mother Teresa was inspired to have the journal of Vilnius published. I have some concern whether or not I can look very far ahead – until April? Will God allow me to live that long?" [p. 311]. On November 18 the Provincial gave permission for the work to be published. The author wished that his name not be mentioned in the book, but the Provincial had other ideas. In January 1900 the work appeared under his name. It was natural Kalinowski should quote his biblical namesake on the first page of the book in words taken from the Chronicle of the Carmelites in Lublin: "The angel Raphael said to Tobias: "Bless and extol his name. Proclaim before all people the deeds of God as they deserve, and never tire of giving him thanks" [Tobit 12:6].[182] For this reason, our holy Mother Teresa wrote a separate book on her Foundations as a testimony for her confessors, and not only has she herself done so, but nearly all religious orders have written chronicles in which they express and describe their purpose and how they were founded by the grace of God. They were concerned with the activities of the members and their holiness of life." [p. 312].

Having thus explained the purpose of his work, Kalinowski gives an overview of the history of Carmelite nuns in Poland during the various disasters that plagued 17th century Poland, Lithuania and other places. He shows how these sisters were forced to leave their quiet convents, carrying the torch of faith and commitment to countries that became known as *the* bulwark of Christianity in the East, just as St. Teresa carried the torch to other countries that were the bulwark of the Catholic Church in the West. He wrote: "During their long forays through Lithuania, Poland, Hungary and Moravia, Carmelites experienced poverty, disease, dangers of various kinds like severe frost in winter, but always and everywhere they were faithful to their religious duties. ... Among them were young sisters, belonging to the foremost families in the country, such as: Tyszkiewiczs, Radziwills, Massalskis, etc." [p. 313].

At the end of the chronicle Kalinowski added a 40-page explanatory note to the work to inspire the Carmelites.

In April 1900 he wrote to Bishop Henry Kossowski in Wloclawek, asking him for help. He met him when he was Pastor at Leszno in Warsaw where every Thursday the bishop received the Catholic elite of the capital in his home. The bishop answered in a lengthy letter, saying how pleased he was with the news that

---

[182] A German account of Kalinowski was entitled (in translation) *An Angel for Tobias.*

Kalinowski was a friar and a priest and was busy working on useful projects for the Lord and for St. Teresa. In the letter to the Prioress of Łobzów, mentioned above, Kalinowski had stated: "Ms. Lubienska almost became a Carmelite nun, 1 hope she will be sufficiently Carmelite to make the trip to Lublin, and let her carefully search the two monasteries and convents of the Sisters and Friars, the latter is probably now the house of the Daughters of Charity. Please do not delay about it." [p. 316].

A Round-up of Old Friends

There were many people who were particularly dear to Kalinowski and whom he never forgot, those with whom he was closely linked by bonds of blood and friendship. Particularly strong were the friendships formed in exile in Siberia. In 1899, after 25 years of separation, a Jewish man named Henry Wohl visited him in Kraków. Kalinowski was delighted to see him, and greeted him like a long-lost brother; they talked about old friends. Kalinowski spoke of other old friends he saw or met again in Kraków – Nowakowski, Wasilewski, Dubiecki, Hofmeister and especially Felix Zienkowicz. The joy that these visits brought to Kalinowski was great and of course he always had an eye to the spiritual welfare of his friends. About one such visit Kalinowski wrote with almost maternal concern to Zienkowicz:

> Dear, loving Felix, I had forgotten your address, but Henry kindly gave it to me. I heard you moved to Warsaw to a permanent abode, and as Henry told me you have found an occupation that will serve as security in the future. Write to me, now that you're the father of several children including a daughter. Do you worry about their upbringing and education? How glad I would be to see you and your wife surrounded by your little ones. Is it God's will that I see you, I wonder? Perhaps not before death! – But I hope

to meet with you and yours in the afterlife. For me, it's not a question of change of state or circumstances, but perhaps only about the state of my soul, which still has to worry about final destiny by removing difficulties and avoiding pitfalls, but always the dangers remain. I read the Chronicle of the convents of Carmelite nuns and I encountered there probably a relative of your family from about the year 1780. She was a nun in the Convent of Vilna, perhaps the aunt of Bishop Zieńkowicz of Vilnius. [p. 318].

Then he discusses a subject dear to his heart – the conversion of his friend Henry Wohl. He invites Felix also to pray for a good outcome for the greater glory of God, and for Henry's good! He suggests Zienkowicz might act as Henry's godfather in that event. "After all, God can do anything, and we must also do all we can. I hug and bless your little children. Tell me their names. Describe your duties and your expectations, and especially let me know if you have enough to live on. Do you go to confession? Felix, let me know if you frequent the sacraments. Give Henry my fraternal embrace. I commend you all to the Immaculate Heart of Mary. Pray to the Lord for me, Your unworthy brother." [p. 319].

A few months later he wrote in reply to Zienkowicz, who informed him he now had a teaching position: "My dear Felix! I received your long welcome letter and I pray that your work and that of your worthy companion will produce much fruit for the good of your home and your dear little ones. Humanly speaking, I would prefer if you had chosen another profession, but if it pleased God to arrange for you the position you occupy today, nothing can be more advantageous to you when it is His holy will. Not being able to do anything else, at least I think of you often." Recalling the days of exile, he adds: "Indeed, the best days of our lives were spent in two places in the East." [p. 319]. He remembers those whom he loved, and who were already dead: Joseph Lagowski, Fiodor Gamello. Then on a sober note:

As for me, I will soon die. When you hear of my death, pray for me and get your children to pray with you. From our old companions in exile I see only Wenceslas, who is now on retreat here, and still works tirelessly; his hair is completely white. Joseph Wasilewski, his nephew, is a professor of philosophy and theology in Jassy. By what wonderful ways does God lead people. What happened to the family of Oledzkich who settled in the area of Zamosc? ... My dear Felix, looking at the current generation, I feel only fear. What confusion of ideas! We are getting closer to cosmopolitanism: broken homes, faith is shaken, religious obligations neglected, nothing, so to speak, is not thoroughly cooked,[183] and how much deceit there is – people live in illusions. Socialism is not only at the threshold, it has come in the door. Hope in God. Only he can inspire people with his grace not to waste life, but seek the truth and devote themselves to honest work. [p. 320].

A letter from Kalinowski in October 1896 further confirms his loyalty to old friends. Mother Mary Xavier told him of the arrival in Kraków of Princess Isabella Czartoryski and asked him to come visit. The princess, of course, had been instrumental in his entry into Carmel. Kalinowki responded to this invitation: "As for Princess Isabella, my deep appreciation for her is well known and I have an unforgettable feeling of gratitude and affection for her in God." [p. 320]. He was nostalgic for the days of "serenity spent in the Hôtel Lambert in the company of the late Gucio. But I do not have enough strength to come, I feel so miserable. Tomorrow will be too late. I will pray more and seek advice from my Guardian Angel." [p. 321]. In fact his guardian angel told him to accede to the wishes of the Princess, to whom after God, he owed his vocation to Carmel!

---

[183] The Polish word here is *dogotowane* which means *cooked*. It is not clear what he means – perhaps something like the English saying, *your goose is cooked!*

There were other people to whom Kalinowski was connected by ties stronger than friendship – by blood. Although his parents, his brothers Victor and Karol, his sisters Monica and Mary were now dead, his sister Emilia and three brothers, Gabriel, Aleksander and Jerzy were still alive. Karol left two sons, Marian and John, and feelings of honor and filial affection deriving from their parents won him the gratitude of the entire family. So Kalinowski, the oldest of the surviving siblings, considered it his duty to watch over them. He prayed for them at Mass daily and when they visited him in Czerna, took the opportunity to commend them to Mary's care, conferring the brown scapular on them. He was also concerned about their temporal wellbeing that often shows in his correspondence. Gabriel did not have long to live and would soon leave Helena alone with four children. Kalinowski cared deeply about them. In the summer of 1898 he wrote to Helena quite poetically:

> Our life, in its various phases, has some similarity with the rotation of the sun. After the fresh morning comes the heat of midday, followed by the soft light of dusk, and then silence. The same thing happens to your soul, reborn by grace. We can't get quite enough of the beauty of the dawn, which rises in our hearts, then we have to endure the heat of midday, but at the end of life in the quiet light of dusk the heat of the day wanes and then comes the darkness of death, followed by the dawning of eternal light. But we keep going. Patience will teach you to bear your hardships readily and your present sufferings, united to the merits of the Savior, will atone for sin to the divine justice. That is the treasury of the troubles you carry for those you love: troubles of a devoted wife, a caring mother and a careful housewife, guard it zealously and do not let the enemy of our soul snatch it away. Cordial and fraternal greetings to dear Bunio. [p. 321].

These are the last words we find in his correspondence about Gabriel (Bunio), who was so dear to him. He died soon afterwards, and Helena more than ever needed consolation. It was also the purpose of Kalinowski's last letter, culminating in this sentence: "I recommend you all to the Heart of Jesus."

Kalinowski had just read the biography of Marie Leszczyńska, Queen of France, written by an influential French writer, L'Abbé Proyart, and reading it, he thought constantly about Poland and his own family in Warsaw. He recommended Helena to read this book: *Vie de la reine Marie Leszczyńska, reine de France*, par L'Abbé Proyart. He wrote: "Order it directly from Librairie Ch. Paussielque, Rue Canette 15, Paris, the best bookstore in Paris." [p. 323]. The reason for this is found in the letter written at the same time to his friend Nowakowski: "A biography of *Marie Leszczynska, Queen of France* was sent to me," he writes, "I'd like to make her known in Warsaw and Kraków as a reminder where to find a model for all age groups and for all states of life. Proyart highlighted her message very well and very clearly. Would it not be good if Stanislaus Tarnowski undertook a summary of the book on Queen Marie?" [p. 323].

Queen Marie Leszczyńska was an exemplar for wives, mothers and children. She married Louis XV, King of France. Princess Louise Marie, her tenth child, mentioned in the previous chapter, entered the Carmelite Convent in St. Denis and her beatification process had just begun. Kalinowski wanted to put Queen Mary forward as a model for Helena and her family. In reply to Helena's letter Kalinowski said he was concerned about the future of children in general and was glad to see in Helena such a well-developed feeling of maternal responsibility. He advises her to look at the true source of fulfilment that lies in frequenting the sacraments and urges her to devote 15 minutes to spiritual reading every day.

Kalinowski continues on a favorite theme: "The confusion and bustle characterizes the spirit of our times, when the social order does so little, or frankly almost nothing, to point out to people where their true good resides. The Sacrament of Penance, by its divine origin, is not only a means of salvation, but is also like an anchor to protect the people on the ship from crashing into the rocks and sinking." [p. 323].

In 1897 Kalinowski's eldest niece was a boarder at the Convent of the Immaculate Conception in Yaroslavi in Russia, a city 250 Km north-east of Moscow. Her mother Helena told him that because of exhaustion, her daughter would be unable to undertake the long journey home to Warsaw for the Easter holidays. Kalinowski wanted to write to her immediately, but he was to begin a ten-day retreat that day, and as he was then Prior, he had still a lot of things to do. On the second day, despite the fact the retreat had commenced, with the permission of the confessor he wrote a touching letter to Marynia which she received before the holidays:

> Dear Marynia! I am writing to you as I begin a 10-day retreat and at the hour of recreation, in which I am about to read the life of a saint. Well, instead of reading, I will write to you.…. Actually I was about to write yesterday, but there were a lot of things to do, so I looked for a dispensation to write to you now, dearest Marynia. The other day your Mother wrote saying you are forced to miss the feast of the Resurrection at Easter away from the family hearth. My dear child you will spend these few days in the care of your venerable Mother Superior. I recommend frequent visits to the Lord Jesus in the Blessed Sacrament of the altar and that you read what I had been reading during recreation hours, i.e., the Lives of the Saints. There will be time for other games and pastimes – which is good. The Lord Jesus and the Blessed Mother, to whom we will pray for your poor Papa and for the rest of the family will take your place in Warsaw and appease their concerns. [pp. 326-327].

Return to Czerna

Kalinowski returned to Czerna in the final years of the century. As Councillor he did not have to lead the community, but even so, people looked to him for guidance. He received numerous letters from Warsaw and from all the Carmelite houses in Poland.

Kalinowski's family told him about their joys and sorrows, and not in vain. He had by no means forgotten family and friends and helped them with prayer and counsel. In almost every letter he advises them to look to the protection of Mary, reminding them in the words of the traditional Memorare: "Never was it known that anyone who fled to your protection, implored your help or sought your intercession was left unaided." [p. 327]. In November 1903 he was visited in Czerna by two sons of his brother Karol. Before leaving, he commended them to the care of the Mother of God, and enrolled them in the scapular.

The new Provincial allowed Kalinowski to remain in his role as Vicar Provincial for the Carmelite nuns. These he visited each year and helped them in every way he could. He would also liaise with the civil authorities, an important job at the time, as he was often called upon for advice because of the construction of several new Carmelite houses. When finances were in a bad state, he would start fundraising, and in fact knew how to do so. Several times in his letters we find the name of Count Stanislaus Grocholski, relative of the Czartoryskis, benefactor of the Convent in Przemyśl.

Kalinowski had to restrain the enthusiasm of Sr. Mary Xavier, and sometimes would insist she take more care of her health. When the triennium ended, he wrote her a commendatory letter: "Reverend Mother! I write today – in the last days of your term as Prioress. Looking back over the past three years I have a real appreciation for you and want to sing to the Lord of Lords a hymn of praise for the blessings received in this three-year period for your community and indirectly for the Order. Three good sisters have been admitted, funds for construction have been donated and dearest Sr. Stefania has departed for heaven." [p. 327].

When Mary Xavier's birthday came round it was always a great joy in the Convent at Łobzów. She had done so much for the Carmelites. She contributed enormously to the reform in Czerna. In many ways Kalinowski owed his vocation to her as he freely admitted. So he couldn't let her birthday pass without showing gratitude. He would send a card each year with an appropriate spiritual maxim. On one such card he wrote: "My most gracious God, in my covenant with you I say: I will die completely to myself, so that you yourself may live in me; I will remain in complete silence, so that you can speak with me, ceasing all feverish activity so that you can work with me. Amen." [p. 327]. And on another card: "St. Francis Xavier was the great apostle of India, and you, who through Mary have been blessed with so many graces, pray to her for me, that she intercede for me, whose name you bear, that she will remember me in life and death. I repeat often: Mother of God, remember me." [p. 327]. A third greeting card contained only these few words: "My God, my only Good, you are mine completely, and I will be completely yours."

The last two years of the 19th century were spent by Kalinowski as Prior and Councillor in Wadowice. He regained some strength, but at the same time they were for him years of strenuous work. Kalinowski worked tirelessly to complete what he had begun to help restore the old Carmel in Poland. He had published the chronicle of Vilnius, and announced that Teresa Marchocka's life was ready to be published. He combined relentless work with conscientious observance of religious life as well as long daily sessions in the confessional. There was much travel involved also in the course of his duties; in early May he was in Vienna and visited the Resurrection Convent.

Kalinowski had been Prior at Wadowice and Definitor for three years so he could not be re-elected. Which was just as well as he was unable to perform any duties, as we see from a letter of May 12: "The use of a pencil indicates my state of health. I now suppose I'm out of the danger but I owe it, after God, to our Father Provincial. How long it may please God to keep me at a low ebb, God only knows. Beginning with the Provincial and ending with the Brother who serves me I have so much experience of care these days that emperors do not have!" [p. 327].

On May 30, he felt better, but still could not leave his room. To save time, he asked for a résumé of Mother Marchocka's life to be sent to the printer and encouraged the sisters to work at it. On August 13 he informed the Convent of Lobzów that he had given the chronicle Lviv – Warsaw to the printers.

The Dawn of Saint Thérèse of Lisieux

Anna Kalstein, in Łobzów, inspired as she was like so many others by Thérèse's *Story of a Soul*, wished to publish a Polish translation. She was one of the prioresses who anticipated the enormous impact Thérèse's story would make, and how it would lead to a renewal of vocations to the Order. But Kalinowski objected because he was not happy with the quality of the translation on offer. He told her: "I advise you to refrain from publishing the translation of *La vie d'une âme*." [p. 340]. Kalinowski himself was the best person to improve the translation of Thérèse but couldn't even think about it at the time – he was completely engrossed in publishing the Convent Chronicles of Lviv and Warsaw, before publishing the biography of Mother Marchocka. Furthermore, he thought the Polish translation failed to capture the flavor of the French original. Now in a letter to Lisieux he refers to "one of those roses that the little sister never ceases to scatter on earth." [p. 340]. In this letter he indicates the need to correct the mistakes in the Polish translation. Being so fluent in French himself he was afraid Thérèse's unique story might be sold short. On October 9, 1902 he wrote to Mother Agnes, (Thérèse's sister) who was now Prioress in Lisieux:

Discalced Carmelites
Wadowice, October 9, 1902.

The inscription at the top of the book indicates my duty to repair a fault committed by me against your little saint, Sister Thérèse of the Child Jesus. Two or three years ago, when I looked over the manuscript of the Polish translation of the life of this little flower of Carmel, I made the observation that the language of our country does not conform to the style of the original, and reading it only causes unease.[184] This might place limitations on the apostolate of this chosen one of God. [He goes on with great good humor:] She had to take me to court, and on the other hand, not only did she take action but she took aim directly at me. For about a week my whole soul was tossed about by the waves of a stormy sea of interior pains, and not knowing where to find shelter, my eyes fell on the French edition of the life of the vengeful sister! Armed with the sign of the Cross I open the book and find the place where the fire in her heart unites with the burning heart of Jesus in *"Vivre d'amour."* [Living on Love] Suddenly the storm dies down, calm returns and something indescribable floods my whole being and changes me completely. This poem became an ark of salvation for me. The dear sister gave me confidence. I therefore conclude that the promises: "I will spend my heaven in doing good on earth." And: "After my death I will send down a shower of roses," is literally fulfilled.

Br. Rafael of St. Joseph, Discalced Carmelite. [p. 341].
This letter demonstrates that Kalinowski was one of the first Carmelites to recognize the importance of St. Thérèse's message.

---

[184] Kalinowski, writing in French, uses the strong word *dégoût*, 'disgust.'

The Prioress of Łobzów, Anna Kalstein, was also rewarded. For ten years the Convent had no novices. In the original small house there was no room for them. But the first novice joined after the completion of the translation of the *Story of a Soul*, and the second came after it was published. These were seen as two lovely roses sent down from heaven by Thérèse of the Child Jesus for the Carmel in Poland, where she was loved so much. Thérèse was beginning to take, not only France and Poland, but the whole world by storm.

Kalinowski's strength was now progressively failing and he felt that death was approaching; on leaving for a long journey to Linz and Lviv with the Provincial, he prepared for it as though he might not return. In a letter written in August 1900 to Sr. Mary Xavier, Prioress of the Convent of Lobzów, he leaves his last will and testament with her.

Testament for the current year from Raphael.

I leave in your careful keeping Mother, until my return from Lviv, the following manuscripts:

1. Description of the foundation of six monasteries of Discalced Carmelites in Poland, Lithuania and Russia.
2. *Life of Mother Barbara*, (Kretkowskich Zadzikowa) founder of the Convents of Lublin and Poznan.[185] This life includes matter of prime importance, the history of both Convents and the exiled Sisters of Lublin at the beginning of the war. Attention! Both these manuscripts belong to the Convent of Wesoła. These are unique, I have not enough time to return them, so please guard them '*ut pupillam oculi*' [as the apple of the eye].
3. *The Life of Mother Teresa of Jesus Marchocka*, through the instrumentality of the Wesoła Sisters.

---

[185] Another great Carmelite mystic. She wanted to become a Carmelite but was first forced to marry. She entered the convent after the death of her husband. She founded the convent of Poznan in 1645. Mother Barbara left an Autobiography containing mystical writings.

Send to the printers at your convenience. I strongly advise you about this and I repeat once again – have it printed without any change in style and layout of copy. [p. 343].[186]

Mary Xavier, who liked to practice instant obedience, wanted to get to work immediately but Kalinowski had to remind her that "the execution of a will can only take place after the death of the testator," so he asked her to wait until his death or return from his journey – whichever came first!

On October 5, he wrote to Mary Xavier who was editing his biography of Blessed Dionysius of the Nativity and Blessed Redemptus of the Cross, Carmelite martyrs of Sumatra. The biography of the martyrs was published in November and Kalinowski ordered a thousand copies for Czerna and two hundred for Wadowice.

The purpose of the biography of Marchocka, so much desired by Kalinowski, and prepared by him amid so many difficulties, was to make known the holiness and admirable qualities of Teresa Marchocka and move forward the process for her beatification. With this in mind he began to study the treatise of Benedict XIV on the beatification and canonization of saints and started to put together a Memorandum for the beatification in accordance with the requirements of the Sacred Congregation of Rites.

---

[186] Helena Kalinowski, Gabriel's wife undertook to pay the printing costs.

Chapter Eight

Vicar Provincial for the Carmelite Nuns (1901)

*I*n June 1901 the Carmelite sisters at Lobzów received the following letter from the Provincial, Chrysostom Lamos: "Mother! I informed Father Raphael of the latest changes. Since June 1 he is the Vicar for the Carmelite Sisters in Poland and from now on the sisters will refer to him in all matters within the Provincial's jurisdiction. I delegate all necessary faculties to him and he will conduct canonical visitations for me. Please tell this to all the sisters, so that they will be aware of who to turn to in order to avoid confusion. Br. Chrysostom." [p. 350].

On May 14, after being notified of his appointment, Kalinowski wrote to Mary Xavier: "In this letter I mention a message for me (from the Provincial) not necessarily a comforting one, and that is finding myself Vicar Provincial of the Carmelite nuns in Galicia. When I was delegated by our Father Provincial a week ago, I cited the pressures of the office, but the excuse was to no avail and I was forced to accept the cross." [p. 350].

And on the previous day he wrote to Przemyśl Convent: "For my final humiliation God was pleased that our Father Provincial appoint me Vicar Provincial for the nuns in the Convents of Galicia.

So in all matters concerning your affairs, that you would normally have put to the Provincial, you can now turn to me instead. I trust in God that they will not be too onerous. What should I do now about the canonical visit? Although I will be obliged to choose the time according to local needs in Wadowice, the Council would also take your convenience into consideration." [pp. 350-351].

As the Austro-Hungarian Province extended from Linz to Lviv, it was difficult for provincials, who lived in Linz, to settle all matters personally, and Carmelites tended to turn to Kalinowski in every need. For that reason the Provincial felt that the sisters might benefit from Kalinowski's experience and prudence. Carmelite nuns tended to write to him frequently, asking for help in difficult and complicated matters both temporal and spiritual that arose from time to time. Already in 1900, when efforts were made to purchase the site for a new Convent in Lobzów, Bonaventure Kirchstein appointed Kalinowski Vicar Provincial for the Carmelites in Poland. "I had been looking out but in vain" writes Kalinowski on April 5 of that year "for promising news about a house and land acquisition, when suddenly a letter comes from our Father Provincial appointing me Vicar Provincial in *partibus Sororum*" [In places where the sisters live].

Chrysostom Lamos [the Provincial] imitated his predecessor and from June 1, 1901, Kalinowski was also appointed Superior for the Carmelite nuns in Galicia. Approaching canonical visitation time and in order to carefully prepare for it, he started to read the instructions of St. Teresa, '*On making the Visitation.*'

The Visitation for 1901 was held on September 9 and was repeated every year at about the same time whenever he was strong enough to undertake the journey. He wrote: "They sent me to you in spite of my unworthiness. In order to carry out this visit well, I would have to have the spirit of our Father Elijah, our Mother Teresa and our Father John of the Cross, which I don't have. So if anything good is to happen, it will be the work of God, but I will boast of my weaknesses." [p. 358].

In the opinion of Kalinowski, the purpose of a canonical visit is found in the Lord's Prayer: "Your will be done on earth as it is in heaven" and he used this as a motto for the nuns. "We are in Carmel," he would say, "to submit to God in giving up the things of this world, and in that way drawing down on ourselves and others the help we need to attain eternal happiness. The best part of this sacrifice, which is also the most pleasing to God, is that we surrender our will to Him by the vow of obedience. Obedience is the death of one's own will, but that's not enough. We need to persevere until death.... Our obedience offers us the perfect opportunity for our will to disappear completely and the will of God to be the guide of our actions. So when is our obedience perfect? We can see it in the mirror which the canonical visitation holds up to us. This is a mirror of our sacred obligations. If you do not obey them perfectly, the visitor will point it out to you, and you should take that as if it came from the lips of God – with respect and joy." [p. 359].

The Prioress in Wesoła commented that during the visits Kalinowski worked tirelessly, paying no attention to his health. One of the sisters of Przemyśl wrote: "Fr. Raphael was always ready to help us. Especially when on a canonical visit he listened and spoke with great patience!" The same sister continues: "He seemed to be immersed in the things of God. He needed to talk about God and promote the service of God, though he was glad he had to deal only with spiritual matters and didn't need to treat of mundane matters at the time of visits.... May the Lord Jesus give our convents more holy people like him!" [p. 361].

When at the end of the visit the nuns gathered for him to communicate his comments and admonitions, he appeared to be somewhat uncomfortable. At the end of the visit Kalinowski quoted the words of the Savior to St. Peter:

"Do you love me?" He asked them to imagine the divine Master calling each of them by name, doing so repeatedly, as he did with St. Peter: 'Do you love me? Do you love me?'

Love gives strength to do the will of God in every situation, to avoid everything that might displease Him, to work and to suffer for His glory. St. Teresa wanted to suffer or to die; St. Magdalen de Pazzi did not want to die, but to suffer. Love is strong as death. And just as nothing can resist death, love gives strength to triumph over every challenge. Then you don't feel pain, and if you do you welcome it. From this fire of God's love the flame of love of neighbor arises. Anyone who loves God with all his heart desires that God be loved by all and this desire pervades his whole life.... But who is able to achieve such a degree of perfect love, which will free our soul from attachment to any earthly goods and completely unite our will with God's will? When the Divine Savior again asks us for our hearts, let us ask Him to take them to Himself; only He can purify them and light the fire of holy love and an ardent desire to be detached from everything and to want only His holy will. To help us to inner freedom and growth, Divine Providence provides us with a number of measures, one of them a visitation. Let each one of the dear sisters try to imagine, as I said, that Christ the Lord asks you by name the question: 'Do you love me? Do you decide to exclude everything in your heart that is opposed to my love?' Maybe you have not received many admonitions during this visit, but you may be aware of hidden attachments: do you make up your mind to exclude these so as to give me your heart completely and forever? [p. 362].

Then he points out what might go to prove that a sister was sincere in her protestations of love for Jesus:

Evidence of this commitment would be this – if each of you in the convent observe strict religious obedience in the task entrusted to you, seeing it as the law engraved in the book of

God's will. When she loves her sisters, is kind to them, gives them good example, accepts her weaknesses and tries to rise above them, and when she forgets the world and the things of this world, except for what is necessary; when she is an apostle of penance and prayer together with the sacrifice of herself on the altar of religious life in order to appease God's mercy and to obtain the conversion of sinners, and when she sees her daily life as a religious martyrdom, as it was so aptly called by St. Teresa, she will possess a courageous and persevering heart. Our life really requires effort and self-denial, but God helps those who ask for it with confidence and humility, and when the struggle is over, God will be her reward. [p. 362].[187]

Sometimes he would send an admonition after the visit: "Mother! Now I want to say I am putting several important observations before you on the matters we discussed at the last visit. I do this to remind you of the requirements regarding our obligations which can be so easily forgotten."[188]

This involved the Convent of Wesoła, the only one remaining from the former Polish provinces. Since the religious houses were suppressed by the Russians, they were deprived of the benefits of the canonical visitation and certain customary practices were overlooked. Kalinowski noticed this and decided to restore former customs. He devoted more effort and time to them than to others and showed sincere dedication to them in spite of fatigue. He continues:

---

[187] This is a summary of the conference, delivered on June 28, 1902 to the community of Łobzów in Kraków at the end of the canonical visitation.
[188] Kalinowski visited the Wesoła convent in August 1902. The letter was addressed to Teresa Joseph Wojnarska, Prioress. The purpose of the visit was to bring the customs of the convent into line with those which prevailed in others in the Province.

I address this letter to you as proof of my sincere affection for your community and I would like to assist the sisters and every individual on the path of your holy calling which leads to heaven. I have already told you, and I repeat once again: God has given you the important task of restoring religious observance in this Convent in which you live out your solemn vows, and thus complete detachment from the world is called for. Let this truth sink deeply into your memory, consider it carefully, and conscientiously adapt your behavior to it. Divine Providence, in its unspeakable goodness towards you, appoints you to live in the Convent far from the world, under the care of the Blessed Virgin and in union with the Divine Master. This thought and the memory of our sins fill our hearts with regret, but the Virgin Mary, Mediatrix of grace will bless us from heaven. [p. 364].

An example of Kalinowski's vigilance, in the spirit of those pre-Vatican times, is shown by the following. The Convent at Wesoła made lace curtains for the grille in the Convent choir so that the nuns could see the Blessed Sacrament when people were in the chapel. "This custom, said Kalinowski, "is not in the other convents, so please dispense with it and let the dear sisters be confident that our Divine Savior will then appear much brighter to the eyes of their souls in which he wishes to live." [p. 364].

In what concerned the parlor and the gate, he insisted that all regulations be strictly observed. This injunction will strike us as rather harsh in the aftermath of Vatican II, but Kalinowski was merely adhering to the strict custom then in vogue. On the same note we find that several people from Mother Teresa Marchocka's family, who wished to pray at her tomb, asked the Bishop of Kraków for permission to enter the cloister. Permission was granted provided the Prioress and Superior agreed. Kalinowski wrote a long letter to the Prioress, informing the family of his decision: He refused permission, because it was Lent: "The Holy See," he writes, "when it gives permission in a similar case gives it on one condition: it had to be outside Advent and Lent." [p. 364].

Kalinowski advised prioresses to ask postulants seeking admission to a Convent to provide necessary and useful information. We often read in his letters, written on this subject: "The prioress decides." Even the decision of the community was not for him a sure sign of a vocation, but the approval of the Superior (himself) was also required.

In his letters he often repeats the same wisdom: "We are in Carmel for the glory of God and the salvation of souls, but by ourselves, we can do nothing, and, we need the help of His grace for the great task which God has entrusted to us. To obtain this assistance we should work continuously and use all means at our disposal to help us unite ourselves with Jesus Christ, the giver and the source of all grace." [p. 364].

Kalinowski insisted that Carmelite nuns be always busy at work according to their strengths and capacities, and recommended to them the apostleship of the Word; but especially he urged them to evangelize by example. We know how they cooperated with him in the immense work of publishing the chronicles of the various Carmels. He would expect the work to be done with all possible accuracy.

He also encouraged the nuns to work willingly and joyfully, because work brings great spiritual benefit, since it promotes a love of solitude, silence and inner recollection. When he wrote to the prioresses and communities he invariably included a few kind words for the lay sisters who worked so hard. He recommended the observance of silence and insisted on the necessity of this important point of the Carmelite Rule.

One of the nuns who endured a lot of sickness asked him for a few words of consolation and she received this response: "What is the real ornament of a church on the outside? It is the crucifix, sign of the Holy Cross which towers above the ground, radiating to the sky and looking down on the faithful. The one who hung on the cross for us sinners now humbly and quietly abides in the tabernacle. Let our merciful Savior give you sufficient strength so that the cross will be your ornament too." [p. 388].

Kalinowski often repeated that perfect love consists of handing everything over to God and he reminded people the Savior gave the Apostles a beautiful discourse at the Last Supper, before he went with them to the Garden of Olives. In this discourse, which can be regarded as his testament, Jesus explained what true love is: "You are my friends if you do what I command you."

"Our main duty in Carmel," wrote Kalinowski, "is to commune with God in all our activities. We should first of all try to get rid of anything that could detain us in our journey and work on this. We should do only what God wants, regardless of the internal and external difficulties that we encounter, not trusting our own powers, but placing all our hope in the infinite mercy of God." Again: "May you desire to love God greatly," he wrote to a prioress, "and let this strong desire increase more and more in you and overflow into all activities of life." [p. 389].

Chapter Nine

Czerna 1903 – 1906

*O*n April 25, 1903 Raphael Kalinowski wrote to the Prioress of the Carmel in Lobzów, Kraków: "I was not expecting this at all, being elected to the Provincial Chapter as a delegate, and today I am leaving Wadowice to spend some days in Czerna, and on Monday at about two in the afternoon, we have to go by train to Vienna. I strongly commend myself to your prayers and those of all the dear sisters. The task is a very difficult one and quite a responsibility." [p. 408].

In this Chapter held in 1903 Bonaventure Kirchstein was elected Provincial, and Kalinowski elected Second Councillor, while Diaz de Cerio was made Prior at Czerna. The previous Provincial, Chrysostom Lamos became Prior in Wadowice and Superior of the seminary. Kalinowski, accompanied by de Cerio went to Czerna, in order to spend the beginning of the new term there and Fr. Albert took the place vacated by the deceased Josaphat. The term started well. In the first days of July the Provincial came on a canonical visitation and met with eight students in Czerna from the seminary in Wadowice who asked to be admitted to the novitiate. It was an impressive ceremony involving these young men following a traditional Carmelite ritual of being received into the Order. One year later, much the same ceremony was repeated, all the novices promising to persevere in their vocation in the service of God and Our Lady of Mount Carmel.

More on the heritage of the past – Chronicles of Warsaw Carmel.

In a letter dated April 1902, we read: "After the Easter holidays I was very tired and was struggling and didn't know if I could do the job…. My head gets tired easily; on the other hand, I cannot remain idle. I do not lack work: I wanted to work on the Chronicles of the Warsaw Carmel." He left that job to another friar whom he asked to do it, and an edition was duly published, namely the Chronicles of the Convent of St. Martin, the first Carmelite convent in Poland. [p. 408].

In the preface he outlined the purpose and significance of this publication. He drew the reader's attention to the names of some of the Carmelite Sisters there – many of them members of the aristocracy – and adds: "We have details of the lives of self-denial of the sisters who cooperate with the grace of vocation through penance and spiritual poverty with the power of the Spirit. Here we have an example of true nuptials, unknown to the wealthy in lofty positions in the world. Such dedication and courageous form of life could not but have a beneficial effect on themselves, on their surroundings, as well as on outsiders." [p. 408].

Kalinowski tells us these Chronicles were preserved in the Krasinski Library in Warsaw, thanks to the helpfulness and mediation of a man called Kallenbach, curator of the library. The Chronicle of the Warsaw Carmel was written in Latin. Kalinowski translated it into Polish and placed it at the end of the Chronicles of the Convent of St. Martin. He also added a brief mention of the Convents of the Discalced Carmelites in Lublin and Wisnicz.

At this stage Kalinowski was nearly seventy, exhausted by age and work. Repeated illness had taken its toll on his health; yet many additional activities will engage him for the rest of his life. And

Carmel in Poland will be forever grateful to him for researching the libraries and rescuing beautiful and touching stories of its history from the dust of oblivion. Kalinowski also wanted to make records in French, so that they might be made known throughout the Order. With the translation and publication of his biography of Mother Teresa of Jesus Marchocka, Foundress of the Polish Carmel, his wish had been partially implemented. Through his efforts several other chronicles and biographies of Polish Carmelites were also translated into French. In a letter to Sr. Mary Xavier at the beginning of 1902, he refers to, "Reverend Mother Catherine Flambeau, an Ursuline nun, translator into French of the Chronicle of Vilnius." On January 1, 1903, Kalinowski wrote to the Prioress: "She, Catherine Flambeau, translated all of your records on French convents. As a token of gratitude I send her a small relic of the hair of Sr. Thérèse of the Child Jesus. Fr. Herman [*sic*] was the spiritual director of this sister before she joined the Order." [p. 413].

These manuscripts are stored in the archives of the Carmelite Convent at Lobzów in Kraków; their publication added precious jewels to the crown of St. Teresa, and as Jean-Baptiste Bouchaud commented: "We expect that the Carmelites won't leave an empty space in the crown of the Virgin for long." [p. 414].

When the Russian government suppressed the houses of the Discalced Carmelites, the house in Warsaw was abandoned in 1864 and taken over by the diocesan Seminary which had moved to St. Petersburg. After the reform of the Carmelites the Czerna community made efforts to regain this house, but there was no money for building a new seminary, and so they had to wait patiently. Containers of books from this extensive library had been sent to St. Petersburg, as had been done in the case of the libraries of other monasteries. Not all the books had been moved, however, and Kalinowski knew this, so he made efforts to reclaim the Carmelite books. The seminary library, now called the Krasinski Library included the Chronicles about the Carmels, mentioned above, together with other valuable manuscripts. Kalinowski enquired: "Have they asked His Grace the Archbishop of Warsaw to try to solve the problem regarding the seminary library?" A month later he wrote again: "The Archbishop of Warsaw could not find a way of releasing the books from our library, which is in the seminary in Warsaw though we asked him to do so." [p. 414].

Kalinowski published old chronicles about the Poland Carmels for two reasons: he wanted to make available to his colleagues, both friars and sisters, the good example shown by those who went before them, encouraging them to follow in their footsteps; he also wanted to remind Poles about the challenges facing the Church and to revive in their hearts sentiments of faith, nobility and sacrifice that had yielded so much renown in the past. "The Polish mission," Kalinowski wrote, "for which our ancestors, especially in the 17th century, shed so much blood was to defend a Church which was hampered by the Orthodox and the Reformers." [p. 414].

Three-way friendship – Raphael Kalinowski, Nathalie Narischin and Hermann Cohen

I referred to Hermann Cohen and also to Nathalie Narischin in Part One, Chapter 1, noting that she and her sister Catherine were known to Raphael Kalinowski. This suggests that we look further at her story in relation to these two Carmelite friars. Nathalie and Catherine were born to parents Gregory Naraschin and Princess Anne Mestechesky in St. Petersburg on August 6, 1820, the year before Hermann Cohen was born on November 10, 1821. Catherine (whom she addresses as Kate in her letters), had two other sisters, Marie and Elizabeth. Hermann Cohen visited Nathalie in Paris whenever he could. On August 9, 1854 she wrote to her sister Catherine: "I have seen the father (Hermann) in our chapel, where he said Mass, during which his own Eucharistic canticles were sung and which everyone who hears them agrees are most beautiful. He turned away from a worldly life and in an instant was transformed into a St. John of the Cross, by the sudden and all-powerful strength of the divine Eucharist." [p. 414].

In the course of the year 1903, with which the present chapter begins, Kalinowski was busy reading and correcting the translation of a biography of Nathalie Narischin, a Sister of Charity, which he had received from his friend, Wenceslas Nowakowski, (later known as Albert) a Capuchin. He wrote: "Sister Nathalie Narishkin was a Russian woman who converted to Catholicism and her valuable biography can help bring back to the bosom of the Catholic Church many Russians of good faith." [p. 414]. Thus did Kalinowski do his best to promote this biography.

Some years previously, 1898, on the occasion of the publication by him of a Polish edition of Hermann Cohen's biography, Kalinowski published a booklet which gives us an interesting description of Nathalie Narishkin. It tried to show that for him only in the Catholic Church can a person find true happiness. In the booklet he says, writing to Sr. Emilia Rostworowska, who had translated Sylvain's biography of Hermann Cohen into Polish:

> I happened to read this biography of Herman [*sic*] and welcomed the opportunity to further explore these two converts and it was impossible not to admire them... Ah, the source from which flow streams of love and strength that brought a previously unknown outpouring of joy – was holy faith... The presence of the Lord Jesus in the Blessed Sacrament won over Herman, and his presence in the Church gained Nathalie. Herman was her spiritual director who designed the final shaping of the beauty of her soul. They met each other providentially, as if the hand of providence brought those two into the bosom of the Church coming as they did from different expressions of hostility to the Church. The former, after a baptism of penance leading to a life in Carmel and dedicated missionary work, by the generosity of his ministry became a martyr to the

French prisoners in Spandau during the Franco-Prussian War. This was the end of his life in exile. The latter – Nathalie... preserved her innocence in a safe refuge in the Congregation of the Daughters of Charity. This was a time of social upheaval (1848–1874) and she worked, sometimes heroically, to assist others in the most varied needs, and continued to sacrifice herself to the last moments of her life. Faithful to her call and mission she could say with St. Paul, Ap.: *"Cursum consummavi, fides servavi"* (I have finished the course, I have kept the faith.) The Catholic faith united them and was the source of their happiness. [p. 416].

Reflecting on the example of their lives Kalinowski continues:

This reminds us that above all, it is impossible not to ask the question: why Herman left the world and did not look for repentance in Judaism? Where the source of the love of God was baptism for Herman, an unknown hand directed Nathalie to the bosom of holy Church. After her reception she wrote: Venice, August 18, 1844. A date forever memorable for me, my dear friends, my dear sisters. Yes, I can tell you now I am a Catholic! My friends, my good Fr Aladel, my good sisters at the Rue de Bac, all of you, whom God and the Holy Virgin have charged to watch over me, you must rejoice today, for you have been heard! I am happy at last! Yes happy to have returned to the fold, but sad to be so unworthy. [p. 415].

Kalinowski only quotes this part of her letter, but I add the remainder, taken from a biography of Nathalie[189] written in French by her friend Augustus Craven:

---

[189] Mme Augustus Craven, *La Soeur Natalie Narischin, fille de la charité de Saint-Vincent de Paul* (Paris: Didier, 1877) p. 50.

Can you imagine how God has given me this grace? Yes, you can, because you have unfortunately such a good opinion of me; but I myself who knows what I deserve and to what degree I am miserable and ungrateful, I cannot understand such a mercy... My friends! What a memory I will keep of this day! It seems to me again that I'm not sufficiently grateful. But God has, and will again have pity on me. How can I thank you, all you to whom I owe my happiness! Circumstances delayed my conversion, until this day consecrated to the Holy Virgin. Will she not protect me all my life as on this day of her glorious Assumption? I have been enfolded and watched over, what more can I say. I only want to tell you of my happiness. Thank the good God for me![190]

Referring to Hermann Cohen, Nathalie writes to her sister Catherine:

Chère [Dear] Kate, How can I thank you for your generous gift? It is in your name that I am enabled to carry out these good works of charity. As for myself, I'm poor, I am unable to recompense you, but this image carries a signature which is that of a *saint* [Nathalie's emphasis]. My companions here are overjoyed and covered by the perfume of such virtue. Yesterday, in signing this little image which I'm sending you, he remarked to me, "Truly I don't deserve to visit this house; I sense Jesus everywhere, in the Holy Sacrament, in the chapel, in your hearts, in the rooms, everywhere, in a word one breathes Jesus our love in this dear house." Our sisters radiate goodness and thankfulness, and you yourself, dear Kate, do please thank God with us for the graces which the visit of this father has brought us. [p. 417].

---

[190] Ibid. p.50

In another passage of that letter to her sister she writes: "Good Father Herman [*sic*] arrives on Monday ... What a delight to love Jesus, love him as holy people do ... Love like a fire envelops and permeates him like rays surrounding his heart." [p. 417].

Nathalie didn't expect, when she wrote these words that he would make a similar assessment of herself. After his conversion and even before joining the Carmelite Order, Cohen called her "an escapee from heaven, one of the most beautiful souls in the Church." [p. 417].

Here is the story of the translation of Hermann Cohen's biography into Polish. On November 11, 1895, Sr. Emilia Rostworowska, a nun from Kraków Monastery of Our Lady of Mercy at Lagiewniki, turned to Kalinowski and asked him to supply her with details of the life of Hermann Cohen. She wrote:

> The Lord Jesus in his great goodness has sent me a chest illness so I may soon depart this world. I am not allowed to talk a lot but instead dedicate myself to the work of our vocation. To profitably use these long free hours I decided on a Polish translation of some good and edifying book if could get my hands on the life of Fr. Herman, a Carmelite, who seemed to me wonderfully fired with the love of God and therefore worthy of translation. The work is almost finished, you may live to see it published, but the question is whether published or not, this Father is well-known ... I come to you Father in need, and at the same time ask if your own recollections could add something to this story? In Paris, you could easily have known the Carmelites or at least heard of Father Herman. [pp. 419-420].

She enquires if he has any such memories which he could share with her.

Because of her illness Sr. Emilia was not able to correct the defects in her translation of the biography. But the situation was saved when she asked Hermann's sister who was the owner of the book, for permission to publish a translation, despite its shortcomings. Printing costs would be covered by the Congregation of Our Lady of Mercy.

Raphael Kalinowski did not personally know Hermann Cohen, but his colleague Bartholomew knew him well in the Novitiate of the Order in Le Broussey, near Bordeaux. Kalinowski's biographer, Jean-Baptiste Bouchaud was actually given Hermann's room next to the chapel in the Novitiate.

Bouchaud knew a lot about Cohen, of course, so Kalinowski was able to satisfy the wishes of Sr. Emilia. In January 1896 Hermann's sister Henrietta Raunheim wrote to the Carmelite Fr. Athanasius who acted as a go-between:

> I would be very happy if the biography of my beloved brother, Father Hermann, is translated into Polish. This book is my own now, because I had to pay a considerable sum to P. Sylvain [author] and M. Oudin [the publisher] for it. Can the good father of Czerna [Kalinowski] ensure that the Polish translation is accurate and well done? Will I be able to show it to Polish experts who would be able to judge this matter? My wish is that no word should be changed. This book has already been translated into German, English and Italian. [p. 421].

In another letter a month later Henrietta explained why she was so concerned to make sure that the translation of the biography of her brother was authentic and accurate:

> The biography written by Fr. Sylvain was done under the guidance of the late lamented Father Martin.[191] Father was a priest in the diocese of Tours, and a professor of rhetoric.

---

[191] This was Felix Fronteau, (1827–1894) who was a General Councillor of the Order in Rome.

He heard a sermon by Father Herman speaking of the inexpressible happiness which he felt at being a Christian and a friar. Under the influence of this sermon, he joined the recently restored Order and the province of Aquitaine as Father Herman did, and he was one of the pillars of the Province for fifteen years. After his release from the office of Provincial, he was appointed to the hermitage in the solitude of Tarasteix, founded by Father Herman. Fr. Martin introduced the eremitical life there in 1869. [p. 421].[192]

In 1872 Fr. Martin was appointed General Councillor, and he held that office for eighteen years in a row. No one in Carmel knew Hermann better than he, and Henrietta was right when she wrote that in a sense he was the author of the biography of her brother, especially the second part, for which he provided Sylvain with the necessary information. Henrietta was really co-author of the first part because the information came from her. It was understandable then that she wished the translation be faithful to Sylvain and so she at first refused permission for a Polish edition. She had learned that it was very inaccurate, and two chapters had been omitted altogether. Sr. Emilia, not having the energy to redo the work, then said she would abandon it.

However, her work was of great value and could have done much good, so this development worried Kalinowski, and he wrote again to Henrietta. She replied graciously: "Please do what you consider to be appropriate. Hermann means the same to you and to me. I agree that the work of beloved Sr. Emilia be transmitted as it is and I repeat that it's better than nothing. Let us ask Our Lady of Mount Carmel that the Polish edition will do as much good as it has done in other languages. Please tell her, Sr. Emilia, that I am united with her in Jesus Christ." [p. 422].

---

[192] Sylvain states that Fr. Martin started the observance of the rule at Tarasteix in 1867.

So in a sense Hermann Cohen began his mission in Poland, where so many Jews lived, in this way. Certainly it brought joy, comfort and courage to those Jews who had converted to the Church and to many other Polish people.

Kalinowski thanked God for that but he was not yet satisfied. He wrote to Nathalie Narischin and asked her to write down everything she knew and remembered about Hermann Cohen. Nathalie complied with his wishes, and her work was published by Kalinowski in the *Chroniques du Carmel*. At the end of the booklet Kalinowski addresses Sr. Emilia: "May those who read your work hopefully bear the fruit desired by you. May the life of Father Hermann and Sister Nathalie Narischin who were first enlightened outside the church, demonstrate that only in the Holy Catholic Church can faith offer eternal life. [p. 422].

Chapter Ten

Pastoral Care: Christian Unity and Growth

Kalinowski spent his childhood near the former Uniate Church of the Holy Spirit in Vilnius and so it had a big place in his heart. He asked Carmelites in Poland to give unity a similar place in their hearts. The proof of this we find in a letter to the Prioress of the Convent in Przemyśl. One of the nuns there was very keen that the Russian Orthodox Church should become part of the Uniate Church in communion with Rome. Kalinowski wrote:

> The more I consider the matter, the more confirmed I am in the conviction that Divine Providence has called on Carmel and the Carmel in Przemyśl in particular to pray for this outcome…During the 15 or 16 hours of my stay in Lviv, where I had to go in order to clarify some matter re Wadowice, I felt a strong urge to request an audience with Cardinal Sembratowicz, the Metropolitan Russian Uniate leader, and although I had no appointment and despite the late hour – it was already after 6 in the evening – I decided to show up at his residence. ... His Eminence was happy to receive me and when I told His Eminence how

much we care about unity, etc., etc. he commented, "Do you know that just a few days ago I received a letter from a French Carmelite, who asked why the Uniate Church didn't establish the Order of St. Elijah here – an Order which arose in the East, and later moved to the West and is called to work for the unity of the Churches." His Eminence called his secretary and told him to bring this letter so that I could read it *propriis* oculis.[193] He concluded that the Carmelite nuns are called by God to ensure that the Orthodox Church comes back to unity with Mother Church. And this is the reason – the Carmelite friar concludes, – that convents of nuns should also exist in the Uniate Church. So Sr. Maria has had this providential duty for many years in Przemyśl and has to grow more and more in perfection and she has the grace and understanding for this…[194]

Mariavite (Christian) Sect

Raphael Kalinowski prayed earnestly for the conversion of a Christian breakaway sect called the Mariavites. Here we have a good example of his zeal for unity in action. The Carmelites at Łobzów (Kraków) give us an account of the beginnings of this sect and their dealings with Carmel. In a part of Poland that was under Russian rule, a number of priests made efforts to carry out a reform of the clergy. They applied themselves fervently to their spiritual exercises, especially prayer. Through a magazine called *Mariawita* they maintained communication among themselves and stimulated their zeal. One of them, a priest called Zenon Kwiek, highly regarded among his peer professors in one of the seminaries, came to Galicia to take a period of rest in Zakopane, a resort in the Tatra mountains. There he met a relative of one of the Carmelite

---

[193] With my own eyes. Ibid.
[194] Jean-Baptiste Bouchaud, p. 390. Here we find one of Kalinowski's apostolic concerns – Christian unity, between Catholicism and Orthodoxy.

nuns and asked her to put him in contact with Carmel because of his devotion to St. Teresa of Avila. He turned up at the Convent and told them about the favors he received from St. Teresa, which was why he wished to have a relic of her which they willingly gave him. Kwiek became a frequent visitor to the sisters on his journeys to and from Zakopane. At the same time, a priest from Warsaw told the sisters about a certain Felicksa Kozlowska, who also wished to reform the clergy and was a driving force among the Mariavites. Some priests gathered around her and she gave them spiritual direction.

Soon, however, they noticed tendencies in these priests to downplay obedience to the bishops. The sisters mentioned this to Kwiek and they saw that he too was an admirer of Kozlowska calling her a new St. Teresa. He explained that she was unjustly persecuted and that the Pope must be thoroughly informed about what was going on. The sisters elicited a promise from him that if the Holy Father condemned the association and the spirit of Kozlowska, he would submit to that decision.

In his talks with the Carmelites, Kwiek told them that he was devoted to penitential practices, to the inner life and to working for people's salvation; he prayed for eight hours a day, was fired with love for the Savior, and his teaching at the seminary was well regarded. The bishop was happy with him. This kind of encomium about himself would hardly appeal to either St. Teresa or St. John of the Cross.

In point of fact, the Mariavites initially did quite a lot of good. They wrote fine books on history, literature, philosophy, etc., but that of course is not the be-all and end-all of the Christian life. The Pope initially issued a strong statement that they should work under the direction of their bishops.

Zenon Kwiek was at first praised by his bishop, but was later reprimanded and deprived of his teaching office in the seminary and sentenced to some months' penance. This happened after the Pope had condemned the sect. The bishop summoned him and one of his colleagues, advising them to submit to the will of the

Vicar of Christ. In the end he did submit but remained anxious and confused. He suffered a lot but didn't know whom to trust or confide in, or where to find answers. His career was destroyed. He came on a visit to Wadowice in August [1906], a year before the death of Kalinowski. He was accompanied by the Provincial, who was visiting the Convent. During the interview someone mentioned Kalinowski and invited Kwiek to open up to him. He did so, and even confessed to him in the chapel. On the Feast of the Assumption he sang Mass with the community. Then he told them that he finally submitted fully to the church and understood the error of his ways. He was ready to return to his diocese and ask forgiveness. After Kalinowski's death he visited the Carmel in 1911, and said with great emotion that he always carried a piece of Kalinowski's habit with him as a relic.

The conversion of this priest dealt a heavy blow to the Mariavites. Many people who had been enticed by the sectarians broke with them and returned to the guidance of their priests. We know Kalinowski prayed a lot for them and in letters to the Carmelite sisters he recommended that they also pray continually for these priests.

Church Unity

Kalinowski's love for the Church prompted him to admire above all the Jesuits and Basilians in Poland and Lithuania who defended the Church against attack. The Jesuits, following the model of Antonio Possevino and Peter Skarga struggled in the 16th and 17th centuries with unexampled courage and talent in revitalizing faith and devotion when needed. It was thanks to them that Poland had not gone over to the Reformation churches. When Czerna celebrated a special feast, he would invite the Jesuits to attend, and similarly they invited him to various ceremonies in Kraków.

Another thing he admired was the contribution made by the Jesuits in the early 17th century to the reform of the Basilian Order.

St. Josaphat was under their direction before becoming a priest, and the famous Archbishop, Joseph Welamin Rutski, the most powerful of his assistants and Josaphat's successor, was a disciple of theirs also. These two men reclaimed for the church all the provinces of the former Dukes of Lithuania. Kalinowski's childhood home of course was near the monastery of the Holy Trinity associated with St. Josaphat, and that fact explains his commitment to this saint and reformer of the Basilian Order. He recalled the happy days of his youth venerating the miraculous image of Our Lady in the Basilian church of the Holy Trinity in Vilnius.

The news of the canonization of St. Josaphat in Rome in 1867 on the anniversary of the death of Saints Peter and Paul, was a source of inspiration for Kalinowski. On that day, Pope Pius IX, in the presence of the College of Cardinals and nearly five patriarchs, with metropolitans and bishops of all rites and all the nations of the world, honored the Saint as the pioneer of ecclesial communion in the East. Several years later, Pope Leo XIII, who wished to unite all the Slavic nations in the faith, promulgated throughout the Church the obligation to recite the Divine Office and to celebrate the Mass of St. Josaphat. Kalinowski recited the office of the holy martyr with devotion and his veneration and love for him grew even more. He prayed the breviary faithfully which fully expressed his own desires and feelings.

There is an extract from the inventory of the Czerna house, where he draws attention to the relic of St. Josaphat, stored there: "Near the altar of St. Joseph in the sacristy, there is a large piece of bone of Bl. Josaphat, martyred archbishop of Polotsk and with autograph and letter."[p.150] Kalinowski made an entry in the chronicles of the priory in Vienna on St. Josaphat: "In this chronicle dated year 1644 there is mention of a precious gift received by the priory of Discalced Carmelites at Graz – a *cilice* [195] of St. Josaphat. Kalinowski added

---

[195] This is a penitential girdle fitted with spikes. Kalinowski himself wore one.

the following note: "This gift had been brought from Vilna by the Carmelite John Mary Centurione, a member of the Colonna family, who helped to found the priory at the Gate of Dawn."[196]

Kalinowski always kept a picture of St. Josaphat on his desk, and he wrote his name in the header of his letters. For him the special mission of Carmel in Poland was to promote union with Rome among Christians, referred to below as the "Sacred Union":

> Only the religious houses of the Reform of St. Teresa had already this goal in mind: to promote the Sacred Union. In 1603 [1604 – correction by the author] Teresian Carmelites were sent to Persia by Pope Paul V. They travelled through Poland on their way to their destination but didn't foresee that their short stay in Kraków and Vilnius would serve as a passport to create two Polish provinces of Carmelites. During their stopover in the Lithuanian capital Hipacy Pociej, the Uniate Metropolitan requested them to ask in Rome for friars to come and promote the Order in Poland and work for unity. He himself had also written to Rome with this in view. His letter was read on May 5, 1605, the very year of the first general chapter of the Italian Congregation of Carmelites. The request of the Metropolitan was adopted and on December 7 of that year the first priory in Poland dedicated to the Immaculate Conception was founded. In the course of 100 years, 15 Carmelite houses were established on the borders of Russia and together with the Basilians they helped bring back the population living there to the Catholic Church. [pp 151-152]

Kalinowski often reflected on the religious situation not only in Ruthenia (Ukraine) but also in Russia. He loved the Russians, and ardently desired their conversion. His brother Jerzy and his

---

[196]   Jean-Baptiste, pp 150–151. The Carmelites dedicated a chapel at the 'Gate of Dawn', or 'Spiked Gate' to display this famous image.

colleague Diaz de Cerio, who knew him well, attest to this fact. In a letter to the Carmelite nuns on the occasion of the revolution in the Polish Kingdom, Kalinowski asked the sisters to pray fervently for the conversion of Russia: "I ask you especially to pray through the intercession of St. Josaphat for the conversion of Russia. Without this, no matter who wins, everything will go wrong" [p.152]. Among his papers also was a draft of a letter by a Russian prince on the occasion of the death of Pope Leo XIII. The author praised him as a great Pontiff who so dearly wished for the conversion of Russia and had done so much to bring it about. Kalinowski knew the Russian people and often said that in the higher social classes you can meet very good people. There were some highly placed people who after converting to Catholicism gained widespread respect and recognition. When he read the above mentioned letter he was pleased and wrote to the author trying to convince him how much Russia would gain by returning to the unity of the Catholic Church. We don't know what effect his letter had, but it is one more reminder of Kalinowski's zeal.

Kalinowski offered to God his own prayers and sufferings for the conversion of Russia and expected this also from Carmelites. During the Japanese-Russian war he wrote to the Prioress in Przemyśl: "I recommend myself to the prayers of the sisters, because I was sick with a severe bout of influenza. There seems to be nothing but suffering while we live in this valley of tears. But it would be wrong to complain about insignificant ailments." In his letter to the Carmel about the Japanese-Russian conflict, he recommended they pray to St. Josaphat the martyr and ask him to intercede with God for the conversion of Russia. "Without repentance it doesn't matter who wins or loses." [p. 434].

In fact Russia was defeated in the Far East, but during the growing danger Carmelites prayed fervently for the welfare of Russia as it was preparing to engage in war. For this purpose Kalinowski wrote to Czar Nicholas II to ask for permission to establish a priory in Warsaw. He also asked Count Thaddeus Grocholski, brother of Mary Xavier, to visit the Empress and submit a request for her intervention in this matter. Grocholski was received very kindly, but without result. The Czar himself was even favorably disposed, but others rejected the proposal. Four months later, in July 1905, Kalinowski wrote to a Carmelite: "In a letter of reply from Thaddeus he tells me the Czarina has no animosity at all, has a good heart... God grant that this mission of Thaddeus may bear fruit." [p. 435].

Around this time Kalinowski's health had once again been in decline but he regained some strength in the summer and used his energy to further his lifelong aims – the development of Carmel in Poland and the spiritual needs of people. In May 1905 he was in Vienna at a meeting of the Provincial Council. For over twenty years the Carmelite friars had envisioned a Foundation in Kraków but some friars resisted the idea for a long time. It had been decided as we saw, to first establish a priory and seminary in Wadowice, thought necessary for the education of candidates for the novitiate. That Seminary had provided twelve friars up to 1905 and this enabled a new foundation to take place. But the question was where should it be sited? It seemed it was needed much more in Galicia than Kraków. Many of the poorer people from there were leaving the country on the trains each day. Some would emigrate to America.

Concern for the Spiritual Growth of All

As he thought about these emigrants to the United States Kalinowski was most concerned.[197] He commented: "What awaits these poor people there? Who will look after their spiritual needs?" And in a letter to the Mistress of Novices he wrote: "Perhaps you

---

[197] In 1950 friars from Kraków would go on mission to the United States and set up a house in Hammond, Indiana. Two years later they moved to Munster, Indiana, in the Chicago area. This was a realization of Kalinowski's hopes. Near the church another chapel has been added under the title of Our Lady of Ostra Brama. A later addition is the St. Raphael Kalinowski Pilgrim Center and Banquet Hall.

should start a new house in America!" [p. 441]. But the Provincial Council decided otherwise and instead to establish a priory in Kraków. A month later, when Kalinowski was asked if he had found a suitable place to build a new priory, he replied: "In regard to my search for a priory the only answer I can give is that I'm feeling weak and something tells me that this will not be established by me because I am weak and a kind of outlaw who is not worthy to do this work; God has someone else in mind to set it up." [p. 441].[198]

It seems that Kalinowski now felt that death was knocking on the door. His eagerness to complete some tasks he set himself took on a new urgency. Sr. Mary Xavier who had done so much to reform the Carmelites in Poland, also helped in the publication of his work on the Chronicles of the Polish nuns and in the construction of a new convent for her own community. Since the arrival of the sisters in Kraków thirty years previously, the community at Łobzów lived in a makeshift home, in uncomfortable and cramped conditions. They had devoted all their energies to new foundations in Przemyśl, Lviv and Wadowice. Mary Xavier, again chosen for the office of Prioress, felt it her duty to build a suitable convent for her sisters before her death. In June 1905, a beautiful convent building was completed and the sisters awaited the arrival of the Provincial to dedicate it.

On July 1 the Polish Provincial Bonaventure Kirschstein came to visit the houses. He didn't come on official business but rather to say goodbye. For more than forty years he had guided the Province with admirable fidelity. Respected and loved by all, he had been provincial of the Carmelite houses in Austria, Hungary and Poland for twenty years on and off. He was now 73 years old and, like Kalinowski, sensed that death was approaching and that this would be his final visit. After a short visit to the houses in Czerna, Kraków, Przemyśl and Lviv he returned to Kraków on July 1. The

---

[198] Kalinowski uses the English phrase 'out of power,' meaning 'powerless.' Again he uses the English term 'outlaw,' perhaps meaning 'exile.'

Carmelite sisters in Łobzów chose his name day [July 13, 1905] for the dedication of the new convent and chapel.

The day after the dedication Kalinowski returned to Czerna and the Provincial went to Wadowice, where on the feast of Our Lady of Mount Carmel he participated in the ordination of two new priests. Before leaving Poland the Provincial wrote to the Prioress at Lobzów as a kind of last will and testament:

> My dear Mother! When I came to Wadowice and opened the envelope I received, I got a pleasant surprise at the sight of the magnificent gift, which by no means I deserved. Now you can go on quietly serving your Divine Spouse, faithfully performing the duties of your vocation and working tirelessly for his glory and for the good of souls. At this difficult time for our Holy Mother Church Carmelites have an important task. Humanity is sliding rapidly toward the precipice, rushing to destruction, and the Church will experience such anxiety as it has not experienced up to this. Salvation is in God's hands alone, and you can obtain it only through noble and ardent prayer for others. God looks at Carmel and seeks people ready to offer their prayers and sufferings to him. God looks to Lobzów, and asks whether the Carmelites will beseech his heart and move him to have mercy on humanity, so that it may return to the path of duty and redemption. What should we do to achieve this? Nothing more than to faithfully fulfil our outer and especially our inner duties that our holy calling asks of us. If a saint has great power over the heart of God, how much more will the whole family of Mount Carmel be able to achieve if we are all saints! Let us go! The creator will strengthen us with an abundance of his graces and help us fulfil our intentions. [p. 445].

It was said of St. Teresa of Avila that her heart was not only in Spain but in France, South America and everywhere else – wherever in fact there were people in need of salvation. The same can be said of Kalinowski. On October 13 he returned from the Provincial Council meeting to spend the winter in Czerna. "If a human being," he wrote to a friend at this time, "sees himself surrounded by limitations, at least the desire to love God more and more will ensure growth that will know no boundaries. May the depth of this desire grow continually in your heart and manifest itself in all the actions of daily life." [p. 449].

Writing to the sisters in Łobzów Kalinowski refers to a book that the Carmelites of Paris, who had been exiled to Amay in Belgium, had sent the Carmelites in Poland. It was *The Third Spiritual Alphabet of Franciso de Osuna*, the Franciscan work which St. Teresa had found invaluable as a spiritual guide to mental prayer and meditation.[199] Then he gives them guidance on completing a translation of *The Carmelites of Compiègne*,[200] and ends his letter: "With nothing of my own to leave behind as a legacy, I borrow from the late Bishop Krasinski the following three verses:

The name is written in heaven,
the victim himself is our daily bread.
Let him remember who has the general welfare in mind,
that the spirit of unity and agreement is a Castle (Carmel).
The Coat of Arms is: persevere to the end;
For perseverance is the steel of the spirit, the mother of martyrs.
Fiat! [p. 449].

---

[199] Francisco de Osuna, *The Third Spiritual Alphabet*, translated by Mary E. Giles (Ramsey, NJ.: Paulist Press) See: The Collected Works of St. Teresa of Avila, Vol. 1, Ch. 4.7.

[200] *To Quell the Terror: The True Story of the Carmelite Martyrs of Compiégne* (Washington, DC.: William Bush, ICS).

To this he would add some further good advice for all the sisters and words of thanks for the kindness that they had always extended to him. Before leaving on his journey, he entrusted them all to the protection of the Blessed Virgin. On May 1 he left Czerna for which he had done so much, and in the company of Bartholomew Diaz de Cerio went to Vienna for the Provincial Chapter.

Back to Wadowice Again

During the Provincial Chapter held in Vienna in early May 1906 the burden carried for so long by Bonaventure Kirschstein was lifted. He had given sterling service to the province of St. Leopold over the years. The Provincial Council elected him to the new priory in Vienna, where he renewed the regular observances and founded a new college of theology. He held the office of Subprior and was also spiritual director of the college and was able to do much good for the province. Chrysostom Lamos, Prior of Wadowice, was re-elected Provincial, and Kalinowski was appointed Prior of Wadowice.

Kalinowski was aware that the burden might be too much for him and asked to be released from it but nevertheless his election was approved. There were many young men in the college in Wadowice who were to become the founders of new Polish provinces. There was a need, especially for good leadership and Kalinowski was the right person for the job. Kalinowski had come to Wadowice on May 11 with Andrew Gdow, outgoing Prior of Czerna, and after a day's rest he bravely took on his shoulders this new burden.

"At the end of life," says his confessor, "he slept very little and meditated most of the night on the passion of Jesus Christ and the sorrows of His Blessed Mother." [p. 451]. Morning choir started around 4.00 am; Kalinowski would kneel throughout without leaning on the bench. He recited the Divine Office with great fervor .... was very fond of the *Canticum puerorum*[201] and wanted

---

[201] Daniel, Ch. 3. Canticle for Sundays and Feast days.

to recite it very slowly. He did the Way of the Cross every day in the afternoon about 4 o'clock. Visits to the Blessed Sacrament would take place at 10 o'clock. With his other work he combined the ministry of priesthood which he exercised conscientiously and with great dedication.

Before celebrating Mass, Kalinowski prepared for it by prior meditation and prayer in private, and made a thanksgiving after its completion. No matter what the circumstances, he never neglected this custom. He gave sermons to the people in the chapel of Wadowice as well as weekly talks to the community. These were always carefully prepared and applied to current needs. His talks often made a deep impact on his listeners. He was a faithful confessor. His knowledge of theology and spiritual things made him capable of answering any spiritual questions and he could safely guide people toward a higher perfection.

Another attribute of Kalinowski was a meticulousness in preserving the rules of the Order. If duty didn't compel him to stay outside the priory, he was always present at community gatherings. Though sometimes fatigued from work he would not consider himself exempt from them.

People talked about the respect which Kalinowski inspired. He seemed to live within himself, always dwelling on the thought of God. But Kalinowski was not a killjoy and even when not Superior at a given time – which was seldom – his colleagues held him in the highest regard. One former student wrote:

> I was lucky to have had talks with him three or four times during recreation while doing my second year novitiate in Czerna. These talks had as their object the past of our Order, about which he was so well acquainted because of the various documents he had collected, and he could share his knowledge of these events with us. He once spoke about Our Lady of Ostra Brama, another time he told us about a Brother who had been tortured for the faith (in Przemyśl, as I

recall), and yet another time about a wonderful Brother from Warsaw, who healed many people. He asked me frequently about my health, about which young people can be careless but later in old age can be sorry for having neglected. These include some of the finest recreational memories I have of him. I always left him encouraged and eager to work for the good of the Order. [pp. 453-454].

An amusing anecdote was recorded by one of his students. On one occasion a student offered him a glass of beer. He accepted it, but put a pinch of salt in the glass, saying that it was good for his health, tasted better that way and he often did this! The student tried it too with predictable results – realising that beer is meant to be drunk without salt. Yet again a student observed: "Fr. Kalinowski never wanted to talk about himself. I remember once when we visited him, we asked him to tell us something about life in Siberia. He said little maintaining that he had forgotten most things, but when pressed he would talk about Siberian forests and rivers with which he was familiar and how to do surveys of these vast areas." [p. 455]. He was of course an expert in this field.

Kalinowski had great insight into the human heart, and in cases requiring great sensitivity he didn't even have to speak, he seemed to understand people without words, and guessed what might be an effective encouragement for them. He also had a habit after confession of recommending prayer for a particular need of the Church or the country.

Kalinowski tried to instil in people the spirit of charity and sacrifice, and thus make them Christlike. To enkindle their zeal, he often spoke to them about the needs of the Church, of the Holy Father, and about the overwhelming sufferings and misfortunes of Poland, especially in the areas under the authority of Russia. In particular, he devoted a great deal of attention to young friars in the community. By word and example, he encouraged them to acquire a love of solitude and recollection, so essential for the life of prayer which is required in Carmel.

The seminary was more specifically the object of his concern and we can say that he watched over the students with great solicitude. His rules of conduct were worked out after careful reflection, then reviewed and confirmed by the General Council.

Anselm Gądek, an Outstanding Student of Kalinowski

As some of the professed students went on to study in Rome, Kalinowski would continue to write to them and show interest in their progress.

I was extremely pleased, [Kalinowski wrote] with the welcome letter from dear Br. Anselm[202] on behalf of you both. Let's give our hearts in obedience to God by doing His holy will. I will try to send you a Greek grammar for greater facility in reading the Holy Fathers in this language (Greek). Some sermons have been translated into

---

[202] Born in 1884 Anselm Gądek became an outstanding Polish Carmelite. After studies and ordination in Rome he returned to Poland in 1908, the year after Kalinowski's death. After a time in Czerna he was sent to Wadowice where he lectured in the seminary and was Master of Students. Later he was appointed professor in Vienna. In 1920 he was elected Polish Provincial. He founded a new Congregation of the Carmelites of the Child Jesus. After a stint of further responsibilities he was called to Rome where he would remain for the next 22 years. He worked on the new Constitutions of the Order and in 1927 he was appointed Rector of the Teresianum, the International College of the Order, a post he retained for 20 years. At the same time he taught Liturgy and Moral Theology. He was General Councillor for a period of 16 years. Pope Pius XI named him Apostolic Visitator for seminaries in Poland and Rome and a Consultor to the Congregation of Seminaries and Universities. He was well-known also for his work for the Carmelite Nuns and other religious and gave them spiritual direction and talks. On returning to Poland in 1947 he became superior of Wroclaw and was Provincial from 1951–54 and again 1957–60. He died on the Feast of St. Teresa, Oct.15, 1969. Such was the outstanding career of one of Kalinowski's first students.

Latin and set out in the so-called interlinear method, e.g., parts of St. John Chrysostom, *The Defence of Eutropius* etc. Also regarding the double text: French and Greek by Schneider which is a book of worship for young people. – Perhaps you may indeed know more about it than me. Now farewell, and I will remember you in our prayer and I recommend you to the Blessed Mother. [p. 461].

Kalinowski cared not only about Carmel – Friars, Sisters, Carmelite Third Order – but also about family and friends, that they might live their lives nourished by grace of the Eucharist. During the summer months his thoughts and prayers accompanied his family on their holiday travels, and in September he wrote to his youngest brother Aleksander: "Perhaps now you have returned safely to Warsaw from Sopot,[203] and Lucio is back from the health spas." [p. 462].

He was apprehensive about contemporary events and his fears were not unfounded. On August 3 he wrote from Lviv, where he had accompanied the Provincial. He read in the Lviv Review that tenants had caused destruction on the estates of the local Duke who was a relative of Nathalie Narischin. On the 20 of the same month he wrote to the Carmelite sisters, "What sad news has just arrived from Warsaw on the feast of the Assumption of Our Lady." He remarked that while there were celebrations in Częstochowa, blood was flowing in Warsaw.[204] In September he wrote again to Aleksander: "The unrest which we saw in Warsaw reminds us that we need to trust God's mercy that it may come to an end." Public offices, churches, municipal buildings and a large granary in the vicinity of Wadowice had been torched, with the loss of all the grain.

---

[203] This was the location of a Carmelite house near Gdansk dedicated to the Holy Family.

[204] International newspaper reports on August 16 described a massacre by revolutionists, killing or wounding 45 soldiers. The troops responded by killing or wounding 145 revolutionists. Then they cleared the streets at the point of the bayonet. Outbreaks of violence were also reported from Łódź.

"The other day," he tells us, "the police managed to catch three of the criminals and some calm has been restored. May Almighty God grant that they may repent...."[p. 462]. And he urged him to pray hard.

At this time the Carmelite Provincial arrived as Apostolic Delegate to the Pauline monastery in Jasna Gora in Częstochowa, to conduct a canonical visitation there. The Paulist community had custody of the miraculous image of the Black Madonna and it was so popular with the people there that the Russians didn't dare expel them. However, they subjected them to laws that greatly hampered the admission of new members. They were only allowed to take as novices those who were exempt from military service and then with the permission of the civil power. There had been difficulties with personnel as a result, and some of the community went to Rome to seek help. The Provincial was appointed Visitator. He addressed the problem discreetly and gained their trust. He restored cloister, removed a variety of abuses and ordered more vigilance to be taken in preserving the rights of the Order and the Church. Kalinowski himself prayed and asked the prayers of the sisters and friars for God's blessing on this important task that the Provincial was commissioned to carry out in Częstochowa.

Another abiding concern of Kalinowski was the spiritual wellbeing of his old friends. Though separated from them for thirty years he still cared about them. In early July 1906 Auguste Iwanski visited him in Wadowice and they talked for several hours. As we saw, Iwanski helped him in Wadowice when he was Mayor of the town. Iwanski had been one of his friends from Siberian days.

Kalinowski wanted people to be always busy with some useful work for the glory of God, for the Virgin Mary, for other people, and for Carmel. This reflects the requirements of the Carmelite Rule. To encourage people to work seriously, he would recall the words of Blessed Mary of the Incarnation: "All our actions are eternal; when you work with love for God and neighbor, our actions deserve an eternal reward." And he insisted: "Idleness is the poison of life, it tires our faculties, introduces anxiety into our lives and disturbs us." [p. 466]. Here we have keen psychological insight – what promises to promote relaxation only induces further fatigue that is fed by boredom. In his correspondence for 1906 Kalinowski returned frequently to an idea that can serve to put things in perspective for all of us:

> But these troubles are insignificant [he stated] and who dares to complain about small matters as against huge disasters happening around the world – horrifying earthquakes resulting in vast areas of land becoming ruined; and these terrible eruptions of Vesuvius with molten lava pouring down on scattered localities.[205] And if you add to these the conflagrations with which society is tearing itself apart, and the various revolutions in the Polish Kingdom, we see a great number of people caught up in a dangerous vortex, and they don't realize where all this is leading. [p. 467].

---

205   Mount Vesuvius is the only volcano in Europe and had erupted many times in the 19th century. Kalinowski is referring to the eruption of 1906. It has also erupted in 2013.

Chapter Eleven

Wadowice: The Curtain Falls (1906–1907)

In 1906, Raphael Kalinowski was again due to go on a visit to the Carmelite sisters in Lviv (Ukraine), but because of his weak health he asked the Provincial to accompany him as he carried out this official visit. You could say that Kalinowski had a particular attachment to the community in Lviv, in somewhat the same way as St. John of the Cross was devoted to the Carmelite community at Beas in Spain. Kalinowski tried to help the sisters in Lviv in their struggles and sufferings, especially in the difficult times they experienced at the beginning. The founding Prioress of the community there, Sr. Teresa Frances, endured a long illness before her death, and this proved to be a painful time for the community.

Now Kalinowski wanted to visit the sisters and say goodbye to them. Prioress Teresa Margaret reports his parting words:

> Insofar as it was the wish of my superiors to entrust your direction to me, I have applied myself to the task during my visits and in my replies to your sincere and direct letters; I've tried to encourage a spirit of unity among you, which, thanks be to God, is noticeable in your community. Saying

goodbye to you, I always think this is the last time, but whether it's this or some other time there is bound to be a last time. Yesterday we had a happy recreation together, but today is another matter: I have to take leave of you. I beg you when you get news of my death to pray for me and to Jesus at that critical time, that he be not my judge but my savior. Remember me also when I'm suffering the pains of purgatory. [pp. 470-471].

He closed his remarks with three words, which he left as a motto: *Ora et labora* – pray and work. At this point, the Prioress tells us, he broke down and quickly left the room.

Also at this time, in a few words of farewell that he sent to the Carmelites at Łobzów, he reminded them not to forget what he had told them as God's representative; he put great emphasis on the responsibility for sustained work in the spirit and letter of the Carmelite Rule: "You shall do some work so that the devil may always find you occupied." And he observed: "It was not for some trifle, that we have come to Carmel, but for God, it was not that we might do what we pleased but to work. Keep before our eyes the goal of our lives – God and heaven; never forget the day of judgement when we have to give an account of everything. Remember '*a chaque l'action repond eternité*' – Everything we do should take eternity into account. Thank you for everything you did for me and may Jesus bless you." [pp. 471-472].

After leaving Lviv, Kalinowski and the Provincial set out for the Convent in Przemyśl. Here Kalinowski suffered his first attack of paralysis. He had to lean on the altar for support during Mass and it was difficult for him to get back to Kraków. But at the end of August he returned to Wadowice and took up his usual duties. He caught up with his correspondence, but his handwriting was very shaky. On September 8 he spent most of the day as usual in the confessional but was confined to bed soon afterwards.

But the end had not yet arrived. A month later he returned to his duties. The Prior of Czerna, his old friend de Cerio, came in October with the architect and asked advice of the former engineer on the building of the projected new foundation in Kraków.

At this time Kalinowski was also engaged in publishing a biography of the Sixteen Carmelite martyrs of Compiégne, which had been translated from French into Polish by Sr. Mary Xavier under his direction. These Sixteen martyrs of the French Revolution were soon to be beatified and he prepared for the event by a solemn Triduum in Wadowice on December 8, 9 and 10. During the Triduum, the influx of people was considerable and remained so during the whole of Advent, a particularly busy time in Poland. Kalinowski, disregarding extreme exhaustion, didn't spare himself, and took part in all community acts, and heard confessions like the others. Any spare time was devoted to the work he had so much at heart – the beatification of the Mother Marchocka, foundress of the Carmelite nuns in Lviv and Warsaw. On December 21 he wrote to the Convent in Łobzów:

> I am under the influence of fever, and I am unable to keep my thoughts in any kind of order. This is also why I do not write to Mother Teresa [Steinmetz], so would you tell her that the Prioress at Wesoła sent me the documents she found in her Convent, and among them were handwritten letters sent to Mother Marchocka by the Carmelites of Alba. My head is done in so I can't very easily examine the documents and edit them. If the merciful God gives me the energy before my death, which is near, I will do whatever I can to honor the Blessed and saintly Mother Marchocka. Please pray for me, a poor sinner. [p. 474].

This is all he could manage to write, but the infirmarian, who looked after him finished the letter for him. One of the community reported to the students in Rome on January 1:

Dear brothers! You are probably curious and want to know without doubt what the Divine Infant brought us for the Christmas festivity. We had everything we needed for a joyful celebration, but we have had to put everything aside to take up a heavy cross this year. On December 20 our dear Father Prior fell ill and soon the sickness got worse. He caught a chill in the church while hearing confessions and bronchitis set in. Finally, in spite of this he insisted in coming to the icy choir and inflammation made rapid progress, so that he had no strength whatever and had to take to his bed. Dr Bukowski came to see him twice a day. On Christmas Day he became so weak that the doctor gave up hope. On the 27 we gave him the Last Sacraments after which there was some improvement and he enjoyed a good night. [pp. 476-477].

People prayed for him in all the houses of the friars and nuns. In Czerna they held a novena to Mother Teresa Marchocka in whose intercession the sick man had so much trust and for whose Cause he had worked so hard.

The Carmelite sisters prayed fervently offering Masses, communions and penances without ceasing. The Sisters in Łobzów were entirely devoted to him. They sent a specialist from Kraków, because the patient had completely lost his appetite and refused food; they inundated him with everything they could think of to whet his appetite – chicken broth, jellies, compotes; they sent air-fresheners so that the sick-room was as redolent as a pine forest on a warm spring morning! By January 5 he had improved, the pneumonia eased, but still the doctors had little hope and gave him two months to live. Before leaving Poland Peter Seul,[206] the community Infirmarian,

---

[206] German-born Peter Seul (1878–1943), made vows in 1903, and was ordained priest on July 8, 1906 in Kraków. He had been a student in Wadowice and knew Polish. In 1907, he left Wadowice for Graz. He then went to the German community in Holy Hill, Wisconsin, USA, where

writing to the Carmelites of Łobzów described the suffering of the sick man:

> I saw that our dear father suffered more than ever and sometimes I was so moved that I asked the Lord to show mercy to him, to give him some relief, or to let me share a little of his suffering. He had indeed a martyred look on his face. But his patience was always greater than his suffering. He suffered but still remained in the presence of God. He frequently used holy water, and often prayed silently to God. His expression was that of someone who didn't belong to this world anymore. He looked at the image of Our Lady of Perpetual Help, then looked at the crucifix, reverently kissed it, then again in a low voice whispered prayers to God, frequently saying: Oh my God, have mercy! O God, God, give me patience! He would strike his chest with such remorse as if he were the greatest sinner. He would thank you for every little favor: God Bless you! Or if unable to speak just smiled graciously. It was a very unique smile. At first he spoke to me in German, and so I distinctly remember that on January 7 at about 12.30 am he said to me, Pater Marian *rufen, meine Sterbestunde ist gekommen!* [call Fr. Marian, the hour of my death has come]. I ran to Fr. Marian and woke him. Then I woke Fr. Nicholas and Brother Bronislas also. They were the closest to him. They used to bring him the Blessed Sacrament. I stayed on with our dear Father and I cried out from grief. I must admit I don't cry easily. He doesn't want to live any longer but rather

---

he died in 1943. Raphael wrote of him in a letter to Theresa Steinmetz: "I have been full of gratitude for Father Peter, a model infirmarian. May God himself reward him." Holy Hill is the National Shrine of Mary, Help of Christians and it was given to Carmelites from Bavaria in 1906. Kalinowski was interested in sending Carmelites from Poland to care for Polish emigrants in the United States.

die soon as he thought he was no longer needed. At the same time he was obedient as a child. He was not too fond of the medicine but he always took it when I told him that Fr. Marian or the doctor ordered it. Sometimes he would eat very little and I said: please Father, that's not enough, you need more! And he would say: Well, let's be obedient and would take more. [pp. 476-477].

He was a somewhat better by the end of January, his strength returning little by little. As the weather improved it exercised a happy influence on his health.

On Good Friday Kalinowski began to complain that he didn't like to see himself lying on a comfortable bed doing nothing and having nothing to suffer. He proposed to the infirmarian that he revert to the plank bed like the rest of the community, but this time his carer was happy to disobey. Kalinowski would say: "What a useless man I am! Others pray, expiate, and I lie here like a beast – I eat, drink, sleep and do nothing." [p. 478]. In fact this was not true because since March he had worked hard on the documents relating to Teresa Marchoka.

A month later, Kalinowski sent his condolences to the Prioress of Lobzów, Mary Xavier who was ill herself at the time and had just lost her brother, Count Stanislaus Grocholski, a great benefactor of Carmel in Poland. He scribbled in pencil: "I asked Fr. Nepomuk yesterday to recommend the late Stanislaus to the prayers of the community. In the *Czas* (*Time*) magazine there is an article on him by Stanislaus Tarnowski ... someone brought it to me to read. He has probably been buried in the family tomb. I first met Stanislaus thirty-two years ago, when I visited Sieniawa for the first time." [p. 480].

In other reports, we read that the change of air and the weather had a positive effect on the health of Kalinowski. One friend writes:

When he first came to himself after his illness and we were allowed to visit we did so with great joy. The weather greatly affected his health and when it was good outside he seemed to derive new life from it and joy was reflected in his face. When I first visited him he received me with a smile. I expressed to him our great joy at his recovery, but he simply pointed to his chest indicating the pain he felt, and a raking cough confirmed this concern. He told me how the illness progressed: "Four days before this illness, I was already weak but I still wanted to throw it off. I did not even call the doctor, because I thought that I just had to go and lie down. I even went to the choir, but on the second day I could not go to Sext and was confined to my room hoping to get better. On the third day I had to lie down. I felt worse and worse. On the fourth day the doctor came and it was so bad I thought it was the end. I was ready to submit to the will of God about which I often prayed ... [p. 480].

Infirmarian Peter Seul also acted as his secretary. In the previously cited memo he wrote: "I transcribed all the documents that father had gathered for the cause of the Beatification of Mother Marchocka." [p. 481].

Mother Teresa Marchocka

In line with his work on the Carmelite Chronicles referred to in chapter 7, Kalinowski wrote a biography in French of Teresa (of Jesus) Marchocka, a saintly nun whose body was preserved incorrupt; she was the founder of the 17 century Carmelite Convents in Lviv and Warsaw.[207] In doing so Kalinowski was extremely anxious to pave

---

[207] *Vie et Vertus heroiques de la M*ère Thérèse de Jesus (Marchocka) (Lille-Paris-Bruges, 1906). Appropriately too he also made a contribution on Teresa Marchocka on the Third Centenary of the death of St. Teresa in 1882.

the way for her beatification. In December 1899 he wrote to his friend Felix Zienkowicz in Warsaw: "The Chronicle of our nuns in Vilnius is ready and will soon be published. Now I would like to do similar work for the convents of our nuns from Lviv and Warsaw, founded by a very saintly nun, Venerable Mother Teresa Marchocka. Maybe you could find the manuscripts in the libraries of Warsaw for me?" [p. 313].

Again he wrote to the Sisters of Łobzów: "A lot of them, (i.e., in the chronicles of Lviv – Warsaw) concern Mother Teresa Marchocka, and we must work for the publication of even a shortened life of the Blessed Mother. Could Sr. Magdalena, with permission, write to the Archbishop in Warsaw to see if we can find accounts of the sisters in the Convent in Warsaw, especially those relating to Mother Teresa Marchocka, may be also they could examine the writings in the Consistory in Wilanow, where the archives of Prince Aleksander Lubomirski are kept." [p. 315].

The same day he wrote to the Prioress in Lviv and asked her to enquire about collections in Ossolinskich's Library in the Benedictine monastery; Carmelites took refuge there on numerous occasions during periods of dispersion in the 17 century. He even suggested the names of people who might do the research – Ladislaus Belz, Director of the Library, and Bishop Weber, confessor of the Benedictines: "During the retreat," he writes at the end of a letter, "I asked Mother Marchocka to intercede from heaven that his successor in Lviv might be pleased to offer support." [p. 315]. A few weeks before that he wrote to the Prioress in Łobzów: "Pray to Mother Marchocka that she will take the case to her heart." [p. 315]. He himself prayed to her constantly.

At the beginning of May the work was completed and sent to Rome. On May 13 Kalinowski wrote to the Prioress of Wesoła to thank her for the outstanding help she had given. "I am sending back the papers," he said, "with an indication of what each one contains. There is a page written in the very hand of the holy mother. You must keep them with the other autographs. Remember also the written testimonies of cures and other favors obtained through the intercession of Mother Teresa." [p. 481].

In the early days of the same year 1907, the Carmelite nuns at Łobzów sent a letter to Rome and many copies were translated into French. The Archbishop of Kraków, Cardinal Puzyna received a richly-bound copy, and on January 17 he came in person to thank the Carmelites. He promised to support the cause of beatification. A few weeks later a letter arrived in Lobzów from Rome with good news; the postulator wrote: "Reverend Mother Prioress, it is with great pleasure that I begin the process that will contribute to the glory of your Convent, and the whole Polish Province. I want to take up the matter of the beatification of the Servant of God Teresa of Jesus and to this end I beg you to send me copies of all documents relating to the matter, indicating the places where they are located, and a complete inventory. Before sending a copy, have it reviewed in the episcopal palace so as to comply with the original." [p. 482].

This work for Marchocka's beatification was carried out over many years as Kalinowski sifted through all the archives in Poland, especially in the Convent of Wesoła, which contains all the documents of the ancient Convents of Kraków (the Convent of St. Martin), Lviv and Warsaw, which were led, or had been established by the servant of God. The letter from the Postulator pleased Kalinowski very much and in early February he wrote: "I still keep my mind active in gathering evidence for the beatification of Blessed M. Marchocka." In March, though he could hardly move he wrote to Czerna: "I thank Divine Providence that has allowed me to employ my weak strength working on a collection of documents necessary for the beatification of the Venerable Mother Teresa of Jesus Marchocka. The box in which they are stored [in Czerna] contains all the relics of the past – chronicles, etc., I placed there the different papers (letters from nuns, notes, etc.) that I had and of which I have need." [p. 483].

In June and July, he continued with the *Codex Postulatorum* in hand, directing the work of the Carmelites in Wesoła and Łobzów and he prepared everything necessary for the committee that would examine the life and writings of the Servant of God. Kalinowski had a premonition that he would die soon and he insisted on preparing for this. "My main task now," he wrote, "is to prepare for death because my sojourn here will not be long." [p. 484].

On July 24 he wrote: "Please recommend an intention to the mercy of God through the intercession of M.Teresa of Jesus." A few days later, the grace was obtained. So Kalinowski could add: "The case, which I mentioned previously, the Lord God in his mercy has successfully realized. I also resorted to the mediation of Blessed *in spe* [in 'hope' of her beatification] M. Marchocka." [p. 484].[208]

And the financial side of things was not forgotten. Processes of beatification and canonization entail significant costs and these had to be anticipated. "In Wesoła," Kalinowski wrote on June 24: "1,000 crowns have already been collected for expenses. Of these, 200 came from the will of the late Father Wenceslas." [p. 484].

Before his death, as we saw, Kalinowski wanted to do everything in his power for the Beatification of Mother Marchocka whose extraordinary virtues he thought would shed new splendor on Carmel and indeed the whole of Poland, because Carmel and Poland had, in his opinion, one and the same mission. What Teresa of Avila achieved in Spain in the 16th century, Carmel in Poland and Poland itself, he thought, should emulate in the 20th century through suffering and prayer. Carmelites should lay siege to heaven and implore mercy for the peoples of the East and the triumph of Holy Church.

Kalinowski, like Mother Marchocka, was a bright light exiled from heaven that lit up the way forward for others. His entire life can be summarized in two words: prayer and suffering; it was his destiny to teach people by word and example how to pray and suffer. In July, he again had an opportunity, for the last time, to give vivid instruction on the apostolate of prayer and suffering. On Sunday,

---

[208] Kalianowski does not identify the special grace.

July 21, the octave of the feast of Our Lady of Mount Carmel, three aisles of the church in Wadowice were too small to accommodate the devout crowds who came from all sides to participate in a profession ceremony. Kalinowski sat down before the altar with downcast eyes, as usual, and five young men knelt at his feet. "What do you ask?" he began and proceeded with the traditional Profession ceremony. Later he presented them with a souvenir card of their profession with the following inscription:

Cor Jesu,
Charitatis Victima,
Fac me Tibi
Hostiam Viventem,
Sanctam,
Deo placentem.

(Heart of Jesus, Victim of love, make me a living sacrifice, holy and pleasing to God). [p. 488]. He then encouraged them to repeat this prayer often in honour of the Sacred Heart.

Love of God and neighbour is a consuming fire. The closer Kalinowski came to the grave, the more he made every effort to enkindle the hearts of those entrusted to him. Speaking to those to whom God had given the mission of education, he advised them not to try to shine in the eyes of the world, but to try to instil in their pupils Christian principles in a simple and direct way, desiring only that God be better known and loved.

Indeed the last instructions which he gave the friars in Wadowice were concerned with fraternal love, and in this he appealed to the words of Christ addressed to the Apostles at the Last Supper, when he was about to part from them. He wrote: "When, after my arrival a year ago in Wadowice, I considered my new position and I asked myself the question, what does Divine Providence plan for me? We have to help each other, you have prepared me for a happy death, and I though unworthy need to spend the remainder of my days in

---

this vale of tears, as an instrument for the working of divine grace, so that in this way I may be of assistance to you." He fretted very much, seeing how the friars worked in the church, in the town and in the parish, without any help from him. Not being able to help them in any way, "I'm just a burden," he would say, "it only remains for me to submit to the Lord with the thought that nothing happens without the will of God." [p. 489].

During a violent storm over the whole of Galicia, he thought of the Carmelite sisters in Przemyśl and Lviv and prayed for them. He expressed his concerns in a letter to the sisters at Łobzów. Both communities in Przemyśl and Lviv suffered from poverty, but did so with great patience, which endeared them to him. In Przemyśl there was a lack of vocations, so one of the sisters in Łobzów offered to go and help out. She arrived there in the first days of July, which caused great joy to Kalinowski, but he was still not completely satisfied. He advised them to storm heaven asking for good vocations. They received them – but that was after his death.

Kalinowski still took an interest in current news especially as it affected the Church. Around this time, referring to trouble in Lublin, he remarked: "What a terrible thing this attack on the bishop of Lublin. Here we go back to the days of Hipacego Pociej, Uniate Metropolitan. We can expect a new St. Josaphat! From Moscow with caution! You cannot trust her sincerity. Until they cease to be afraid of spreading the truth among their own, they will put obstacles in the way. The Uniate Metropolitan Szeptyckim wanted to send a Basilian to Chelm and Lithuania but the Synod of Swjatiejszyj refused." [pp. 489-490].

Again on July 20, he noted: "A scapular procession in Rome was insulted by a group of troublemakers, though the security forces restored order and dispersed the attackers. Progress is very slow! *Usquequo Domine*?! [How long Lord?] ... All trials only strengthen our faith: Non *praevalebunt* [They shall not prevail]. You need to have a strong attitude so as not to lose peace of mind." [p. 491].

In his last letters Kalinowski indulged in an orgy of self-condemnation, comparing himself to the prodigal son. He wrote to the Prioress of one Carmelite convent:

> You did all you could do for the benefit of this son of the Fatherland and the Church, who had once wandered through this world caught up in the turmoil of life. You are still praying for unfortunate people and for me, who has so little to offer, or worse has made only a return of ingratitude for the gifts of God. I have pierced the Heart of our Savior with a spear, not once, but thousands of times. These last words apply only to me, not to the reader or anyone else. The past is so vividly engraved within me – the magnitude of my ingratitude, and the many wounds inflicted by me on our Savior; and I have added to the agony of His Heart. But what's the point of crying, at the end of life. [p. 491].

But Kalinowski found the way to transformation in the act of perfect love of God. He entrusted himself completely to God with full submission of his will to that of God. In a message to one of the young men he stated: "When someone comes to me and complains about suffering and crosses, I say to him: It is God's will. And this is the best advice I can give to everyone: recognize the will of God." [p. 491].

Soon he would be writing letters of farewell to his former comrades in exile, the last one on August 7 to Fr. Fiszer who was his confessor and friend in Perm: "I am on the edge of the tomb. I must shuffle off this mortal coil and hold myself ready." [p. 492]. When the supreme moment of his life arrived, he accepted it not simply in yielding up his life, but even doing so with joy, because he had finally come to an end of his second exile; he was about to join the company of Him whom he had loved above all else and for Whom he had worked and endured so much. After his former illness he was in fact worried that he had come back from the brink. "I've been so happy but now I must return again to life." Now, however, his desire was about to be fulfilled and there was to be no return.

From the feast of the Trinity on, Raphael Kalinowski was unable to celebrate Mass daily. In July and early August he came down to the garden for a walk, leaning on his cane, and he turned up in choir several times.

August 20 was the last time he celebrated the Eucharist. He then developed pneumonia and suffered from arthritis in his knees. He had to take to his bed again, but this time was unable to rise. His last letter was dated September 25. He wrote it in pencil in bed, with a trembling hand so that it is almost illegible. It was addressed to the Carmelite nuns at Łobzów and is an expression of his usual concern for his sisters there and in Przemyśl and Lviv: "News of the possible profession of 30 sisters means the Lord will multiply vocations and this really opens the way to sustaining both houses of God in Przemyśl and Lviv." [p. 492]. Later, referring to deceased brothers and sisters of Carmel in Poland he mentions his own death, which was now inevitable, and adds words of comfort: "The actions of Divine Providence follow one another to maintain continuity between heaven and earth." His letter ends: "Please remember this Lazarus in your prayers. I am grateful to God for everything." [p. 493].

Cardinal Gotti, learning of Kalinowski's dangerous illness wrote him some words of consolation. He expressed his gratitude for the kindness and favors rendered to him during canonical visits, but the patient immediately guessed what was going on, stopped reading and gave the letter to the infirmarian. He didn't want to hear any words of praise like what followed in the letter: "Your kindness, gentleness and obedience during illness as well as your humility, deserve admiration." [p. 494]. The Provincial had told the General that in all that related to his illness he was obedient to Father Marian who was now in charge. If given something that in his sobriety he was unaccustomed to drink, such as wine, he looked at the infirmarian and asked, "Do I need to drink this?" [p. 493]. If the answer was affirmative, he would drink it! Father Marian informed the sisters at Lobzów that the patient was so weak that he could hardly speak. A friend came to visit but he could only respond with a smile.

Towards the end he developed tuberculosis which completed the breakdown of his body. He was constantly troubled by a raking cough with the result that he was deprived of the consolation of the Holy Communion which he could not retain.

Final Reprieve

On November 1 Father Marian wrote to the Carmelite sisters: "The doctor said that there is no hope, and that death will occur in a few days. Tonight I want to give him Extreme Unction." [p. 494]. At three o'clock after lunch his coughing stopped, and the patient himself asked for Holy Viaticum, which he immediately received. After receiving the last Anointing, at the request of the friars kneeling beside the bed, he barely raised a trembling hand and blessed them for the last time. In fact he was hoping to die on November 2, the feast of All Souls.

The next day was one of recollection, prayer and suffering. He often looked at the crucifix saying, "Jesus! Mary! My God! My God! I will be filled, Lord, when I see your glory." [p. 494]. He rallied on for almost two weeks. A few hours before his death, sitting up in bed, he took his breviary to recite the daily liturgy. He opened it at the Sunday and began to read. When the attendant reminded him that he was exempt from reciting the Divine Office, and it would be better if he just rested, he replied: "How is it, today is Sunday, and I indulge myself." [p. 494]. The infirmarian reminded him that it was November 15. At approximately 7 o'clock he murmured: "Now take your rest." [p. 494]. He died an hour later. Berthold Schorman wrote: "On November 15, the feast of St. Leopold, the patron saint of our Austrian provinces, and also the day for commemorating

the deceased members of our order, he was called home by God."
[p. 494].

At 8 am the mournful sound of the bell called the friars together.
With candles lit they began to pray for the dying friar which was a
signal for the end. Soon afterwards his emaciated body was again
clothed in his brown habit and white mantle. The sound of the bells
had alerted the people who arrived at the church as Mass was about
to be celebrated.

The Provincial arrived from Vienna for the funeral and next
day the mortal remains of Fr. Raphael Kalinowski were transported
to Czerna where they would be buried in the priory cemetery. The
funeral took place on November 20. The Church in Czerna was
too small to accommodate the large numbers of people who wished
to pay him a final tribute. The Third Order, the clergy in the area,
religious and friends came from afar, especially from Kraków. His
family was represented by his brother Jerzy, now a priest, who had
arrived in time for the end. Helena, widow of his brother Gabriel
and her children were present to represent the family.

Fr. Martin Czermiński, a Jesuit priest, entered the pulpit. He
was editor of the monthly *Catholic Missions*, and a close friend of
Kalinowski. With more than a touch of eloquence he began:

> The soul of the late Fr. Raphael, mature in virtue, after a
> long, hard and busy life already stands before the righteous
> judgment of God. We gather sadly to honor his remains
> which have always been the dwelling place of God. And we
> gather to give vent to heartfelt feelings for our country; with
> this person here one of the last links connecting us with a
> heroic past is broken and a modest coffin encloses someone
> who, for more than seventy years, seemed to embody the
> history of our nation. But this death too suggests to us
> tidings of a happier future. He is buried in the ground
> but alive in heaven, adding to that powerful company of
> intermediaries with God. [And the speaker ended saying]

Fr. Raphael is not dead, but lives the life of the chosen – and he who on earth was an example for you today – let us have confidence in God – he is now our advocate. [p. 499].

A friend of Kalinowski, a Mr. Golab, recalled his great contribution to the Order and Poland before the open coffin and ended saying: "We are left with the consolation that the late Father Raphael, at the throne of God can obtain for our country a better fate, and add to this, faith, hope and love for each other and the strength to endure the hardships of life. After this brief journey on earth, may we sooner or later reconnect with this our Star of the Sea in heaven."

Others paid tribute to Kalinowski in letters of condolence. Cardinal Puzyna himself, Archishop of Kraków, wrote the day after his death: "Cardinal Puzyna offered Mass today for the repose of the late Raphael, who, I trust has entered into his eternal reward." [p. 499]. Archbishop Bilczewski of Lviv wrote to the Prior: "I would like to share my sorrow for the loss of dear Father Kalinowski. Our consolation lies in the great confidence we have that we have gained in him an intercessor with God. I celebrated Mass for him." [p. 501].

The new Archbishop of Warsaw, Aleksander Kakowski, wrote to Czerna, asking the community to pray at the tomb of Father Raphael on his behalf, before he got the opportunity to do so personally, which he did in due time.[209] The Superior of the Ursuline Sisters of Kraków, wrote: "Surely this is a big blow, an irreparable loss, but on the other hand a sweet consolation: the awareness of a new advocate in heaven, because the unique sanctity of the deceased will have immediately opened the gates of heaven." [p. 501].

Raphael Kalinowski more than fulfilled the trust the Czartoryska women placed in his potential even before he became a Carmelite. His work led to the expansion and growth of the Carmelite Order

---

[209] Before leaving for the Conclave in Rome that elected him Pope in an historic election, his successor in Kraków, Karol Wojtyła, prayed at the tomb of Raphael Kalinowski.

in Poland. He can truly be called the Restorer of Carmel in Poland. Here again he bears a distinct resemblance to Hermann Cohen, whose biography he promoted, and who did so much to restore the Teresian Carmelites in France and England some years previously.

The Prioress of Łobzów Convent, Mother Mary Xavier ought of course to have the last word – even if a long one – on the influence of Raphael Kalinowski on her and her sisters in her own and other convents. She to whom the Polish Carmel owed so much including the vocation of Kalinowski, informed the Carmelite communities about Fr. Raphael's death in these words, so painful as it was for everyone:

> Dear mother and dear sisters! Everything passes on this earth!... We ought to preserve the memory of this father who gave himself for so many years for the good of the Order, for each one of us, wanting only to guide us to heaven and form in us a true religious spirit, always wishing to see that each one walked in the steps of our mothers in the past and become holy Discalced Carmelites. His own life itself pointed out to us the way to go to achieve this holiness. He was for us a model of mortification, both exterior and interior, his total detachment from all earthly things, of all that didn't lead to God. His life was one continual death, a heroic death to all created things. He only wanted God's love to have first place in his heart and with God's love, love of neighbour. We never heard the least word escape from his lips that could cause offence to neighbor. Never. On the contrary he always jumped to the defence of others. He had a horror of entertaining the least thought capable of hurting charity or of troubling the peace of his soul, always united to God and pure as crystal. He seemed to pass through this world without touching the ground. He seemed to be an intermediary between God and people and obtained for them grace and comfort. His profound humility and his

mortification, one can say without fear, worked miracles of grace: and the more he obtained from God, the more he concealed it, so that God might be glorified and reign in the hearts of people. Let us pray, dear mother and sisters, pray for the peace of his soul for which he asked us to pray. In all his letters and cards and in his last farewell he recommended himself to the prayers of Carmel which he loved so much and for which he laboured for so many years. Give him eternal rest O, God, and let perpetual light shine upon him. [p. 502].

It is obvious that all who knew him revered Fr. Raphael as a saint. After his death, requests for his relics came from all sides, people wanting a particle of his clothing or some other souvenir. Many people of Wadowice, Kraków, Galicia, and even Austria wrote in about the extraordinary graces received through Father Raphael. There was already talk of his beatification.

Raphael Kalinowski was beatified in Kraków by Saint John Paul II on June 22, 1983, during his historic homecoming to Poland, in the presence of two million people. He was canonized by the same Pope on November 17, 1991 at St. Peter's in Rome.

Epilogue

Spiritual Legacy

In the course of this biography of Raphael Kalinowski, I have had occasion to refer to spiritual themes on which he laid special emphasis, notably his devotion to Mary the mother of Jesus. This required a special chapter of its own – "Carmel is all Mary's". [Part Two, chapter 3] In this final section I would like to draw attention to additional spiritual topics that figured prominently in Kalinowski's prayer life, eg, the person of Jesus Christ, priesthood and Eucharist, etc. By way of introduction to these themes I refer to his call to experience the joy of Christian living.

"Rejoice in the Lord always," says St. Paul, "again I say, rejoice" [Phil 4:4]. Whenever he gave spiritual direction Kalinowski reminded people of the need for joy. He made every effort to detach directees from anything that would impede their joy in the Lord; above all taught them to avoid an air of sadness as well as anxiety of conscience, which he felt only serve to niggle people and hinder real devotion.

St. Teresa would exhort her followers to serve the Lord with joy, and Kalinowski tried to maintain this joy in communities by every means at his disposal. When he had to give what little admonition he was expected to give in community chapters, he would do so in such a witty and sensitive way that his wishes were usually complied with.

The Convent in Przemyśl is situated on the slope of the hill near the fortress which dominates the town and surrounding areas; Kalinowski made the first canonical visitation there which involved a lot of work. One of the sisters, seeing him very tired, cheerfully told him that he would probably die in Przemyśl! However, this didn't happen and he referred to it on his next visit a year later! This community was made up of young and zealous sisters and there was scarcely any need to urge them forward in the spiritual life. He remarked: "Let us ensure that the members of the community of Ulica Fortu (Przemyśl) Convent are cheerful and strong, maintain a good mood and enjoy good health." [p. 393]. Inner peace is important also because it enables people to attain quiet enjoyment of the God who dwells within them. Kalinowski's dealings with the sisters shows sufficiently clearly that he could direct people in all those various and difficult trials they met with, and how much effort he required from them. He was anxious to accept into Carmel only strong and courageous people who would gladly take up the challenges facing them. [p. 394].

When one of the sisters confided her worries to him, Kalinowski responded: "The best way to restore peace is to humbly admit our faults, not to think about what happened yesterday, and then devote ourselves entirely to today's occupations because that is God's will. Let you, dear sister, engrave deep within the truth that our whole strength lies in a life of faith, not a life of feeling. Then you will be like an unshakeable rock and will pay no heed to turmoil and storms, and even less to a light wind: you need to use the experience that the good Lord sends. Ask for this grace above all in Holy Communion." [p. 394].

Kalinowski reminded Carmelites of the sublime teaching bequeathed to them by St. Teresa and wished that they would apply this teaching to their own situation. For him doing the will of God in all things was a necessary and reliable means of achieving all that is needed for the spiritual growth of the community. The Rule and customs of the Order as approved by superiors are an expression of God's will, and the greatest efforts should be made to fulfil these faithfully and fully, without the need to add anything else.

Keep it simple.

Kalinowski preached Carmelite simplicity of life both personally and in one's surroundings. For instance as prior he discouraged any lavish art or adornment in the chapel and elsewhere. He rebuked a painter who demonstrated his talent in the chapel as being against the Carmelite way of simplicity and poverty. "Even in the matter of the altar," he said, "in no way do I advise overdoing things, not to mention the expense involved; for what purpose does it achieve?" He felt this tendency to over-decorate was due to a lack of a serious and devout style in the work of artists of the 19th century. "Better to settle for a modest altar," he thought, "by painting the walls of the chancel and chapel in an appropriate color that will best befit the chapel and the spirit of humble simplicity. But for my own part I don't insist on this, however." [p. 395]. Naturally the artists involved were of a different opinion and a few months later, Kalinowski wrote to the prioress: "Apart from the style of contemporary artists, I am afraid of the very big expenditure involved."

Dealing with scruples.

Kalinowski came across an Italian book by a contemporary author Joseph Quadrupani (1846), which was translated and called *Light and Peace, Instructions for Devout souls to dispel their doubts and allay their fears.* He read it carefully and as usual with such books, wanted to share it with those who had not yet enjoyed the blessing of interior peace. The author Joseph Quadrupani, a Barnabite religious, believed that teaching the Gospel clearly to the faithful is not in itself sufficient. Preachers and ascetical writers go to great lengths, he thought, to tell people when their actions are sinful, but fail to explain when they are not! Because of this neglect, the lives of many people who by nature were generous and capable of high spiritual achievement, were plagued by unnecessary scruples and so fell into a state of discouragement. To prevent this to sisters, Kalinowski's long experience and deep knowledge of people convinced him that this book could do much good in Poland. For that reason, linguist that he was, he began to translate the book. When he found out that a translation had already been made and given to the Warsaw community, he ceased further work on it and merely recommended the Warsaw publication. So we can gather from this how Kalinowski wanted people devoted to the service of God to enjoy complete freedom and detachment of spirit. He required detachment from every pressure – even in carrying out spiritual exercises – if obedience and love of neighbor required it. An expression of this precious freedom is the filial confidence that we show towards God. In this respect of course St. Teresa was an excellent model and Kalinowski wanted her daughters to seek this spiritual perfection: Quadrupani's book would help them achieve this.

Kalinowski pointed out that in the Eucharist the Lord unites himself with us. He advised directees to contemplate the Passion of Jesus Christ and receive Holy Communion frequently as a powerful means to union with God. He would insist, however, that these measures are not foolproof and will not be effective if they are not accompanied by a right approach to the will of God. "Holy Communion," he said, "is only a means, and if we accept it without the proper disposition, rather than allowing it to bring us closer to Jesus, it will only keep us from Him." [p. 396]. He insisted on proper preparation for the Eucharist, and also pointed out the practical benefits of this food from heaven in acquiring virtues and avoiding faults.

Devotion to the Infant Jesus.

Devotion to the Passion of Christ and the Eucharist were certainly part of the Carmelite tradition; this was emphasized by St. John of the Cross and St. Teresa, as well as devotion to the Infant Jesus which she also recommended to her followers. And no one took her recommendation more seriously that St. Thérèse who chose as her religious title 'Of the Infant Jesus'. Kalinowski reminded the sisters: "Among the items in the church, which pleased Teresa when she went to the Convent of Villanueva de la Jara, was a statue of the Infant Jesus, carved in wood. Appointing Sr. Anne as portress and procurator of the new foundation, she told her to ask the Divine Infant for all that was needed for the sisters, assuring them that their requests would be heard. Anne placed the Infant near the gate, and she often prayed before the statue. When they were in need, she turned to him with great faith, and her prayers were answered so generously that she called him the founder and steward of the Convent!" [p. 398].

Francis Pascual Sanchez, whom we met earlier, spread this devotion in Spain, Sister Margaret Parigot spread it in France,[210] and Cyril Barberi did the same in Prague, where the Holy Infant Shrine is world-famous. It spread also from the Carmelite houses in Kraków and from Ostra Brama in Vilnius. Kalinowski, who was at the heart of the Polish and Lithuanian restoration, anxious to revive the great Carmelite tradition of past centuries and restore it to its former glory, could not ignore the Infant Jesus. "May the Child Jesus possess the hearts of the dear sisters so that they may sing Glory to God here on earth and forever possess the Infant Jesus through His Blessed Mother!"[211]

---

[210] She belonged to the Carmel of Beaune in France and died in 1648.

[211] The Church where the present writer ministers is dedicated to the Infant Jesus.

Holiness for all.

Kalinowski worked not only for religious but also for the laity. What he did at the beginning in Czerna, he continued doing in Wadowice, and information about this work can be found in his letters from this time. In 1899 he wrote from Kraków to Louise Młocka, that his life was spent in the confessional. In the jubilee year at Wadowice in 1901 he wrote: "People flock to the sacrament of penance as a deer to springs of water." This was during Lent, and in July he wrote again: "The faithful besiege the confessionals, really guided by God's grace." And in October: "Only at night do I find some time to answer even a few letters or to read those I get from the dear sisters. The eagerness to resort to the grace of the sacrament of penance came upon the faithful, and it as if we are under siege from early morning until evening – without a break from day to day. But what a great thing is repentance? What an abyss of God's mercy is shown in the establishment of the Jubilee! In *Aeternum Misericordias cantabo Domini*. [p. 401].[212] Undoubtedly Kalinowski loved people and devoted himself to their service without stint; people reciprocated this, and entrusted themselves to his care. It could also be said Kalinowski enjoyed scarcely more peace in his cell than in the church! If, for instance, a friar needed help in publishing work, or students needed guidance in clarifying various questions or solving difficult mathematical problems they knew where to go.

Sacred Humanity of Jesus

The Sacred Humanity of Jesus Christ and his suffering for us was something that greatly motivated Kalinowski with a desire to give of himself fully to the Lord as promised on the day of his profession. In this, of course, he was a true disciple of St. Teresa of Avila. The vows which he faithfully kept, kindled his enthusiasm.

---

[212] *Forever I will sing the mercies of the Lord.* [A favorite verse of St. Teresa taken from Ps. 89:1].

But that was not enough for him, he wanted to give everything, following the example of his Divine Master. "True," he wrote, "I am probably just looking for sweetness deriving from the nearness of Christ, but that tends to turn me away from suffering! I say that I love and it seems to me that my heart doesn't lie, but I'm aware that in order to obtain this love I need to go his way, the way he himself chose, and not turn my eyes away from the way of the cross. Can we meet on any other road? Dear Christ I beg you to enter my heart, and lift me up when my feeble strength falters! O God, if I live, it matters only if by my actions I have lived only for love of you." [p.137]

Kalinowski's brother Jerzy also wrote, in a memo: "Raphael had a spirit of sacrifice in the highest degree and gave himself completely to the love of God, without reservation, and he lived only for Him. His inner eye turned to the Heart of the Savior and he made every effort to imitate His life and be humble as he was." [p.138]

Kalinowski spoke of three points needed to effectively achieve this goal: self-renunciation, focus, prayer. The first two he would consider a preparation for the third – prayer of the heart; they kindle the fire of love for God and neighbor. Kalinowski was himself very faithful to prayer. His confrère Diaz de Cerio, who often accompanied him on his journeys to Kraków, Przemyśl and Lviv, wrote that he also prayed while traveling, or read a spiritual book, which he always carried with him: "Do not shorten the time devoted to prayer, he advised, "during prayer be filled with reverence for the Divine Majesty and the carrying out of your duties with enthusiasm. The heart must work more than the mind. Then make practical well-defined resolutions. After the prayer, reflect on it; a well-made meditation cleanses and heals."[p.138]

What transpired in his heart, loving and generous as it was during his prolonged conversations with the Lord? He gives us a clue in his notes:

> Ask for repentance and true sorrow for past and present infidelity. Have no fear other than that of not pleasing God.

Love God above all things and place all your trust in Him... Be attentive to the voice of God. Desire that all hearts be filled with the fire of divine love. In this love find all your happiness, aligning your will with His. Desire to depart and be united with God in heaven. Jesus desires to find someone worthy and capable of receiving Him and keeping Him lovingly in His heart. Jesus seeks me out, but so does the world, the devil and the lust of the flesh. But no one can possess me without my consent. May Jesus alone find me. He alone is sufficient for me. He is our King and we ought to serve Him. We have chosen Him as King on the day of our baptism and profession, and He in turn chose us as His people. He leads us, supports us, arms us, fights for us and wins the victory for us. He first carried the cross, which is our shield, our defender, our salvation. He died for us, and His death is our life. If we follow Him in faith and without fear, we can be confident of victory and know that eternal glory awaits us. [p.139]

Kalinowski gravitated towards the Eucharist like steel to a magnet. His brother Jerzy, who from early childhood admired and loved him, wrote in his notes, that "his only happiness was the Eucharist, and nothing worried him more than to be deprived of it." [p.139]

When he moved to Smolensk as noted in Part One, he could receive the sacraments with renewed zeal. This is evidenced in a prayer found in his papers relating to that time:

> "Lord, look kindly on those inadequate confessions, the coldness of heart preventing us from visiting you in the Blessed Sacrament, the distractions and dissipations of mind to which I admit. Spare my weakness and have mercy on me a sinner; the weak cannot make strong acts of faith, hope and love. Preserve me, O God, in your continual

presence. When I write these words, may I write them in your presence, O Holy Trinity, and in the presence of Mary our Queen, and the whole communion of saints!" [p.140]

Priesthood and Eucharist

Obviously Kalinowski had a deep appreciation of his priesthood which he had sought for so long. With approval he quotes St. John Chrysostom, who had such an exalted idea of priesthood, and wrote a little treatise on it. He meditated constantly on an influential book called, *Guidelines for the Priests*, written by Antoine Moline de Chartreux.[213] What he read here he carried out in practice: frequent confession, and deep devotion at the celebration of the Eucharist.

"If Eucharistic life expresses itself in fulfilling the greatest commandment, that is to say, love of God and neighbor, then this love finds its source in the sacrament of the Eucharist, which is commonly called the sacrament of love." [p.141] These words quoted from a letter of the late Pope John Paul II, demonstrate the truth about the role the Eucharist plays in the life of the Christian. Those who make use of this school of love and apply the lessons learned there to their lives are known as saints. And the Church, through the teaching and witness of the saints acknowledges this fact, and offers people a reliable means of reaching the goal. There is no saint indeed in the Church who has not lived by the Eucharist, and we need look no further than Teresa, John and Thérèse. This is the source of all holiness and full Christian life. Raphael Kalinowski is among the number of those who derived constant strength from Christ's presence in the Eucharist.

After his conversion Kalinowski always tried to receive the Eucharist each morning. Before his arrest by the Russians as we noted in Part 1, he hurried through the streets of Vilnius to attend

---

213   Ibid., p 141. His teaching follows that of the French Sulpician model which derives from J.J Olier.

Mass each day, usually in St. Elisabeth's Church of the Benedictine Sisters and occasionally in the church of the Bonifrats' monastery.

Again, like Hermann Cohen in France some years before, while still a layperson he became something of a herald of devotion to the Eucharist, anticipating future developments by decades. Indeed it was only as late as the beginning of the 20 century that Pope St. Pius X promulgated frequent Communion for all. In this he was said to have been influenced by St. Thérèse of Lisieux.

Kalinowski believed that frequent presence at the Lord's table would make it easier for Auguste Czartoryski, his aristocratic pupil – who was very absent-minded by temperament, and not helped by illness – to attain the necessary concentration for study. Through the school of Eucharist Kalinowski led Czartoryski to the Salesian Order and today his pupil has been beatified.

As a convict imprisoned for his role in the leadership of the January uprising in 1863, Kalinowski was deprived of Communion, but was delighted to be able to follow the Eucharist being offered in the nearby church, and join spiritually in Holy Communion.

When he lived briefly in Perm, a town where he was deprived of the Eucharist, he felt very bereft. The Catholic Church here had been taken over by the Orthodox and the nearest church was some distance away, and it had not been possible for him to attend there. This lack of the Eucharist caused him great suffering.

No matter where he stayed in Siberia – places like Smolensk or Irkutsk, Kalinowski tried to live as near as possible to a church. He gladly spent time in Eucharistic adoration whenever he could. Here again we have a distinct echo of his fellow Carmelite of only a few years earlier, Hermann Cohen, who became known as an Apostle of the Eucharist. In the letter to his family Kalinowski wrote: "I live close to the chapel so I can have my daily spiritual nourishment and I am troubled when I think of losing it by being transferred from here, as therein lies my strength." On another occasion he wrote: ... I see the Eucharist in my dreams and I prostrate myself and, if I can, I choose something from sacred doctrine or a theme from our Savior's passion to meditate on. Strengthened by Spiritual Communion I arise, ready to accept anything peacefully, united with the Lord."[214]

Kalinowski showed by his example, not with words only, what living by Eucharist is about. After his return from penal servitude, while in Davos, Switzerland, with no Catholic church in the vicinity, he felt miserable without access to the Eucharist.

The direct and honest content of his letters is a key to Kalinowski's experience of Eucharist. In one of them he wrote: "Since the time I believed in Jesus Christ present in Holy Sacrament, all my being has been concentrated on the high altar; even in Czestochowa I just glanced at souvenirs, not to mention other objects." In his letter from Menton, he confessed: "My only entertainment is to relax in God's presence and be replenished with the treasure left us by our Savoir on the Holy Altar." [p.143]

It is worth emphasising that as a lay person, 30-year-old Kalinowski wrote to his family from Siberia in these words: "God devoted himself entirely to us. How can we not devote ourselves to God?" He perfectly understood the Lord's utter dedication to his mission, showing himself madly in love with us until the end. The Eucharist especially expresses the self-giving of Jesus, who identifies with everyone, especially those who suffer.

Kalinowski's response to God's love was complete, expressed in his priestly life in Carmel. His happiness reached its peak when he could offer the Eucharist every day and dispense this precious treasure of the church. As a friar he was happy to live under the same roof as Christ present in the Sacrament.

Altar boys who served Kalinowski's Mass in a chapel in Łobzów near Kraków, later wrote: "When he approached the altar his face looked solemn and during the Mass all his composure seemed to be

---

[214] Ibid., p 143. Here we have yet another echo of Hermann Cohen. It was always his wish to be next door to the chapel and even as a novice he was given this privilege.

focused on the holy Eucharist. People liked looking at him and many of them could not take their eyes off him." [p.143]

Kalinowski once noted: "We are reminded that we should try as much as possible both to pray the Eucharist and to listen to it, so as to have the spiritual attitudes required by the Holy Mystery." [p.144]

Witnesses of his life during the canonical process unanimously testified to his great love for the Eucharist. He celebrated it with great fervor and reverence, according to some witnesses appearing to be in ecstasy; his whole demeanor was transformed during the liturgy. Veronika Smoczynska, a Carmelite sister and a directee, considered his Eucharistic life to be: "The basis of his whole life and activities. You should have seen him at the altar celebrating the Eucharist. What concentration and care! He seemed to contemplate the mystery he was celebrating right at that moment. What respect, what love in distributing Holy Communion. A vivid faith revealed God's secrets to him. He brought to the altar his soul prepared for the grace he received for his faithfulness." [p.144]

Kalinowski never spoke to people after Mass before making thanksgiving in the sacristy. In his opinion the fruits of Eucharist depended not only on its frequent reception, but also on proper preparation and thanksgiving for this event. In his letters and during conferences he recommended saying thanksgiving prayers after receiving Holy Communion. He wrote: "When can prayer be more ardent and deserving of acceptance by God if not after receiving our Lord Jesus Christ's body?" In this he followed the example of St. Teresa of Avila, who seemed to have received her deepest spiritual experiences after Holy Communion. Her masterpiece *The Interior Castle* was written at white heat in the mornings after receiving Holy Communion.

Kalinowski spoke to Carmelite sisters about Pope St. Pius X's decree recommending frequent Holy Communion: "I remind you that it's not the frequency of Holy Communion itself that benefits us, but preparing for it, trying to improve our lives, and by adorning ourselves with the flowers of virtues, in silence and recollection and with love towards all." His words to the same Carmelite nuns pointing out specific requirements following participation in Eucharist are worth noting: "First of all, remember that frequent Holy Communion requires that you aim at religious perfection, growing in the love to God and a neighbor." [p.144]

In addition to speaking about the Eucharist from the pulpit or in the confessional, Kalinowski also spoke about it in letters to his family. He frequently returned to this point: "In the Eucharist Jesus unites himself with us, bestows enlivening grace on us, strengthens us with the bread of life and desires that through this we try to be like Him."

To preserve internal joy and peace in his addressees' hearts, he recommended in his letters frequent confession and Holy Communion as spiritual food.

The Church

Kalinowski loved and worshipped the Lord, not only hidden in the Eucharist, but also as he encountered him in the Church, the dispenser of the Eucharist. The Church is a community reborn in baptism, united by the grace of Jesus Christ, animated by his Spirit, and called to share in his inheritance. During long years of exile, as we saw previously, Kalinowski carefully studied the history of the Church, and summarized it in his notes. He admired the spirit of unity and love that he found in the Church, and encouraged his friends to love the Church as well. These characteristics marked his apostolate of writing. For instance:

> The Church is the assembly of people committed to work for salvation on this earth by faith and good works. Faith reveals the one, true Church of Christ also and it can only be one. The Catholic Church professes the truth, and clearly proclaims and makes it known that Christ is the only mediator between God and humankind, and that faith

is the only true path to salvation – outside the Catholic Church there is no salvation – and it calls all people to unity with the Church; therefore we should pray for the conversion of dissenters back to the communion of faith with the Catholic Church as the only means of entering the path of salvation, while there is still time on earth[215].

Kalinowski refers to what he called the humiliating position of women before the birth of Christ, and he adds: "in the Catholic Church of the Redeemer women were already liberated. Indeed Mary was even called Queen of the Angels." [p 144] In his Siberian Notes he talks about the religious discussion group he had organized that often included mariological themes – such as the role of the Mother of God in the work of redemption, the principal Marian dogmas, Mary as an outstanding example of the emancipation of women and similar themes.[216] Kalinowski held that the words of the Book of Proverbs: *Mulierem fortem quis inveniet…..[217]*, which the Church reads on the feast of the holy women, can be applied directly to Catholic women.

---

[215] Ibid. p 143. *Extra Ecclesia nulla salus*, "outside the church there is no salvation," has always been a bone of contention. American Jesuit Leonard Feeney was condemned by the Vatican for holding a strict interpretation of this adage. Kalinowski holds to the correct position: "If the deceased person was outside the Catholic Church by *ignorantia invincibilis* he or she ipso facto, belongs to the soul of the Church, and has a share in the graces that God grants the prayers of the faithful of the Church. But as the state of the soul of the deceased may in this case be known only to God, the church can offer public prayers and even encourages people to pray for the souls of the faithful departed as the priest does while celebrating Holy Sacrifice.

[216] Teresianum, Romae, XLI 1990/I, *Szczepan T. Praskiewicz OCD*. Again in this chapter I am indebted to Szezepan for material from his unpublished notes on the Eucharist.

[217] *Who shall find a valiant woman? She is more precious than any jewel.*

When he was ordained priest, it opened before Kalinowski a new field of apostolic work of course. He liked to talk to his penitents about the Church, he taught them to explore the treasures the Church puts at our disposal and how the Church expects us to respond. Here is what we read in one of the conferences:

> O holy Church, the Lord Jesus said that 'the gates of hell shall not prevail against it', and, 'I am with you until the end of time. You are Peter and on this rock I will build my Church.'[p.145] The Lord Jesus lives in the Church and is present in the Blessed Sacrament. The Church is governed by our Holy Father, the Pope (from Greek: papa – father); he gave him the keys of the kingdom of heaven and has given the power of binding and loosing: Those you forgive will be forgiven, those whom you bind will be bound. Feed my lambs, feed my sheep. The Church is infallible in matters of faith and morals. The Church also established the sacraments and gave us other various aids also, gave us a mediatrix in his Blessed Mother, gave us the angels as guardians and the saints as companions... In moments of temptation against faith we can say: I believe in everything that Holy Church proposes for belief. [p.145].

More on Kalinowski's human and spiritual qualities.

It should also be noted that Raphael Kalinowski had a soft spot for children and for the poor. One eyewitness tells he was sometimes seen by the nuns in Łobzów, loaded with sweets, medals, images, etc., which he himself didn't need, and children would be waiting to receive them, kissing his hands. A truck loaded with vegetables was often seen outside the gates of the Convent in Kraków – courtesy of the prior of Czerna.

When his brother Jerzy was doing a retreat under his guidance, he came to him at breakfast and after a while Kalinowski had to leave saying, "I'm going to do sacrifice." This was code for: "I'm going to the confessional," and indeed it was. [p.154] There, despite poor health and often extremely cold conditions in the church at Czerna, he spent hours and sometimes days on end hearing confessions. As prior, he was already sufficiently weighed down administering a large property, but he still carried out this ministry in the church. The community would try to dissuade him from doing so but he would continue at his post until a fever or flu forced him to keep to his room.

In 1888, the Provincial Chapter elected him for a second time prior of Czerna. Already at the beginning of 1889 his health began to decline, so he went to visit a doctor in Kraków who prescribed some treatment and insisted on complete rest. The Carmelites of Łobzów wished to look after him and asked the Provincial if he might be allowed to follow up the treatment in Kraków. Sr. Sophia from Łobzów Convent comments:

> "I was then on duty at the turn and I was glad to be able to able to help him. Every morning he came to the turn for medicine, into which he poured a few drops of Lourdes water. Before taking this medication he recited a Hail Mary. He ate little, and once, when he left the meat untouched we camouflaged it with porridge so he didn't notice next time. He liked fruit, but also left some uneaten. As soon as he improved a little he would spend hours hearing confessions, not only those of the nuns, but also of many people from the city, religious, laity, etc. One of them, especially Princess Moruzi, a Pole from Podolia, who was married to a Romanian prince, made me very impatient. She came to Kraków for a retreat, and hearing a lot about Fr. Raphael, whose patience must have been sorely tested by her, she would come every year to affirm her devotion.[1]"

Another account in the Convent of Łobzów reads: "Those who have to deal with Father Raphael said that it felt as if they were talking to a saint. He had an ascetic appearance and while he was polite and gentle in manner and inspired respect and trust, he spoke with each according to his or her age and position. He was very good with the children and tried to teach them about God. One of his nieces, still a baby, whom he occasionally visited in Kraków, didn't want to see him leave." [p.155]

All the usual people benefited from Kalinowski's presence in Kraków and they would come to the Convent chapel for a long chat. Among them was Julia Labedzka, a nun from Warsaw and Teresa Moruzi, both of whom suffered from scruples; Kalinowski was the most patient confessor they could find. All came to him for reassurance and he welcomed them always with unfailing kindness and patience. One day he was kept for a long time in the confessional and he later commented that such a person such as she suffers greatly and requires a lot of pity and compassion.

In one of his letters he writes of Teresa Moruzi: "She is very down and endures the severest external and internal struggle. This is the penitent for whom I spent most of my efforts... and God saw fit to give her the strength to stand beneath the cross, which the Lord laid on her." [p.154] In this case he hadn't worked in vain. Here is what we read in a letter from her husband Prince Dmitri Moruzi to Kalinowski: "Dearest and reverend Father! God indeed hears your prayers in the spiritual direction given my wife, myself and the city of Sulina, because half the miracle has already occurred; there has been almost complete moral change. I do not doubt that she will heal physically also. If this miracle continues I will come as a pilgrim to thank you. Please accept most dear and Reverend Father, my words of deep gratitude and heartfelt reverence." [p.156]

Certainly Prince Moruzi was a great benefactor of Carmel in Poland, and the same can be said about Julia Labedzka, mentioned above. For 23 years she was under his direction. One of the sisters in her community wrote to him: "First, I have no words to thank you enough for the frequent help dear Father, you gave that poor sister. Neither can you imagine dear Father, how your work has borne fruit at present."[p.155]

The priests who came to celebrate Mass in his community also benefited from the presence of Kalinowski. He treated them with respect and reverence and they held long spiritual conversations with him.

The compassion, kindness and dedication of Kalinowski attracted a great variety of people to him: small and great, rich and poor, saints and sinners, and he became all things to all in order to win all for Christ. Diaz de Cerio, who had lived with him in the same house, wrote of him:

> Father Raphael was only in Czerna for a few months, when people of the area already knew what a treasure they possessed. They came to him in distress, in suffering and in all their deepest needs and not for nothing did they come. He always received them with great kindness, compassion, throwing light in time of doubt and gaining the hearts of all by his goodness....He liked to talk to the village people... I loved him as a father, and sought his advice. In particular, he gave advice in sensitive family issues, especially to those troubled in conscience; and everyone went away enlightened, comforted and ready to withstand the troubles of life, if not with joy, at least with patience and resignation. This Christian charity that people sometimes so desperately needed was never refused, and for that purpose he never hesitated to sacrifice his rest and health. [p.165]

Union with God.

Union with God is our primary goal in life, since, as St. Augustine says, only therein can we find true happiness. Christ has shown us how to achieve this. Kalinowski tells us: "Blessed are the pure in heart, for they shall see God. Whoever decides to return to God should first of all regain this purity of heart, if it has been lost and if so desired, make a general confession. After recovering purity of heart one should always be vigilant lest it be lost again. After this meditation that should be our daily bread, we should tread firmly on the right path, looking inwards on ourselves in prayer and following through with perseverance." [p.166]

He further advises: "Keep in mind the presence of God, because if God is with you, you will be close to God and be protected against danger. God is faithful to his promises, and if you truly love God you need have no fear." [p.166]

Kalinowski paid special attention to the need for frequent renewal of the intention to please God in all our actions, because it's the intention that gives them value. To be holy, you do not need to do great things, simply do little things well. Here are a few thoughts which he left us: "There are people whom God has chosen to become holy through performing insignificant things. God allows everyone access to perfection, that is, to sanctify even the simplest activities of everyday life, by doing their best to carry out the will of God. Being faithful to God even in the trifling affairs of everyday life is the secret of holiness. Do not depart from the tried and trusted way, but settle for a humble and hidden life." [p.167]

Here he would cite the example of the Holy Family of Nazareth: "Maybe today the holiest and highest person in heaven is an anonymous Christian of humble origin, who lived a quiet life, hidden from the world, devoted to ordinary duties... That which is little in the estimation of people, is often great in the sight of God. It is written that God sees our outward actions but only looks at the heart." [p.168] By this Kalinowski means that the Lord assesses the measure of love with which we carry out our tasks. He writes: "It would be wrong to think that little things are devoid of importance, each action is great, if it is joined to a deep love for God and a strong desire to please Him. Remain silent instead of uttering a harsh word, be patient with the mistakes of the neighbor, forgive an insult, anticipate the wishes of superiors, or even equals or subordinates. Try to lighten people's workload, comfort the afflicted, postpone a task to help a neighbor, etc. Living out one's normal daily duties in this way is the best way to make progress in the inner life."[218]

Penance, mortification, meditation, practicing the presence of God, and the oft-repeated intention of doing everything with the desire to please God – that was the means of sanctity which Kalinowski would recommend to the people he directed. In order to help them achieve this sense of the presence of God, he advised people to carefully avoid unnecessary talk and shun idleness. He encouraged them to continue to perform every action well, without regard to human respect.

Kalinowski followed the spiritual direction methods of St. John of the Cross which he learned from a repeated reading of his works. To encourage us to use this rich resource, he left the following memo: "One of the fathers wrote of St. John of the Cross: I advise all my friends to have a special devotion to this saint, to read his works, and choose him for their guide and a guardian. To me, this is the most effective means to progress in virtue. Those who heed my advice will do well." [p. 169]

Kalinowski also carefully searched out and cultivated religious vocations among his penitents. In the early years at Czerna a girl came for the Sacrament of Penance. She received her First Holy Communion from her uncle who was a priest. The girl had been well brought up and from what she later wrote one could see that she had been a beautiful person. It occurred to Kalinowski to recommend her to join a convent. He tried to develop good qualities in her, and especially the spirit of sacrifice, that can so readily take root in young hearts. Ten years later she entered Carmel.

His brother Jerzy commented: "After the death of our dear brother Karol, I came for comfort to Father Raphael, because his

---

[218]   Ibid., p 168. Here Kalinowski echoes again the teaching of the French Carmelite Ferdinand Wuillaume referred to in Ch. 1.

death had plunged me into deep sorrow. I asked him then if I would not do well to seek admission to the congregation of Father Bosco, who became the guardian of orphans. He replied without hesitation, Try it, – so then I decided to go to Italy." [pp. 169-170]

Jerzy Kalinowski was attracted to the Salesian Congregation. He was a devout person and spoke several European languages, so he thought he could use them to work for the benefit of the Church in that Order, which was beginning to spread around the world. He was admitted to the novitiate. But after a trial period his health began to deteriorate; he returned to Warsaw where he finished his theological studies and was ordained a priest.

Apropos of Jerzy's desire for religious life, Kalinowski wrote to his brother Gabriel in June 1889:

> After his troubled journey to Kissingen and other spa mineral waters, Jerzy thought he had achieved peace and calm. As soon as he was rested I thought it right to suggest that Juras[219] should explore a vocation to see if God had really called him to join the Salesians. Juras listened to me. He left us on Thursday, and on Saturday morning, on the eve of Pentecost, he approached the Salesians, and by the evening he had joined them. He felt happy to undertake the work for which the Order was established, and asked us to pray for the spirit of perseverance for him. I am convinced that when Juras submits himself to the leadership of his superiors and enters the way of obedience that he will acquire peace of mind and joy in the Lord. In fact what each of us needs to do is to prepare for the hardships and dangers of our earthly pilgrimage before we come before the judgment of God. [p. 170]

---

[219] Ibid., p 170. Juras was a pet name for Jerzy, which was a usual practice in the Kalinowski family.

A few days later he wrote these simple words to Jerzy: "You need to persevere – imitate our Savior, who was obedient unto death, even death on a cross. In the virtue of obedience, you will find all treasures." [p. 170] Kalinowski held that if God calls a person to his service, they should respond promptly to this call. But if you don't see signs of a true vocation, if the person is guided by purely human considerations, or if unstable, sullen, or had been expelled from another religious congregation, he was adamant that that person should be refused permission to join. In that case no amount of pleading would sway him. As a spiritual director in Kraków he enjoyed general respect. Here's what one of the Polish Carmelites wrote; "My cousin, being in great uncertainty and anxiety about choice of career, told me that in Kraków she was advised to go and see Fr. Kalinowski (she did not know that I knew him), because he is a holy priest and has a very enlightened and impartial manner and whose opinion can be completely relied on." [p.171] Surely a fitting endorsement of a reliable spiritual guide!

Appendix

Miracles Approved for the Glorification of Raphael Kalinowski

$\mathcal{T}$here are strict guidelines enshrined in Canon Law for a person to be declared Blessed or Saint. In order that the Pope can proceed with the beatification of a candidate, known for his or her holiness, certain conditions need to be in place. In addition to proving his or her heroic virtues, there is also the need to find that a miracle has taken place, i.e., an unexplained phenomenon from the point of view of the experimental sciences, and originating from God through the intercession of the candidate. Furthermore, the condition for the canonization of Blessed is the extension of his or her veneration to the whole Church and canonical proof of a second miracle through the holy person's intercession after the beatification.[220]

The miracle then for the beatification of Father Raphael Kalinowski concerned the healing of a priest Fr. Ladislaus Misia from Krakow who suffered from an incurable disease of the spine. The miracle for the canonization occurred five and a half years after the beatification of Raphael Kalinowski. This happened in

---

[220] Again, I am indebted to Fr. Szczepan Praśkiewicz OCD for information included in this appendix.

Wadowice, the place of his death, and the locus of his cult. The miracle consisted of a child, Aleksander (Olek) Roman, returning to full health after sustaining near fatal injuries in a car accident.

The Beatification Miracle

Fr. Ladislaus Misia, a zealous pastor from the parish of All Saints, Krakow, was arrested in September 1942, and deported to Auschwitz; from there he was transported to Mauthausen and finally to Ebensee, where he lived to see the liberation of the camp. He returned home, however, sick and supporting himself on two walking sticks. He tells us: "I felt constant and extreme pain in my spine, both while sitting and standing, and even while lying down. In a word – it was unremitting. In July 1945, I had a medical examination using radiography on the spine. The diagnosis was: 'damage to the second vertebra of the spine with consequent deformity and a tendency to further complications.'"[221]

Doctors recommended complete rest for the patient, professional massages, and the wearing of a back brace. Misia, however, devoted as he was to the service of his parishioners, failed to comply with these guidelines. He was getting worse and in great pain. The priest – witnesses testified – found it difficult to rise from a chair, or kneel in church. So he decided to ask for an exemption from his parish duties. On May 4, 1948 he went to see his bishop, Stanislaus Rospond together with Fr. Benedict Szczesny, a Discalced Carmelite. During the interview, the Bishop advised him to ask the intercession of Father Raphael Kalinowski, whose process of beatification was then in place. Taking these words as a sign sent him by God, Misia went to Czerna a few days later, to the house of the Discalced Carmelites, and asked them to begin a novena to the Servant of God for his healing. The Novena ended on May 19, 1948, and his healing coincided with completion of the Novena – as he himself

---

[221] Beatification and Canonization Process, Rome, 1982.

has testified and is confirmed by witnesses. To quote: "At the end of the Novena the pain in my spine finally ceased. I threw away my walking stick, and celebrated Mass with total freedom of movement; I could kneel easily. The healing was instantaneous together with the disappearance of all pain – an overall recovery. The first witnesses to this were people living in the rectory. I participated in the Corpus Christi procession in the Church of the Franciscan Fathers and sang the gospel. I went on walking tours several times in the vicinity of Krakow."[222]

One of these trips was a pilgrimage to Czerna, to visit Father Raphael's grave and thank him for his intercession before God and the grace of healing.[223]

The extraordinary nature of the healing attracted the attention of the church authorities and the Metropolitan Curia in Krakow. Between March 30 and June 30, 1950 the canonical process was carried out with the aim of proving the alleged miracle. Twelve witnesses testified, plus three medical doctors. The certificates were compared with the reports of three other doctors who commissioned an analysis of the X-rays, those that had been made both before as well as after the healing.

When the records of the trial were transferred to Rome, a censor of the Congregation for the Causes of Saints reported: "With regard to the full testimony of the witnesses, the accompanying documentation and the statements involved in *Summarium*, it seems that the files submitted are sufficient to continue to pursue the case."[224]

A Decree of October 27, 1980 officially stated the importance of the process at Krakow and on December 17, 1981 the Consultative Medical Committee met to discuss the alleged miracle. This group consisted of seven doctors and the Consulters of the Congregation.

---

[222] Summary of Beatification Process.

[223] Fr. Misia died in the sixth year after his cure, i.e., October 31, 1954. The cause of death was not spinal disease, but cancer of the colon.

[224] *Relatio*, p 7.

Here are the results: the diagnosis – the loss of the second vertebra of the spine, "non-life-threatening, but unfavorable for recovery or return to independence; therapy was fruitless, the healing, extraordinary."[225]

However, there was disagreement among physicians regarding the inexplicability of the healing. Three of them found it indisputably extraordinary, while two preferred to talk only about the 'how of the cure' rather than 'the nature of the cure.' The latter two commented that the cure could have happened naturally, and cited possible psycho-somatic factors (unspecified by them), of which the patient was unaware.

Summing up the deliberations of the Consultative Committee, the General Promoter of the Faith said: "There was a great diversity of opinion in this case concerning the heart of the matter, i.e., inexplicability of the healing from the point of view of medical science.... Considering the fact that three doctors found an inexplicable recovery, two found it a progressive cure and two were not opposed to the favorable finding, but explained the healing naturally, the Committee decided to pass on the documentation for examination by theologians."[226]

Discussion of the documentation took place on October 26, 1982. The majority of doctors considered the healing extraordinary from the point of view of medical knowledge, and found there was no discrepancy in the testimony of witnesses in relation to the fact of invoking the intercession of the Servant of God Raphael Kalinowski. The patient carried out the Novena with the community of Discalced Carmelites of Czerna for his healing and experienced it at its completion. For these reasons the theologians unanimously decided that the cause of healing should be attributed to a miracle. Congress confirmed the opinion of the theologians, cardinals and bishops, and the members of the Congregation for the Causes of

---

[225] *Relatio*, p 7.
[226] *Relatio*, p 7.

Saints, that was held on December 7, 1982. At the end of January 13, 1983, Pope John Paul II issued a decree about the miraculous healing of Fr. Misia through the intercession of Father Raphael Kalinowski.

The Miracle for the Canonization

On January 18, 1989, a seven-year-old boy named Aleksander (Olek) Roman was crossing a street in Wadowice, when suddenly a car approached at 80 km per hour. It struck the boy with full force and threw him into the air. The child fell hitting his head on the asphalt and lost consciousness.

Aleksander's sister, Agnes, who witnessed the accident, rushed home to their parents. They called an ambulance and the unconscious boy was transported immediately to the district hospital in Wadowice. An X-ray was carried out and the result showed evidence of multiple fractures of the skull. The diagnosis was very serious.

In order to save the child's life it was decided to proceed immediately with surgery, which lasted two hours. After the operation the unconscious boy was sent to Intensive Care. However, the child did not regain consciousness, and the prognosis was bad. On the day of the accident Fr. Rudolf Warzecha, a Discalced Carmelite, was present in the hospital and gave the boy the last rites; then he asked Olek's mother to go with him to the hospital chapel, where they prayed together for a good outcome for the operation. The next day they started a novena to Blessed Raphael Kalinowski and encouraged the whole family to join in. On the eighth day of the novena the mother touched the boy's head with the relics of Bl. Raphael. Next day to everyone's surprise, Olek regained consciousness and immediately showed awareness of his surroundings. He was able to respond to questions, could read, write, draw, and perform tasks he had learned in the first five months of primary school. He joined in singing songs with his sister. He took meals, and even asked his mother to bring him his favorite cakes.

The canonical process for the alleged miracle took place in the Metropolitan Curia in Krakow from May 29 to June 5, 1989, and eight witnesses were interviewed. Aleksander's mother states: "Fr. Rudolf encouraged us to do the novena to Blessed Raphael Kalinowski. I didn't pray to any other saints. I trusted Bl. Raphael. I was given his relics by Fr. Rudolf, with which I touched my son's head on the eighth day of the novena. We prayed as a family, joined by my mother and brother and we kept Bl. Raphael's image before our eyes."[227] Dr. Stanislaus Chmura commented: "My experience and medical knowledge have taught me that most similar cases are fatal. Personally, I thought that the boy would not survive the accident, so I cannot explain to myself in a natural way how he managed to survive and recover so quickly after surgery."[228] Fr. Rudolf recalls: "When I asked the doctor what he thought about the case, he said that from what he knew on the basis of experience, Aleksander's healing cannot be explained by any natural means."[229]

Records of the process were sent to Rome, and were tested by the Consultative Medical Committee at the Congregation for the Causes of Saints. On November 15, 1989 five medical experts discussed the case and unanimously concluded that the healing of the boy was extremely rapid, complete and permanent, without any after-effects. They found it impossible to explain it with current medical knowledge.

The doctors handed over their reports to seven theological Consulters of the Congregation, to discuss the healing. The theologians met on February 23, 1990 and they and the general Promoter of the Faith unanimously found that sufficient evidence had been submitted to the canonical and theological committees, that a healing miracle could only be attributed to the intercession of Raphael Kalinowski.

---

[227] Process of Canonization, Rome, 1990.

[228] Process of Canonization, Rome, 1990.

[229] Process of Canonization, Rome, 1990.

The unanimously positive judgment of the theologians on the alleged miracle was confirmed collectively by the cardinals and bishops, and on July 10, 1990, in the presence of Pope John Paul II, a decree on the miracle was proclaimed enabling the canonization of Bl. Raphael Kalinowski to go ahead.

Principal Dates in the Life of
St. Raphael Kalinowski

September 1, 1835	Birth
1843	Higher Education, Hori-Horki
1857, Professor of Mathematics, Military Academy, St. Petersburg	
June, 1863	Joins Polish Insurrection in Warsaw.
April 15, 1865	Begins Exile in Usolye, Siberia
February 2, 1874	Ends Exile
October 27, 1874	Becomes tutor to Prince Auguste Czartoryski
November 26, 1877	Kaliinowski Enters Carmel
January 15, 1882	Ordained Priest.
October 9, 1882	Prior at Czerna
1897-1899	Superior at Wadowice
November 15, 1907	Dies at Wadowice

Prayer of St. Raphael Kalinowski to Our Lady

*H*oly Virgin, Immaculate Mother, look with compassion on the oppressions of my soul that is forever wedded to You. Be my protective shield against the missiles of an evil spirit, calm the storms of my own untamed spirit, engrave upon my heart the suffering of Your Divine Son, instill in me contrition purely out of love for Him, point out the path of sincere penance for my repeated unfaithfulness, prepare me for a death out of longing for God, preserve for the Kingdom of Saints and of just ones, the least of all who belong to You, but do not delay, rather lead me out of my incessant anxieties over salvation from the snares of earthly life, and through Your mercy remove me, who am full of wickedness, into everlasting rest with God Himself. Amen.

(Your prodigal son, Raphael of St Joseph.)

Bibliography

Mateusz Siuchiński	*An Illustrated History of Poland* (Interpress: Warsaw 1979).
Czeslaw Gil OCD,	*Father Raphael Kalinowski* (Kraków: 1984).
Lipson, E.,	*Europe in the Nineteenth Century* (London: Adam and Charles Black, 1944).
Blanc, Henri C.,	*Un Grand Religieux* (Carpentras: Chez les Soeurs Carmelites, 1922).
Peltier, Henri,	*Histoire du Carmel* (Paris: Editions du Seuil, 1958).
Haton, Rene (ed.),	*Hermann au Saint-Desert De Tarasteix* (Paris: 1877).
Silverio, P de Santa Teresa,	*Historia del Carmen Descalzo* (Burgos, 1979).
Hussey, Andrew, *Paris,*	*The Secret History* (Penguin Books, 2006).
Bouchaud, Jean-Baptiste,	*Joseph Kalinowski* (Liège: 1923).
Bouchaud, Jean-Baptiste,	*Miłość Za Miłość* (Kraków:2006)
Rohrbach, Peter-Thomas OCD,	*Journey to Carith* (Doubleday and Company Inc,1966).
André De Sainte-Marie,	*L'Ordre De Notre-Dame De Mont-Carmel* (Bruges: 1910).

Praskiewicz, Szczepan T OCD,	*Saint Raphael Kalinowski* (Washington D.C.: ICS Publications, 1998).
Hazan, Eric,	*The Invention of Paris* (London and New York: Verso, 2011).
Sylvain, Abbe Charles,	*The Life of Father Hermann* (Translated by Mrs. Raymond- Barker), (New York: P.J. Kennedy and Sons, 1925).

Richard, Copsey, O.Carm (edited and translated), *The Ten books on the Way of Life and the Great Deeds of the Carmelites* (Kent: St. Albert's Press, 2005)

Index

Printed in the United States
By Bookmasters